Inside
the Adobe®
Photoshop® 6
Studio

Check the Web for Updates:

To check for updates or corrections relevant to this book and/or CD-ROM visit our updates page on the Web at **http://www.prima-tech.com/updates**.

Send Us Your Comments:

To comment on this book or any other PRIMA TECH title, visit our reader response page on the Web at **http://www.prima-tech.com/comments**.

How to Order:

For information on quantity discounts, contact the publisher: Prima Publishing, P.O. Box 1260BK, Rocklin, CA 95677-1260; (916) 787-7000. On your letterhead, include information concerning the intended use of the books and the number of books you want to purchase.

Inside the Adobe® Photoshop® 6 Studio

Eileen Mullin

A Division of Prima Publishing

A Division of Prima Publishing

Prima Publishing and colophon are registered trademarks of Prima Communications, Inc. PRIMA TECH is a trademark of Prima Communications, Inc., Roseville, California 95661.

Adobe, Acrobat, Acrobat Reader, Illustrator, ImageReady, and Photoshop are either registered trademarks or trademarks of Adobe Systems Incorporated in the United States and/or other countries.

Apple, Mac, Macintosh, and QuickTime are either registered trademarks or trademarks of Apple Computer, Inc. in the U.S. and other countries.

Microsoft, Microsoft Windows, and Microsoft Internet Explorer are either registered trademarks or trademarks of Microsoft Corporation in the United States and/or other countries.

Important: Prima Publishing cannot provide software support. Please contact the appropriate software manufacturer's technical support line or Web site for assistance.

Prima Publishing and the author have attempted throughout this book to distinguish proprietary trademarks from descriptive terms by following the capitalization style used by the manufacturer.

Information contained in this book has been obtained by Prima Publishing from sources believed to be reliable. However, because of the possibility of human or mechanical error by our sources, Prima Publishing, or others, the Publisher does not guarantee the accuracy, adequacy, or completeness of any information and is not responsible for any errors or omissions or the results obtained from use of such information. Readers should be particularly aware of the fact that the Internet is an ever-changing entity. Some facts may have changed since this book went to press.

ISBN: 0-7615-2884-9

Library of Congress Catalog Card Number: 00-109082

Printed in the United States of America

00 01 02 03 04 II 10 9 8 7 6 5 4 3 2 1

Publisher:
Stacy L. Hiquet

Marketing Manager:
Judi Taylor Wade

Managing Editor:
Sandy Doell

Acquisitions Editor:
Jawahara Saidullah

Senior Editor:
Kevin Harreld

Technical Reviewer:
Bob Breece

Copy Editor:
Kezia Endsley

Interior Layout:
Danielle Foster

Cover Design:
Prima Design Team

Indexer:
Sharon Shock

Proofreader:
Jessica McCarty

To my mom and dad,
for all the good things they taught me.

Contents at a Glance

1 System Essentials 1

2 File Format Essentials 31

3 Toolbox and Palette Essentials 67

4 Color Essentials 141

5 Layering Essentials 173

6 Path Essentials 207

7 Channel and Mask Essentials 243

8 Filter Essentials 277

9 Scanning Essentials 337

10 Retouching Essentials 367

11 3D Rendering Essentials 415

12 Web Graphics Essentials 443

13 Using ImageReady 483

14 Print Production Essentials 507

15 Automation and Batch Processing Essentials 527

A Setting Photoshop Preferences 553

B Sources for Further Information 569

C Vendor Directory 577

Contents

Introduction xxii

 System Essentials 1

Hardware and Memory Needs 2
    Assessing Your System 3
    CPU 6
    RAM 7
    Scratch Disks (Hard Disk Space) 11
    General Suggestions for Speeding Up Photoshop 15
    Monitor Basics 16
    Removable Storage 17
    Internet Connection 18
Printers 19
    Inkjet Printers 20
    Laser Printers 20
    Dye-Sub Printers 20
Imagesetters 21
Scanners 21
    Flatbed Scanners 22
    Slide Scanners 22
    Drum Scanners 22
Calibrating Your Monitor 23
    Crash Course in Calibration Terminology 24
    Calibrating Your Monitor in Photoshop 25
Acquiring Images 27
    Scanning 27
    Digital Clip Art 27
    Online Image Archives 28
    Video and Digital Cameras 29
    Drawing Tablets and Software 30
Summary 30

 File Format Essentials 31

Computer-Rendered Graphics: Bitmapped vs. Object-Oriented .. 33
    Bitmapped Graphics 33
    Object-Oriented Graphics 34

Color Depth and Resolution 37
    Filling in the Bits 37
    Resolution 37
Graphics File Formats 41
    Native Photoshop 42
    Online Standards 42
    Print Formats 46
    Onscreen and Multimedia Standards 51
    Special Interest Formats 52
    When You're Left Guessing: Photoshop's Raw Format 53
Understanding Compression 53
    Lossy Compression 54
    Lossless Compression 55
Image Modes 55
    Bitmap 56
    Grayscale 57
    Duotone 57
    Indexed Color 58
    RGB Color 59
    CMYK Color 60
    Lab Color 61
    Multichannel 62
Online and Print Formats 62
    Putting It on Paper 62
    Multimedia Applications 66
    Web Graphics 66
Summary 66

3 Toolbox and Palette Essentials 67

Toolbox Overview 71
Viewing and Navigating Images 77
    The Hand Tool 77
    The Zoom Tool 78
    The Navigator Palette 79
    The Measure Tool 80
    The Notes Tool 81
    The Audio Annotation Tool 81
Selection Tools 81
    Marquee Tools 82
    The Crop Tool 87
    Lasso Tips 88
    Magic Wand Tips 91
    The Move Tool 94

Cutting Up Graphics with the Slice and Slice Select Tools ... 96
The Pen Tool, Points, and Paths 99
Saying It with Type 100
Painting and Drawing Tools 106
Paintbrush Tips 107
Airbrush Tips 111
Rubber Stamp Tips 112
Paint Bucket Tips 113
Gradient Tips 114
Pencil Tips 122
Lines and Shapes 123
Rectangle and Rounded Rectangle Tips 125
Ellipse and Polygon Tips 126
Custom Shape Tool 126
Eyedropper and Color Sampler Tool Tips 127
Eraser Tips 129
Rewriting History: The History Palette and Brush 131
Reverting to an Image State 131
The History Brush Tool 132
The Art History Brush Tool 133
Editing Tools 134
Blur and Sharpen Tips 134
Smudge Tips 134
Dodge, Burn, and Sponge Tips 135
Summary 136

4   **Color Essentials** **141**

Precision, Precision: Photoshop's Color Models 143
RGB 144
CMYK 145
HSB 147
Lab 148
Web Colors 149
The Color Picker 150
Using the Color and Swatches Palettes 153
The Color Palette 153
The Swatches Palette 154
Predefined and Custom Color Sets 155
Third-Party Commercial Inks 156
Using Indexed Color Palettes 160
Color Options in Painting and Editing Modes 164
Managing Color Consistency 167
Summary 171

5 Layering Essentials **173**

Creating New Layers 174
    New Layer Options 176
    Establishing What Layer to Work On 177
Deleting Layers 180
Manipulating Layers 180
    Moving Layers 181
    Linking Layers Together 181
    Viewing and Hiding Layers 182
    Scrolling through Layers via Keystrokes 182
    Copying Layers between Documents 183
    Rearranging Your Layers' Order 183
    Creating Layer Sets 185
    Locking Layers 186
Editing and Manipulating Layer Styles 187
Creating Fill Layers 191
Creating Translucent Overlays 192
Using Adjustment Layers 193
Changing Mode Settings to Create Special Effects 195
Combining Layers 198
    Cutting and Pasting into Layers 199
    Clipping Groups 199
    Editing More than One Layer at Once 202
    Blending Options 202
Creating Layer Masks 203
Merging and Flattening Layers 205
Summary 206

6 Path Essentials **207**

Path Fundamentals 209
    Path Tools 211
    Paths Palette Menu Items 213
    Icons in the Paths Palette 214
Drawing with the Pen Tool 215
    Taking the Guesswork Out of Drawing Paths 215
    Straight Lines 217
    Bézier Curves 219
    Drawing Precise Selections 226
Saving and Deleting Paths 228
Importing and Exporting Paths 230
Converting Paths to Selections—and Back Again 231
    Converting Paths to Selections 231

Converting Selections to Paths 232
Filling and Stroking Paths 233
    Filling a Path 236
    Stroking a Path 236
Making Silhouettes with Clipping Paths 237
Summary 240

7   Channel and Mask Essentials 243

Introduction to Channels 245
    Viewing an Image's Color Channels 246
    Looking at Individual Channels 248
Using Spot-Color Channels 254
Creating Alpha Channels 255
    Saving a Selection in a New Channel 255
    Loading a Selection 260
    Adding to, Subtracting from, and Intersecting Channels 261
Understanding the Channels Palette Menu 263
    New Channel 263
    Duplicate Channel 264
    Delete Channel 264
    New Spot Channel and Merge Spot Channel 264
    Channel Options 265
    Split Channels 265
    Merge Channels 266
    Palette Options 266
Creating Effects with Masked Type 267
Using Quick Mask Mode 272
    Editing in Quick Mask Mode 272
    No More Marching Ants 273
Summary 274

8   Filter Essentials 277

Putting Filters to Work 278
    Applying Filters at Partial Strength 281
    Why Are Filters So Slow? 282
Artistic Filters 284
    Colored Pencil 284
    Cutout 286
    Dry Brush 286
    Film Grain 286
    Fresco 287
    Neon Glow 287

Paint Daubs 287
Palette Knife 288
Plastic Wrap 289
Poster Edges 289
Rough Pastels 289
Smudge Stick 289
Sponge 290
Underpainting 290
Watercolor 290
Blur Filters 291
Blur and Blur More 291
Gaussian Blur 291
Motion Blur 292
Radial Blur 293
Smart Blur 294
Brush Strokes 295
Accented Edges 296
Angled Strokes 297
Crosshatch 297
Dark Strokes 297
Ink Outlines 297
Spatter 298
Sprayed Strokes 298
Sumi-e 298
Distortion Filters 298
Diffuse Glow 298
Glass 299
Ocean Ripple 300
Pinch 300
Polar Coordinates 301
Ripple 301
Shear 302
Spherize 302
Twirl 303
Wave 303
ZigZag 304
Displace 305
Noise Filters 308
Add Noise 308
Despeckle 310
Dust & Scratches 310
Median 311
Pixelate Filters 311
Color Halftone 312

Crystallize 312
Facet 312
Fragment 313
Mezzotint 313
Mosaic 313
Pointillize 313
Render Filters 313
3D Transform 314
Clouds 314
Difference Clouds 314
Lens Flare 315
Texture Fill 315
Lighting Effects 315
Texture Channel 317
Sharpen Filters 320
Sharpen and Sharpen More 320
Sharpen Edges 320
Unsharp Mask 320
Sketch Filters 321
Bas Relief 321
Chalk & Charcoal 321
Charcoal 321
Chrome 322
Conté Crayon 323
Graphic Pen 323
Halftone Pattern 323
Note Paper 324
Photocopy 324
Plaster 324
Reticulation 324
Stamp 325
Torn Edges 325
Water Paper 325
Stylize Filters 325
Diffuse 325
Emboss 326
Extrude 328
Find Edges 328
Solarize 329
Tiles 329
Trace Contour 329
Wind 329
Texture Filters 330
Craquelure 330

Grain 330

Mosaic Tiles 330

Patchwork 330

Stained Glass 331

Texturizer 332

Video Filters 332

De-Interlace 332

NTSC Colors 332

Other Filters 332

DitherBox 333

High Pass 333

Minimum and Maximum Filters 334

Offset 334

Custom 334

Digital Watermarking 335

Embed Watermark 335

Read Watermark 336

Summary 336

Scanning Essentials 337

Scanner Specifications 339

Choosing Good Scanning Material............................... 340

Installing Scanning Software 341

Scanning Options.. 342

Preview 343

Color Mode 343

Cropping 344

Sharpening 344

Descreening 344

Black Point and White Point 345

Resolution 346

Considering Resolution Issues in Depth 346

Scanning for Print Production 347

Scanning for Web or Onscreen Production 347

Interpolation Issues... 348

Changing Resolution and File Size 349

Halftone Scanning 354

Eliminate Moirés Using Your Scanning Software and
Photoshop Filters 356

Adjusting Brightness and Contrast 357

Setting Black Point and White Point Values 357

Setting Brightness and Contrast 360

Sharpening with the Unsharp Mask Filter 362

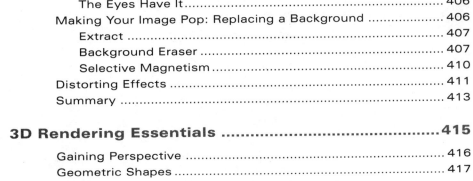

Removing a Color Cast 362
Photo CD—An Alternative to Straightforward Scanning 363
Summary 366

 Retouching Essentials **367**

Taking Stock 368
  Checking Color Values in the Info Palette 369
  Keeping Backups Close By 371
Can This Photo Be Saved? 377
Making Tonal Corrections in Grayscale Images 378
  Variations 383
  Levels 385
  Input Levels 386
  Output Levels 387
  Curves 388
Making Color Corrections 391
  Taking Eyedropper and Color Sampler Readings 393
  The Color Balance Command 393
  The Hue/Saturation Command 394
  Using the Histogram Command 395
  Setting Black, White, and Neutral Points 396
  Variations 397
  Levels 398
  Curves 399
  Using Adjustment Layers to Preview Corrections 399
  Using the Dodge and Burn Tools 400
Removing Dust Spots and Blemishes 401
  Using the Clone Stamp and Pattern Stamp Tools 402
  Using Feathering to Smooth Transitions 404
Making Picture-Perfect Facial Corrections 404
  Keeping It Natural 406
  The Eyes Have It 406
Making Your Image Pop: Replacing a Background 406
  Extract 407
  Background Eraser 407
  Selective Magnetism 410
Distorting Effects 411
Summary 413

3D Rendering Essentials **415**

Gaining Perspective 416
Geometric Shapes 417

Overlaying Images on 3D Graphics 429

Using the 3D Transform Plug-In 433

Using Layer Styles to Create 3D Edges and Realistic Shadows 433

    Creating Buttons with Beveled Edges................................ 433

    Creating 3D Lettering 436

Adding Shadows 436

Summary 437

 12 Web Graphics Essentials 443

Design Considerations for Web Graphics 445

File Formats Revisited 447

    JPEG 449

    GIF 450

Optimizing Your Web Graphics and Minimizing
    Download Time 455

    Using Fewer Colors 455

    Studying the Save for Web Interface 458

    Maximizing Image Compression 463

    Cropping Your Graphics 464

    Creating Thumbnails 464

    Creating Low-Resolution Versions of Images 464

Functions of Web Graphics 468

    Splash Pages 468

    Background Patterns and Colors.. 469

    Background Images and Tiling 470

    Navigational Buttons and Icons... 473

    Splitting a Large Web Graphic into Smaller
        Contiguous Pieces 474

Using Color Palettes Throughout a Site 480

Protecting Your Web Graphics 481

Summary 482

 13 Using ImageReady 483

Assessing When to Use ImageReady vs. Photoshop 484

Examining ImageReady's Tools and Palettes 485

Creating Image Maps 491

    Creating Hot Spots 492

    Sliced Images vs. Image Maps 495

    Design Considerations for Image Maps 496

Using Animated GIFs 496

    Animated Banners and Buttons... 498

Creating Rollover Effects 499

Summary 503

Print Production Essentials 507

Preparing Graphics for Use in Page Layout Programs 508
Changing from RGB to CMYK 511
Changing File Formats 511
Color Settings 513
Helping Your Service Bureau and Yourself, Too 514
Building Better Design from the Screen Up 518
How Your Service Bureau's Imagesetter Works 519
Halftone Screening 519
Stochastic Screening 520
Process vs. Spot Color 521
Duotones 522
Printing Spot Colors from Photoshop 522
Quick Tips for 2-Color Print Jobs 523
On the Press 524
Dot Gain 524
Trapping 525
Summary 526

Automation and Batch Processing Essentials 527

Exploring the Actions Palette 529
Playing an Action 531
Predefined Actions 533
Recording and Editing Actions 535
Duplicating Actions 536
Deleting Actions 536
Editing Actions 540
Using the Insert Menu Item Command 540
Hold It! or Stopping Actions 541
Acquiring Additional Actions 543
Droplets: Drag-and-Drop Actions 544
When Actions Go Wrong 544
Playback Options 544
Troubleshooting Tips 546
Using the Automate Commands 547
Organizing Your Actions 549
Summary 551

Setting Photoshop Preferences 553

General Preferences 555
Saving Files 558
Display & Cursors 559

xviii CONTENTS

Transparency & Gamut 560
Units & Rulers 561
Guides & Grid 562
Plug-Ins & Scratch Disks 563
Image Cache, or Memory & Image Cache 564
Preset Manager 565
Color Settings 566

B Sources for Further Information 569

Photoshop-Related Tips, Tricks, and Techniques 570
Photoshop-Related Actions 571
Free Filters and Plug-ins for Photoshop 571
Free Web Graphics 572
   Buttons and Icons 572
   Backgrounds and Textures 572
   Animated GIFs 573
   Free HTML Templates and Interfaces 573
Free Stock Photos and Clip Art 573
Free Fonts 574
Periodicals 574
Professional Organizations 575
Related Usenet Newsgroups 575
Discussion Groups and Forums 576
   Photoshop Discussion List 576

C Vendor Directory 577

Employment Services 578
Hardware and Software Products 578

Glossary 585

Index 591

Acknowledgments

Every day, every day, every day I write the book.

—*Elvis Costello and the Attractions*

Special thanks to the people who help me every day:

Above all, I want to thank Ross Rubin, my true companion, for his unfailing ability to make me laugh, as well as his encouragement, unconditional support and patience, and all the good bits. His willingness to constantly fetch Diet Coke and Chinese food, make hundreds of cups of tea, and belt out musical numbers on demand is deeply, deeply appreciated. Ross, you're Macy's.

My family, friends, and colleagues offered enthusiastic support and critical feedback. Warmest thanks go to my siblings, Kathleen, Kevin, James, Bill, and Thomas, and to my photogenic, well-behaved nieces and nephews, Caitlin, Johnny, Julia, Erika, Kevin Patrick, and Sean who provided so much subject material in the photos that grace these pages. My extended family—including Irene, Nat, Jared, and the whole Terry clan—always lent a collective sympathetic ear, especially during the holidays.

I'm grateful to Leslie Fagenson and the whole Global HR Information Systems & Solutions team at Merrill Lynch for kindly enduring my sleep-deprived demeanor during office hours. Joanne Kissane, Anne Savino, Tom Eyestone, Inara Angelis, and Michele Durst deserve special thanks for helping the crises pass and ensuring that employees could find the help they needed online.

I'm obliged to Neil deMause, Mich Nelson, Abigail Collings and the whole IBM gang for providing fun and distraction at much-needed times. Finger, Tivo, and Sophet were also always there for me.

My sincerest thanks go to the team at Prima Publishing who helped make this new edition possible: Jawahara Saidullah, acquisitions editor; Kevin Harreld, senior editor; Kezia Endsley, copy editor; Bob Breece, technical editor; Jessica McCarty, proofreader; and Sharon Shock, indexer. Credit on the design end belongs to Danielle Foster for the interior layout, and the Prima Design Team for the cover.

Thanks and extra kibble to my furry companions Starsky and Hutch, who provided many hours of entertainment and middle-of-the-night companionship. And every Saturday, the people and cats at Bide-a-Wee provided a welcome respite from my computer-based responsibilities.

And thanks to Adobe for giving graphic designers such wonderful tools!

Eileen Mullin

–November 2000

About the Author

Eileen Mullin is vice president of global HR Internet strategy for Merrill Lynch, where she manages the firm's Web sites for human resources. Previously, she was program director of content programming for ibm.com. Eileen lives in Manhattan with her husband and cats.

Introduction

Whether you're upgrading to Photoshop 6.0 or are relatively new to designing computer graphics, this book offers you a solid grounding in the program's basics so you can create and edit images with great results. As you expand your core design skills, you'll learn key techniques that will help you successfully complete professional-quality assignments for print publications, Web sites, multimedia presentations, or for your own portfolio.

Many companies manage to stretch just a few people over a lot of different jobs, and you might need to get up to speed on creating graphics for all kinds of projects in a hurry. As you gain Photoshop skills, you can save a lot of time and money in the long run by doing the kinds of tasks that once could only be outsourced to specialists. Aspiring Web designers will especially appreciate learning how to take advantage of Photoshop's features for quickly and automatically slicing Web images for splash screens or navigation bars—not to mention using the bundled ImageReady 3.0 program to create rollovers or image maps. Best of all, you'll find out how great it feels to have that measure of control and opportunity to showcase your talents.

That's what led me to write the previous editions of this book. I wanted to help other people learn these kinds of computer skills quickly so they could keep pace with a changing workplace. I also saw it as a way to help empower people who were looking to land that first position, grow beyond their present job, or open new avenues and make career changes even if they had been computer-phobic in a previous life. In this Internet-powered economy, especially, mastering Web design and production skills is a fast track to increasing your marketability to any potential employer, if you have interest in developing in that area.

I think that becoming proficient in Photoshop is a lot like learning how to swim—there's a certain amount you can do with no problem at the shallow end, but it takes a lot of initiative to become really good at it. One of the greatest barriers to taking the plunge, so to speak, is information overload—there's a confusing array of instructional videos, online courses, instructional CD-ROMs, and seminars about Photoshop all clamoring for your attention. And then there's the intimidation factor of striving to keep up with the ever-changing world of new technologies—even if they contain many time-saving features, like Photoshop 6.0 does, you still have to learn how to use them.

My approach is one I developed after reading one of Calvin Trillin's wonderful columns from *The Nation*. In this essay, entitled "Iran for Christmas," he described how he and his wife, Alice, dealt with their information anxiety about current events.

Specifically, Trillin was worried about appearing ill-informed at dinner parties and the like when asked to give his opinion about the state of affairs in parts of the world about which he knew nothing. His solution was to divide with his wife the responsibility for keeping up to date about different topics, each providing the other with relevant information on a need-to-know basis. Thus, he could blissfully ignore news reports on "her" topics without fearing he might miss something, knowing he would be apprised on events as he needed to know them.

Similarly, I organized the material in this book on a need-to-know basis. There is a lot of introductory material in the first few chapters that will increase your understanding of the more advanced features—which sounds obvious, I know, but it's sorely lacking in many Photoshop books, which often tend to showcase special effects or single-use tips and tricks.

The exercises in each chapter focus more on achieving specific common effects—from creating images masked within another object's outline to warped text and fuzzy drop shadows to removing color casts. As you might have found already, there's almost always more than one way to achieve a particular effect in Photoshop—so the best method to use should depend more on your level of Photoshop expertise and your ultimate use for a particular graphic than on any single shortcut. Although I give step-by-step information on how to achieve certain effects, I want to emphasize that there's a continuum of Photoshop techniques, and various methods are suited to different skill levels and the final use of your graphics.

In short, I'm leery of tips-and-tricks techniques that show you just one way of doing things. I hope you'll use the exercises in this book to get up to speed on using Photoshop's features and that you'll continue to

explore—for example, by tweaking combinations of filters and figuring out how the elaborate images you see in other print publications were created. The examples in this book demonstrate a range of real-world uses of Photoshop features—and you can extend them to situations or assignments far beyond those shown here.

What's New in Photoshop 6.0

Here are some of the major improvements added to the latest version of Photoshop—all good reasons for bringing this upgrade to a computer near you:

- **Editable, flowing text.** For the first time in Photoshop, you can enter text directly on the image's canvas instead of in a separate dialog box. You can also now produce text in paragraph format; you designate an area for flowing in text and let it wrap and hyphenate according to settings you specify. You can readily select any letter or word and apply particular color or font attributes to just those characters instead of the whole block of text.

- **Warped text.** Photoshop 6.0 includes 15 preset contour effects for distorting text, including arcing, bulging, fisheye, inflated, squeezed, and twisted.

- **Vector artwork.** This feature provides a shortcut approach to some of the smartest-looking popular effects that artists create in Photoshop. Now it's much easier to create clipping paths (for masking images within the outline of another objects) and edit the content contained therein separately from the outlined shape.

- **Custom shape tools.** These tools provide the easiest way to see Photoshop 6's new vector capabilities in action—and easily create starburst effects, callouts for magazine or book cover artwork, polygons, and unique navigational buttons for Web sites.

- **Editable type.** You can easily enter type and later modify it, specifying all kinds of typographical formatting on a character-by-character basis. It's most impressive because Photoshop's type capabilities left a lot to be desired in older versions.

- **Layer styles.** These commands allow you to manage popular graphic effects such as drop shadows or embossing for an element, and then apply that style immediately to other elements. In this way, you can create a variety of stylistically identical navigational buttons in a couple of fell swoops.

- **Layer sets.** Experienced users can typically create dozens of layers in a single photocomposition. The new ability to create group layers into sets might help you better organize and manage your collections of layers in your images. Previously, a Photoshop image could contain up to 99 layers; this limit has been drastically extended into the thousands.

- **Slicing and dicing.** Photoshop 5.5 users were introduced to ImageReady's tools for preparing images for the Web. Now, slice capabilities—used most frequently for dividing navigational graphics or large images for faster online display—have been more tightly integrated into Photoshop. ImageReady 3.0 is now bundled with Photoshop 6.0 with more extensive Web-production capabilities, such as generating HTML and code for rollover effects (in which a graphic changes to a highlighted state as a user's cursor passes over it).

- **Contextual options bar.** Options palettes for individual tools have been replaced by a constant options bar that updates to reflect the features available with each tool for that specific situation. Palettes for brushes, patterns, and a number of additional useful presets are well-integrated with each tool that uses them. Up until now, to change the style and opacity of a paintbrush's strokes, for example, you had to display both the Paintbrush Options palette and a separate Brushes palette. In Photoshop 6.0, though, you access all Paintbrush features in one context-sensitive toolbar that spans the width of your monitor.

What's Inside the Book

Here are the topics you'll find addressed in the chapters ahead:

Chapter 1: System Essentials affords you an opportunity to assess whether your computer setup is equipped to handle your Photoshop

work. It includes an overview of third-party software, printers, and scanners, plus some resources for obtaining source artwork online or for a low cost.

Chapter 2: File Format Essentials addresses the range of graphics formats and Photoshop image modes available to you, and how to pick what's best depending on your ultimate uses for your graphics. You'll also learn about how image compression works.

Chapter 3: Toolbox and Palette Essentials is a tour of Photoshop's most functional tools and some accompanying power-user techniques. This chapter includes the book's first hands-on exercises for creating a couple of all-purpose effects, such as warping type and gradated shapes that look three-dimensional.

Chapter 4: Color Essentials guides you through the optimization of your images' colors both onscreen and in print, and offers a quick overview of the basics of color theory. Exercises include a walkthrough of how to create a duotone image and how to convert a graphic to hand-tinting parts of an image.

Chapter 5: Layering Essentials explains Photoshop's powerful layer style features and some of its potential uses. In this chapter's exercises, you'll learn how to put layer styles to work to create drop shadows and pattern files, and use layering to create outlined images that contain other images within their borders.

Chapter 6: Path Essentials provides a step-by-step guide to creating paths and Bézier curves with the Pen tool. The chapter's exercises include a hands-on use of clipping paths, which are essential for creating silhouette images in Photoshop for export to page layout programs.

Chapter 7: Channel and Mask Essentials breaks down Photoshop's powerful but initially confusing channel capabilities into manageable steps that you can use to create unique composite images. In one exercise, you'll learn how to add a spot color channel to an image for print production.

Chapter 8: Filter Essentials demonstrates the range of unusual special effects you can create with Photoshop filters. You'll see the basics of each standard filter's controls and preview the unique results.

Chapter 9: Scanning Essentials explores the steps you can take to ensure your scanned images look good. This chapter offers tips on using different kinds of scanner controls, adjusting gamma (which controls how your scanner handles the contrast of your images' midtones), and avoiding problems when you're scanning halftone images (that is, images that have been printed previously in a book, newspaper, or magazine).

Chapter 10: Retouching Essentials covers an essential, real-world application of Photoshop—retouching and correcting less-than-perfect images. This chapter's exercises help you create stunning "after" artwork from all your "before" photographs.

Chapter 11: 3D Rendering Essentials shows you how to add depth to two-dimensional objects with realistic textures and shadow effects. You'll also use the 3D Transform rendering filter to improve perspective in your images, rotating 3D images so they fit smoothly into place.

Chapter 12: Web Graphics Essentials shows you how designing graphics for a Web audience differs from designing for print. You'll begin to create images optimized for the Web, such as interlaced GIFs and seamlessly tiling background images, and use the Save as Web command to optimize image color and size.

Chapter 13: Using ImageReady helps you move your Web design skills into high gear to generate the JavaScript for rollover states. You'll also learn how to turn layered Photoshop files into animated Web graphics.

Chapter 14: Print Production Essentials includes the hard-and-fast rules for ensuring that your Photoshop creations look as good in print as they do onscreen. The chapter covers RGB-to-CMYK conversion, duotones for two-color printing, and examples of putting clipping paths to use.

Chapter 15: Automation and Batch Processing Essentials shows you how to go on autopilot when it comes to handling rote tasks that you do in Photoshop again and again. You can take advantage of the program's predefined actions, or designate your own custom set of the routine Photoshop tasks you perform most frequently.

Appendix A: Setting Photoshop Preferences addresses how to change the default settings that affect many of the Photoshop dialog boxes and displays what you see. It's a one-stop resource for learning how to change any interface preference that might be bothering you, from the units of measurement to the type of cursor used.

Appendix B: Sources for Further Information lists a number of other useful resources, including prominent Web sites that offer Photoshop-related tips and techniques, computer magazines, and e-mail lists.

Appendix C: Vendor Directory lists contact information for many hardware and software manufacturers whose products can be used with Photoshop.

Glossary: The worlds of print production and Web design are rich with their own unique terminology. If you run across a term that's not fully explained in context—or that comes up in the course of your graphics work!—here's a quick reference to get the definitions you need.

Conventions Used in This Book

Photoshop's menus contain many submenus and commands. I try to give directions in the order in which you'd navigate the menus. For example, "Choose Adjust from the Image menu, and then select Channel Mixer from the Adjust submenu." This might sound like quite a mouthful, but I find it more readable than a purely hierarchical description.

The vast majority of figures in this book show the Macintosh version of Photoshop. If you're a Windows user, don't worry—the menu commands and functions in the Windows and Macintosh versions of Photoshop behave the same way and are what's important to focus on, not the minutiae of the interface. The instructions given should prove just as useful for Windows users as for Mac users. Wherever necessary, I've included separate steps for what to do if the type of computer you're using makes a difference. For the most part, this only affects instructions for pressing key commands. (Wherever a Mac user presses Cmd or Option, a Windows user presses Ctrl or Alt.)

Getting Additional Help

I've tried to answer as many of the pressing questions as possible that plague professional Photoshop designers, but there are always more that will crop up—some that require exhaustive detail, others that in-

volve emerging technologies yet to come. To that end, the listings for online resources in Appendix B should prove more helpful than any print publication.

Sometimes finding the right answer is a matter of knowing where to look, but all too often it's also a matter of building up the courage to ask. "Did you hear they discovered the gene for shyness?" comedian Jonathan Katz once said. "They would've found it years ago, but it was hiding behind a couple of other genes." Don't hide behind a couple of other Photoshop designers. If you're struggling with a thorny what-scanner-should-I-buy question or puzzling over creating a certain effect, chances are that others are too. Start by asking your circle of acquaintances for help, but you can also get a wider perspective by seeking help on an online forum.

There are many online resources where you can get a quick answer to a specific question—or at least a push in the right direction if your query is more broad-based. Deja.com's Usenet Discussion Service at **http:// www.deja.com/usenet** is a great up-to-the-minute resource. The Usenet newsgroup **comp.graphics.apps.photoshop** is a good first stop; for Web graphics, **comp.infosystems.www.authoring.images** covers a wide range of Internet graphics topics. On America Online, you can post messages in the Photoshop Special Interest Group folder (keyword: Photoshop) for Photoshop help. Appendix B also contains pointers to many additional online resources where you can find the answers to specific Photoshop questions.

Before you post to a newsgroup or online message board, there are three rules of netiquette to follow that will save you from unwittingly raising your fellow readers' hackles. First, check for a FAQ (Frequently Asked Questions) list, and read it to see whether your query is answered there. Second, catch up on the messages and topics currently in circulation; people will forgive you for asking a question that was discussed and answered a month ago, but not one that just came up two days ago.

The third rule relates not to the content of your question but to how you ask for replies. Many fledgling Internet users post help requests in so many areas—including newsgroups they don't visit regularly—that they ask people to send responses via e-mail rather than post them to

the online forum. This will infuriate many other users because it violates the spirit of the group as a forum for shared information, and you'll stand the risk of being perceived as a taker, not a giver. If you decide you must ask for responses via e-mail, make it clear in your original post that you will summarize the most helpful hints and post accordingly—and then do it!

Feedback

If you have any comments or suggestions about this book, I look forward to receiving e-mail about it; please write me at **eileen@interport.net**.

Eileen Mullin

–November 2000

System Essentials

IN THIS CHAPTER

Hardware and Memory Needs

👁

Printers, Imagestters, and Scanners

👁

Calibrating Your Monitor

👁

Acquiring Images

You're all set to put Photoshop to work for you, but first you need to make sure—sooner rather than later—that your computer system is up to the task. Whether you're preparing graphics for the Web, print publications, or multimedia presentations, it's important that your computer can handle the demands you'll place on it.

This chapter helps you determine what to do if, for example, Photoshop chugs along at a snail's pace during processor-intensive tasks, or if your work is frequently interrupted because you don't have enough room on your hard disk. Straight ahead, you'll get a look at the following topics:

- 👁 How to determine your hardware and memory needs and get the best performance out of your system

- 👁 What printing and scanning capabilities are available to you— whether you're looking to buy your own equipment or just need to call your service bureau to conduct some printing tests

- 👁 How to make sure your monitor is properly calibrated, and what kind of difference that really makes

- 👁 How to find good source materials for your images

If you're using Photoshop in your daily work now, you may already have a handle on some of this material. If that's the case, keep this chapter in mind as a ground-level reference and feel free to skip ahead to Chapter 2, "File Format Essentials," which covers the different graphics file formats used in various real-world applications.

Hardware and Memory Needs

Whether your interest in Photoshop is driven by a personal motivation to become an accomplished computer graphics user or by fast-approaching deadlines at your job, you should take to heart the Boy Scout motto and be prepared. One of the first things you need to do is ensure that your computer's *infrastructure*—its hardware and memory—is up to the task.

It may surprise you at first, particularly if you're new to computer graphics in general, how far you have to extend most out-of-the-box computer setups to optimize for professional design use. When you add up

memory upgrades, third-party filters, utilities, tools, scanner software, Photoshop, and other graphics software packages, you can spend as much on extras as you did on your CPU, hard drive, and monitor.

Outfitting a computer system for intensive Photoshop use is like decorating a new home: there's simply an enormous range of things you need. When I moved into my current apartment, I had a shopping list that began—and at the time it didn't seem strange to me at all—as follows:

 Corkscrew

 Light bulbs

 Sofa

The remainder of this section addresses how to get a handle on the same kinds of juxtaposed needs; that is, picking up the simpler stuff while you're also facing more pressing problems. First, you'll take a look at your system components—including your CPU, RAM, and hard disk space—and see whether any major purchases should be in your near future.

Assessing Your System

At some point, most computer owners want a bigger hard drive, more RAM, or a larger monitor. Photoshop users probably reach that point sooner—and start wishing more fervently—than almost anyone else.

Photoshop can place the kind of heavy-duty strain on your computer's memory resources that messy children do on their clothes in those TV laundry detergent commercials. You don't necessarily need a top-of-the-line computer to run Photoshop—but you'll find that the amount of RAM you have, your processing speed, and the amount of free space on your hard disk directly affects how much work you can accomplish and how quickly.

Table 1.1 shows an at-a-glance checklist to make sure you have at least the minimum system requirements for running Photoshop. Some additional system recommendations are also listed; most software developers—and Adobe's no exception—tend to understate the minimum requirements for its products in terms of real-world performance drains.

Table 1.1 System Requirements for Running Adobe Photoshop 6.0

IF YOU'RE USING A MAC

CPU

Adobe says a PowerPC model is required. For serious usage, however, a G3 or G4 will greatly improve performance. Any model iMac is a good baseline.

RAM

At least 64MB (with virtual memory on). A minimum of 128MB of RAM is required to run Photoshop and ImageReady at the same time. For optimal performance, you should have at least 128MB even if you are running only Photoshop. To run both Photoshop and ImageReady concurrently and optimally, you'll want 160MB of RAM.

Hard Disk Space

You'll need at least 125MB of free hard disk space. On a practical level, though, you'll probably need much more. Storage should not be an issue if you're buying a new machine, which typically include 6GB to 10GB or more of hard disk space.

IF YOU'RE USING A PC

Adobe says a Pentium-class processor is required. For new mainstream PCs that use Intel chips, you'll typically find models that use either a Celeron chip (on the low end) or a Pentium 3 (on the higher end). Also note that more PC makers are using AMD chips; the high-end one is called Athlon and the lower-end version (or Celeron competitor) is called the Duron.

At least 64MB. A minimum of 128MB of RAM is required to run both Photoshop and ImageReady at the same time. For optimal performance, you should have at least 128MB even if you are running only Photoshop. To run Photoshop and ImageReady concurrently and optimally, you'll want 160MB of RAM.

You'll need at least 125MB of free hard disk space. On a practical level, though, you'll probably need much more. Storage should not be an issue if you're buying a new machine, which typically include 6GB to 10GB or more of hard disk space.

Table 1.1
(continued)

IF YOU'RE USING A MAC	IF YOU'RE USING A PC
System Software	
MacOS version 8.5 or higher. See following note for MacOS X information.	Microsoft Windows 98, Windows Millennium, Windows 2000, or Windows NT 4.0 or later. With Windows NT, the NT 4 Service Pack 4, 5, or 6a is required. In general, Windows NT and 2000 tend to require more memory than a comparably configured PC running Windows 98.
Monitor	
A 256-color (8-bit) or greater video card is required with an 800×600 monitor resolution or greater. A 24-bit color or a 32-bit video display card is even better, of course. You can still use images with more colors on a 256-color monitor, but you won't get an accurate screen display. For any new monitor purchase, 24-bit color is standard.	A 256-color (8-bit) or greater video card is required with an 800×600 monitor resolution or greater. A 24-bit color or a 32-bit video display card is even better, of course. You can still use images with more colors on a 256-color monitor, but you won't get an accurate screen display. For any new monitor purchase, 24-bit color is standard.
CD-ROM Drive	
Required.	Required.

note

Early in 2001, Apple is scheduled to release a rewrite of the Mac operating system from the ground up dubbed Mac OS X. This new system will include a new colorful graphical user interface (called Aqua) and, more importantly, will create a more robust environment for handling application errors and crashes. Mac OS X will run three kinds of Mac programs—today's Mac software will run in a compatibility layer called the "classic" environment. With minimal changes, developers will be able to create versions of their programs that take advantage of more of Mac OS X's features. Developers can also take advantage of Cocoa, which provides a way of creating Mac applications more quickly.

CPU

A computer's *CPU*, or central processing unit, is the main chip that processes software instructions. Typically, the CPU is the most significant factor in determining a computer's price.

As per the system requirements Adobe has issued for Photoshop 6.0, Windows users need a Pentium processor or better, whereas Macintosh users need at least a PowerPC-based machine; Table 1.1 lists additional CPU recommendations.

The faster your computer processes your commands, the faster you'll be able to complete operations in Photoshop and knock off work early for the day. If your processing speed is less than optimal, you'll feel every extra second of processing time as it creeps by.

note

To make it easier for you to follow the discussion of microprocessor chips if you're only familiar with one system, let me draw rough comparisons between the chips found inside Windows PCs and Macintoshes. A Pentium processor on a Windows machine is akin to a PowerPC 60x processor on a Macintosh. Moving up the value chain, a Pentium II or Celeron processor on a Windows machine is roughly equal to a PowerPC G3 processor on a Macintosh. The Pentium 3 is more comparable to a PowerPC G4.

If you have the opportunity to run Photoshop on two computer models, it should be an eye-opening experience—and drive home the difference in operating speed that a faster microprocessor chip makes.

Additionally, your computer's ability to run Photoshop at a fast clip is partly determined by its CPU's operating speed, or clock speed, which is measured in megahertz (MHz). For example, a 350MHz G4 might be faster than a 400MHz G3. This only happens at the margins, however; a 500MHz G4 will trounce a 500MHz G3. Clock speed is not a valid way of comparing the speeds of Pentium and PowerPC systems to each other.

note

> Photoshop 6.0 takes advantage of the *velocity engine* in G4 chips, which can greatly accelerate certain operations, such as applying Photoshop filters.

Some computers ship with multiple processors, but it's important to note whether your operating system supports multiprocessing. On the Mac, Photoshop 6.0 can take advantage of computers with multiple G4 processors through an add-on that Adobe provides. On PCs, Adobe supports multiprocessing under Windows NT or Windows 2000. Adobe will also likely support multiprocessing under Mac OS X. Adobe supports multiprocessing through an add-on; Mac OS X will support multiprocessing in all native ("carbonized") applications (see the earlier note about Mac OS X).

Because it's hardly practical to replace your computer every time a new model with a faster CPU is announced, there are a couple of ways you can improve your existing machine's clock speed and thus its performance: upgrade your computer's CPU or the motherboard.

RAM

RAM, or *random access memory*, is where your computer stores the information it is currently using. Accessing information from RAM is much faster than accessing it from even the fastest hard disk, so the more RAM you have, the faster your machine will run. After the CPU, the amount of RAM in a computer is typically the second-largest factor in a computer's price. It is usually easier—and sometimes cheaper—to upgrade a computer's RAM than its CPU.

Photoshop's operation in particular is inextricably tied to how much of your computer's RAM it can use. The single best way to improve

Photoshop's performance on your computer system is to increase the amount of RAM you have installed.

Before you save a file for the first time, that data is stored in your computer's RAM. But with Photoshop files, the program keeps a copy in RAM even after you save a file to disk. In fact, Photoshop constantly manages large amounts of your file's data during your image editing. This is what powers Photoshop's multiple levels of undo, which let you revert to earlier stages of your editing sessions as you want if you decide you don't like the results of your image manipulations.

Photoshop's memory management needs are so complex and funky that I want to take time out from this buyers' discussion to cover the basics of how the program's memory-caching scheme, called *virtual memory*, works.

Virtual Memory

Virtual memory is a technique Photoshop uses to substitute hard disk space for RAM. When Photoshop doesn't have enough RAM to complete an operation, it makes use of free hard disk space on your computer. This will get the job done, but because accessing hard disk space takes a lot longer than accessing RAM, Photoshop operates much more slowly.

Users with older versions of MacOS may remember turning off virtual memory in order to improve Photoshop's performance—but that won't be necessary when you're upgrading to Photoshop 6.0, which requires at least MacOS version 8.5 for your operating system. That's because the built-in virtual memory scheme for Mac software before version 8.1 conflicted with Photoshop's virtual memory. If you're running Mac system software that predates version 8.1, you'd do well to just turn off Apple's virtual memory when you're using Photoshop.

In this case, you should turn on virtual memory only if you don't have enough RAM to run Photoshop otherwise. Similarly, Adobe advises against using programs like Connectix's RAM Doubler that aim to extend your RAM or hard disk space in a virtual way.

With virtual memory turned on, remember that you should never allocate more RAM to Photoshop than you physically have. Also, don't allocate all the RAM you have just to Photoshop—you have to account for what

your system software uses and subtract at least that much from your total RAM before assigning RAM to Photoshop.

Allocating Physical RAM to Photoshop under Windows

If you're using Windows, Photoshop automatically allocates 60 percent of whatever RAM is available for its own use. Under Windows NT, this amount is set to 50 percent. You can increase this setting, but the optimal RAM settings really depend on what else you're doing at the time—for example, if you need to print files or use other applications, you wouldn't want to turn over a much greater amount of RAM for Photoshop's exclusive use. You can change this physical memory amount within Photoshop by choosing Preferences from the File menu, and then choosing Memory & Image Cache (see Figure 1.1).

Allocating Physical RAM to Photoshop on a Mac

The following steps walk you through allocating RAM to Photoshop on a Mac. It may look familiar to you—it's the same way you increase the memory for any Mac application—so you should feel free to skip it if you already know how to give a program more RAM.

1. Make sure that you've quit Photoshop and are working from your Mac desktop. Select your Photoshop application icon and choose the Get Info command from the File menu (or press Cmd+I).

Figure 1.1

Windows users can use the Memory & Image Cache settings in the Preferences dialog box to change the amount of RAM that Photoshop allocates for its own use. Under Windows NT, the default is 50 percent; for other versions of Windows, the default is 60 percent.

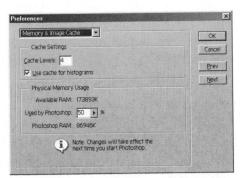

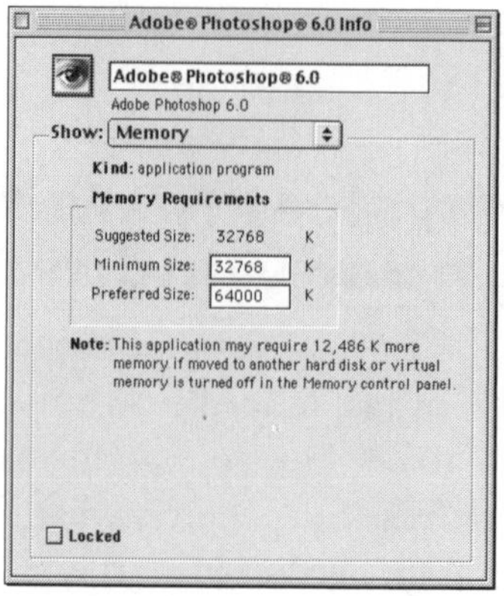

Figure 1.2

Mac users can allocate more RAM to Photoshop via its Get Info dialog box.

2. Once you launch the Adobe Photoshop 6.0 Info dialog box, choose Memory from the Show drop-down list. Enter a higher number in the Preferred Size box to allocate more RAM to the application.

3. Remember the warning about not allocating more RAM to Photoshop than you physically have. If you have 64MB of RAM installed in your machine and your system software uses 6MB of RAM, don't make Photoshop's Minimum or Preferred Size larger than 58MB. (You can determine the amount of RAM your system software uses by choosing About This Computer from the Apple menu in the Finder.)

Figure 1.2 shows the dialog box for allocating more memory to Photoshop directly.

Clearing RAM within Photoshop

Whenever you cut or copy a large selection in Photoshop, that selection stays in the active part of your RAM and can slow down the program significantly. The quickest solution for avoiding this problem is to use Photoshop's drag-and-drop feature to move selections from one layer or document to another, instead of cutting and pasting.

A more far-reaching solution is to use the Purge command from the Edit menu (see Figure 1.3). Use this command to clear any data currently saved to the program's Clipboard or to clear the step-by-step recording of your image editing stored in the History palette.

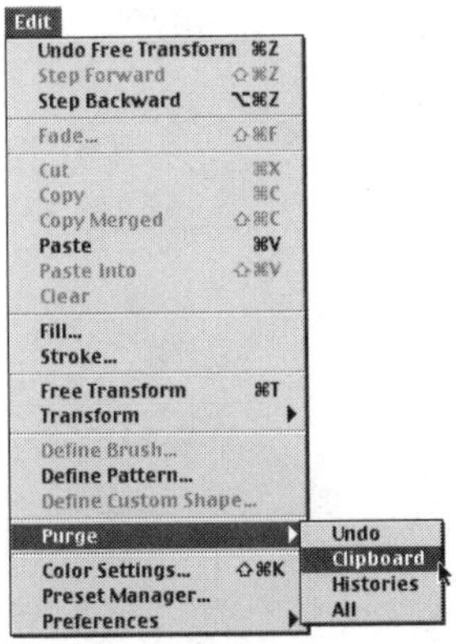

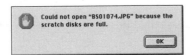

Figure 1.3

By choosing Purge from the Edit menu, you delete the image data from memory to free up RAM.

Scratch Disks (Hard Disk Space)

Photoshop will start using your hard disk space when it runs out of RAM. So, what happens when you don't have that much free disk space to spare? Photoshop calls the hard disk it's using for virtual memory a *scratch disk*. When that's no longer available, Photoshop displays an error message that says the scratch disk is full (see Figure 1.4).

Photoshop requires that you have at least as much free hard disk space as you have RAM allocated to run the program. If you've allocated 72MB of RAM to Photoshop, you must have at least 72MB free on your scratch disk—even if you're only trying to open a tiny file.

To avoid running out of scratch disk space while working in Photoshop, however, you should keep considerably more than that available— at least three to five times as much free hard disk space as you have RAM. So if you're using 64MB of RAM, try to keep 192MB of free hard disk space available before launching Photoshop.

There's an easy way within Photoshop to check your scratch disk efficiency and keep track of how much RAM your commands are using: let your status line display it for you. The status line is a little text blurb

Figure 1.4

When your scratch disk is full, Photoshop stops working until you free up more space for it.

Could not open "BS01074.JPG" because the scratch disks are full.

OK

Figure 1.5

Changing your status line to Scratch Sizes gives you a running count of how much memory you're using.

that appears in the lower-left corner of your document window in Photoshop. The default line reads Document Sizes. You can click the status line to display a pop-up menu with your other options. You can select Scratch Sizes, which shows you how much RAM Photoshop is using and how much you have allocated—as shown in Figure 1.5. If the amount of RAM used (the first number shown) is larger than the amount allocated (the second number), you'll know that Photoshop's virtual memory has kicked in.

 *tip*

Let Photoshop Tell You About Your Documents

You've just seen how to look up your scratch disk usage in Photoshop via the status line—but what other information can you glean from this line? Here's an overview:

👁 **Document sizes.** Here you'll see two file sizes separated by a slash mark (/). The file size on the right shows the current open size of your graphic, with all layers and channels in place. The value at left shows what the file size would be if the layers were flattened and alpha channels removed—in other words, when the native Photoshop document is prepared for final output.

👁 **Document profile.** This refers to the color-mode profile information saved with the file, if it is saved in a file format that supports embedded ICC profiles. By default, untagged documents are saved without embedded profiles; here, their document profiles might say "Untagged RGB" or "Untagged CMYK."

👁 **Efficiency.** This value indicates whether Photoshop is operating using only RAM, or whether it is using the scratch disk for more memory. A value close to 100 percent indicates that the scratch disk is not very much in use, so increasing RAM would not improve performance at this point. If the value is hovering at about 75 percent, though, you can boost performance by increasing RAM.

👁 **Timing.** The value shown here reports how long it took to carry out the last operation. If certain operations (such as applying complex filters) take so long to apply that you tend to leave your machine for the duration, this is one way to determine exactly how long that operation took and keep that in mind when you need to repeat that step.

👁 **Current tool.** If your Photoshop view temporarily hides all palettes including the toolbar, you might have difficulty immediately sensing what tool is currently active. This value lets you instantly see what tool is selected without needing to backtrack or change the view.

Assigning Additional Scratch Disks

Photoshop lets you specify a total of four scratch volumes, using up to 200GB of scratch space. If you have an external hard drive you use for extra disk space or one that runs faster than your primary one, for example, you can tell Photoshop to use this drive as a scratch disk after it runs out of room on your primary hard drive.

To designate additional scratch disks, choose Preferences from the Edit menu, and then select Plug-Ins & Scratch Disks (see Figure 1.6). Click the First pop-up menu and select the drive you want. Repeat this for the Second pop-up menu as needed. You don't need to restart after adding a new scratch volume.

Any volumes you designate as additional scratch disks should be local, nonremoveable storage devices. In other words, don't specify a disk drive that you access over your local area network, or something like a Zip or Jaz drive. Heavy users may benefit from installing a disk array using a system called RAID, which stands for *redundant array of inexpensive disks.*

USB (*Universal Serial Bus*) disks are an easy way to add storage to a modern Mac or PC. Their speed is comparable to SCSI disks of yore on the Mac. FireWire drives can achieve greater throughput but are probably overkill for most Photoshop tasks.

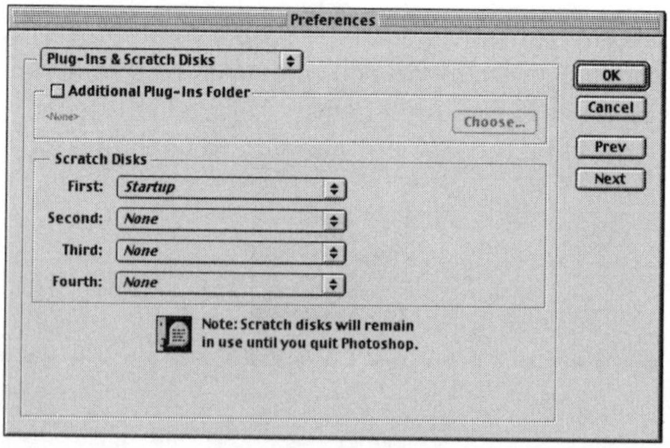

Figure 1.6

The Plug-Ins & Scratch Disks Preferences dialog box allows you to designate additional scratch disks.

General Suggestions for Speeding Up Photoshop

In addition to optimizing RAM and virtual memory, there are a few other instant fixes short of a major hardware purchase that can help your performance. Here are some everyday, all-around tips to help you on the spot when Photoshop suddenly goes sluggish:

- **Partition or defragment your drive**. Photoshop runs most smoothly when information on the hard disk is contiguous and unfragmented.

- **Close other applications**. Background operations can occupy CPU time and slow down Photoshop.

- **Reduce your image cache settings**. In the Memory & Image Cache Preferences dialog box you saw in Figure 1.1, you can enter a lower cache level (the range is 1 to 8) to use less RAM and speed up the time it takes to open a file. You'll find more details about how cache levels work—and the trade-offs of increasing or decreasing this number—in Appendix A, "Preset Manager and Photoshop Preferences."

- **Decrease the disk cache if you're using a Mac**. If your RAM is very limited, you can free up more by lowering the disk cache. This setting is found in the Memory control panel. Use the arrow keys to reduce the disk cache size and close the Memory control panel; you need to restart your machine for the changes to take effect.

- **Remove unnecessary utilities, plug-ins, and extensions**. You can help free up memory by removing unused plug-ins, and this can extend the functionality of Photoshop. On a Mac, you can try rebooting with unnecessary extensions turned off before launching Photoshop.

- **Cut down on your fonts**. A font-management program like Suitcase (for Mac users) or FontMinder (for Windows users) reduces the number of fonts available at any given time, which can cut down on the time it takes for Photoshop to build its font list.

Monitor Basics

A large color monitor is another must-have in your daily Photoshop work. Its screen size, sharpness, and color accuracy are all crucial factors in how comfortably and efficiently you'll be able to produce your designs.

As their costs decrease, flat-panel LCD (liquid crystal display) monitors have become more attractive because they consume less desk space, are often brighter than their traditional CRT (cathode ray tube) counterparts, and just look cool! However, CRT monitors still retain a significant cost advantage. Hooking up flat-panel monitors can also sometimes be more complex because they tend to use different kinds of connectors than CRT monitors.

Because Photoshop is a 24-bit color application, you'll get the best results with a screen set to 24-bit color (also described as "millions of colors"). If you're considering buying a new monitor, you'd do well to conduct some hands-on experiments at a local computer dealer. You'll also be able to judge for yourself whether you really need a 20- or 21-inch monitor (if you can afford it) or whether you can live with a 17- or 19-incher.

Other features to look for in a monitor are a high refresh rate (at least 75Hz), which helps prevent screen flickering, and a small dot pitch (under 29mm), where reducing the amount of space between the dots on your screen produces a sharper image. You'll find more details on how colors are stored in computer memory in the "Filling in the Bits" section in Chapter 2.

Video Display Cards

Video cards determine several factors in conjunction with your monitor. First is the maximum resolution of the screen image, reported as the number of pixels displayed *horizontally* by the number of pixels displayed *vertically*, such as 1280×1024 or 1600×1200. Note that certain monitors may place real or practical limitations on how high a resolution you can display. For example, using a 17-inch monitor at 1600×1200 will result in tiny onscreen objects that are very hard to see.

The second determination is the number of colors that the screen can display at a given resolution, such as 8-bit color (256 colors), 16-bit color (65,536 colors), or 24-bit color (16.7 million colors). If your

video card allows you to add more memory, you can increase the number of colors it can display at higher resolutions.

Leading video card manufacturers include 3dfx, ATI, Diamond Multimedia (a division of S3), and Matrox. Some newer video cards work on both Macs and PCs.

Video Accelerators

Some vendors sell accelerated video cards that help speed up screen redraws, but they might not do much to significantly enhance Photoshop's performance beyond that. If you have an accelerated video card, you should install the maximum amount of video RAM (or VRAM) allowed for the card for best performance. The memory on the card affects only maximum resolution and bit depth, not speed.

note

If you're considering buying an accelerated video card, remember that a 3D accelerator card won't significantly boost Photoshop's performance much because Photoshop only renders 2D graphics. However, most 3D video cards also include some 2D graphic acceleration. You should look for a card that specifically mentions facilitating screen redraw.

Removable Storage

A high-capacity removable storage device like an Iomega Zip drive, Jaz drive, or Castlewood Orb is a must-have for transporting large digital files to service bureaus and printers, as well as transferring them from your home computer to a co-worker's.

For long-term archiving, though, these devices have a failure rate high enough to make safe storage an iffy prospect. You'd do far better to back up your files to tape or an external hard drive, or burn your own CDs with a CD-R or CD-RW drive.

CD-ROM Requirements

CD-ROM drives are almost universal in new computer systems, and make reading and installing software and digital files much faster. You'll need one for installing Photoshop and working with any Photo CDs or clip art CDs you run across in your work. Note that DVD-ROM drives can also read CD-ROMs.

CD-Recordable and CD-Rewritable Drives

Recent price drops have put CD-Recordable (or CD-R) drives within reach of consumers for long-term storage; some are selling for under $200. CD-ROM drives have always let you read CDs, but you've never been able to write to them before. CDs created with these drives work on any computer with a CD-ROM drive or a DVD-ROM drive. With a CD-R drive, you can write once to a new CD you create but not edit the contents further. For works-in-progress, a CD-Rewritable (or CD-RW) drive is a better choice for storing very large files that you are continuing to edit.

These drives are available in both internal and external models, and tend to come bundled with user-friendly software for burning your own CDs. Plextor, Hewlett-Packard, and Philips are some leading manufacturers of these drives.

Internet Connection

Although not essential for your Photoshop work, you'll need a fast modem for communication and your Web projects. A 56Kbps modem is typical of systems sold today; a 28.8Kbps modem is the bare minimum you'll need for Web surfing.

In addition, several forms of broadband connections are becoming increasingly available and affordable. For most users in urban areas, the two best choices are cable modem and DSL (digital subscriber line), which can sometimes be had for less than $40 per month. To take advantage of these connections, your Mac or PC should have an Ethernet connector. Check with your local cable provider or local telephone services provider for information on their broadband offerings.

If your computer can connect to the Internet, clicking the eye icon at the top of Photoshop's toolbox (see Figure 1.7) will launch a splash screen for connecting to the Adobe Online Web site. Click the Refresh

**Click here to
access the Adobe
Online Web site**

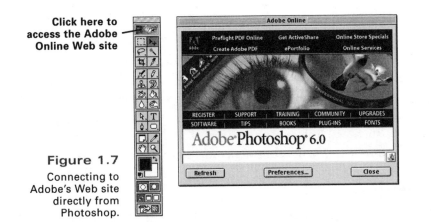

Figure 1.7
Connecting to
Adobe's Web site
directly from
Photoshop.

button to launch your Web browser and connect to Adobe's Web site to find the latest Photoshop downloadables.

Now that you've had a chance to review the various components in your system, you should have a good sense of whether you're well equipped to do intensive Photoshop work with your current setup. Next, you can take a look at some additional equipment you might be considering to round out your hardware arsenal for heavy-duty graphic design work: a printer and scanner.

Printers

As a Photoshop designer, you'll find that complicated printing demands come with the territory. You may have an office (or home office) laser printer to take care of checking designs-in-progress on paper, but still need full-color printouts for a client presentation. Or you may have to send out to your service bureau for color proofs, but also need to determine what option will save money while providing good color accuracy.

At some point you might debate purchasing a new laser printer. A definite sign is when you engage in freelance design—or work you'd rather take home at the end of the day—yet find yourself at your (or your client's) offices at godforsaken hours of the day or night, just to use the equipment!

With so many printers to choose from, comparing models is beyond the scope of this book—but there are a number of more timely resources that can help you out. Periodicals for graphic designers, such as *Publish*, include product roundups and reviews of new printers; computer magazines such as *MacWorld*, *PCWorld*, or *PC Magazine* offer similar help for the specific platform you want. Once you've narrowed down your choices, Web sites such as DealTime (**http://www.dealtime.com/**) and cNet's Shopper.com (**http://www.shopper.com/**) can help you compare prices.

Inkjet Printers

Inkjet printers, which produce colored dots from disposable ink cartridges, are the most affordable option for color printing. They run about half the cost of a color laser printer. There are also very high-end inkjet prints you can order from your service bureau, such as Iris prints.

Laser Printers

Like a photocopier, a laser printer transfers finely powdered toner—please try to avoid breathing the stuff when you change the cartridge!—to paper to re-create the original image, and then applies heat to hold it in place. One of the important factors that determines print quality is the *resolution*, or how many dots per inch the printer can create. A minimum resolution of 300 dpi is standard; an increasing number of models now offer 600 dpi and higher. You can find both black-and-white and color laser printers, which are increasingly affordable. Color laser printers use separate toner cartridges for cyan, magenta, yellow, and black in separate passes to produce full-color pages.

Dye-Sub Printers

Dye-sublimation printers are the highest quality (and priciest) of the color printers described here, although some color laser printers have begun to rival dye-sub printers in quality. Dye-sub printers use four separate dyes—cyan, magenta, yellow, and black—to produce a continuous-tone image with good color accuracy. You can order dye-sub prints from your service bureau; ask what options they offer.

Imagesetters

A service bureau's imagesetters, or typesetters, typically output photo-sensitive paper or film that then needs to be developed in a separate step, like film from a camera. Imagesetter output is usually at a high resolution, such as 1,270 or 2,540 dpi.

If you have a full-color print job to send to film, your service bureau will output a separate piece of film for each color—cyan, magenta, yellow, and black (these four are collectively called *process colors*), and any additional colors (called *spot colors*)—in your job. This film is often used to generate an *off-press proof* (so-called because they're making it from film alone, and not on the press) that gives you a good indication of the final color output. These proofs are used by commercial printers at press time to help color-check the final product. If you're asked to look at and approve color for off-press proofs of your work, you'll probably see laminated proofs, such as Matchprints, FujiArt proofs (for process color work), or Chromalins (for spot color jobs).

Scanners

Scanners really boost the range of source materials you can use in your Photoshop graphics. With a scanner, you can copy old photographs, hand-drawn or painted artwork, textures from fabric swatches and household objects, doodles on napkins—almost anything you can put on a flat surface.

There are quite a few scanners in the home office category, generally priced from $99 up to about $1,000. Many low-end models aren't well suited for high-resolution Photoshop use, however, because they tend to produce muddy colors or dark overcasts on every scan—problems that will take valuable time to correct. Before you buy a scanner, solicit as much feedback as you can through Web sites. You can discuss models with fellow users at Deja.com, Productopia.com, CreativePro.com, or the i/us forums (at **http://www.i-us.com/pshop.htm**).

Depending on the level of design work you'll be doing, you might be able to contract out your scanning to a service bureau. You might really just need to work with low-resolution scans to position type and photos

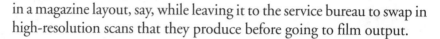

in a magazine layout, say, while leaving it to the service bureau to swap in high-resolution scans that they produce before going to film output.

Whether you plan to purchase a scanner yourself or you have others do your scanning for you, you'd do well to understand the fundamentals of how scanners work and what quality you can expect from different kinds of scanners.

Flatbed Scanners

Most scanners sold for office and home office use are flatbed scanners, which resemble copying machines to a certain extent. After you place your artwork under the machine's cover, thousands of light beams pass over the original and reflect back information for a digitized reproduction. Leading manufacturers of flatbed scanners include Agfa, Canon, Hewlett-Packard, Microtek, Epson, and Umax.

Resolution is just as important in scanning as it is in printing. The greater the resolution (measured here in pixels per inch, or ppi), the sharper your final image. Lower-cost scanners generally produce 600-ppi output; some boast 1200-ppi resolution but really use *interpolation*—filling in more colors and pixels after an initial scan—to approximate the claimed resolution.

Slide Scanners

If you ever have to digitize slides, you'll need a slide scanner to get the job done. These tend to have much better resolutions than flatbed scanners, up into the 5,000- to 6,000-ppi range. Leading slide scanner manufacturers include Nikon and Microtek.

Drum Scanners

The most professional scan output you can get is from a drum scanner, which rotates the original material on a drum and uses a stationary light source to scan the image. Because a drum scanner can cost $30,000—and is pretty massive, to boot—you'll probably have the service bureau produce these high-quality scans (at $25 to $100 a pop) for you.

• •

Show Your Scanner a Little TLC

To produce the sharpest scans, it's very important to keep your scanner as spotlessly clean as possible. Ideally, it should be clean enough to eat off of (not that I'd recommend doing so). Every time you lift the cover and use your flatbed scanner, the glass platen is vulnerable to dust, fingerprints, and grime. Keep a container of glass cleaner and a soft cloth handy to wipe off the platen as needed; a can of compressed air is also handy for getting rid of dust. If you ever need to scan something heavy or metallic that might scratch the platen, it's a good idea to place a sheet of clear plastic down first—also spotlessly clean, of course.

• •

Further details on good scanning techniques appear in Chapter 9, "Scanning Essentials."

Calibrating Your Monitor

Calibrating your monitor will help you match the colors on your computer screen with those in a full-color image that appears in a printed publication. By properly calibrating your monitor, you can help ensure that your full-color printouts turn out the way you expect—and avoid running up a tab because of color reprints.

There will always be a difference between the colors you see on your computer monitor, which uses the RGB (red, green, blue) color gamut, and the colors you see on a printed page, which are produced via the CMYK (cyan, magenta, yellow, black) printing process. And there are some very bright, saturated hues you can see onscreen that just can't be matched in print—they're simply outside the color range achievable by printing presses. Chapter 4, "Color Essentials," covers in greater detail what monitor calibration can—and can't—do for you.

Monitors are also subject to a lot of variance every time you turn them on and off and as they warm up. They wear out over time, so the monitor you bought two years ago is probably a lot dimmer than it was when you first got it.

Despite all the good reasons to calibrate your monitor, it's something that many designers just never get around to doing. Many art directors and entire professional art staffs never fine-tune their monitors but still manage to get by. Maybe it's human nature, but it's the way people treat their television sets too: through careful tweaking you can add never-before-seen vivid and realistic colors, yet almost everyone settles for just plugging the thing in and turning it on.

Calibration programs judiciously reduce the brightness of your monitor's red, green, and blue channels. As a result, your monitor will be somewhat dimmer after you've calibrated it than before.

You can calibrate your monitor either through the Adobe Gamma utility included with Photoshop, or with any hardware-based monitor calibration program included when you bought your monitor. If you have a hardware-based color calibration utility that can generate an ICC-compliant profile, it's a better choice than the Adobe Gamma utility. Now take a look at what you need to know before putting these tools to work in calibrating your monitor.

Crash Course in Calibration Terminology

Here are the basic settings that you're tweaking when you calibrate your monitor. The next section—on using Photoshop's own built-in calibration—walks you through how to refine these settings.

- 👁 **Gamma**. A numerical representation of an image's contrast. As the gamma increases, the contrast gets higher and the images get lighter. Lower gamma means less contrast and darker images.

- 👁 **White point**. The lightest shade of white that your monitor can display. It should be set to the same color white as the paper stock you print on. Uncalibrated monitors tend to have a blue overcast that can be difficult to compensate for when you're trying to picture what an onscreen image will look like in print. Your monitor's white point is measured in degrees.

- 👁 **Black point**. Similarly, the heaviest shade of black that your monitor can display. Setting the black point, also measured in degrees, helps ensure that shadows and dark areas show up properly on your screen.

- 👁 **Phosphors**. The values for your monitor's pure red, green, and blue hues.

Calibrating Your Monitor in Photoshop

No matter which calibration method you use, there are some good all-purpose steps to take beforehand:

- 👁 Leave your monitor turned on for at least half an hour to stabilize the monitor display.

- 👁 Make sure the room's lighting is set to the ordinary conditions you plan to maintain. It's best to shut off all outside lighting as much as possible, because natural light tends to make colors look different on the screen at different times of day.

- 👁 Set your desktop pattern to a solid gray. Dithered gray or colored patterns can play tricks on your eyes during the calibration process. Mac users with System 8 or later can change this by using the Desktop Pictures control panel; those with earlier system software can use the General Controls control panel. Windows 95 users can change background color by using the Display control panel.

- 👁 Fine-tune your monitor's brightness and contrast to the levels that look best to you.

Now you're ready to calibrate your monitor:

1. Open the Adobe Gamma control. On a Mac, choose Control Panels from the Apple menu and then pick Adobe Gamma. On a Windows machine, choose Settings from the Start menu, select Control Panel, and then click the Adobe Gamma icon.

2. Choose either of the two options given for running the utility: Step By Step or Control Panel. If you choose Step By Step, a series of dialog boxes prompts you for input and guides you all the way through the calibration process (see Figure 1.8). If you choose Control Panel, all the input you are asked for is presented in a single dialog box; proceed with the steps listed here to find the values to enter (see Figure 1.9).

3. You can load your computer monitor's ICC profile, if one exists, as a starting point for calibrating your monitor. Click Load, and select the monitor ICC profile that matches your computer monitor.

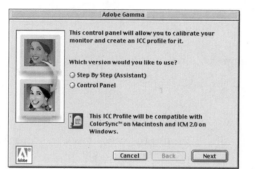

Figure 1.8
Launching the
Adobe Gamma
control panel.

Figure 1.9
If you choose the
Control Panel
option, you
manually set
your selections in
a single dialog
box. The options
shown are similar
whether you're
using a
Macintosh
(at left) or
Windows NT
(at right).

4. Turn your monitor's contrast and brightness controls to their highest settings. Now adjust the brightness to darken the alternating gray squares in the top bar while keeping the bottom bar as white as possible.

5. Under Phosphors, you can use the drop-down list to choose a monitor type if an incorrect one is selected. If you don't know what values to enter, just leave this setting alone.

6. Set your monitor's gray levels next. Click the Gamma Adjustment slider left or right until the center box seems to fade into the patterned frame. If you uncheck the View Single Gamma Only check box, you can adjust separate settings for red, green, and blue.

7. You can vary the White Point setting next, but you'd do well to leave it set at the Hardware default.

8. Click the Desired drop-down list to enter a value for target gamma. If you're running Windows, the default is 2.2; on a Mac, this is 1.8. Click the Adjusted drop-down list, and choose the Same as Hardware setting.

9. Click the OK button on the control panel (or click Finish if you're running the Step By Step wizard) to save your settings.

Acquiring Images

Although Photoshop is an incredible photo-realistic editing program, you'll probably use it more for altering images than for creating them from scratch. The following methods describe some of the main ways designers acquire base images they use in creating their stunning compositions.

Scanning

As mentioned earlier, most designers regard scanning as a prime method for obtaining source material for new digital compositions. Typical uses include scanning photographs or original artwork, but a little brainstorming will help you come up with additional effects. For example, if you need an image of a household object like a safety pin or a textured pattern like denim, you can place the object right on the scanner's glass and scan the original.

I've seen people scan telephone receivers, dinner napkins, leaves, and a roll of metallic wrapping paper. Please take care, though, not to scratch the scanner's platen and not to scan anything that can get inside the scanner and damage it. For example, if you're going to scan a pile of sand, put it in a clear plastic bag, not on the glass platen directly!

Digital Clip Art

Packaged clip art and stock photos can provide a quick fix if you need, say, a photo of a typewriter or a Stetson in a hurry. There are a lot of software vendors who sell clip art on CDs. These clip art CDs contain graphics in many formats such as Kodak's proprietary Photo CD format or TIFF. The Photo CD format is especially useful for stock art purposes, because you can open Photo CD files in several sizes and resolutions. Check your mail-order catalogs for Mac or PC software collections.

The best advice here is to view as much of the collection as you can before buying it. You'll feel swindled if you wind up purchasing a lot of cheesy images that don't really suit your needs.

Online Image Archives

You'll find many Web sites at your disposal that are devoted to providing free and for-cost image archives. There are Web sites that specialize in providing images devoted to a specific genre—say, scientific illustrations or celebrity photos. Many of these sites make public domain images available for free downloading, use, and alteration. Appendix B, "Sources for Further Information," lists the URLs for some noteworthy Web-based image archives.

One nice feature about many of these online archives is that they are searchable—if you need a photo of a frog in a hurry, say, you can do a search on the word "frog" and generate a list of all the images in the library that include "frog" in their file description.

 note

Not all the images you'll find in online archives are in the public domain. Some were uploaded by graphic designers advertising their services; others are copyrighted images that belong to companies or commercial photo archives and have been uploaded without their owners' knowledge. The "do unto others" rule is always a good one to live by: just as you wouldn't want others to reproduce your artwork without your permission and credit, don't take advantage of others by passing off their work as your own. (And if virtue doesn't appeal to you, try caution—pirating images is illegal, and you can get sued for copyright infringement even if you aren't selling the images you've used!)

Video and Digital Cameras

If you're going to shoot a lot of your own photos for use in your Photoshop work, it might be worthwhile to invest in a video or digital camera to create electronic images on the spot.

There are a number of ways to capture video from a computer to a video source such as a video camera, VCR, or television. Some video cards from companies such as ATI or Hauppague include video capture capabilities. In addition, USB devices such as those from Eskape Labs can substitute for such video cards. If you have a digital video camera that uses standards such as Digital 8 or MiniDV, you might be able to connect these cameras to your computer via a connection known as IEEE 1394, i.Link, or FireWire. Software such as iMovie 2.0 or Windows Movie Maker (part of Windows Me) allow you to manipulate video capture through these devices. Leading manufacturers of video cameras include Sony, Canon, and JVC. Windows users may want to check out a device that grabs images from video such as the Snappy from Play, Inc.

 note Bear in mind that stored video can consume a tremendous amount of disk space, even more than large Photoshop files.

Digital cameras look like ordinary 35mm cameras for the most part, but save their images to the camera's built-in storage. Some digital cameras have built-in LCD screens so you can immediately see what you've shot; these models, however, really wear down batteries at a rapid clip if you leave the screen on. Leading vendors include Sony, Kodak, Casio, Epson, Canon, Olympus, and Nikon.

There are a number of ways to connect digital cameras to your computer. Some lower-end cameras use a serial connection, whereas newer or higher-end models generally use a USB connection. In addition, most cameras use some form of removable memory that can be read on the PC or Mac with a card reader. The two most popular forms of removable memory are Compaq Flash and SmartMedia. Sony cameras use a format called Memory Stick, and its Mavica line of digital cameras can store images on a standard floppy disk.

Digital cameras can capture images that range from 320×240 pixels to 2,048×1,536 pixels, and beyond. Digital camera capacity is often measured in *megapixels* (1,000 pixels). In general, the higher the number of megapixels, the higher the photo resolution that can be produced.

For print output, in general a 2.1-megapixel image can produce a clear, high-resolution image for a 5×7 photo. A 3.3-megapixel image can produce a quality 8×10 photo.

Drawing Tablets and Software

If you're adept at traditional illustrating or cartooning, you can sketch straight into Photoshop. You'll probably be able to draw faster and more accurately with a pen-based graphics tablet than with a mouse or trackball, however. Wacom is a leading manufacturer of pressure-sensitive drawing tablets, which let you draw thicker lines by pressing harder on the tablet.

Many artists also use other software such as Adobe Illustrator, CorelDRAW, or Macromedia Freehand to create images that they later edit in Photoshop.

Summary

In this chapter, you've learned about the system requirements needed for running Photoshop as smoothly and consistently as you want, the basics of printing and scanning terminology, what monitor calibration can and can't do for you, and obtaining source material for your Photoshop creations.

Straight ahead in Chapter 2, you'll get a chance to look at the basics of opening and saving files in Photoshop. (What? A whole chapter? Yes—the subject has hidden depths...read on!)

File Format Essentials

In This Chapter

Color Depth and Resolution

👁

Graphics File Formats

👁

Understanding Compression

👁

Image Modes

👁

Online and Print Formats

Whenever graphic designers and art directors discuss exchanging files, they always ask the same question: "How do you want me to send that?" This isn't a question of FedEx versus UPS, though—rather, the question is, "Which of the many available graphics file standards and which color mode (RGB or CMYK, for example) is appropriate for your needs?"

Like many other graphics applications, Photoshop has its own native file format, which shows up as Photoshop in your Save As option under the File menu. (A much earlier version of the program, Photoshop 2.0, appears as a separate format.) If you're using Windows, a file in native Photoshop format is saved with the extension .PSD.

In practice, though, you'll probably only use the native Photoshop format during the creative process. When you're ready to send your images to a client or use them in a page layout or multimedia program, you'll turn to one of the acronymized file standards: TIFF, EPS, JPEG, or GIF, among others.

This chapter aims to demystify graphics file formats by explaining the importance of and the role played by the following factors:

- The differences between bitmapped and object-oriented graphics

- Color depth and resolution

- The kinds of files Photoshop can save and open

- The kind of compression best suited to your particular images, and how it affects their quality

- How to work with Photoshop's eight modes: Bitmap, Grayscale, Duotone, Indexed Color, RGB Color, CMYK Color, Lab Color, and Multichannel

- The file formats most commonly used for print publication, multimedia presentations, and Web graphics

You'll find that this chapter really only introduces the file formats and color modes; the real get-down-to-business examples and exercises are still to come in later chapters. If you have a burning graphics file format question, you should feel free to turn ahead to the appropriate

section now. But do come back and read this chapter all the way through, because it will give you a good grounding in the reasons why you might choose one format over another, given the many options you have as a Photoshop user.

Computer-Rendered Graphics: Bitmapped vs. Object-Oriented

Your graphics software has two methods that it uses to store your images: bitmapped (or raster-based) and object-oriented (or vector-based).

From a designer's perspective, the terms also describe the different ways you edit these graphics—with bitmapped graphics you edit the picture dot by dot, whereas with object-oriented graphics you can move lines, curves, and shapes independently of other image elements.

Bitmapped Graphics

Bitmapped graphics use a grid made up of dots, or picture elements (pixels), to present the image (see Figure 2.1). The number of dots in a bitmapped graphic can vary, as can the number of colors available to each pixel, depending on the precise format and the parameters specified for that particular graphic.

You'll see how this works a little later in this chapter in the section entitled "Color Depth and Resolution." Scanned images are always bitmapped, as are graphics you get from paint or image-editing programs (such as Photoshop), screen shots, and images captured on video. There are several standard file formats for bitmapped graphics, both

Figure 2.1

A sample bitmapped graphic; a close-up look reveals the dots that form the image.

platform-specific like BMP (under Windows), PICT (for Macintosh), and cross-platform like GIF (Graphics Interchange Format), TIFF, and JPEG. You can save your Photoshop images in any of these file formats, depending on what's most appropriate for your needs.

Object-Oriented Graphics

When you draw a shape in a program such as Adobe Illustrator that uses object-oriented graphics, you designate its size, border, fill colors, and so on. You can edit and move each shape around onscreen or between documents without affecting the other shapes. It's kind of like playing with Colorforms; you can layer your image's elements, move them, and then place them somewhere else—all without disturbing the rest of the scene.

You can resize elements in object-oriented graphics as much as you want without adversely affecting image quality. Other programs that use these kinds of graphics include Macromedia Freehand, CorelDRAW, and AutoCAD. Object-oriented graphics files tend to be much smaller than bitmapped ones, which makes sense if you think about it—describing an object's general properties and dimensions is more efficient than storing all of an image's information on a pixel-by-pixel basis (see Figure 2.2).

Treating Bitmaps as Objects

It's possible to import a bitmapped image into an object-oriented graphics software program as an independent object. For example, you can

Figure 2.2
A sample object-oriented graphic; a close-up still shows the image's curves.

include a scanned image saved as an EPS (Encapsulated PostScript) file in an Illustrator file. You'll be able to rotate and stretch the object but not touch up individual pixels—those aren't editable within Illustrator.

There's another situation where it's useful to treat a Photoshop graphic like an object-oriented graphic, and that's when you want to use a Photoshop image as a *silhouetted image* in a page layout program. Silhouetted images let you overlap an object with other separate images or make text run around an image easily. You need to save these files within Photoshop in EPS format, incidentally. Chapter 6, "Path Essentials," describes the intricate but manageable process of creating *clipping paths* that let you treat bitmapped graphics like object-oriented ones.

Bringing Object-Oriented Graphics into Photoshop

You can open object-oriented EPS files such as Adobe Illustrator images in Photoshop, and the program will *rasterize* the image elements—that is, turn them into pixels so it can work on them. There are three basic ways to bring object-oriented EPS files into Photoshop:

👁 You can open an EPS file from within Photoshop by choosing Open from the File menu, and then selecting the file you want. This calls up the Rasterize Generic EPS Format dialog box shown in Figure 2.3. From this dialog box, you can change the image's width, height, resolution, and color mode before you load it. You can also choose anti-aliasing, which will apply blended shades of gray to the edges of the image's objects to simulate the smooth curves in the original.

👁 You can place an EPS file within an existing Photoshop document by choosing Place from the File menu, and then selecting

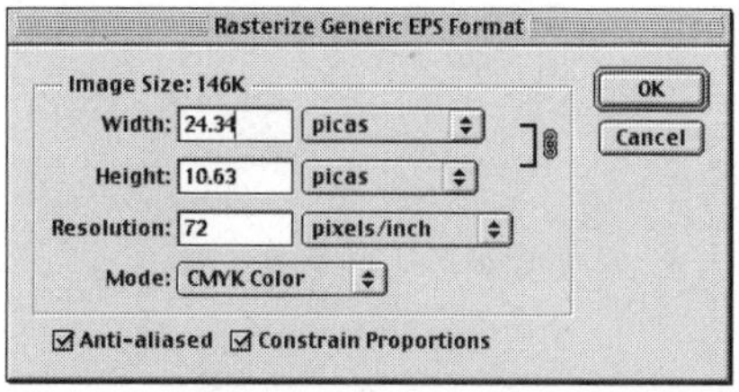

Figure 2.3

Opening an Adobe Illustrator file or generic EPS file in Photoshop.

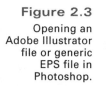

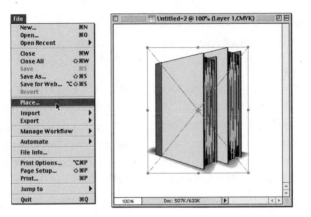

Figure 2.4

Placing an Adobe Illustrator file or generic EPS file in Photoshop.

the file you want. After you choose Place from the File menu, the file will appear in a bounding box that you can click and drag to reposition (see Figure 2.4). You can also change the placed image's proportions. When you've finished repositioning the placed image, double-click it to begin the rasterization process.

👁 If you're using Adobe Illustrator, you can also simply copy selections from an Illustrator document and paste them into Photoshop. After you copy the image in Illustrator, return to Photoshop and choose the Paste command from the Edit menu. The keyboard command is Cmd-V (on a Mac) or Ctrl-V (on a PC). The Paste dialog box appears(see Figure 2.5), asking whether you want to paste the selection as a path, pixels, or a shape layer. The default selection (Path) gives you the same flexibility as the Place command. If you choose Pixels, the Illustrator object will rasterize, so any further resizing will degrade your image's quality. The Shape Layer option makes Photoshop paste your vector shape on a new layer, where it can be edited independently of other parts of your image. You'll learn about how layers work in Chapter 5, "Layering Essentials."

Figure 2.5

The Paste dialog box appears when you paste an Adobe Illustrator file in Photoshop.

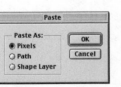

Color Depth and Resolution

One reason for the variety of graphics formats in current use is that different kinds of images lend themselves to different methods of information storage. Two properties that come into play here are *color depth* (how many colors an image has) and *resolution* (how many pixels it uses).

Filling in the Bits

Bitmapped file formats differ in terms of how many colors each pixel can hold. At this point it's necessary to digress a little into the fundamentals of computer memory. Each byte of computer memory includes 8 bits, and each bit has a value of 1 or 0. Thus, 1-bit graphics can only contain pixels with one of two values—black or white. In an 8-bit graphic, each of the 8 bits could have a value of either 1 or 0; totaling up the potential color combinations gives you 2^8, or 256 possible colors.

In 24-bit graphics, each pixel has 3 bytes—that's a whole byte (8 bits) of information each for red, green, and blue hues. This yields 2^{24} or 16.7 million possible colors—which, as it turns out, are too many colors for the human eye to process. A 24-bit graphic, therefore, should appear very realistic to the viewer.

Naturally, 24-bit or larger images use a lot of memory (see Figure 2.6). To reduce those memory requirements, in certain circumstances Photoshop can employ an *indexed color palette* (also called a *color lookup table*, or CLUT) to display or convert your image to 8-bit by distilling the closest 256 colors. I'll revisit this scheme later in this chapter in the section on Indexed Color mode.

Resolution

I've already discussed how a bitmapped image really comprises a large collection of pixels laid out on a grid. When you measure a bitmapped image, it's not enough to know how many inches tall or wide the picture is—you also need to know its *resolution*, or how many pixels fit in a certain unit of measurement, usually pixels per inch (ppi).

Say you have a 72-ppi image that measures 3 inches square. It's possible to resize that image to only 1.5 inches square without changing

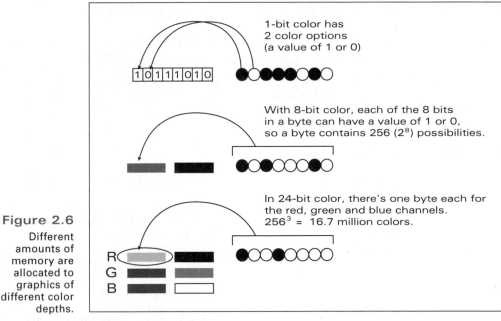

Figure 2.6

Different amounts of memory are allocated to graphics of different color depths.

the number of pixels in it—instead they'll just be doubled to 144 pixels per inch. Doubling the physical measurements—6 inches across now, instead of 3 inches—lowers the resolution to only 36 pixels per inch.

You can see this for yourself by creating your own sample RGB image in Photoshop measuring 3×3 inches with a resolution of 72 ppi. Choose Image Size from the Image menu, as shown in Figure 2.7, and note how the resolution changes when you alter the height and width.

Here's a real-world example using your 72-ppi image measuring 3×3 inches. Service bureaus and professional printers will output your job using one of several standard line screens. A *line screen* refers to the number of dots per inch used to reproduce photos and tints; for your professional print jobs, your printer will need to tell you what line screen to use. Some typical values are a 133-line screen for one-color (black and white) print jobs and a 150-line screen for full-color work.

For best results, your graphics' resolution should roughly double that of the line screen. If the job will print using a 150-line screen, the general rule for you is to use a 300-ppi resolution for all your graphics.

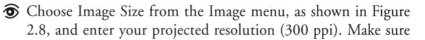

Figure 2.7

Resizing an image to change the resolution. With the Resample Image option left unchecked, the number of pixels per inch changes, but not the number of pixels altogether.

(Chapter 14, "Print Production Essentials," covers this process at much greater length.)

So now you need to convert your 72-ppi image to a 300-ppi one. The math used here is a simple ratio, but Photoshop has a couple of automatic schemes to figure the math for you. Either of the following methods works:

◉ Choose Image Size from the Image menu, as shown in Figure 2.8, and enter your projected resolution (300 ppi). Make sure

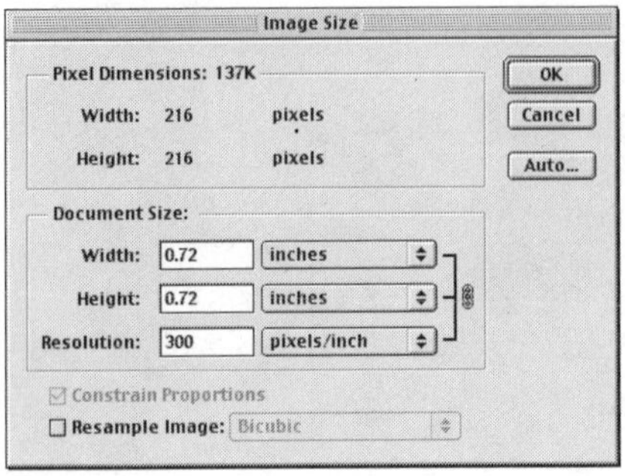

Figure 2.8
The Image Size
dialog box.

the Resample Image check box is not checked. As you can see, your original 3×3 inch graphic now measures .72 of an inch on each side.

👁 Or, choose Image Size from the Image menu, and click the Auto button. Again, you should make sure the Resample Image check box is not checked first. The Auto Resolution dialog box opens (see Figure 2.9). Enter your line screen in the Screen field—again, the professional printer that's outputting this job for you can provide that number. Here, I've entered 150 lines per inch (lpi). Under the Quality heading, check the Best radio button—this setting makes your resolution double your line screen. In this case, the new resolution will be 300 ppi, and Photoshop will work out the 72-ppi to 300-ppi resolution conversion automatically.

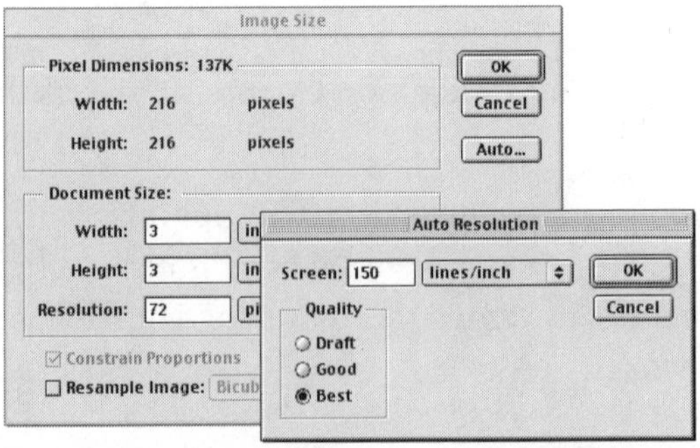

Figure 2.9
Clicking the Auto
button in the
Image Size dialog
box launches the
Auto Resolution
dialog box.

Figure 2.10
After resampling, the image on the right loses the clarity of the image on the left.

note

When the Resample Image check box is not checked, you'll notice that a link icon (⚮) appears in the Image Size dialog box with lines that indicate a connection between the Width, Height, and Resolution values. What happens if you leave the Resample Image check box checked? Well, resampling means that pixels will be added to or subtracted from your image to meet whatever ratio you've imposed—this can adversely affect the quality of your final image, as Figure 2.10 demonstrates. Changing the width, height, or resolution while the Resample Image check box is checked will also change your image's file size.

Graphics File Formats

I've mentioned some file formats for bitmapped images but haven't yet talked about what these different formats will mean to you in your Photoshop work. Before I go any further, it's important to introduce the different kinds of file formats you can save and open in Photoshop.

Photoshop—which originated, incidentally, as a file format translation program—has over 20 graphics built-in formats. It also lets you add plug-ins so you can open and export even more graphics file formats.

Here, I'll just touch on the formats that you're most likely to use and the common applications in which you'll find them. The sections that follow contain more practical information for how you'll use and think about these file formats—some contain compression

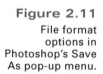

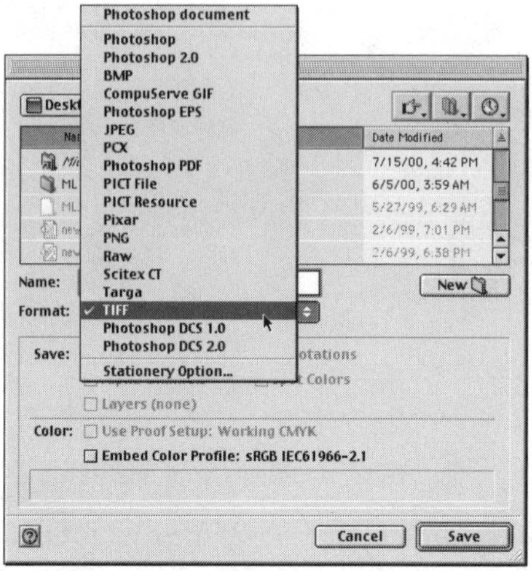

Figure 2.11

File format options in Photoshop's Save As pop-up menu.

schemes for keeping the image's physical file size low, and some should have certain color models (such as RGB or CMYK) assigned, depending on what their end use is. Figure 2.11 shows some of the file formats you can use.

Native Photoshop

While you're editing and tweaking your images, you'd do well to save all your files in Photoshop's native format. It lets you use all of the program's editing tools, commands, and filters. There is a separate Photoshop 2.0 format, which doesn't support features included in Photoshop 3.0 and later versions, such as layers (which are covered in Chapter 5). If you save an image in the Photoshop 2.0 format, you'll see that its file size is often substantially larger than the same file saved in the standard native Photoshop format. Photoshop's proprietary compression scheme was built into the program with version 3.0, so earlier versions don't understand compression and will produce larger file sizes as a result.

Online Standards

If you're creating graphics for Web sites or other online distribution, you need to save them in a format that can be understood by a Web browser, which is the kind of software that displays Web pages.

Graphics Interchange Format (GIF)

CompuServe originally designed the GIF format to enable users to transfer graphics files across its online service. Now available on nearly all computer platforms, GIF is a standard format for Web graphics. It uses compression and limits the number of colors that can be displayed—two features that make it a logical choice for online transmission and display.

GIF is the best file format choice when you're saving flat-color artwork—say, for Web buttons, icons, or other navigational graphics. GIF is not as good as JPEG when saving photos for use on the Web, though, because GIF files contain only up to 256 colors.

note

The format's widespread use was threatened in the mid-1990s because the compression scheme that CompuServe chose for GIF, called LZW (Lempel-Ziv-Welch), is patented. After Unisys, one of the patent holders, discovered the violation, it eventually reached an agreement with CompuServe over licensing software that displays GIFs.

GIF also supports *interlacing* (also called *interleaving*). First a rough preview of the image appears, and then gradually more detail emerges, as you can see in Figure 2.12.

When you choose GIF from the list of file formats when you save your file in Photoshop, you'll be able to include this interlacing feature if desired (see Figure 2.13). If you try to save an image as a GIF without first reducing your full-color image to 256 colors or fewer (through the Indexed Color mode), you will see an Indexed Color dialog box, which forces you to reduce the number of colors in your image.

When you export images in GIF89a format, you can also specify one or more transparent colors (or knockout colors). These colors will not show up when the image is viewed in a Web browser. This will help you create images with irregularly shaped borders for your Web pages. You'll find more details about the GIF89a format in Chapter 12, "Web Graphics Essentials."

Figure 2.12
An interlaced GIF, shown in mid-display and as a completed image.

Figure 2.13
The GIF Options dialog box lets you save a GIF file as interlaced.

Joint Photographic Experts Group (JPEG)

JPEG is a popular Web graphics format named for the group that collaborated on its design. The group's goal was to develop a compressible format for high-quality images—accordingly, JPEG is the file format to choose when you need to place full-color digital photos on a Web site. JPEG shrinks files by using a *lossy* compression method, one that

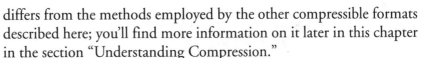

differs from the methods employed by the other compressible formats described here; you'll find more information on it later in this chapter in the section "Understanding Compression."

There is also an interlaced JPEG format, called *progressive JPEG*. Photoshop has built-in support for progressive JPEGs; when you save a file in JPEG format, you simply check the Progressive radio button in the JPEG Options dialog box (see Figure 2.14). Checking the Progressive radio button activates the Scans drop-down list, which lets you choose how many times the image should preview, gradually sharpening before displaying in full.

Note that the JPEG Options dialog box also includes a Size section that estimates both the file size of the image and how long it would take to download at several dial-up modem speeds. This dialog box does the math for you in demonstrating that an 85KB file, for example, would take 59.05 seconds to display at a 14.4Kbps modem speed, or 15.02 seconds at a modem speed of 56.6Kbps (which is four times faster than a 14.4Kbps modem). You can even see the estimated file size change before your eyes if you experiment with the quality settings (Low, Medium, High, or Maximum) under Image Options in the JPEG Options dialog box.

To really take the guesswork out of comparing levels of JPEG image compression or how far you can reduce the number of colors in a GIF, though, you should use Photoshop's Save for Web interface. When you choose Save for Web from the File menu, an interactive interface launches that lets you preview your image in four JPEG, GIF, or PNG file compression schemes. You'll learn how to fine-tune the settings in the Save for Web interface in Chapter 12.

Figure 2.14

The JPEG Options dialog box lets you specify a progressive JPEG format.

Figure 2.15
The PNG Options
dialog box.

Portable Network Graphics (PNG)

The PNG format was designed by a number of software developers after the licensing flap over GIF. PNG has a couple of advantages over GIF—it supports 64-bit images and uses a better and unpatented compression scheme. PNG also supports interlacing. It became a standard file format included with Photoshop as of version 4.0. However, despite its useful features, PNG has made little headway as a popular Web graphics format to date.

If you're using a Macintosh, you'll see the dialog box shown in Figure 2.15 when you save a file in PNG format. Here, you can specify interlacing—PNG's interlacing scheme is called *Adam7*—or file compression, which PNG includes via a filter algorithm. If you're unsure which filter to use—Sub, Up, Average, or Paeth—just choose Adaptive. Windows users see a dialog box that allows you to choose interlacing.

Print Formats

When you're ready to finalize your images for print publication, you'll want to save it in one of the following major graphics file formats.

Tagged-Image File Format (TIFF)

TIFF is a scanning standard for high-resolution grayscale or color images. It is a very flexible file format that is supported by almost all paint programs and page layout applications. If you digitize images with a scanner, you also know that desktop scanners use TIFF as a prominent format for saving files.

TIFF makes use of LZW compression and supports several color modes, including grayscale, RGB, Indexed Color, and CMYK. However, TIFF

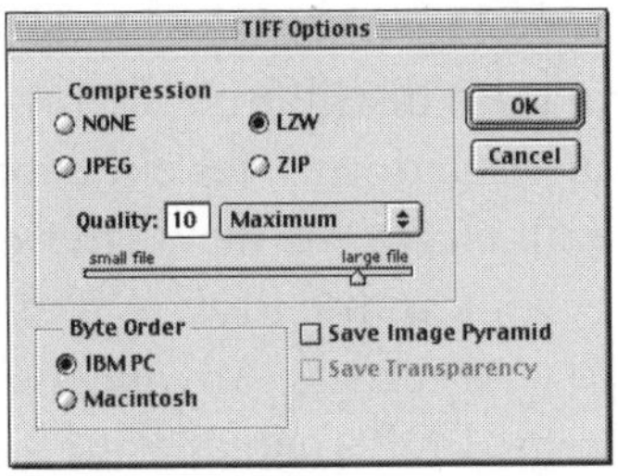

Figure 2.16

When you save a TIFF file, you can choose Mac or PC format. Checking the LZW Compression checkbox is a good idea for reducing file size.

is also a platform-specific setting, because Macs and PCs store TIFFs in slightly different ways. Figure 2.16 shows how you specify Mac or PC format when you save a TIFF file. TIFF is well suited for manipulating large images. Along with EPS, it's one of the main formats for preparing graphics for page layout programs. To compress a TIFF file automatically, check the LZW Compression checkbox.

note

Windows users will find that TIFF is one of several file formats to which you can add file information (such as captions, copyright lines, or notes about your color settings). Mac users can add this information to any file format; Windows users are limited to TIFF, JPEG, EPS, PDF, and native Photoshop formats.

To add file information to your images, choose File Info from the File menu. When the File Info dialog box displays (see Figure 2.17), you can categorize the file information you're including under Caption, Keywords, Categories, Credits, Origin, or Copyright & URL.

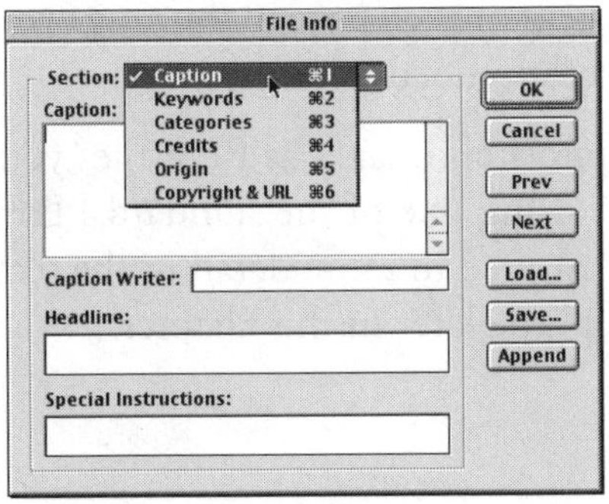

Figure 2.17

The File Info dialog box.

Portable Document Format (PDF)

Adobe's PDF is a file format for distributing highly formatted, typeset publications across computer platforms, for either onscreen viewing or print output. If you have an electronic newsletter or some digital design samples, for instance, you can use PDF to post these files on your Web site or e-mail them to your readers. Anyone using the free Acrobat reader can easily view them. PDF enables your audience to see the highly formatted design and page layout you intended. The major benefit is that your readers don't need access to the same page layout software, fonts, or computer platform you used. You can also make PDF files a very useful online tool by embedding hyperlinks in your document for search and navigation purposes.

You can open and rasterize any PDF file—both single- and multi-page documents—which allows you to add a lot of creative effects to PDF files. For example, you can take a typeset page designed in a page layout program—say, a typeset magazine spread or a book cover—convert it to PDF, and then open the file in Photoshop to apply fun effects. You can continue to work with these files as Photoshop documents or save them in PDF format again by choosing Save As under the File menu.

PDF is based on PostScript, a language invented by Adobe. PDF files can incorporate object-oriented and bitmapped graphics as well as text. They can retain font information and formatting from the original page layout program used, and their file sizes are relatively small—especially when compared to the PostScript files they're built from.

To open a multi-page PDF file in Photoshop, choose Automate from the File menu and then choose Multi-Page PDF to PSD; the Convert Multi-Page PDF to PSD dialog box opens (see Figure 2.18). Each page in your PDF document or each page in the range you specify is saved as an individual Photoshop document.

When you save Photoshop images as PDF files you can choose to reduce your file's size using one of the standard PDF data compression formats. These are covered in more detail in the section "Understanding Compression" a little later in this chapter.

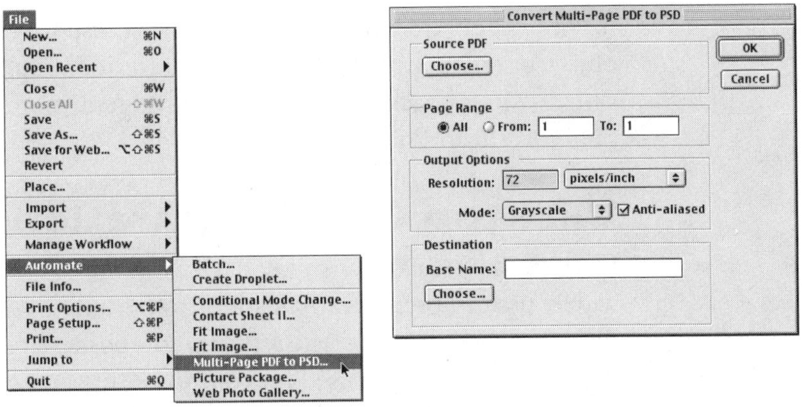

Figure 2.18

When you open a multi-page PDF file in Photoshop, you can specify the file's resolution and color mode, as well as the page range of the input file.

Encapsulated PostScript (EPS)

The main advantage of the EPS format is that it lets you save graphics with *clipping paths*—images with transparent backgrounds that can be silhouetted against others or against other elements in a page layout program. The TIFF format now also has capabilities for including clipping paths, but because not all page layout software supports these kinds of TIFFs, for most printing purposes it's a safer bet to use EPS to create images with clipping paths. Figure 2.19 shows the dialog box for specifying EPS format.

Another benefit is that EPS graphics are already translated into PostScript, so you can usually print them more quickly than other kinds of graphics on PostScript output devices.

EPS is a popular file format for object-oriented graphics in programs like Adobe Illustrator but, as mentioned earlier, the EPS files you open

Figure 2.19

Adding a clipping path to an EPS file lets you create silhouetted images for use with page layout programs.

in Photoshop are already rasterized. As a result, if you want to resize object-oriented artwork placed in Photoshop, you'll get smoother results if you go back to your drawing program to resize the image and then place it in Photoshop again.

Desktop Color Separation (DCS)

Developed by Quark, Inc., DCS is a variation of the EPS format that is widely used in prepress applications to pre-proof CMYK color separations. You can use it to create a 72-dpi composite version of your CMYK document that can be used for color proofing and checking before the final film is output. Photoshop supports DCS 1.0 and 2.0. The difference between the two versions is that DCS 1.0 can only handle CMYK proofs; it cannot be used to proof print jobs with spot colors, die cuts, or other special printing requirements.

DCS 2.0 lets you add to your Photoshop files any spot colors, spot varnishes, die cuts, or other special print needs that are part of your professional print projects. Your DCS 2.0 files can be composite images or can save each channel in a separate file. After you save files in DCS 2.0 format (see bottom half of Figure 2.20), you can place them

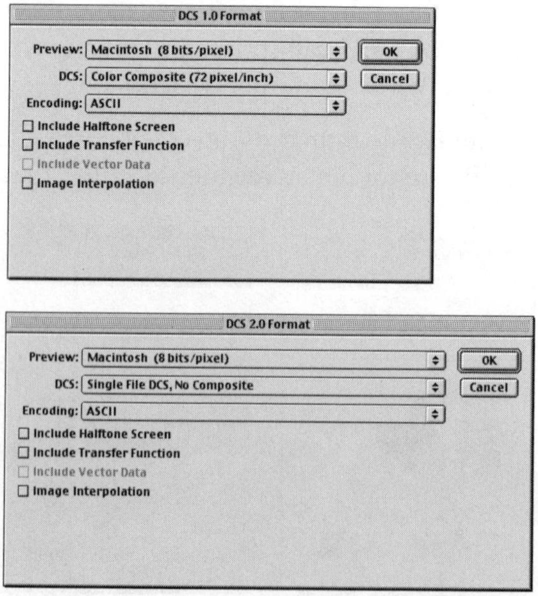

Figure 2.20

Saving files in DCS 1.0 or DCS 2.0 formats, respectively.

in page layout applications that support DCS 2.0 files, such as QuarkXPress or Adobe PageMaker.

Onscreen and Multimedia Standards

The following low-resolution formats are optimized for onscreen viewing; Adobe supplies plug-ins for viewing these and several other formats. For the most part, these formats have been in wide use with platform-specific paint programs.

PICT

PICT is the Macintosh native image resource format; if you take a screen capture on a Mac, it's saved as a PICT file. You can import PICT files into page layout programs, but it's not recommended for print production because it's a low-resolution format (72 ppi). Because PICT has also developed a reputation for choking PostScript devices, these files are best used for onscreen display purposes only.

You can also open and save a Photoshop file as a *PICT resource*. This is a preview of a PICT image that can be stored in the resource fork of a Macintosh file. EPS files, for example, all contain a PICT preview in their resource forks.

BMP and PCX

BMP is the Windows native bitmap format; it is supported by many Windows and OS/2 applications. It can save up to 24-bit images, and has optional compression capabilities.

PCX originated as the native format for PC Paintbrush, the first paint program to run under DOS. The PCX format evolved and accumulated quite a bit of redefinition in a less-than-orderly way; as a result, the BMP format has generally replaced it.

Filmstrip

This format is for opening and resaving a collection of frames from the Adobe Premiere video editing program. You can only open an existing Premiere document in Photoshop; however, there's no way to save a file created in Photoshop as a Filmstrip document.

When you look at a Filmstrip file in Photoshop, you'll see a gray bar underneath each frame that shows the timestamp for that frame in the video. You can toggle quickly from one frame to the next by pressing Shift+Page Down or Shift+Page Up.

Special Interest Formats

A number of file format plug-ins come bundled with Photoshop, and I've already showed you a few of them (GIF, BMP, and Filmstrip). Most of the others, though, are of limited use to designers in general, and need only the briefest of mentions just in case the question "What're these for?" ever comes up. You can use these formats if you need to open (and sometimes save) files sent to you from anyone using one of these systems.

- **Amiga IFF**. The native file format for the now-defunct Amiga from Commodore. These files end with .IFF as a file extension.

- **FlashPix**. This file format—created by Live Picture and endorsed by a host of leading computer companies (Kodak, Microsoft, Hewlett-Packard, and Adobe, among others)—enables multiple resolutions of images to be stored within the same file. You can use this format to open photos captured with a Kodak digital camera. These files end with .FPX as a file extension.

- **Pixar**. Remember Pixar, the brains behind the *Toy Story* movies and *A Bug's Life*? This format is for opening and saving still images for use with one of their 3D-rendering programs, like RenderMan. These files end with .PIC as a file extension.

- **Scitex CT**. A format used by high-end Scitex computers, which professional service bureaus use to produce color separations; the CT stands for Continuous Tone and is also the file extension. Check with your service bureau first before sending images in this format; they'll probably tell you not to bother and just use TIFF instead.

- **Targa**. This format for TrueVision's video boards really belongs with the multimedia category, but its proprietary nature limits its use. You use it to superimpose still images and animation graphics onto live video. These files end with .TGA as a file extension.

When You're Left Guessing: Photoshop's Raw Format

Has this ever happened to you? You've received an image from a client for a project, but there's no indication what file format it's saved in and Photoshop won't open it for you. In desperation, you click the Show All Files check box in the dialog box you get when you choose Open from the File menu; now you can choose from a drop-down menu of file formats, and try to open the file in specific file formats. After unsuccessfully trying to open the image in BMP, PICT, or other formats, you try Raw.

A Raw Options dialog box opens and your heart soars—perhaps you can read this picture after all—but your hopes are soon dashed when you see the garbled mess that fills the screen.

The Raw format is designed as a free-for-all format for reading image data that's unknown. It might be possible for you to recover the image data, although it helps if you know ahead of time what the image's dimensions should be. The Raw Options dialog box asks for several general kinds of information common to all graphics files.

It first asks for the image's width and height in pixels; if you don't know them, leave both boxes blank and press the Guess button. The Photoshop program will then figure out likely dimensions. The Raw Options dialog box also asks you to identify how many channels are in the image, so it helps if you know if this should be an RGB file (with three channels: red, green, and blue) or a CMYK graphic (with four channels: cyan, magenta, yellow, and black). Finally, the dialog box prompts you to answer whether the image file has any header information at the beginning of the file, as some graphics do. As you can see, though, if you already knew this kind of information about your file at hand, you'd probably know what kind of graphics program you should use to display or edit it!

Understanding Compression

It's not unusual for even a single Photoshop image to take up a significant amount of space—10MB, 20MB, or even more—especially when you're dealing with 24-bit color images. Most graphics seem to travel in herds—you might have to wrangle dozens or hundreds of images for a full-length magazine, brochure, or book project. As a result, compression is a crucial feature built into many graphics formats.

Lossy Compression

Lossy compression shrinks an image by averaging the color values of blocks of adjacent pixels and changing them all to the same value. Although some colors are lost, the overall difference to viewers is usually not noticeable. Hence, there is a loss of data, though a virtually imperceptible one, after the image file is decompressed. The JPEG method is the main lossy compression scheme.

For scanned and photographic images, like those shown in Figure 2.21, lossy compression creates a significantly smaller file without much degradation of image quality. It's less suitable for line drawings or graphics containing only a few solid colors. Because lossy-compressed files can't be totally reconstructed, it's a good idea to save an uncompressed version of the image if you plan to edit it any further.

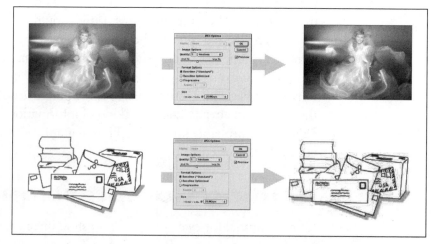

Figure 2.21

Lossy compression is better suited to photos than to simple line art.

Lossless Compression

Formats that use lossless compression, such as TIFF or GIF, have only moderate levels of compression, but retain image data in its entirety. Although the resulting file size of a lossless-compressed image is larger than the equivalent file saved as a JPEG, it will appear onscreen more quickly. Lossless compression formats are better for reducing file sizes for uncomplicated images such as icons or logos than for detailed photographs.

There are several popular schemes for lossless compression. Photoshop's native format and BMP use one called *Run-Length Encoding* (RLE). GIF uses the general-purpose LZW (described earlier in this chapter), which is not specifically tailored to compress graphics images. TIFF can use a variety of compression methods. ZIP encoding is one compression technique used by the PDF format; it's most effective when used with images that contain large areas of a single color.

For most of these formats, there's no way to turn this compression off. With TIFF, however, you do have the option not to use any compression at all. You can go back and check the TIFF Options dialog box in Figure 2.16 to check this for yourself.

Image Modes

As you create new documents in Photoshop, you'll notice that its default image mode is RGB Color. Many of your design projects, however, will probably require you to convert to another color mode. Some examples include:

- ◉ Converting to CMYK color mode when preparing graphics for four-color printing.

- ◉ Saving in Indexed color mode when you're designing icons or other graphics for a Web site.

- ◉ Switching to Duotone mode when using *duotones*, (images in which two inks, usually black and one other color, are superimposed on each other).

Additionally, to make use of some file formats or apply various Photoshop filters, you need to convert to a different image mode. For example, to save in GIF format you'll need to convert to either Indexed color mode or Grayscale.

I've included some brief descriptions and features of Photoshop's color modes. You can find and experiment with them by choosing each item separately in the Mode submenu under Images. These descriptions are very introductory—you'll get a better look at each mode's features as you progress through these pages.

Bitmap

Photoshop's Bitmap mode describes 1-bit images—black-and-white only, no colors or grays. This mode is the most limited; you can't use any filters, and you can't scale or distort images in Bitmap mode. Because you can't use any shades of gray, any features that compel their use—such as anti-aliasing, the Smudge tool, and the Blur tool—are unavailable.

Because 1-bit graphics are pretty basic by nature (see Figure 2.22), there aren't any restrictions in terms of what file format you can save them in.

Figure 2.22
Bitmap images are made up of black and white pixels only.

Figure 2.23
Grayscale images, like the one shown at the top, have greater depth and dimension than their bitmapped counterparts, shown at the bottom.

Grayscale

In Grayscale documents, you have access to all of Photoshop's filters as well as its editing and painting tools. Most of the time that you're in Grayscale mode, you'll be working with 8-bit images including up to 256 shades of gray (see Figure 2.23). If your final printed piece is one-color, however, the number of visible shades of gray will be cut way down. Like Bitmap mode, Grayscale mode lends itself to saving in any of Photoshop's available file formats.

Duotone

Duotone mode lets you enhance grayscale images so you can print them using one, two, three, or four colors of ink (called monotones, duotones, tritones, and quadtones, respectively).

If you work on two-color print pieces, the Duotone mode will be your friend. It lets you produce a greater range of tones than is available with either single ink alone. Say you're designing a two-color newsletter in black and one other ink, or spot color. Your range of possibilities for introducing color includes all shades and blends of the black ink, all shades and blends of your second color, and—with duotones—combinations of both inks together.

Before you can convert an image into a duotone, it must first be in Grayscale mode. To save your duotones for use with page layout programs, you need to save them as EPS files. (The only other file formats available are Photoshop's native format and Raw.) You'll find step-by-step details for converting a grayscale image into a duotone in Chapter 4, "Color Essentials."

Indexed Color

Indexed color mode is useful if you specifically want to limit the number of colors in your images, for example, controlling the way images appear to users whose monitors have limited color capabilities. Probably the most popular use for this mode is in creating GIFs for Web pages; it's also a natural for multimedia and onscreen presentations. With Indexed color mode, you can limit your files to 8-bit, 256-color images.

Indexed-color images draw from a table of 256 colors, called an *indexed color palette*, chosen from the full 24-bit palette. You can create a new indexed color palette every time you convert an RGB or CMYK image to Indexed color, but it's also useful to save a custom palette if you want to create a number of related graphics that all use the same color palette—say, a number of very well-coordinated related icons.

There are some limitations to editing in Indexed color mode. Anti-aliasing and a number of tools (including the Blur, Sharpen, Smudge, and Gradient tools) are unavailable, because using them can introduce new colors that are not in the indexed color palette.

You can save indexed-color images as CompuServe GIF, PICT, Amiga IFF, or BMP files, or in Photoshop's native format. If you need to export an indexed-color image to a page layout program, you should

convert it to CMYK color mode; the image will still only contain 256 colors at most, though. See Chapter 12, "Web Graphics Essentials," for some roll-up-your-sleeves details about working with Indexed color mode and using indexed color palettes.

RGB Color

The RGB color mode, which is what your computer monitor is based on, defines all possible colors as percentages of red, green, or blue. Devices such as televisions and computer monitors produce color by emitting red, green, and blue light beams. As a result, RGB mode is appropriate for any kind of onscreen graphics viewing or editing.

As mentioned earlier, RGB color is Photoshop's default mode. With an RGB color document open, you have access to all of Photoshop's image-editing menus, filters, and commands. RGB color is one of several modes in which you can view the separate color components, or channels, that make up the format. Here's how to use the Channels palette:

1. Open or create any document in RGB color mode.

2. Choose Show Channels from the Window menu.

3. After the Channels palette opens, you should see four channels: each of the RGB channels, and a composite channel on the top (see Figure 2.24).

4. You can view and edit each channel individually, if you like. Toggle between channels by clicking the name of the channel you want

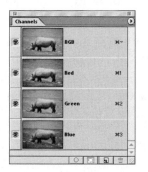

Figure 2.24
The Channels palette.

in the Channels palette. You can also toggle between channels by pressing their assigned key combinations, which show up next to the channel's name. To view the Red channel alone, for example, you press `Cmd`+`1` on a Mac (or `Ctrl`+`1` on a PC). Press `Cmd`+`2` (`Ctrl`+`2` on a PC) for the Green channel, and `Cmd`+`3` (or `Ctrl`+`3`) for Blue. Go back to the composite view by pressing `Cmd`+`~` (or `Ctrl`+`~`). Notice that the viewable channels appear colored in gray in the Channels palette.

● ●

tip

Channel Palette Shortcuts

You can choose to view and edit more than one channel at a time. Highlight the first channel you want to view by clicking its name in the Channels palette, and then hold down Shift as you click the second name. As Figure 2.25 shows, you can see how the color channels contribute to producing your composite image by viewing them singly or in combination—in this example, just the Red channel is visible in the top picture, and both the Red and Blue channels are in view in the bottom picture.

● ●

You'll find out all about how channels work in Chapter 7, "Channel and Mask Essentials."

CMYK Color

If you create graphics for four-color print production, you need to save your images in CMYK format. CMYK color mode divides an image into four channels—one each for cyan, magenta, yellow, and black—corresponding to the inks used in four-color printing.

You can convert from CMYK color to RGB color and back again, but you should try to avoid this because there are some hues in each mode that don't exist in the other, which can cause you to lose some colors along the way. For this reason, if you obtain an image to edit that's already in CMYK color mode—for example, if your service bureau returns a high-end, drum-scanned CMYK image—you're better off keeping it in CMYK.

Figure 2.25

Viewing a single channel, then selecting more than one channel to view at once.

CMYK images can be saved in many formats, including TIFF, EPS, JPEG, native Photoshop format, Scitex CT, and Raw. For four-color printing and exporting to page layout programs, TIFF and EPS are the most common.

Lab Color

Lab color is a device-independent mode designed to display consistent colors no matter what kind of computer system or monitor is in use. It's actually the internal color model that Photoshop uses when converting between RGB and CMYK.

Although not as well known as RGB or CMYK, it's really the safest color mode choice when you need to export an image for editing on another computer system, because you don't risk converting any information or changing how it looks. Files in Lab color mode can be saved in TIFF, EPS, native Photoshop, or Raw format.

Multichannel

Multichannel is a general-purpose mode that can contain a number of 8-bit channels. If you delete a channel from an RGB, Lab, or CMYK image, Photoshop automatically switches over to Multichannel mode.

If you want to experiment with channel conversions or import extra channels into your images, you'll probably find the Multichannel mode very useful for intermediary steps. Otherwise, you might never find uses for Multichannel mode in your daily work. Images in Multichannel mode can be saved only as native Photoshop or Raw files.

Online and Print Formats

When you're ready to distribute your artwork, you need to know which file formats make the most sense for your purposes, and then save and distribute your images accordingly. To that end, this section covers how to make your images readable whether they'll appear in print, in an onscreen presentation, or online.

Table 2.1 summarizes the potential applications for your graphics and what the most appropriate color modes and file formats are for each situation.

Table 2.2 shows what file formats can be opened, imported, saved, or exported from Photoshop itself or from ImageReady (which enhances what you can do with Web graphics). The menu options from the File menus of each file format are shown as well.

Putting It on Paper

Whenever you create graphics that will be imported into a page layout program like QuarkXPress or Adobe PageMaker, you should convert

Table 2.1   Matching Uses with Image Modes and File Formats

REAL-WORLD USE	SAVE IN THIS IMAGE MODE	SAVE IN THIS FILE FORMAT
Artwork for full-color printing	CMYK	TIFF or EPS; check with your image-setting service bureau for their requirements
Graphics with one or more spot colors	CMYK	TIFF or DCS 2.0
Duotones, tritones, or quadtones	First convert to Grayscale mode; then choose Duotone, Tritone, or Quadtone from the Duotone Options dialog box	EPS
Grayscale halftones for printing	Grayscale	TIFF
Simple Web graphics	Indexed Color	GIF
Highly detailed, photorealistic Web graphics	RGB	JPEG
Graphics for slide shows and digital video	RGB	TIFF, BMP, PCX, or PICT for single frames; Filmstrip (for a collection of frames); Targa (if you're using a TrueVision video board)
Reserve for future editing in Adobe Photoshop	RGB	Photoshop

Table 2.2   Matching File Formats with Available File Menu Options in Photoshop and ImageReady

FILE FORMAT	FILE MENU OPTIONS IN PHOTOSHOP	FILE MENU OPTIONS IN IMAGEREADY
Photoshop	Open, Save As	Open, Export Original
Photoshop 2.0	Open, Save As	
Amiga IFF	Open, Save As	Open, Export Original
AVI		Open
BMP	Open, Save As	Open, Export Original
CompuServe GIF	Open, Save As	Open
DCS	Open	
EPS	Open	Open
Filmstrip	Open	Open
JPEG	Open, Save As	Open
PDF	Open, Save As	
PCX	Open, Save As	Open, Export Original
PhotoCD	Open	Open
PICT	Open, Save As	Open, Export Original
PICT Resource (for Mac users only)	Import	Import
Pixar	Open, Save As	Open, Export Original
PNG	Open, Save As	Open
QuickTime		Open, Export Original
Raw	Open, Save As	
Scitex CT	Open, Save As	
Targa	Open, Save As	Open, Export Original
TIFF	Open, Save As	Open, Export Original

them to CMYK (for full-color print jobs) or grayscale (for one-color printing) and save them in TIFF or EPS format.

I mentioned earlier that if your Photoshop graphics use clipping paths to simulate object-oriented graphics, you'll need to save your files as EPS; this is the main reason for choosing EPS over TIFF as a file format for images in print publications. Some page layout programs like Adobe PageMaker can handle clipping paths in TIFF files, but I would still recommend EPS over TIFF for images with clipping paths unless you ascertain that your page layout software has this capability.

Service bureaus that make high-resolution scans for their customers often use EPS format. When they save these high-resolution CMYK images in EPS format, they might turn to the DCS options mentioned earlier in this chapter. DCS saves an image in multiple files—one for each color channel, plus a low-resolution composite file. The service bureau then returns the much smaller low-resolution composite file to the customer to work with. When the time comes to print the job, the service bureau swaps in the other image files. Service bureaus like these EPS variants because graphics print faster, instead of tying up their image-setting equipment for many hours.

However, TIFF has many advantages over EPS. With a TIFF, you can make some changes in QuarkXPress or PageMaker, such as applying a new background color to a graphic or changing its halftone frequency. EPS doesn't let you do that; its file information is a self-contained unit and is simply downloaded straight to the printer when called upon.

TIFF also often cuts processing time when your print job is output. If your printing uses only a fraction of your graphic's information—say, only one corner of an enormous graphic will appear on the page—then using TIFF will speed things along. An EPS must be processed in its entirety even when only a small portion will actually print. Similarly, TIFF is a little more efficient in printing (when the settings call for a lower resolution than the image is optimized for) and in color separation (although it takes time to generate an image preview, which EPS files already contain).

The different uses for TIFF and EPS formats are discussed further in Chapter 14.

Multimedia Applications

If your images are going to be included in presentations viewed onscreen—for example, in slide shows or demos—your requirements are less demanding than for print output. You can keep the image mode at RGB because you're still adhering to an onscreen format; bitmapped file formats like PICT, BMP, or PCX are usually suitable. Your best guide is to find out what file formats the multimedia software you're exporting to can accept.

As mentioned earlier, Photoshop also includes a Filmstrip file format that specifically lets you open and save files from multimedia authoring programs such as Adobe Premiere. You can use a number of other common formats, including PICT, to create and edit images as single frames for Macromedia Director or Adobe Premiere files.

Web Graphics

If you are creating graphics that are destined for Web sites, your most likely choices come down to the two most popular Web graphics formats: GIF (using lossless compression) or JPEG (using lossy compression).

The discussion earlier in this chapter about which kinds of graphics are better suited for lossy or lossless compression should help simplify your decision for your Web design efforts. You should also consider that GIF is an 8-bit format, so it can only represent up to 256 colors. Save in JPEG format to ensure that your full-color or photorealistic graphics retain as much clarity as possible without losing much quality in the trade-off to decrease download time.

Summary

This chapter covered a lot of ground to prepare you for working with all kinds of graphics file formats with various color models, compression schemes, and end uses. With all this material in mind, you're well equipped to start planning what shape your creations will take.

Coming up in Chapter 3, I dip into Photoshop's tool palettes and get you started with some tips and techniques for painting and image editing.

3

Toolbox and Palette Essentials

IN THIS CHAPTER

Viewing and Navigating Images

❂

Selection Tools, Editing Tools,
and Type Tools

❂

Painting and Drawing Tools

❂

The History Palette and Brush

When you're ready to start tooling around in Photoshop—literally—you'll want to take a good, long look at the toolbox (the unlabeled box with all the little icons in it) and experiment with your options there. Although most Photoshop tools are easy to understand, their best features are not very intuitive. This chapter aims to help you discover the powerful uses you wouldn't find through casual dabbling.

Straight ahead, I'll cover the following topics to give you a thorough grounding in how to manipulate Photoshop's tools, their associated palettes, and the other icons represented in the toolbox:

- Explore each of the tools

- Change the foreground and background colors

- Select and manipulate specific parts of an image

- Master the painting and drawing tools and Brushes palette

- Create typographic effects with the Type tool, greatly improved in Photoshop 6.0

- Slice images into smaller pieces for Web sites, by using the new Slice tools or by launching Adobe ImageReady

- Use the History palette and Art History Brush to undo and redo changes you've made to your images

- Add subtle touch-ups with the editing tools

When you launch Photoshop, the toolbox should appear by default on the upper-left side of your screen; however, you can move it anywhere on the screen or even make it disappear entirely. If you moved or hid the toolbox the last time you used Photoshop, it'll remain moved or hidden until you change its position. In other words, you can always find your tools just where you left them.

The toolbox is one of a number of palettes in Photoshop. Similarly, you can put Photoshop's other palettes anywhere you want onscreen. You can show any of these palettes onscreen by choosing the corresponding menu item on the Window menu. These floating palettes

Figure 3.1

You can reposition the toolbox and palettes anywhere you like on your screen. You can hide the status bar, as in this example, but it cannot be moved from the bottom of the screen.

remain in those positions until you move them, or choose a menu command from the Window menu to hide them (see Figure 3.1).

The palettes are also highly customizable; most are represented by a folder-like display. You can pick up these folders by their tabs and reposition them into groupings with other palettes. As you grow more accustomed to using Photoshop, you might find there are certain palettes that you use more frequently; you can then take advantage of their customizable design to keep together the palettes you like to use the most.

One feature in Photoshop 6.0 that has changed significantly from earlier versions is each tool's options settings. No longer a folder-like tab to be mixed-and-matched with the other palettes, Options is now a toolbar that spans the greater part of your monitor's real estate. By default it's positioned at the top of your screen, just below Photoshop's menu bar, but you can click its handle at left and reposition it elsewhere with the mouse.

You'll continue to encounter these extremely useful palettes and toolbars as you progress through this book. For now, just take a look at the commands listed under the Window menu. They let you view and hide the Photoshop palettes and tool information:

- 👁 The Navigator palette provides an easy way to view your images at different magnifications. Info is a highly useful reference palette that tracks your mouse coordinates and color values in two different color spaces.

- 👁 The Options toolbar relates to whichever tool is currently active and updates as you switch tools.

- 👁 The Color and Swatches palettes involve the choosing of colors by entering specific values or clicking color chips, respectively.

- 👁 Several new palettes, discussed later in this chapter, enhance the display of editable type in your images. The Styles palette applies complex special effects and blending options that you can apply to parts of your image (covered ahead in Chapter 5, "Layering Essentials") with a single mouse click. The Character and Paragraph palettes let you specify type characteristics on a par with any word processing program, from font and point size to hyphenation settings, alignment, and hanging indents.

- 👁 The History palette lets you undo multiple steps in your image editing.

- 👁 The Actions palette (covered in Chapter 15, "Automation and Batch Processing Essentials") automates repetitive steps.

- 👁 Layers (covered in Chapter 5) provide a means of editing or photocompositing portions of your image without affecting other parts.

- 👁 Channels (covered in Chapter 7, "Channel and Mask Essentials") are used to manipulate parts of an image based on color or selection area.

👁 Paths (covered in Chapter 6, "Path Essentials") can be used to define a selection area; they work like the Paths feature in Adobe Illustrator or Macromedia Freehand.

note You can press ⸤Tab⸥ to toggle between showing and hiding the toolbox. This also hides and reveals any floating palettes.

Toolbox Overview

Many icons in the toolbox actually contain more than one tool. These multipurpose icons have a tiny arrow in the bottom-right corner that you can click and hold to display a pop-up menu of other tools that share the space. For the icons that contain more than one tool, Mac users can hold down ⸤Option⸥ (Windows users can press ⸤Alt⸥) while clicking an icon to toggle to the next option. For example, ⸤Option⸥-clicking the Lasso tool (or ⸤Alt⸥-clicking for Windows users) will display the Lasso, Polygonal Lasso, and Magnetic Lasso tools in turn. Figure 3.2 shows the toolbox and its parts.

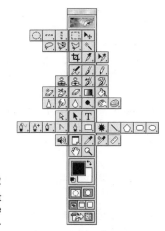

Figure 3.2

The icons that make up the toolbox.

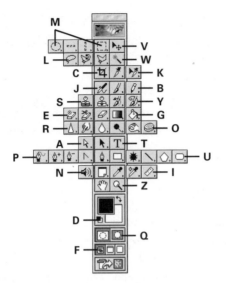

Figure 3.3

The toolbox icons and their associated keystrokes.

 *tip*

● ●

Using the Keyboard to Select Tools

In addition to just clicking the tool you want, you can also select an icon by pressing its assigned key on the keyboard. These key assignments are the same for both Mac and Windows users. Figure 3.3 shows the keystroke you press to select each tool.

For the icons that contain more than one tool, you can hold down Shift as you press that icon's keystroke again to toggle to the next option. For example, pressing and holding Shift while pressing the letter O three times will select the Dodge, Burn, and Sponge tools in turn. Any time you click and hold a tool that has other tools housed at that position, you will see a full list of the tools contained therein showing the icon, name, and associated keystroke.

● ●

Photoshop has a built-in Help option that explains the name and function of each of its tools. If you let the mouse pointer rest for several seconds on any tool, you will see a pop-up menu containing the name of the tool and, in parentheses, the keystroke shortcut that can be used to select that tool. Photoshop calls this feature its *tool tips*. Figure 3.4 shows the tip for the Custom Shape tool.

Figure 3.4
The Custom
Shape tool tip.

You can turn off tool tips if you find them distracting. First, choose Preferences from the Edit menu, and then pick General from the Preferences submenu; uncheck the Show Tool Tips check box in the Preferences dialog box (see Figure 3.5).

You can fine-tune any tool's settings using the options bar. Note that when you switch tools, the toolbar's display changes to show the current options for whichever tool you have selected.

tip

Any modifications you make to a tool's options remain in memory until you actively change them. There is a drop-down menu on the left side of any tool's options bar you can use to either reset that tool's settings or to reset all the tools to their default values (see Figure 3.6).

Figure 3.5
You can use the
Preferences
dialog box to
turn off tool tips.

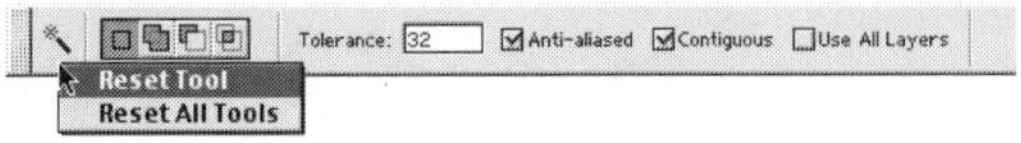

Figure 3.6

Resetting a tool's options to its default values.

Before discussing the tools themselves, it's useful to take a look at the bottom of the toolbox—it contains some special controls that affect the whole process:

- **Color Selection box**. This area controls the current foreground and background colors. If you delete an area onscreen, it will fill with the background color you've chosen. If you add anything to an image, such as drawing a line or filling in a selected area, you'll apply the foreground color.

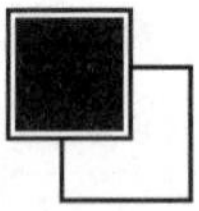

  Clicking either the foreground or background color will call up Photoshop's Color Picker dialog box, in which you can click to choose from a dazzling array of colors. Alternatively, you can type in a color's numeric value from the RGB, CMYK, or Pantone color models or a hexadecimal value (most commonly used in specifying colors on Web pages).

  You can quickly revert to Photoshop's default foreground (black) and background (white) colors by clicking the Default Colors icon or just pressing D.

  The Switch Colors icon lets you reverse your foreground and background color selections. You can click the icon or press X to activate this.

- **Mask Mode box**. In Quick Mask mode, you can use painting tools to extend the boundaries of a selection area—that is, you can make a selection on a pixel-by-pixel basis if you're having difficulty defining a precise area onscreen with just the ordinary selection tools (Marquee, Lasso, or Magic Wand). Don't worry, you don't need to understand at this point how or when to use this option; I just feel compelled to mention the Quick Mask mode here because it does appear in the toolbox. When no document is open onscreen, this option is unavailable. I'll cover masks in fuller detail in Chapter 7.

Clicking here will bring you into Quick Mask mode.

 Clicking here will return you to Normal mode.

👁 **Screen Mode box**. Photoshop gives you several options for hiding or displaying whatever else is on your screen besides the image you're editing.

> The leftmost icon shows the Standard Screen Mode, which is your default display. With this option, your document's title bar, scroll bars, and status bar (for showing memory usage and tool tips) are all shown onscreen; you also see your menu bar at the top of the screen.

> The center icon activates a setting Photoshop calls Full Screen Mode with Menu Bar. This hides all the extras—the title bar, scroll bars, and status bar. The menu bar remains at the top, and a gray background fills the rest of your screen except for the toolbox, any active palettes, and your image. Figure 3.7 shows the same image in Standard Screen Mode and in Full Screen Mode with Menu Bar.

> The rightmost icon activates a setting Photoshop calls Full Screen Mode. Now even the program's menu bar is hidden, and a black background fills in behind your image. Because the scroll bars are still hidden, the easiest ways to move around an image in this mode are to use the Hand tool or the Navigator palette. Figure 3.8 shows the image from Figure 3.7 in this mode.

👁 **Jump To button**. Click this button at the bottom of the tool palette to launch directly into Adobe ImageReady 3.0 for all kinds of image creation and editing tasks related to Web graphics. These include slicing images into sections for faster page loading, editing buttons, adding links to image maps, building animated GIFs, and preparing alternative versions of graphics for rollovers.

 When you click the graphic at the very top of the toolbox, Photoshop launches a dialog box for connecting you with Adobe Online, an online customer support and marketing area.

Figure 3.7

A document in Standard Screen Mode (top), and hiding interface elements in the Full Screen Mode with Menu Bar (bottom).

Figure 3.8
Hiding all
interface
elements—
including the
menu bar. You
can still toggle
floating palettes
on and off.

When you click the graphic at the very bottom of the toolbox, Photoshop will move you directly into Adobe ImageReady (covered ahead in Chapter 13, "Using ImageReady"), which lets you create and refine Web graphics—including creating JavaScript rollovers and GIF animations—that extend beyond Photoshop's core capabilities.

Viewing and Navigating Images

Need to look at different parts of your image, and find it takes too long to use the scroll bars to move around? You can use the Hand or Zoom tools to change what part of your image is shown onscreen without affecting its placement. If your editing work requires a lot of zooming in and out to appraise your changes at different sizes, you can use the Navigator palette controls to take in different views most easily.

The Hand Tool

The Hand tool drags your image so you can see a different portion of it onscreen. It's helpful for scrolling through an image that's too large to

fit in the active window. No matter what tool is selected, you can always temporarily access the Hand tool by pressing [Spacebar].

tip A quick way to fit the entire image in your window at once after looking at a magnified view is to double-click the Hand tool.

The Zoom Tool 🔍

With the Zoom tool, you can change the magnification of the image you're working on. Select the Zoom tool, and then click anywhere in your image to increase the magnification; the spot you've clicked becomes the new center point of the zoomed image. Or, you can also draw a marquee with the Zoom tool to magnify just that selection. If you want to zoom out instead of in, hold down [Option] (or [Alt]) as you click to reduce the magnification. Your document's title bar gives information about the percentage of magnification that you're using. Figure 3.9, for example, shows the same image at 16.7% and 46.91% magnification, as stated in the status bar.

The Zoom tool's options include a check box labeled Resize Windows To Fit (see Figure 3.10). If your image's window size is not large enough to display the entire image at the specified magnification, Photoshop will resize the window to attempt to accommodate the new magnification when this option is checked. If you have floating palettes open on your desktop, by default the resized window will only extend to the edge of where these palettes begin. In order to make Zoom take full advantage of your screen's width, you need to check the Ignore Palettes check box first. The Zoom tool also contains three buttons—Actual

Figure 3.9

Two views of the same image, after magnification with the Zoom tool.

Figure 3.10
The Zoom
options bar.

Pixels, Fit On Screen, and Print Size—that can be used to resize your image's display quickly.

The Navigator Palette

Want to zoom around your image at different magnifications even faster? Choose Show Navigator from the Window menu to display the Navigator palette (see Figure 3.11). This palette has intuitive controls for choosing an area of an image to magnify or specifying an exact zoom percentage.

The main part of the Navigator palette shows a thumbnail view of your image; a red rectangle (called the *view box*) contained therein shows the area of magnification. The Navigator palette controls include:

- A zoom percentage field in the lower left corner that shows the current percentage of magnification. To change to a new percentage, double-click this field, enter the number (without the % sign), and press (Return) (or (Enter), for Windows users).

- The Zoom Slider at the bottom of the palette offers a good quick-and-dirty method for fast zooming: drag the slider left to zoom out, right to zoom in.

- The Zoom In ⏷ and Zoom Out ⏷⏷ buttons on either side of the Zoom Slider do their jobs based on Photoshop's preset percentages; they give you results much like using the actual Zoom tool.

Photoshop has a preset list of magnification levels from 0.65 percent all the way up to 1600 percent. You can see them all by experimenting with the Zoom In and Zoom Out icons on the Navigator palette.

Figure 3.11
The Navigator
palette.

Here are some useful shortcuts I've found for zooming in and out of images:

- 👁 You can click and drag with the Zoom tool, creating a marquee on a portion of your image, to magnify just that selected area.

- 👁 If you're using the Navigator palette, you can easily focus on another part of your image and control its magnification by holding down Cmd (Windows users choose Ctrl) as you click and drag the view box in the thumbnail. Your cursor will change to a magnifying glass icon that looks much like the Zoom tool.

- 👁 You can also control image magnification with keyboard commands alone: Cmd+[+] and Cmd+[−] for Mac users; Ctrl+[+] and Ctrl+[−] for Windows users. That is, by pressing Cmd or Ctrl and the plus (+) or minus (-) keys.

- 👁 You can zoom out to the maximum magnification possible by pressing Cmd+Option+[+] (for Mac users) or Ctrl+Alt+[+] (for Windows users). Similarly, Cmd+Option+[−] (for Mac users) or Ctrl+Alt+[−] (for Windows users) will zoom in to minimum magnification.

- 👁 When another tool is selected, you can zoom in quickly by pressing Cmd+Spacebar (for Mac users) or Ctrl+Spacebar (for Windows users). Adding Option (for Mac users) or Alt (for Windows users) lets you zoom out.

The Measure Tool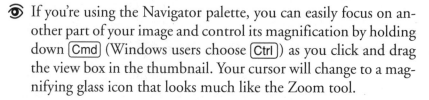

Want to make sure that two parts of your image are aligned? If you add or edit objects that need to look right at an angle, you can use Photoshop's Measure tool to ensure the overall perspective looks right.

After you choose the Measure tool, click the cursor to create a starting point, and then drag to the ending point you want. Holding down Shift will restrain the Measure tool to angles of 45-degree increments.

tip You can set the unit of measurement used by the Measure tool (and elsewhere in Photoshop) in the Units & Rulers Preferences dialog box. Choose Preferences from the Edit menu, and then select Units & Rulers.

Figure 3.12

You can attach messages of any length to your images with the Notes tool; a scroll bar will appear if necessary.

The Notes Tool

If you've ever looked for a way to attach a message or caption to an image before forwarding it to someone else, you might want to try the Notes tool. When you select this tool, you can attach a small message window to your image and begin typing away (see Figure 3.12). You can enter an author name that will appear in the title bar of the message window. You can choose your own font and size for the message text as well as colors for the note icon and the title bar.

The Audio Annotation Tool

If you still have more to say—literally—about your images, you can use the Audio Annotation tool to record a personal message and embed it in your file. You'll need to have audio capabilities on your PC and a microphone hooked up. When you select the Audio Annotation tool you're prompted to enter an author name and a color for the message's icon, just as with the Notes tool. Next, click where in your image you want the annotation icon to be placed. Click the Record button onscreen and then begin speaking into the microphone. There is a Pause option if you need to stop and resume recording. When done, click the Stop button and then click Save.

Selection Tools

Making selections in Photoshop is what gives you so much control over editing parts of an image. The selection features let you apply effects like blends and filters to portions of your image while leaving other parts untouched. The areas you select are displayed onscreen within a crawling, blinking border of *marching ants*.

tip

Hiding the Marching Ants Border

After you apply a special effect to a selection, you might want to see what your image looks like without the marching ants border in place. You can deselect the border (Mac users press Cmd+D; Windows users press Ctrl+D), but what if you need to keep that area selected for other effects? You can just hide the marching ants (Mac users press Cmd+H; Windows users press Ctrl+H) instead of deselecting them entirely. Click this key combination once again to cause the marching ants to display again.

Marquee Tools

A slew of related selection tools occupy the upper-left tool in the toolbox: the Rectangular or Elliptical Marquee tools, and the Single Row and Single Column Marquees. When you're in ImageReady, you'll see an additional Rounded Rectangle tool, which is especially useful for creating Web buttons. You can access these tools in a couple of different ways:

- ◉ Hold down Shift and press M repeatedly to toggle among the different Marquee tools.

- ◉ Click and hold the tiny arrow in the bottom-right corner of the Marquee icon to display all available tools; choose your selection by clicking the tool you want.

Rectangular and Elliptical Marquee Selections

When you select one of the Marquee tools, your cursor will change to a crosshair. Clicking your image creates a starting point for your selection, and you can drag your pointer in any direction to enlarge your selection area.

You can also make your first click on the center of the selection instead of an edge point. To accomplish this, Mac users can hold down Option

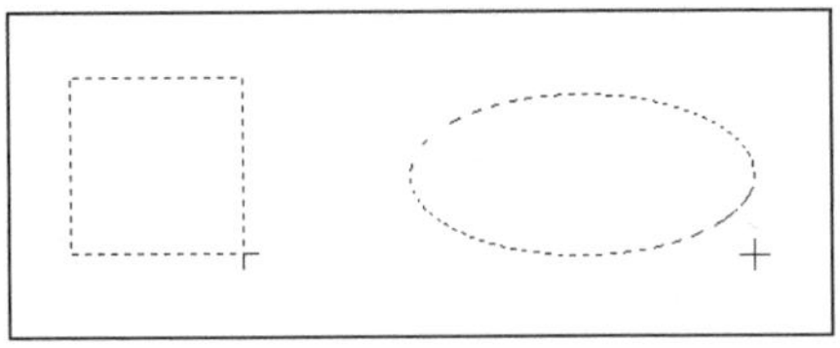

Figure 3.13

Clicking and dragging to create rectangular and elliptical selections.

(Windows users hold down [Alt]) before clicking. Figure 3.13 shows the results of clicking and dragging to create a selection.

note

You can reposition a marquee selection after you've created it. After you've made your selection, position the cursor on or in the marching ants. You'll see the cursor change slightly to an icon that looks like an arrow with a marquee image ( ). Click the selection; you'll be able to move the marquee anywhere you want in your image.

The options you see in the Marquee Options display vary depending on which Marquee tool is selected. See Figure 3.14.

Along the left side of the Marquee Options toolbar, you'll see four tiny icons that illustrate options for adding to or subtracting from a selection.

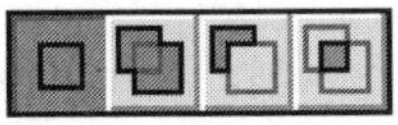

Say you want to apply a filter or some other effect to two separate, noncontiguous areas. It's possible for you to make multiple selections at once by clicking the Add to Selection icon, and then using any selection tool to choose one highlighted area after another.

Alternatively, you can subtract a portion of your current selection by clicking the third icon as you carve out a second selection. To create a selection made up of the overlapping area between two selections, choose the fourth icon in the options bar and then select both areas. I think of

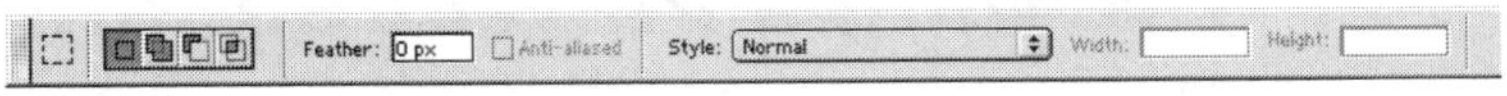

Figure 3.14

The Marquee Options toolbar.

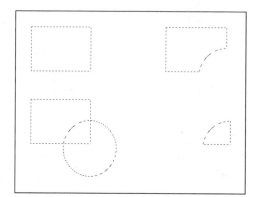

Figure 3.15
Making complex
selections.

these as "subset" selections because they remind me of those illustrations of sets and subsets from math class in grade school. Figure 3.15 demonstrates how to add and subtract from selections and create subset selections.

tip

There are also keyboard equivalents for adding and subtracting from selections. For example, you can hold down (Shift) after you make one first selection, and then use another selection tool to grab another portion of your image while the first selection remains highlighted. To subtract from a current selection, hold down (Option) (for Mac users) or (Alt) (for Windows users).

To create a selection made up of the overlapping area between two selections, hold down (Option)+(Shift) (for Mac users) or (Alt)+(Shift) (for Windows users) as you select both areas.

The other options in the Marquee Options bar vary depending on which Marquee tool is selected. When the Rectangular or Elliptical Marquee tool is selected, for example, you can pre-set the size or shape of a selection via the Marquee options. From this palette, you can also control your selection's *feathering*, an effect that smoothes the transition between the areas inside and outside the selection's border.

Drawing a Perfect Square or Circle

The simplest method for drawing a perfect square or circle using the Rectangular or Elliptical Marquee tool is to press (Shift) as you click and

Figure 3.16
The Constrained
Aspect Ratio
setting for the
Marquee tool.

drag your selection. This will constrain your selection's height and width to identical dimensions.

You can also constrain the selection's dimensions by using the Marquee Options bar. Choose Constrained Aspect Ratio from the Style drop-down list (see Figure 3.16). The default settings that display show a 1 in both the Width and Height boxes, which will create a perfect square or circle. The Constrained Aspect Ratio setting is also useful if you're creating a design that requires shapes with the same proportions but different sizes.

Creating a Selection of Fixed Dimensions

The Marquee options bar also lets you indicate in pixels the exact size of the selection you want. Choose Fixed Size from the Style drop-down menu, and type in the desired Width and Height. Among other uses, this comes in handy if you need to create several objects with the same dimensions for a tile or brick pattern.

Feathering a Selection

As I mentioned earlier, feathering is used to soften the transition boundaries between a selection and the rest of your image. It's a great technique for adding shadows to type and objects in an image, and for creating vignette effects. Figure 3.17 shows an example of adding a vignette effect to a photograph. Here, I've cropped the image with the Marquee tool set to 10 pixels of feathering. This softens the edges and makes them look like they're disappearing gradually into the background.

Feathering vs. Anti-Aliasing

Both the Rectangular and Elliptical Marquee tools have an option for feathering, but the Elliptical Marquee tool has an additional setting for

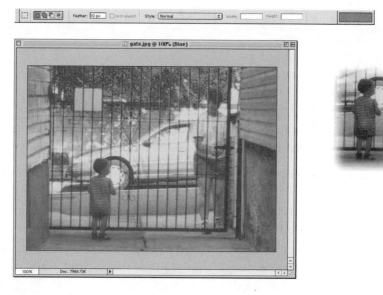

Figure 3.17
Setting a
selection's
feather radius to
10 pixels.

anti-aliasing. Both feathering and anti-aliasing are useful when creating a composite image by blurring the boundaries between an irregularly shaped object and the background. The difference is that feathering blurs pixels on both the inside and outside of a selection, whereas anti-aliasing only introduces blurred pixels on one side of the boundary.

You can also adjust how much feathering is used to affect how the selection will blend with the surrounding pixels. Higher feathering values create a more gradual blend; you can add up to 250 pixels of feathering to a selection. You don't have the same kind of control with anti-aliasing; its blend is always limited to one pixel. Other Photoshop tools that allow for anti-aliasing include the Lasso, Magnetic Lasso, Polygonal Lasso, and the Magic Wand.

Single Row and Single Column Marquee Selections

The Single Row and Single Column Marquee tools are very useful for making a one-pixel-wide (or deep) selection that measures the full depth (or width) of your image. I use this tool when I'm touching up scanned images, to nudge a misaligned one-pixel-deep line back into place. You

might also find these tools very useful to touch up image borders or to visually divide an image in some way.

The Crop Tool

With the Crop tool, you can select part of an image and discard the remainder. This is a useful feature if you've scanned a large image but only wanted to capture a smaller portion. I also use this a lot for sectioning part of an image for use in a page layout program when I don't want to compel the program to load a huge graphics file.

You can also crop an image by making a selection, and then choosing Crop from the Edit menu. When you use the Crop tool, though, you have extra options for specifying the image's height, width, and resolution. Clicking the Front Image button will automatically enter the dimensions—width, height, and resolution—of your current image in the Crop options bar (see Figure 3.18).

The Crop tool gives you corner handles so you can further adjust the size and shape of your selection before you actually crop the image (see Figure 3.19). Click inside the marching ants to implement the cropping change.

Figure 3.18
The Crop
options bar.

Figure 3.19
Using the
Crop tool.

Here are a few useful pointers for cropping that I've run across:

- 👁 If you change your mind about cropping your image after you've already outlined the selection, you may find it difficult to back up. You can start over by pressing Esc.

- 👁 You can rotate your selection by clicking and dragging clockwise or counterclockwise anywhere outside the marquee. You can also reposition the axis for rotating your shape by clicking and dragging the crosshairs that automatically appear at the center of your marquee drawn with the Crop tool. Double-click inside the selection or choose Crop from the Image menu to implement the cropping change.

- 👁 You can also click the OK button in the options bar to crop the image, or click the Cancel button in the options bar to cancel the cropping operation.

- 👁 You can make your first click on the center of your selection rather than on one of the edges by pressing Option (for Mac users) or Alt (for Windows users).

Lasso Tips

The Lasso is the tool of choice for making freeform selections. You can use it to select irregularly shaped areas that are difficult to capture by other means.

The Lasso tool variants, the Polygonal Lasso and Magnetic Lasso, are extremely useful for making other special kinds of selections. They also overcome some of the frustrating limitations of the bare-bones Lasso tool.

The Polygonal Lasso Tool

If you stop clicking as you drag your cursor with the regular Lasso tool, the beginning and ending points will connect and automatically close the selection. By contrast, with the Polygonal Lasso, you click once to begin a selection and then click at every point where you want to place a corner. The selection won't close until you connect with the starting

point again. As its name implies, the Polygonal Lasso is optimized for making selections with numerous corners.

> *tip*
>
> Once you start clicking with the Polygonal Lasso or Magnetic Lasso tool, you'll realize that you need to close the selection before you can move on to using another tool. But what if your selection doesn't turn out quite right, or you lose track of where your starting point was? You can escape from your predicament by pressing ⎋Esc⎦. If your previous action had been to make an earlier selection, that selection will be made active. Otherwise, you will simply escape from your selection-in-progress gone wrong.

The Magnetic Lasso Tool

The Magnetic Lasso also overcomes one frustration of using the regular Lasso tool—namely, the difficulty in controlling a selection with great precision if your hands are less than perfectly steady or if you take a wrong turn halfway through. When you drag the Magnetic Lasso, however, the selection area is formed by the automatic detection of contrasting image areas rather than the strict path you've outlined manually. This makes the Magnetic Lasso tool especially well suited for making complex selections against high-contrast backgrounds.

The Magnetic Lasso options bar differs somewhat from that of the other two Lasso tools (see Figures 3.20 and 3.21). With the regular Lasso or Polygonal Lasso, you can use the options bar to specify anti-aliasing or set values in pixels for feathering. With the Magnetic Lasso tool, you can also set several additional values—Lasso Width, Edge Contrast, and Frequency—to indicate how far the selection area can stray from where your cursor indicates.

Figure 3.20

The options bar for the regular Lasso and Polygonal Lasso tools.

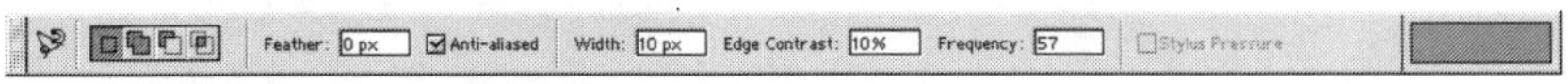

Figure 3.21

The options bar for the Magnetic Lasso tool.

Modifying Selections with the Lasso Tools

After you make a selection, you may sometimes find that you want to add to it. You can do this by pressing the same icons for adding to and subtracting from selections described earlier for the Marquee tools. The previously mentioned keyboard equivalents—such as holding down Shift while you outline an additional selection, for example—work here too. In Figure 3.22, after outlining the dress of one of the seated figures, I've traced a second selection around the dress of the woman standing at right.

Similarly, you can subtract from a selection by clicking the Subtract from Selection icon in the Lasso options bar or using the keyboard equivalent: Option (for Mac users) or Alt (for Windows users). The second selection I made in Figure 3.22 was too wide; I wanted to trace just the dress, not part of the background as well. To fix this, I subtracted several smaller selections from the larger one, as the top half of Figure 3.23 shows. Using this technique to remove the extraneous portions of a selection is much more efficient than just tracing your selection again from scratch.

tip You can draw straight lines and angles restricted to multiples of 45 degrees with the Lasso tool by holding down Spacebar as you click and drag.

Figure 3.22
Using Shift with the regular Lasso tool lets you add to a selection.

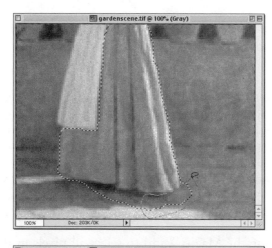

Figure 3.23
Click the Subtract from Selection icon in the Lasso options bar to remove pieces of a selection.

Magic Wand Tips

It's not just for Tinkerbell anymore. With the Magic Wand tool, you can select areas of your image based on the colors they contain. Like the new Magnetic Lasso tool, the Magic Wand is great to use if you need to select parts of an image bounded by a border in a clearly contrasting color. You can specify how choosy the Magic Wand tool should be in selecting pixels by setting its tolerance level.

Setting Tolerance Levels

It sounds like it should describe the limits you set for how long you can stand being around people you don't like, but tolerance level really just

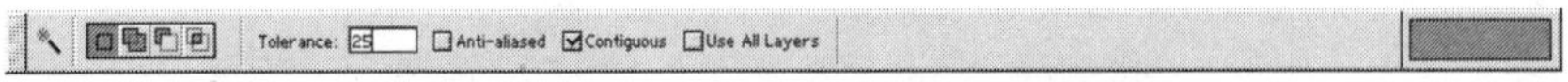

Figure 3.24

The Magic Wand options bar.

defines how many similarly colored, contiguous pixels the Magic Wand tool will pick up after you click in an image. You can enter a numeric value for your tolerance settings in the Magic Wand options bar (the default is 32).

If you choose a tolerance level of 0, the Magic Wand selects only pixels that have the same color as the one you first click. The higher the tolerance setting, the greater the range of pixels the wand will select for you.

You can use the Magic Wand to select all pixels in the color range—whether or not they're touching—by unchecking the Contiguous box (which is checked by default) in the Magic Wand options bar. This only applies to the current layer, though. If your document has different graphic elements on separate layers (covered in Chapter 5), you need to check the Use All Layers box in the options bar to select all colors in the range on all visible layers.

In many cases, you probably won't be able to guess the best tolerance level for grabbing the exact selection you want on the first try. Photoshop uses its own calculations, based on hue and luminance, to figure out what pixels will and will not be selected. For example, if you set your tolerance level to 20 and click a pixel with a value of 100, the Magic Wand will pick up all pixels that have a value between 80 and 120. Figure 3.24 shows the Magic Wand tool's default settings, including anti-aliasing, which smooths out the edges of your selections.

Choosing Smart Tolerance Settings

There can be a lot of trial and error in using the Magic Wand to select the exact area you want. If your first selection doesn't grab enough of the right area, it's easy to raise the tolerance level to allow for a wider range. Most of the time, however, this can backfire and make Photoshop grab much more of your image than you really want. You can retain more control by keeping the tolerance levels low, and then clicking the Add to Selection icon on the Magic Wand options bar (or holding down (Shift)). You then just add a separate selection based on a new color value.

The Magic Wand in Action

The picture in Figure 3.25 shows a straightforward use of the Magic Wand tool. You can select just the Buddha's silhouette in this image by first clicking the light-colored background, and then choosing Inverse from the Select menu to select the opposite of your original selection.

What if you need to select not just a solid object, but an image in which part of the background shows through? After you click the Magic Wand on the background, choose Similar from the Select menu—it will pick up all other instances of the background color—and then choose Inverse from the Select menu. An example is shown in Figure 3.26.

This technique is especially helpful for hard-to-select items—picking up a doughnut but not the hole, for example. Another way to accomplish this is by unchecking the Contiguous box before you make your first selection on the background color—but this solution applies only if you know for certain that you want to select all instances of that color. For example, as Figure 3.27 shows, you can select a sky background including small patches between tree branches by unchecking the Contiguous box—but this works well only if there are no other blue-colored areas in your image.

Figure 3.25
Selecting objects by a slightly roundabout means with the Magic Wand tool.

Figure 3.26
Select a background color, and then choose Inverse from the Select menu.

Figure 3.27
To select all instances of a certain color, just uncheck the Contiguous box in the Magic Wand tool's options bar.

tip You can make selections using the Magic Wand tool in any single channel or layer, and then load it for use on the entire image or any combination of channels or layers. This is good to remember if you're having trouble selecting an item that doesn't stand out well against its background—in such a case, there's bound to be one color channel where the contrast is more prominent, and it might be easier to make your selection in that channel.

The Move Tool

You can use the Move tool to reposition your image selections with great precision. If you try to click and drag a selection when you still have a selection tool chosen, only the selection outline will move. To really move the selected pixels, choose the Move tool immediately after you make your selection.

The Move tool is also frequently used to reposition part of an image without needing to make a selection first. For example, you can use it to move whole layers or channels between documents.

When the Auto Select Layer check box is checked, Photoshop will automatically find the uppermost layer that has pixels under the Move tool and make that your selected layer. As a result, repositioning the mouse pointer will actually move the layer containing the pixels the Move tool had been positioned over.

You may find this feature a little disconcerting at first—as you'll see in Chapter 5, it's important to always keep track of which layer you're working with—but it can be a real timesaver if you do a lot of photocompositing with multi-layer Photoshop files.

tip
You can also always use the arrow keys on your keyboard to move a selection up, down, left, or right. Your selection will move one pixel at a time with each press of an arrow key.

The Move options bar (see Figure 3.28) also contains many options for aligning different layers in your image. These options are available only when you are working in an image that contains at least two layers (see Chapter 5). Make a selection, and then choose the Move tool. You'll see icons for aligning dual layers along your selections' top edges, vertical centers, bottom edges, left edges, horizontal centers, or right edges—as well as comparable selections for distributing your layers across these same parameters. As you begin to create complex photocompositions, this can provide a precise way to line up two layers before you begin to apply effects that blend the two together. Or, if you have linked layers that somehow become separated during your editing sessions, this function can offer an easy solution for getting your separate layers back in sync again.

Figure 3.28
The Move tool's options bar.

Cutting Up Graphics with the Slice and Slice Select Tools

Because a large image on a Web site tends to display faster when sectioned into multiple smaller graphics than as a single large graphic, many Web sites make a practice of *slicing* their splash page images or navigational bars into a series of smaller, interlocking graphics files. You can use Photoshop 6.0's new Slice tool to quickly divide any image into multiple sections. At that point, you can then use the new Slice Select tool to add all kinds of Web features to individual slices.

You can add and specify the Web address (known as an URL) that Web users are taken to when that particular slice is clicked, as well as an alternative "rollover" image that displays when a user's mouse moves over this image. Later on, in Chapters 12, "Web Graphics Essentials," and 13, "Using ImageReady," you'll learn more about the tools and commands within Adobe ImageReady that further automate how you create and edit slices. If you're not currently concerned with learning how to cut up images for Web page display, feel free to skip past this discussion of the Slice and Slice Select tools.

When you first select the Slice tool, you will see the icons for your initial slice display in the upper-left corner of your image (01 ⬚ 8). These indicate the number of each slice, whether your slice is based on a layer, whether it's linked, and whether it contains image data or (as you'll see in Chapter 13) whether you've created a slice that contains other Web page data like a background color or HTML code. When you choose either of the Slice tools within any document, any existing slices will automatically display.

tip You can prevent slice numbers from displaying by unchecking the Show Slice Numbers check box in the Slice tool's options bar.

Next, if you know the exact dimensions of the slice you want to create, you can enter these in the Slice tool's options bar. Choose Fixed Size from the Style drop-down menu and enter the width and height in pixels. The other available style settings in the options bar include Normal, where you just click and drag to indicate the proportions of a

Figure 3.29

The Slice tool's
options bar.

given slice, and Constrained Aspect Ratio, where you set up a height-to-width ratio. To create a slices that measures a perfect square, for example, you can choose Constrained Aspect Ratio and use the default settings where width and height are both set to 1 (see Figure 3.29).

After you create an initial slice, several auto slices are generated to complete the division of your image. The initial slice that you create here is known as a *user slice*, because you have defined its dimensions and placement. After you create this initial slice, several other *auto slices* are dynamically created by Photoshop to fill in the remaining areas of the image. Every time you define an additional slice in this image, more auto slices are generated to divide any remaining unportioned areas. The top image in Figure 3.30 demonstrates how this displays after an initial user slice is created. I then created a second user slice around the word "books" to prevent that part of the image from being divided inappropriately.

tip
Another way to constrain your slice's shape to a square is to hold down Shift as you click and drag. To start drawing a slice from the center, position your mouse at the desired starting point and hold down the Option key (for Mac users) or Alt (for Windows users).

Onscreen, user slices and auto slices display slightly differently. You'll see user slices bounded by a solid line—you can choose the color via the Slice tool's options bar—whereas auto slices are indicated by a dotted line.

Slices are numbered in chronological order from left to right and top to bottom beginning in the upper-left. If you don't want to see the numbers attached to each slice, just uncheck the Show Slice Numbers check box in the Slice tool's options bar. Once you create a second user slice, you'll see that the positions and the number of auto slices displayed will change. If you decide you want to hold on to an auto slice

Figure 3.30

The top image shows the first user slice that's created. At the bottom, a second user slice is added.

to ensure it is not changed, you should switch to the Slice Select tool, choose the auto slice you want, and then click Promote to User Slice in the options bar.

With the Slice Select tool chosen, you can resize any given slice by grabbing a side or corner handle and then dragging to resize it. You can move a slice by placing your pointer inside the selected slice's border, and then dragging to a new position. Hold down (Shift) to limit your repositioning to multiples of 45 degrees.

The Slice Select tool is used most frequently to hyperlink a slice to a Web page. It's also used for entering text that displays in any sliced area once you generate a new Web page based on the image that you're

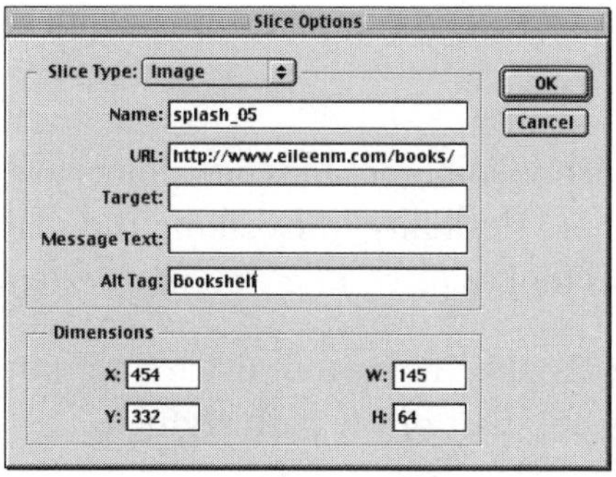

Figure 3.31

The Slice Options dialog box, accessed through the Slice Select tool.

editing here. Because this text is HTML markup, you can format it using any standard HTML tags. You won't see the HTML text displayed here in Photoshop; you'll need to preview it in a Web browser (covered in Chapter 12). To reach these options, click the Slice Options button in the Slice Select tool's options bar. Use the resulting Slice Options dialog box (see Figure 3.31) to enter this additional data for each image slice.

The Pen Tool, Points, and Paths

The Pen tool and its variations are used for creating *paths*, which are object-oriented selections made up of precise lines and curves. If you've ever used a drawing program such as Adobe Illustrator or Macromedia Freehand, you've already learned how to create paths by drawing Bézier curves—you specify anchor points that lie along the curve and manipulate control points that set the shape of the curve. Paths are best suited for placing cutout images into page layout applications or for creating elaborate border effects on selections. I mention them here just to introduce the tools, but you'll see how they work in Chapter 6.

Click with the Pen tool to place a single point in a path. Click again where you want the first segment of the straight line to end, or press ⟨Shift⟩ as you click to constrain the angle of the segment to a multiple of 45 degrees. When you click a second time, a line connects the new point with the first one. These segments ultimately form an entire path.

 The Freeform Pen is designed for sketching Bézier curves easily. With the Freeform Pen tool selected, you use the cursor to sketch the path you want; the tool automatically places points where appropriate.

The Add Anchor Point tool adds new points to existing paths, which gives you more flexibility in tweaking the shape of the path. You can't use this tool to place a new point to extend a path, though.

The Delete Anchor Point tool deletes a point in a path without eliminating any part of the path segment.

The Convert Point tool can turn right-angled corner points into smoothly curved ones, and vice versa.

The Path Component Selection tool lets you quickly move all points in a path.

With the Direct Selection tool (or Arrow tool), you can manipulate and reposition individual points in a path.

Saying It with Type T

The Type tool lets you add text and a vast range of text effects directly to your images. Before Photoshop 6.0, selecting the Type tool launched a Type tool dialog box where you specified typeface, style, font size, color, spacing, and the text you wanted to appear. Now, in 6.0, you can position your cursor directly in your image and instantly see how your type additions appear within the context of your entire image. You can now also click and drag with the Type tool to create a *bounding box* into which you can flow blocks of text that will wrap to fit within the box's boundaries.

You can also use the Type tool to control various typesetting options that you may be familiar with from word processing programs. These include leading, tracking, baseline shift, alignment, and kerning (spacing letters closer together for greater readability). New in 6.0, you can apply *warp styling* to your type selections to align the text along the shape of a wave, arc, or another path.

Photoshop has now added in version 6.0 many features designed to accommodate the display of large amounts of type. To produce posters,

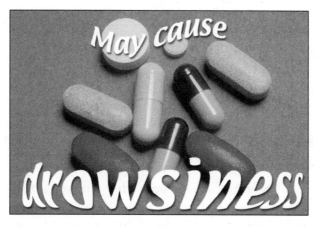

Figure 3.32
The type style effect at top is called Flag, whereas the word "drowsiness" uses a warp styling effect called Fisheye.

brochures, or other complex print materials, many professional designers are used to employing the type features in drawing programs such as Adobe Illustrator or page layout programs such as QuarkXPress on top of base images imported from Photoshop. The new type features in 6.0 are designed to replicate much more of these programs' functionality from within Photoshop. For the first time, you can now set hyphenation and word wrap options within Photoshop, or specify indentation in paragraph settings. You can mix typefaces, styles, and size—if desired, you can even choose different colors within type blocks and mix alignment on a paragraph-by-paragraph basis (see Figure 3.32).

The first drop-down menu in the options bar for the Type tool (see Figure 3.33) shows the font choices that are available in your computer system, or the ones currently available through a type management program such as Suitcase (for Mac users) or Adobe Type Manager (for both Mac and Windows users). I've learned the hard way that having a large number of fonts can severely lengthen the time it takes for Photoshop to build the font menu. (I'm a firm believer in the old typography credo that the one who dies with the most fonts, wins.) If your fonts take an unbearably long time to load, you should probably consider installing—and using!—one of these typeface-management programs.

After you choose a typeface and point size, the next setting in the Type options bar is for anti-aliasing. By default, this is set to Crisp; along with Strong, these two settings especially enhance the onscreen display

Figure 3.33
The Type
options bar.

of your type. Choose the Smooth setting if your graphics will eventually be used in print work. You can turn off anti-aliasing, but this will produce jagged edges on your text's display, especially on the curves of your letterforms.

Next, you can click to apply left-, centered-, or right-justification to any paragraph. If you are editing multiple paragraphs within a bounding box, you can apply this alignment to one or more paragraphs at a time. Similarly, you can click the color swatch in the Type options bar to change the color of any amount of text, from an entire bounding box's content to a single character.

If you click the Create Warped Text button, the Warp Text dialog box will display (see Figure 3.34). Here you can have a lot of fun experimenting with the different warp styles shown in the Style pop-up menu. You should then choose the orientation of the warp effect—that is, whether it should be applied with a Horizontal or Vertical setting. You can also enter a percentage for how much warp is applied to your type layer; remember that entering 0 percent is equivalent to choosing None for the warp style. Finally, entering a value for Horizontal or Vertical Distortion

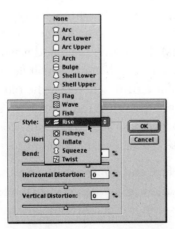

Figure 3.34
The Warp Text
dialog box.

will apply perspective to the warp effect—experimenting with the values will help you determine how useful this effect is for your work.

Clicking the Palettes button will launch both the Character and Paragraph palettes for the Type tool (see Figure 3.35). Here you can fine-tune your text's display in typesetting terms. Don't let it throw you if these terms are new to you—most are readily understood by looking at a few examples. Here are a few definitions for the previously uninitiated:

- **Leading** (pronounced *ledding*). Specifies in points how much vertical space is between the baselines of two lines of type. If the leading value matches the point size of your type—say, if you have 36-point type with a leading of 36—then your leading value is said to be *set solid*.

- **Kerning** and **tracking**. Values that affect how close together (or far apart) pairs of letters are set. If you want to set the spacing for more than just a single pair of letters l i k e t h i s, use a positive *tracking* value instead.

- **Baseline**. The imaginary line that your type sits on. A positive *baseline shift* value raises your type above that point, whereas a negative value lowers it.

The default settings for kerning (which read Metrics) in the Character palette are fine for creating highly readable type, unless you plan to modify your type or its outlines. For those situations, you might want to add extra space (tracking) in order to leave room for drop shadows or other effects.

The Horizontal and Vertical Scale settings can be useful for distorting the size and shape of your letterforms within your Type layer; these settings are new in Photoshop 6.0, but will be familiar to users of Adobe Illustrator.

Figure 3.35

The Character and Paragraph palettes for the Type Tool.

EXERCISE 3.1

Using Type Palettes to Warp and Format Text

Because the Type tool is exponentially more useful in Photoshop 6.0—especially for manipulating large blocks of text for print production or creating special effects—you'll use it here in the book's first hands-on exercise. In these steps, you'll use the Warp Text dialog box to stylize the shape of text. You'll also create a bounding box in which you can paste in and format blocks of text of any length.

① ②

1. For this exercise, you'll need to open a source image to which you'll add some type. If you like, you can use one of the images included with Photoshop when you first installed the program. Here, I've used a stock image of a pencil sharpener.

   If you need the elements in the underlying image to show through, you should take care in choosing your source image to find one that leaves you room for adding text.

2. Click the Type tool in the toolbox to select it. Your cursor will change to a horizontal I-beam.

3. Click anywhere in your image to position your cursor.

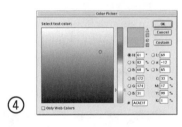

④

4. Choose the color in which you'd like your type to appear by clicking the Color swatch in the toolbar or the Type options bar. By default, the current foreground color is shown. Clicking one of these color swatches will open the Color Picker dialog box. You can enter a specific color value (in the RGB or CMYK fields, for example). You can also make your choice by moving the color slider, clicking anywhere in the color field, or by dragging the circular marker to choose an appealing shade. I'll cover the Color Picker dialog box in greater depth in Chapter 4, "Color Essentials."

⑤

5. Enter the text for your type selection. Here, I've typed **Join the Clean Desk Club!**. You can change the type characteristics by dragging your cursor over the letters to highlight them, and then making new selections from the typeface or size menus in the Type options bar. Or, you can click the Palettes button in the Type options bar to display the Character and

⑥

⑦ ✓

⑧

Paragraph palettes. You'll use these palettes to tweak your text's display, from kerning between a pair of letters to modifying the space before or after a block of text. You can even format your type on a letter-by-letter basis.

6. Click the Warp Text icon (𝐓...) in the Type options bar to launch the Warp Text dialog box. Select one effect after another to see how your text is rendered differently each time. Choose a warp style that suits the text you've entered and the overall image. Here, I've chosen Arc Upper.

7. You can reposition this block of text, warp style and all, by switching to the Move icon to click and drag your type block wherever you like in your image. You can continue to enter and edit text at this point—however, you must commit to your type changes before Photoshop will let you perform most other operations. For example, you can't select any of the painting tools while the Type tool is in this editing mode. Look in the options bar to determine whether the Type tool is in edit mode. If you see the OK and Cancel buttons, the Type tool is in edit mode.

8. Each time you select the Type tool to add a new type selection to your image, you're creating a new type layer in the Layers palette. Choose Show Layers from the Window menu so you can see for yourself the type layers in your document. Here, I wanted to create a block of text that should flow in a column to the left of the pencil sharpener image. In order to make the text flow naturally within a specified area, use the Type tool to outline a *bounding box*, and then position your cursor within the box's marquee.

As you enter text, it will wrap and hyphenate within the bounding box's borders.

You can also take advantage of the special characteristics of Photoshop layers to further influence your type effects. Here, I added a drop shadow to the words in the type layer from the Drop Shadow submenu under Layer Style in the Layer menu. You'll see more examples of layer effects in Chapter 5. Figure 3.36 gives you a good look at the results of this exercise.

In Photoshop 6.0, you can return to edit your text by selecting the appropriate type layer, choosing the Type tool, and positioning the cursor anywhere in the text block.

Figure 3.36
Creating warped text and formatted paragraphs: the finished effect.

The Paragraph palette includes the alignment settings you saw earlier in the Type options bar, with several additional settings for indenting and adding extra leading before or after each paragraph. The most compelling addition in this new palette is hyphenation; this feature makes it truly feasible to wrap and edit large blocks of text within a Photoshop image.

Photoshop has two approaches for enabling hyphenation: every-line composition and single-line composition. Every-line composition considers the big picture: What line breaks and hyphenations should be effected for the best overall look for the entire text block? Single-line composition is a more traditional typesetting approach; if you prefer to manually control how lines break, this is the better option for you.

Painting and Drawing Tools

Of all the good reasons to brush up—excuse the pun—on using Photoshop's painting and drawing tools, the best one is that these are the most fun tools to use. You'll find many of these same tools in art creation software aimed at the children's market. Those programs also tend to have rubber stamps, paint buckets, pencils, and a zillion paintbrushes in wacky shapes.

Does this mean your kids (if you have them) will paint circles around you if they ever get their grubby little hands on Photoshop? Well, maybe, but I'm going to share some less-than obvious tips for using these painting and drawing tools that'll take you worlds away from finger painting or casual scribbling.

Paintbrush Tips

Although several of the painting tools in Photoshop have a Brush drop-down menu on the tool's option bar, the Paintbrush tool is where you can really go wild with them. You can dab on color with brushes that paint fuzzy-edged or smooth strokes; brushes with fine tips, fat heads, or custom shapes; brushes where the paint is applied continuously or in dotted lines; and even brushes that lighten or darken only selected pixels.

The next section discusses how you can create new brushes or sets of brushes and then save or reload them. You can also experiment with Mode and Opacity settings, which affect which pixels are painted and to what extent. Next, you can select Wet Edges, which produces the effect of painting with watercolors or felt-tip markers. To round out the examination of the Paintbrush options bar, the Brush Dynamics menu lets you set options for fading and stylus pressure to reproduce the effect of applying pressure as you apply brush strokes.

Brushes and the Preset Manager

Just as fine artists keep a goodly supply of different-sized paintbrushes on hand to achieve various effects, you can use various brushes to gain more control over Photoshop's Paintbrush tool. Photoshop 6.0 has removed the Brushes palette found in earlier versions, but you can see the brushes at your disposal via the Brush drop-down menu on the tool's option bar.

The active brush appears bordered in black. To choose another brush, just click any of the other icons in the palette. Photoshop remembers the last brush you used with each tool, which makes it easier to switch between tools and varying brush sizes.

Photoshop includes several alternative sets of brushes that you can load by choosing Preset Manager from the Edit menu. Click the Load button in the Preset Manager dialog box to see the additional sets of brushes (see Figure 3.37).

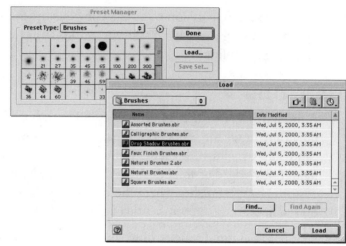

Figure 3.37
Loading additional sets of brushes using the Preset Manager.

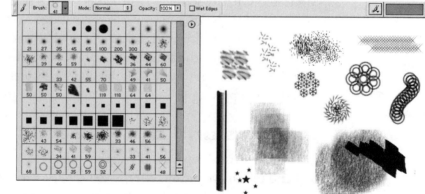

Figure 3.38
Using the Paintbrush tool with various brush effects.

You can load these instead of the default set or append them to the current array. These brush shapes let you add all sorts of creative effects; some samples are shown in Figure 3.38.

Making Your Own Texture Brushes

One really fun thing you can do is create your own custom paintbrushes. You can turn any collection of selected pixels into a custom brush shape. This feature opens up a lot of possibilities for creating incredible interwoven collages of any texture or scanned image, and achieving effects that may elude you with Photoshop's standard tools.

Figure 3.39

When you create a custom paintbrush, a preview icon is added at the end of those shown in the Brush drop-down menu. Here, I've dabbed with two new brushes I've defined.

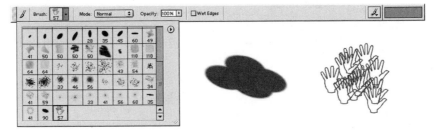

To create your own custom paintbrush pattern, you first need to create an image selection. Try small, distinct shapes—for example, select some lettering, or load the brushes from Photoshop's Preset Manager for ideas.

Next, choose Define Brush from the Edit menu. If you haven't chosen an active selection, the Define Brush option will be grayed out. Once you've chosen Define Brush, you should see your new brush added to the Brush display (see Figure 3.39) when you select it from the Paintbrush or another painting tool's options bar. If your brush is too large to display in full—the preview image is limited to 27 by 27 pixels—only the upper-left corner will be visible in the Brushes palette.

You can also create a new brush by clicking the brush display in any paintbrush tool's options bar, and then clicking the arrow in the display's right corner to display the brush display's pop-up menu. This will cause the New Brush dialog box to display (see Figure 3.40). The preview box in the lower-right corner of the New Brush dialog box shows the shape of the brush that is currently selected. The box at lower-left indicates the current brush angle and roundness. As you enter new options, the brushes in these boxes will update accordingly.

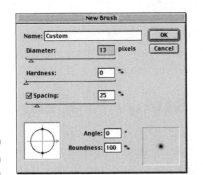

Figure 3.40

The New Brush dialog box.

Figure 3.41

The Mode pop-up menu in the Paintbrush options bar.

Mode and Opacity Settings

As you begin to experiment with Photoshop, you should try exploring different settings in the Mode pop-up menu in the options bar for the different painting and editing tools. The various settings shown in Figure 3.41 affect how you apply color to your image. For example, if you use the Paintbrush tool in Lighten mode to paint a selection with a yellow hue, only the underlying pixels in the image that are darker than your yellow are lightened with your color. If you swab in Darken mode, only those pixels lighter than your yellow are filled in with your chosen color. The specific effects of each of these mode settings are described in fuller detail in Chapter 4.

Entering a new value for Opacity—or clicking to launch and adjust the slider—on the painting tools' options bar affects how transparent your painting effects are. The lower the Opacity setting you choose, the lighter the amount of color applied is.

note

> The percentage box and accompanying slider in the options bar also changes depending on which tool is currently selected. For the Paint Bucket, Gradient, Line, Pencil, Paintbrush, and Rubber Stamp tools, the slider controls opacity. On the Airbrush, Smudge, and Blur/Sharpen tools, the slider controls the applied pressure. With the Dodge/Burn/Smudge tool, the slider sets exposure.

Fading and Stylus Pressure

As you apply pressure to the stylus of a drawing tablet, you dynamically change the way the selected brush works. You can control this effect by setting options for fading and stylus pressure in the Brush

Figure 3.42

The Brush Dynamics drop-down menu in the Paintbrush options bar.

Dynamics drop-down menu (see Figure 3.42). You can apply these to the brush stroke's size (a range of thickness), color (either the foreground, background, or a median color between the two), and opacity.

Fade measures the distance in pixels over which the Paintbrush's stroke are applied before fading out. You can choose whether to fade out to the background color or to transparency. If you have a pressure-sensitive drawing tablet (such as a Wacom tablet) hooked up to your computer, you can access the Stylus Pressure options.

Airbrush Tips

The Airbrush tool puts a diffused spray of the foreground color on your image, which can produce good effects when coloring grayscale images or when creating soft gleams of color to touch up objects and images. In Figure 3.43, I used the Airbrush tool to add a burnt effect to an image with a torn-edged border. To create the appearance that the

Figure 3.43

Using the Airbrush tool to create a burnt-paper look.

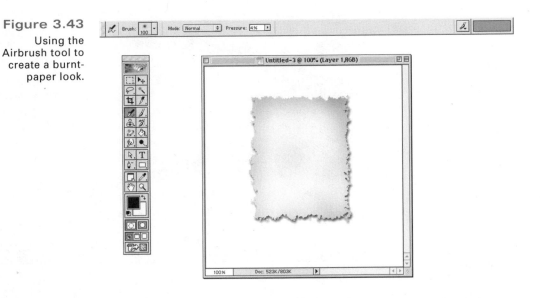

edges of this piece of paper were burnt, I selected a large, soft brush for use with the Airbrush tool as I sprayed a line filled with a medium brown color across each side.

Like a real airbrush, paint builds up if you hold the cursor in one place for a while. In the Airbrush options bar, you can choose a new airbrush nozzle from the Brush drop-down menu and adjust the Pressure settings (increasing the percentage makes the paint flow heavier).

Rubber Stamp Tips

With the Rubber Stamp tool, you can copy portions of an image to another part of the same document or a different one. You can add leaves to a picture of a tree that's looking a little sparse after a cold snap, or use flesh-tone selections to remove a pair of glasses from a subject's face. Figure 3.44 shows the Rubber Stamp tool in the process of creating the metal pieces sprinkled across the bottom of the image.

As the Rubber Stamp options bar shows (see Figure 3.45), it uses opacity settings as well as a brush to let you incorporate your cloned additions more naturally.

You can use the Pattern Stamp tool, a variation of the Rubber Stamp tool, to tile a defined pattern over and over as you paint. Remember,

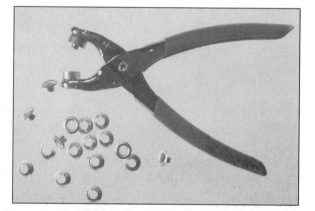

Figure 3.44
The Rubber Stamp tool in action.

Figure 3.45
The Rubber Stamp options bar.

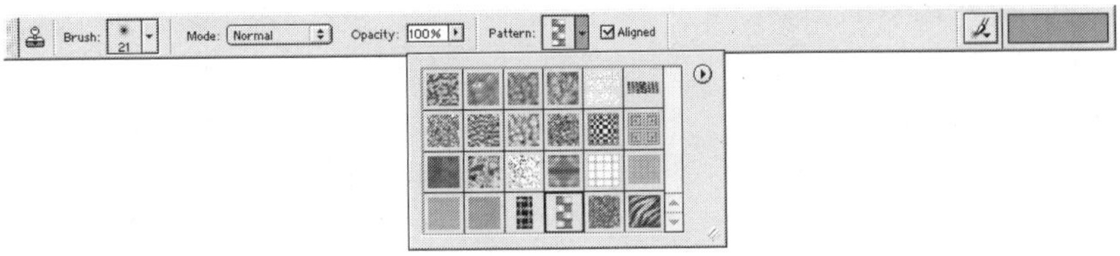

Figure 3.46

The Pattern Stamp options bar.

you can define any rectangular area of an image as a pattern by dragging a rectangular marquee around a portion of your image, and then choosing Define Pattern from the Edit menu.

If you don't click the Aligned check box in the Pattern Stamp options bar (see Figure 3.46), the pattern starts over each time you release the mouse button and start painting again. You'll use the Rubber Stamp tool extensively in Chapter 10, "Retouching Essentials."

Paint Bucket Tips

This one's an easy-to-use tool: click your image (with either a selection or no selection in place) to fill a contiguous area of similarly colored pixels with the foreground color or a selected pattern.

Just like the Magic Wand, the Paint Bucket tool has tolerance settings for how many pixels it'll reach out and touch. The Paint Bucket works a lot like the Magic Wand tool and the Fill command (from the Edit menu). If you select an area of pixels with the Magic Wand tool and then fill that selection with a certain color, that's basically what you can accomplish with the Paint Bucket tool and in one less step to boot. Figure 3.47 shows the Paint Bucket options bar.

The Fill pop-up menu in the Paint Bucket options bar lets you specify whether you want to fill an area with the foreground color or a predefined pattern. You can define any rectangular area of an image as a pattern. To do so, drag a rectangular marquee around a portion of your image, and then choose Define Pattern from the Edit menu. You can also load a number of great-looking predefined patterns by choosing Preset Manager from the Edit menu. Once you have selected a pattern,

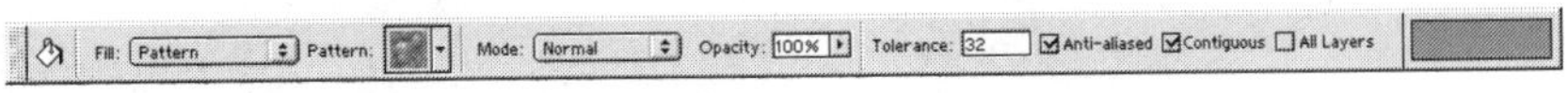

Figure 3.47

The Paint Bucket options bar.

Figure 3.48

Choosing a new pattern from the Pattern drop-down menu in the Paint Bucket options bar.

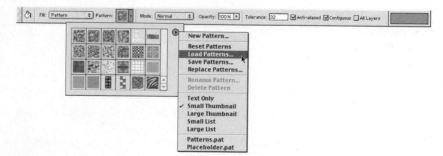

you can click the Pattern button in the options bar to choose another Pattern in the display or load a new set (see Figure 3.48).

Gradient Tips

The Gradient tool lets you create smooth blends—transitions, really—between two or more colors. You can also set options for many kinds of gradient styles, including blends from your foreground color to the background color and vice versa, and blends that fade away into transparency. It's especially useful for creating 3D effects such as adding depth and shadows to objects. In Photoshop 6.0, after you choose the Gradient tool, you can choose from one of five gradient variations in the options bar:

- **Linear fills**. Applies color in a straight line from the beginning to the ending point you select.

- **Radial fills**. Radiates color outward from a central point that you define.

- **Angular fills**. Emanates color clockwise 360 degrees in a circle from the angle you draw.

- **Reflected fills**. Creates blends with an illusion of depth via two opposing lighting effects.

- **Diamond fills**. Reflects a linear fill both vertically and horizontally, for blends with a 3D, diamond-shaped effect. These fills also remind me of tie-dyed effects.

Once you choose the type of fill you want, you can click in the gradient sample in the options bar to launch the Gradient Editor dialog box (the tool will then change to the Eyedropper). This dialog box lets you specify what kind of blend you want and what colors to use—typically foreground to background or vice versa, but you can also set up and save settings for blending multiple colors in as many transitions as you like. You can also choose Preset Manager from the Edit menu to load predefined gradients, much as you did for adding predefined brushes for the Paintbrush tool and patterns for the Paint Bucket to use.

From the options bar, you can also specify a blending mode and opacity for the paint; these mode and opacity settings are the same as those you saw a little earlier for the Paintbrush tool. To reverse the order of colors in the gradient fill, just select Reverse. The Dither check box in the options bar lets you create a smoother blend that has less banding. Figure 3.49 shows the Gradient options bar and Figure 3.50 shows the Gradient Editor dialog box.

Next, you simply click and drag your cursor over part of your image. If an area of the image is currently selected, the blend will only apply to that selection. The first place you click determines where the blend will start, and the point at which you release the mouse after dragging is the blend's endpoint. Holding down (Shift) as you drag will constrain the gradient angle to a multiple of 45 degrees.

Figure 3.49
The Gradient options bar.

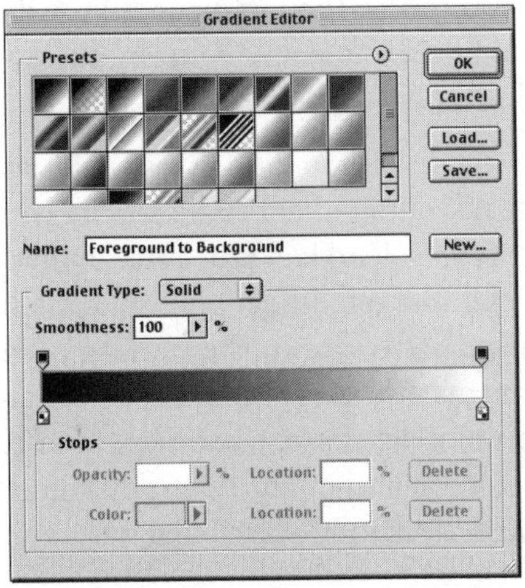

Figure 3.50
The Gradient Editor dialog box.

To create a new type of gradient, you launch the Gradient Editor, and then click the New button and assign your new gradient a name. Click the leftmost marker under the gradient bar to modify the starting color; the triangle above the marker turns from white to black, indicating that this is the part of the gradient currently being modified. You can then define the starting color in one of several ways:

- 👁 Click the color swatch in the Gradient Editor dialog box, which will launch the Color Picker dialog box. You can enter specific color values (in RGB or CMYK, typically) or make your choice by moving the color slider and clicking the circular marker in the color field to choose an appealing shade.

- 👁 Click the foreground or background color selection icon in the Gradient Editor dialog box to make one of those the starting color.

- 👁 Position your cursor over the gradient bar in the Gradient Editor dialog box; as your cursor turns to an Eyedropper icon, you can click to select a color in the gradient as the starting color. This really only works for editing preexisting custom blends; if you're creating a new blend, the whole gradient bar will show the shade of your foreground color.

You can then define the ending color by clicking the rightmost marker below the gradient bar and using one of the color selection options I just described. When you finish creating a custom gradient, save it by clicking the Save button in the Gradient Editor dialog box. You can reopen your custom gradient at any point by clicking the Load button in the Gradient Editor dialog box.

With the Gradient Editor, you can also specify whether you want a certain percentage of your gradient to fill solidly with your starting (or ending) color before the blend kicks in. You can do this by clicking and dragging one of the markers under the gradient bar, depending on whether you want to apply this to the starting or ending color, or by selecting one of the markers and entering a percentage in the Location box. The Location box defines at what percent of the gradient length the color should stop blending. For example, Figure 3.51 shows a linear blend from 100% black to 0% black that starts at 25% of the gradient

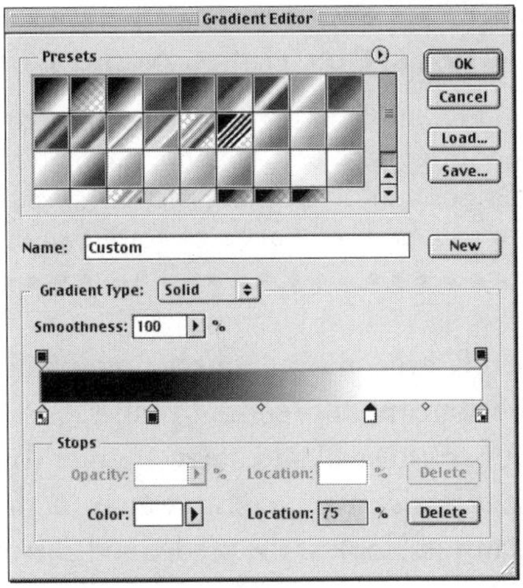

Figure 3.51

You can control the starting and ending points of a blend by moving one of the markers under the gradient bar or by entering a value in the Location field.

width and ends at 75%. Essentially, the first quarter of the image is filled with solid black and the right quarter is filled with 0% black. The actual blend takes place within the middle half of the image.

Another way to adjust how long it takes to blend one color into another is to adjust the midpoint of a gradient, which appears in the Gradient Editor dialog box as a diamond above the gradient bar. Click and drag the diamond left or right to mark at what point the midpoint color between the starting and ending colors should be reached (see Figure 3.52).

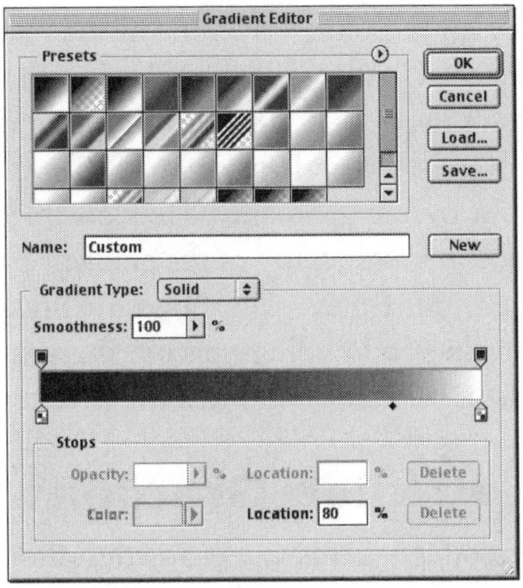

Figure 3.52

In this linear blend from 0% to 100% black, the midpoint has been placed at 80% of the width of the gradient.

tip   **The Dither Check Box Helps Avoid Color Banding**

When there are too few steps in the transition from one color to another, your gradients might print with color banding, which ruins the look of the smooth blend. It's a good idea to select the Dither check box in the Gradient options bar to reduce the chance of color banding.

To make your blends even more complex, you can add intermediate colors between the starting and ending points. Just click in the space under the gradient bar; this will add a new marker (by default, the color is set to whatever appears in the color swatch in the Gradient Editor dialog box). For examples, look at the predefined custom blends included with the Gradient Editor, such as Spectrum or Transparent Rainbow.

tip   **For Print Images, Make Blends in CMYK Mode**

Chapter 2, "File Format Essentials," talked about how you'll often edit your print production images in RGB mode (which is optimized for onscreen viewing) and switch to CMYK mode when you're done. But if you need to add gradient fills, you're better off switching to CMYK mode early on because you can get significant color shifts in blends if you switch from RGB to CMYK after you use the Gradient tool.

Gradient fills also contain an opacity mask that determines how transparent the fill is at any given point. Click one of the markers on top of the gradient bars within the Gradient Editor dialog box to see what percentage the opacity is set to. If the opacity is set to 100% throughout the gradient, you'll completely overlay the underlying image if you draw a blend right over it. But you can overlay gradient blends on images by clicking the leftmost or rightmost marker on top of the gradient bar and reducing the opacity (see Figure 3.53). Figure 3.54 shows the finished effect. You can enter values for starting and ending opacity; the values you set are previewed on the gradient bar at the bottom of the Gradient Editor dialog box.

Creating a Noise Gradient

Besides creating smooth gradients, the Gradient Editor dialog box also lets you define a new noise gradient or edit an existing one. A noise gradient

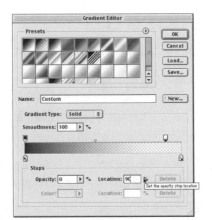

Figure 3.53

The Opacity options in the Gradient Editor dialog box.

Figure 3.54

By adjusting opacity percentages in the Gradient Editor, you can overlay blends on images, as shown here.

contains random components that cause a random brightness pattern at the pixel level that lends an exaggerated film grain effect to your gradient.

To create or edit a noise gradient, first select a gradient tool and click in the gradient sample in the options bar to launch the Gradient Editor. If you want to create a new noise gradient, choose New Gradient from the pop-up menu; enter a name for the gradient, click OK, and then change Gradient Type to Noise.

You can also base your noise gradient on an existing one by selecting an available gradient from the list before choosing New Gradient. Make sure that the Gradient Type is set to Noise. You can add, remove, and reposition colors and set transparency as described earlier in the Gradient Editor. Here, you can also set the roughness for the gradient fill, which has an impact on how distinct the color bands become. If you're just experimenting with colors, try clicking the Randomize button until you find a setting you like. When you're done, click OK to add the new noise gradient fill to the list or to update the one you're editing.

EXERCISE 3.2

Using the Gradient Tools to Create 3D Shapes and Text

You can use the Gradient tools to create some realistic-looking 3D shapes. I usually create spheres and other simple 3D objects in Photoshop as icons for Web sites. In this exercise, you'll first create a round selection, and then add a gradient fill to create the 3D illusion; next, you'll create a square selection and add a diamond fill. Both finished objects can be used as decorative bullets or icons on a Web page or in a printed piece.

1. In a new document, choose the Elliptical Marquee tool. Hold down (Shift) as you click and drag to form a perfect circle.

2. Make the foreground color a bright color – in this example, this will be the primary color used for a 3D ball. Set the background color to black.

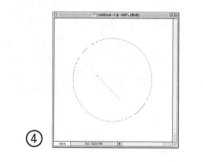

3. Choose the Gradient tool and select the Gradient Fill icon in the options bar. Make sure the selected Gradient swatch box reads Foreground to Background. Set the Opacity to 100% and the mode to Normal.

4. Position the cursor inside the selection areas and drag to apply the gradient fill. The first place you click will be where your bright color is most highly concentrated, blending into solid black at the position where you release the cursor.

5. That's it! Your finished sphere should look something like Figure 3.55. By clicking the gradient's color swatch in the Gradient tool's options bar, you can use the Gradient Editor dialog box to experiment with different cursor starting and ending points and with changing the midpoint value.

Figure 3.55
The finished
results of the
sphere icon.

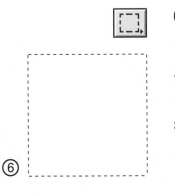

6. Now try creating the diamond icon. Create a new document and choose the Rectangular Marquee tool. Hold down ⟨Shift⟩ as you click and drag to form a perfect square.

7. Make the foreground color a bright color for the finished square, and set the background color to black.

8. Choose the Gradient tool, and then click the Diamond Gradient icon on the options bar. Make sure the selected Gradient swatch is set to Foreground to Background. Set the Opacity to 100% and the mode to Normal.

9. Position the cursor at the center of your selection. Hold down ⟨Shift⟩ to limit your dragging to 45-degree increments. Drag your cursor diagonally to one of the four corners of your selection to apply the gradient fill. The first place you click will be where your bright color is most highly concentrated, blending into solid black at the position where you release the cursor. When you release the cursor, your shape will fill in with the diamond gradient.

That's it! To make variations in a rainbow of colors, choose Adjust from the Image menu, and then Variations from the Adjust submenu. In Figure 3.56, I defined my new icon as a pattern in order to create a studded decorative border for other images.

Figure 3.56
Besides icons and bullets, 3D shapes can also be used to construct a decorative raised-looking border.

Pencil Tips 🖉

As you'll discover with casual doodling, the Pencil tool lets you color in pixels in either a freeform or straight-line manner. It's most useful for changing the color of single pixels. You can use the Brushes palette in conjunction with the Pencil tool to select a pencil with a coarser or finer drawing surface. As with so many of the other tools, though, exploring the options bar is the key to extending its use. Just as with the paintbrush tools, you can use the Brush Dynamics menu in the Pencil tool's options bar to adjust fade and stylus pressure.

Auto Erase

The other neat feature about the Pencil tool is Auto Erase, an option you can check in the Pencil tool's options bar (see Figure 3.57). With the option checked, you can click and hold to draw a line as usual. After releasing, though, when you click a second time you can draw with the background color over areas you've colored with the current foreground color. So if you draw one line and then draw another line back over the first one, it will look as though you are erasing over it. This can be useful if you regularly need to toggle between drawing with your foreground and background colors.

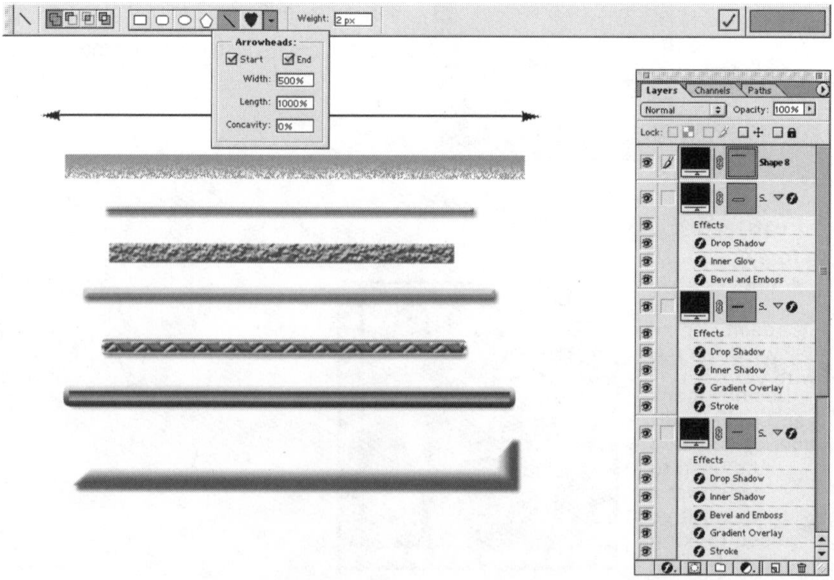

Figure 3.57

The Pencil tool's options bar.

Lines and Shapes

You can produce many useful graphical effects in Photoshop by starting with basic lines and shapes. The new shape tools in Photoshop 6.0 let you easily create rectangles, ellipses, polygons, stars, and a bevy of custom shapes. These new shapes share a spot in the toolbar with an old Photoshop standby, the Line tool, which has also been greatly improved in version 6.0.

Before you start drawing, you need to specify how you want to incorporate this shape with the rest of your image editing. You have three options, indicated on the options bar for all the line and shape tools (see Figure 3.58). They may sound confusing at first, so it's good to walk through them briefly:

 Create new shape layer. If you create a new layer with what's called a *vector mask*, your shape can be edited separately from the rest of your image on any underlying layers. In this chapter, you use this option because it gives you the most flexibility in manipulating shapes separately from your image.

 Create new work path. As you'll see in Chapter 6, you can use the pen tools to edit your shape's path, which can then be a powerful tool for making selections with interesting outlines.

 Create filled region. This tool will add the selected shape to your current image layer, filled in with the foreground color. This obliterates the part of your image that previously appeared underneath the added shape.

Figure 3.58
Before you create a line or shape, you need to specify how it will integrate with your overall image.

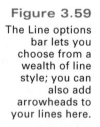

Line Tips ╲

A little experimentation with the Line tool (which shares a toolbox space with the new Rectangle tool and other shape tools) shows you how you can draw lines in any direction. If you hold down ⟨Shift⟩ as you click and drag your cursor, you can constrain the angle of your lines to increments of 45 degrees.

The real oomph added to the Line tool in Photoshop 6.0, though, comes with the palette of Layer styles for lines. As you experiment with the styles in the Line tool's options bar, you'll see that lines produced this way combine into a single step a number of useful effects that take considerable effort to create by hand. You can load more predefined styles by choosing Load Styles from the pop-up menu on the Layer Styles display.

As Figure 3.59 shows, by selecting a new line style you can quickly create the look of shaded pipes, lines with shadows, and 3D buttons and bars. You can also draw lines with arrowheads; just click the drop-down menu that follows the shape icons in the Line options bar.

Figure 3.59

The Line options bar lets you choose from a wealth of line style; you can also add arrowheads to your lines here.

Rectangle and Rounded Rectangle Tips ☐ ⬭

As Figure 3.60 shows, creating marbled, textured, or 3D buttons for Web graphics is a natural use for the tools in Photoshop 6.0's shape arsenal. The styles you've just seen with the Line tool come to full fruition when applied to shapes such as the Rectangle or Rounded Rectangle.

To create a rectangular shape using one of these predefined styles, choose the Rectangle tool or Rounded Rectangle tool (if you want the appearance of rounded edges). From the tool's options bar, click the triangle next to the Layer Style swatch to display all the available styles. You can load more predefined styles by choosing Load Styles from the pop-up menu on the Layer Style display.

Drag in your image to draw your shape. Hold down Shift as you drag to constrain a rectangle or rounded rectangle to a square. You can hold down Option (for Mac users) or Alt (for Windows users) to draw from the center of the object. By holding down the Spacebar, you can move the object without changing its size or shape.

tip

• •
Leveraging Layers

Most of the effects you're achieving by applying these predefined styles are simply good combinations of a number of layer effects, which can be applied manually via the Layer Style submenu underneath the Layer menu. You can further tweak any effect you create by applying more layer effects manually—for example, if your predefined style didn't include a drop shadow, you can add one by choosing Layer Style from the Layer menu, and then selecting Drop Shadow from the Layer Style submenu.

• •

Figure 3.60

Using the Rounded Rectangle tool to create graphics well suited for use as Web site buttons.

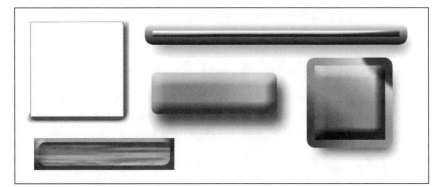

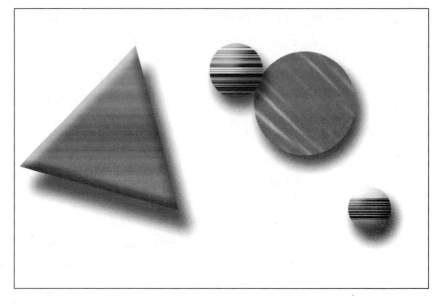

Figure 3.61
Using the Ellipse
and Polygon
tools.

Ellipse and Polygon Tips ◯ ◇

The Ellipse and Polygon shape tools are well suited for creating distinctive cutouts and button shapes for Web graphics (see Figure 3.61). As with the Rectangle or Rounded Rectangle tools, you drag in your image to draw your shape, and then click the OK icon when done. To constrain a rectangle or rounded rectangle to a square, hold down [Shift] as you drag. You can hold down [Option] (for Mac users) or [Alt] (for Windows users) to draw from the center of the object.

When you select the Polygon tool, you have an additional option, labeled Sides, in the tool's palette bar. You can create a polygon containing anywhere from three (yes, a triangle!) to 100 sides.

Custom Shape Tool ✳

Rounding out the shape tools, the Custom Shape is a fun one—on a separate layer, it lends itself well to use as a starburst or callout image added to other images (see Figure 3.62).

You can readily save shapes you've created as custom shapes for this tool. To do so, first piece together the new shape using the other shape tools or

Figure 3.62

With the Custom Shape tool, you can add starbursts— common fixtures on book or magazine covers—to your Photoshop images.

Figure 3.63

The Custom Shape tool's options bar and drop-down menu for selecting a shape.

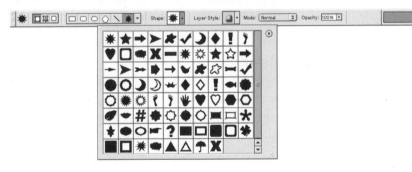

path tools. Choose Define Custom Shape from the Edit menu and type in a name for the new shape. From then on, you can select your custom shape from the Shape list in the options bar (see Figure 3.63).

Eyedropper and Color Sampler Tool Tips

With the Eyedropper tool, you can *sample* (that is, pick up) colors from your images to designate as the foreground and background colors. Simply click with the Eyedropper tool on a section of your image to change the foreground color; hold down Option on a Mac (or Alt for Windows users) when you click to assign the background color. This is a useful tool for touching up image flaws.

By default, the Eyedropper picks up the exact color value of the single pixel you first click. With the Eyedropper's options, you can change this sample size to the average value of a 3-by-3 pixel area or a 5-by-5 pixel area around the pixel you've clicked.

When you're looking at pixel colors as closely as the Eyedropper tool warrants, it's often useful to keep the Info palette open so you can note new color values as you click and sample. A variation of the Eyedropper tool called the Color Sampler tool—which shares a spot on the toolbar with the Eyedropper and Measure tools—stores Info palette information on up to four color values at a time.

You don't need to focus on the Color Sampler much at this point, but you'll see later on, in Chapter 10, that this tool is easier to compare and contrast color values in an image after you make modifications. It gives you valuable data when you're trying to fix color problems or an image with not enough contrast, for example, because you can see how the changes affect a range of color values at once.

Whenever you use the Color Sampler tool, make sure the Info palette is also visible. As you click in your image for the first time, note that the number 1 appears next to the area chosen, and a corresponding #1 with color values appears in the Info palette. You can continue to click to store up to four points for sampling color values. If you change your mind about any color sample, you can discard it—and free up its position for reuse—by Option-clicking or Alt-clicking it. Figure 3.64 shows an image with samples in values #2, #3, and #4; the next color sampler click would fill #1.

Figure 3.64

The Color Sampler tool lets you store values for up to four color samples in the Info palette.

Figure 3.65

The Eraser
options bar.

Eraser Tips ✎

As the name implies, the Eraser tool erases pixels. If you're working on a transparent layer, the Eraser fills in erased spots with transparency. Otherwise, the erasures fill in with the designated background color. Perhaps surprisingly, there are some pretty powerful options in the Eraser options bar (see Figure 3.65).

First, you'll notice that you can define the eraser's shape to reproduce the effect of an airbrush, pencil, paintbrush, or its default block shape. When you choose the Eraser tool's paintbrush option, you can click a check box labeled Wet Edges to produce an effect akin to erasing with a watercolor brushstroke.

The most amazing Eraser effect, though, is one you'll see when you click the Erase to History check box in the tool's options bar. Say you've made some changes to a saved image. If you change your mind about some of those changes, you can always revert to the saved version—but perhaps you don't want to undo *all* the work, just a few changes. Check the Erase to History check box in the tool's options bar and position your cursor over just one part of the image you want to change back. You can also produce similar—and actually, more versatile—results with the History Brush tool and History palette, covered a little later in this chapter. When the Erase to History check box is checked, portions of your saved image will reappear with each stroke as you drag the Eraser over your image. Spooky, huh?

The Magic Eraser ✎

First added in version 5.5, the Magic Eraser helps you silhouette items in a layer by making transparent only the contrasting pixels surrounding that part of the image as you begin to erase. You can choose to erase only contiguous pixels (through the Contiguous check box in the Magic Eraser's options bar), or—as Figure 3.66 shows—have your erasures apply to those colors throughout the layer you're in—or even to all layers. When

Figure 3.66
Erasing with the
Magic Eraser.

you use the Magic Eraser, you can enter a tolerance value to define the range of colors that can be erased, as well as an opacity value.

The Background Eraser

When you select the Background Eraser, you can turn the pixels on a layer transparent as you drag over them. It's especially useful for silhouetting objects with difficult edges. The tool works by continually sampling the colors underneath, based on the sampling and tolerance options you've set in the options bar (see Figure 3.67), and evaluating which should be erased. You can choose a brush shape for the Background Eraser and erasing mode. Discontinuous lets you erase the sampled color wherever it appears in the layer you're in, whereas Contiguous only erases similarly colored areas attached to the pixels that you pass the Background Eraser over. The Find Edges mode operates like Contiguous, but pays attention to preserving sharp edges.

Figure 3.67
The Background
Eraser's
options bar.

Brush: 17 Limits: Contiguous Tolerance: 100% Protect Foreground Color Sampling: Continuous

Rewriting History: The History Palette and Brush

If you don't like the way your image editing is turning out, you don't have to scrap all your changes or revert to a previously saved version of the file. With Photoshop's History palette, you can now undo and redo multiple image-editing steps.

Reverting to an Image State

The History palette records every action you take in an editing session and lists each *image state* on its own line (see Figure 3.68).

The oldest actions appear at the top of the History palette list, and each new step you take is added below. You can then jump back to any given image state to view your image at that point; all the states below it become grayed out on the palette (see Figure 3.69). If you start to edit an image upon returning to a previous image state, all the steps that come after are eliminated.

Figure 3.68

The History palette lists your editing changes as image states.

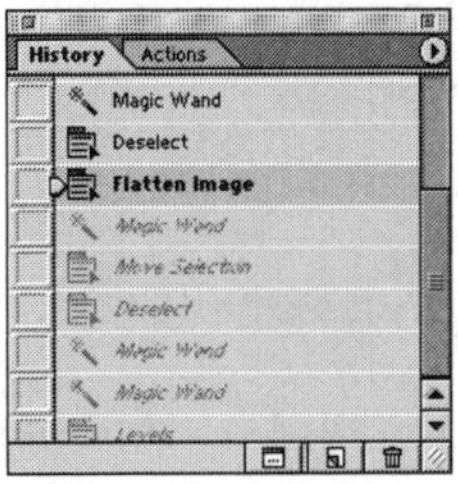

Figure 3.69

You can click any image state to view it. The states below it immediately turn dim.

note

> The History palette works independently of Photoshop's traditional Undo command, so you can actually undo an image edit that eliminates image states. Those once-deleted image states then reappear. This is helpful if you change your mind frequently about how you want to edit an image!

When you display the History palette, you'll see three icons along the bottom of the palette:

- **New File icon.** Saves the current state as its own Photoshop file.

- **New Snapshot icon.** Creates a new snapshot of a current state.

- **The Trash icon.** Gives you a place to dump image states, effectively deleting them.

tip

Photoshop has keyboard shortcuts for skipping between states in the History palette. To move to a previous state, press Option+Cmd+Z on a Mac (Windows users press Alt+Ctrl+Z). To move ahead to the next state, press Shift+Cmd+Z on a Mac (Windows users press Shift+Ctrl+Z). You can also go back and forth between states by choosing Step Forward or Step Backward from the History palette pop-up menu.

The number of actions that the History palette can capture depends on certain memory and size limits—such as how much memory is available, how large your image is, and how memory-intensive your actions are. When memory gets tight, the History palette begins to discard the oldest actions. However, to guard against losing that image state information, the History palette lets you take what's called a *snapshot* of a image. These snapshots remain in the History palette even after you or Photoshop delete the steps associated with a given image state (see Figure 3.70).

The History Brush Tool

The History Brush tool lets you paint a copy of an image state or snapshot into your current image. For example, you can apply a filter to an image, take a snapshot of it, and then undo the filter. Then, with the

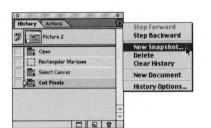

Figure 3.70
Creating a
snapshot in the
History palette.

History Brush tool, you can paint the filter change onto selected areas of the current image. This lets you use features specific to Photoshop's Paintbrush tool and Brush palettes—such as control over opacity or brush shape—in applying filters and other effects to selections.

Clicking the box at the left of any image state will make that state the basis for the History Brush tool's effects. More tips for taking advantage of the History palette and the History Brush tool are in Chapter 10.

The Art History Brush Tool

Here's another immediate use for the History snapshots you just learned about: The Art History Brush tool interprets the History snapshots in your image via the options you set as you paint, to create different colors and artistic styles with each stylized brush stroke. So, whereas the History Brush applies brush strokes to "uncover" the past, the Art History Brush produces an artistic rendering based not only on the history snapshot but also on your settings for style, fidelity, and opacity, among others.

Before you begin to use the Art History Brush tool, make sure that you click the left column of the History state or snapshot that you want to use as the source for the art history brush tool. A brush icon appears next to the source history state or snapshot. Just as with any paintbrush tool, when you select the Art History Brush tool you can choose the brush, mode, and opacity you want.

The Style and Fidelity menus are unique to the Art History Brush tool. Experiment with the Style modes to control the shape of each stroke; enter a numeric value (or drag the slider) for Fidelity to affect how your paint color can deviate from the color in the History state or snapshot.

You can use the Area field to indicate how much of your image is touched with each stroke; larger values, naturally, indicate a wider area. Just as with the Magic Wand tool, the Tolerance field in this tool lets you indicate a range of pixels that your actions apply to.

Editing Tools

The editing tools primarily retouch the pixels in your document instead of applying paint or some other new content to the image. Using them judiciously can lead to dramatic improvements in your images.

Blur and Sharpen Tips

The Blur and Sharpen tools affect the color contrast between neighboring pixels. Apply the Blur tool to lessen the contrast, and you'll start to think your glasses are fogging over; use the Sharpen tool to make specific parts of an image come into closer focus. The options bar for both tools lets you decide whether you want to sharpen or blur all visible layers; to do so, click the Use All Layers check box (see Figure 3.71). Leave the box unchecked if you want to sharpen or blur only one layer at a time.

Both tools have counterparts under the Filter menu; their tools simply allow for a more hands-on, concentrated control over this effect.

Smudge Tips

The Smudge tool shares a spot on Photoshop's toolbar with the Blur and Sharpen tools. The cursor for the Smudge tool is very cute: you use a

Figure 3.71
The Blur options bar has the same features as the Sharpen options bar.

Figure 3.72

The Smudge options bar.

little finger to smudge a color as if you've stirred a little water into some paint or smeared a charcoal stroke. In portraits, you can use the Smudge tool to soften wrinkles and to enhance eyelashes—it's like instant mascara! You can use it to smooth out blemishes too, but for retouching substantial parts of an image it can produce an artificial-looking effect; if this happens, you're better off trying the Rubber Stamp tool.

As Figure 3.72 shows, the Smudge options bar includes Finger Painting; if you check this box, your smudging begins with the foreground color smearing into the image's colors. For Mac users, pressing and holding Option (or for Windows users, Alt) automatically activates Finger Painting as you work with the Smudge tool.

Dodge, Burn, and Sponge Tips

This three-in-one tool builds on traditional film exposure techniques. It lets you tone an image by lightening or darkening portions of it (using the Dodge and Burn tools, respectively), or by adding or removing saturation and contrast (via the Sponge tool).

To me, the Dodge tool looks like a little pushpin, but it's really supposed to represent a small paddle that a photographer might use to cover an image to diffuse the amount of light that reaches a piece of photographic paper as it exposes, thereby lightening the finished print. The Burn tool looks like a little hand cupped in a circle and is also an allusion to a traditional photography technique for concentrating light on an image, thereby darkening it. The Sponge tool lets you selectively affect the contrast levels in portions of your image.

Figure 3.73 shows the effects of applying each of Photoshop's editing tools. I used the Dodge tool to lighten the model's skin overall. Her features looked a little washed out then, so I used the Sponge tool to draw out the contrast. I used the Burn tool to darken the shadow on the right cheek and emphasize her lips.

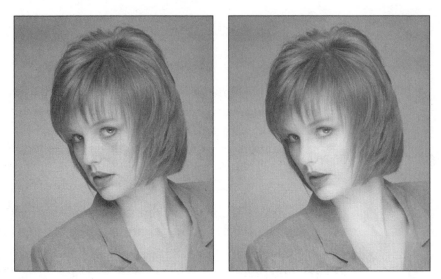

Figure 3.73

The Dodge, Burn, and Sponge tools in action.

Summary

By now you've learned a great many need-to-know techniques for using Photoshop's tools efficiently and effectively. In this chapter, you got a chance to try some of these tools individually; in later chapters, you'll use them in conjunction with each other and with Photoshop's layers and masks for even cooler effects.

Table 3.1 gives you an at-a-glance reference to matching tool names with their icons and their gotta-know-'em keyboard shortcuts. Next up in Chapter 4 is an in-depth look at using color in Photoshop.

Table 3.1   Photoshop's Tools, with Icons and Keyboard Commands

ICON	TOOL NAME	KEYBOARD COMMAND
Image Navigation		
	Hand	H
	Zoom	Z
	Measure	I
	Notes	N
	Audio Annotation	N
Type		
	Type	T
Additional Toolbox Controls		
	Foreground and Background Colors	
	Default Colors	D
	Switch Colors	X
	Standard Mode	Q
	Quick Mask Mode	Q
	Standard Screen Mode	F
	Full Screen Mode with Menu Bar	F
	Full Screen Mode	F

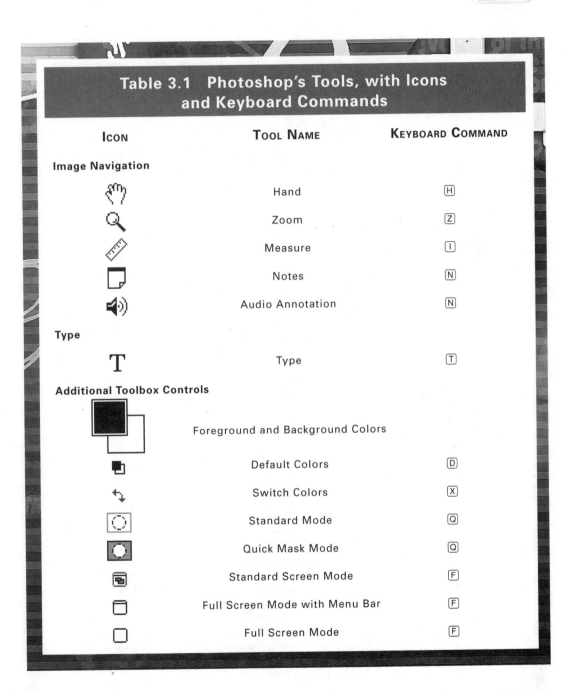

Table 3.1 (continued)

ICON	TOOL NAME	KEYBOARD COMMAND
Selection		
	Rectangular Marquee	M
	Elliptical Marquee	
	Single Row Marquee	
	Single Column Marquee	M
	Crop	C
	Lasso	L
	Polygon Lasso	L
	Magnetic Lasso	L
	Magic Wand	W
	Move	V
	Slice	K
	Slice Select	K
	Pen	P
	Freeform Pen	P
	Add Anchor Point	
	Delete Anchor Point	
	Convert Point	
	Path Component Selection Tool	A
	Direct Selection	A

Table 3.1 (continued)

ICON	TOOL NAME	KEYBOARD COMMAND
Painting and Drawing		
	Paint Bucket	G
	Gradient	G
	Line	N
	Rectangle	N
	Rounded Rectangle	N
	Ellipse	N
	Polygon	N
	Custom Shape	N
	Eyedropper	I
	Color Sampler	I
	Eraser	E
	Background Eraser	E
	Magic Eraser	E
	Pencil	B
	Airbrush	J
	Clone Stamp	S
	Pattern Stamp	S
	Paintbrush	B
	History Brush	Y
	Art History Brush	Y

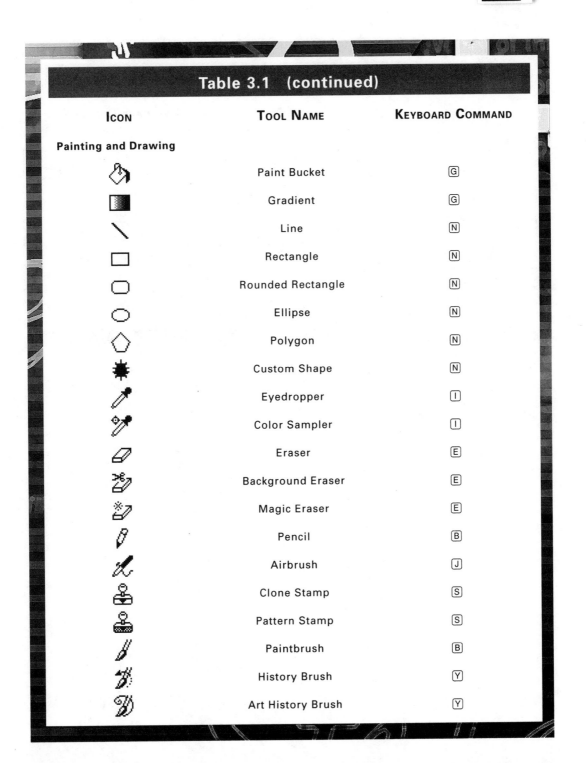

Table 3.1   (continued)

ICON	TOOL NAME	KEYBOARD COMMAND
Editing Tools		
	Blur	R
	Sharpen	R
	Smudge	R
	Dodge	O
	Burn	O
	Sponge	O

Color Essentials

IN THIS CHAPTER

Photoshop's Color Models

❂

Using the Color and Swatches Palettes
and the Color Picker

❂

Predefined and Custom Color Sets

❂

Managing Color Consistency

Predictability—it's a bad thing for a movie plot but something you really want to strive for in terms of making your onscreen color images match your final print output. Matching colors onscreen with those in the print output is a big concern for any Photoshop designer, because human eyes perceive color on a computer monitor differently from how they perceive it on paper.

You're bound to face additional print costs (and lost time on press) for corrections if your colors don't turn out right in the first place. Likewise, you might face color-matching dilemmas when you're working with images for the Web or multimedia presentations; your images look vivid and well coordinated on your Mac, so why do they sometimes look so lousy when viewed in Windows?

To transmit the colors in your mind's eye to your monitor's screen and then faithfully reproduce them in their final form, you need to know the basics of what influences color in your Photoshop documents. This chapter provides an overview of how to predict good results when producing full-color print pieces and onscreen graphics. It also aims to fill in any gaps in your knowledge of color theory—that is, what colors mix and match well. Some specific topics addressed here are as follows:

- 👁 The basics of the RGB, CMYK, HSB, and Lab color models

- 👁 How to use Photoshop's Color Picker dialog box along with the Color and Swatches palettes

- 👁 Commercial color systems such as Pantone and Trumatch

- 👁 How to use indexed color palettes, especially for Web graphics

- 👁 Ensuring your Photoshop graphics match well with other elements of your Web pages

- 👁 The fundamentals of color-management systems

- 👁 How Photoshop's painting and editing modes affect color in your images

Precision, Precision: Photoshop's Color Models

The way people perceive colors can be very subjective. According to some estimations, the number-one reason why mail-order customers return merchandise is dissatisfaction with the color. It's a good demonstration of how often something gets lost in the translation between product photo shoots and final images in print catalogs.

There are several models for translating subjective color terms to precise values that can be reproduced consistently. When you're choosing colors in your Photoshop work, at various times you may use its different color models: RGB, CMYK, HSB, and Lab. You can specify values in any of these four models in the Color Picker dialog box (see Figure 4.1). As you saw previously, you display the Color Picker dialog box when you click either the foreground or background color in the toolbox.

In the RGB (red, green, blue) model, a monitor displays color formed by a mixture of red, green, and blue dots emitting beams of light. The dots are so tiny and tightly concentrated that you see the color formed by the mixture of light rather than individual dots. Full-color printing uses the CMYK model, which combines four inks (cyan, magenta, yellow, black) to produce a wide spectrum of color. The HSB (hue,

Figure 4.1
Color model options in the Color Picker dialog box.

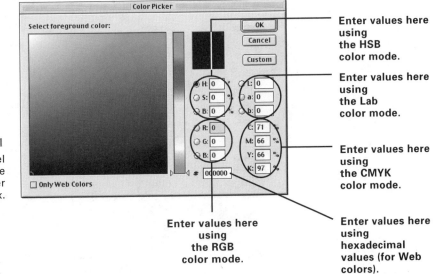

Enter values here using the HSB color mode.

Enter values here using the Lab color mode.

Enter values here using the CMYK color mode.

Enter values here using the RGB color mode.

Enter values here using hexadecimal values (for Web colors).

saturation, brightness) model is a viewing option that describes color components as they relate to the properties of light, or how people perceive color subjectively. The Lab model helps produce device-independent color, that is, colors that remain the same no matter what monitor or printer you use to render them. A fuller description of each of these four color models (also called *color spaces*, or *color gamuts*) follows, along with suggestions on when you'd want to use them.

RGB

The human eye sees color as wavelengths of red, green, and blue. These three additive primary colors combine in varying levels to form all other colors. In additive color reproduction, colors become lighter as you add more red, green, and blue light. Combining the highest levels of red, green, and blue forms white (see Figure 4.2). Any device that mixes, transmits, or filters light uses the additive color model—your TV and computer monitor, for example, as well as movie projectors and theater spotlights.

In Photoshop's RGB Color mode, each of the three additive primary colors has 256 levels of intensity; they take values in the range of 0 to 255. Setting all three to 0 produces solid black (because you're adding

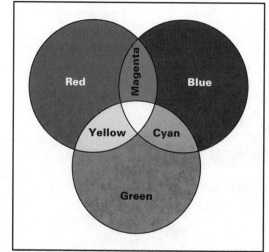

Figure 4.2
The RGB color
model.

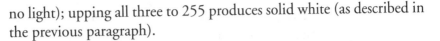

no light); upping all three to 255 produces solid white (as described in the previous paragraph).

Why are there 256 levels in RGB mode, and why do the numbers run from 0 to 255? With RGB, you have access to the full range of the 24-bit color spectrum. Think back to Chapter 2, "File Format Essentials," which described how 24-bit graphics assign 1 byte of memory each for red, green, and blue values. One byte is equal to 8 bits, and a bit can have one of two possible values (on and off). Thus, a byte can have 28 (or 256) possible values. In binary notation, the bit-numbering scheme standard on most computers, a byte can range in value from 0 (with every bit turned off) to 255 (with every bit turned on). This makes RGB an ideal color mode for image editing and for saving images designed for onscreen viewing.

CMYK

If you've worked on full-color print publications, you may be most comfortable with the CMYK model, which is the basis for four-color process printing. The CMYK model is based on *subtractive color reproduction*—that is, subtracting light instead of adding it. Unlike a TV or computer monitor that emits light (in the RGB model), a printed page doesn't emit light—it reflects the light that hits it. So to produce color images in print, pigments are used—such as printing inks, dye, or toner—that absorb some colors of light and reflect others.

The primary colors of these pigments are cyan, yellow, and magenta. They're called the secondary colors or subtractive primary colors because subtracting these colors brings you closer to producing white. They're complementary to the additive primaries of red, green, and blue. For example, cyan absorbs all the red light, magenta absorbs all the green light, and yellow absorbs all the blue light.

Cyan, magenta, and yellow come from the highest concentrations of two of the three additive primary colors (and by no amount of the third color). The light that's reflected is the color that you actually see. When you look at a picture of a frog, you see the color green because the paper has absorbed everything that's not green inside the outline of the frog. A solid white surface reflects all wavelengths of light; a solid black surface absorbs all wavelengths and reflects no light.

Here's how the additive primary colors combine to form the subtractive primary colors:

Blue + Green = Cyan

Red + Green = Yellow

Red + Blue = Magenta

Conversely, two subtractive primary colors combined produce an additive primary color:

Magenta + Yellow = Red

Cyan + Yellow = Green

Cyan + Magenta = Blue

These relationships also point out how each of the additive primary colors is the direct opposite of a subtractive primary color. For example, cyan is the opposite of red, because all the red is absorbed and the blue and green are reflected. Opposite color pairs (such as cyan and red) are called *complementary colors*. Figure 4.3 shows the additive primary and subtractive primary colors, and their respective complementary colors.

In theory, printing solid concentrations of cyan, yellow, and magenta inks should produce black, but printing with ink is an imperfect process.

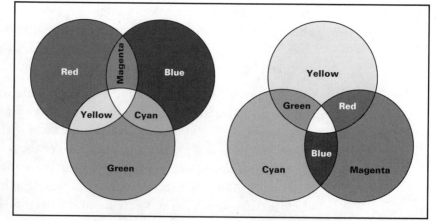

Figure 4.3
The additive primary and subtractive primary colors.

Printing with the highest combination of cyan, yellow, and magenta tends to produce only muddy browns, so the system calls for black ink to make up for the problem. Black is the K part of CMYK (the letter K is used instead of B because B could potentially be mistaken for blue). Photoshop's CMYK mode measures values for the colors in percentages.

HSB

As nice as RGB and CMYK are for defining colors in fairly precise terms, neither model is particularly intuitive for differentiating colors the way the human eye does. The HSB (hue, saturation, brightness) model is based on how people perceive color and lends itself well to many subjective terms used to describe color. Hue is determined by the wavelength of the reflected light; it's described in terms of the names people generally give to colors—purple, reddish-yellow, or what's on the label of any crayon in a box of Crayolas. Saturation (also called chroma) defines a color's purity, that is, how much gray is mixed in. Zero saturation results in plain gray, whereas full saturation results in the purest (or strongest) version of a hue. Brightness measures a color's intensity—how light or dark it is.

Hue is measured in a 360-degree circle, a literal color wheel. Saturation and brightness are both measured in percentages. When you set both saturation and brightness to 100 percent, you get the fullest, most vivid representation of any hue. See Figure 4.4 for a representation of how the HSB color model works.

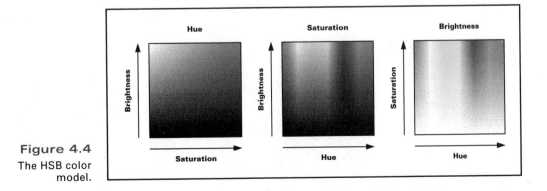

Figure 4.4
The HSB color model.

Lab

The Lab mode is the diplomat of Photoshop's color modes; it attempts to transcend color differences between monitors and print devices and produce device-independent color. The Lab color model is based on a mathematical model of all colors visible to the human eye, which was developed by a French standards committee, the Commission Internationale d'Eclairage (CIE), also known as the International Committee on Illumination.

When Photoshop converts between RGB and CMYK, it first internally converts to Lab. It then uses the settings in Monitor Setup and Printing Inks Setup in the Preferences submenu under the File command to complete the conversion. (This is another reason why it's important to calibrate your monitor—your Monitor Setup preferences are then optimized for your monitor type and you'll have more accurate RGB-to-CMYK conversions.)

Lab measures color across three axes; it essentially does the work of RGB in only two channels, with a third channel thrown in for controlling brightness. Its name is actually an acronym for its three axes. L stands for luminosity, which is similar to brightness in the HSB model, and is measured in percentages. The other two stand for imaginary color ranges, known by the initials a and b. Based on the expansive CIE color wheel, the a axis traces a wide span of colors in the green-to-red range; the b axis traces a wide blue-to-yellow range. Calling up the Color palette for the Lab color mode is the best way to see how these other two axes work, as shown in Figure 4.5. You can enter values ranging from 0 to 100 for the L channel, and values from 120 to -120 for the other two.

Figure 4.5
Lab color in the Color palette.

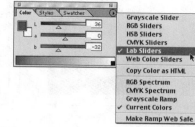

You might want to use Lab if you're most concerned with changing the lightness (not the colors) of an image, or if you edit Photo CD images frequently. The proprietary color model Kodak uses in its Photo CD format is virtually identical to Lab. If you print using several output devices—for example, a Canon Color Laser Copier and a QMS Colorscript 100 model—but need to match the color printouts from all of them, you'd do well to save in Lab and create custom Printing Inks Setup settings for each device.

Web Colors

If you toggle back and forth between Web browsers and Photoshop as you create graphics for Web sites, you may find yourself creating graphics to specifically match colors in your HTML pages. Although the Netscape and Microsoft browsers let designers specify some colors by name, chances are that you refer to colors in your HTML markup—whether for backgrounds, table cells, or text colors—by their *hexadecimal* (or *hex*) values. Each RGB value (from 0 to 255) can be represented by a two-digit or two-letter hexadecimal value; strung together, an RGB value can be represented as a six-character alphanumeric hexadecimal code.

You can specify any RGB value in Photoshop by using its hexadecimal equivalent in place of the 0 to 255 range used for RGB values. As you modify RGB values in the Color Picker, take notice of how the six-character hex value that appears beneath the RGB values change. This field is labeled only by the pound sign (#)—that's because HTML tags that use hex values precede this alphanumeric value with the pound sign, as follows:

```
<FONT COLOR="#336699">
```

One of Photoshop's built-in indexed color palettes, labeled Web, is optimized for creating Web graphics. It contains 216 colors common to both the standard Mac and Windows 8-bit color system palettes. Among Web designers, this palette is also popularly known as the *Netscape 216*. The Only Web Colors check box limits the color field's display to this 216-color Web palette. When you click in this check box, you'll see the Select Color field display suddenly adopt a banded look as the number of available colors is greatly restricted (see Figure 4.6).

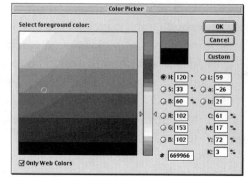

Figure 4.6

Activating the Only Web Colors check box in the Color Picker greatly limits the colors you can select by simply pointing and clicking.

The Color Picker

Now that you've had an introduction to each of Photoshop's color models, you'll have a better grasp on how to choose the precise colors you want. You're ready to call up the Color Picker dialog box, which appears when you click either the foreground or background colors icon found in the toolbox or the Color palette.

Figure 4.7 shows what you see when you click either the foreground or background color icon.

Here's a brief rundown on how you can use each part of the Color Picker in your color selections:

👁 **Select Color field**. This field takes up most of the Color Picker's left side. You can click and reposition the circular marker in the

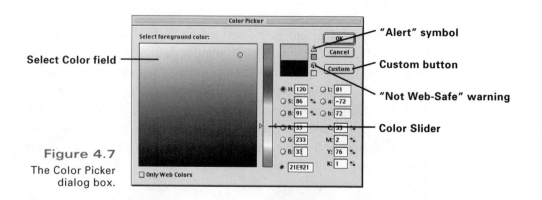

Figure 4.7

The Color Picker dialog box.

color field to select different color values. This is a straightforward, click-and-point method for color selection—no messing with exact color values necessary!

👁 **Color Slider**. Appears just to the right of the color field and is equipped with a pair of slider triangles that you can drag to select and display different sections of the available color spectrum. For example, with the R radio button clicked, dragging the slider triangles lets you change red RGB values. Dragging the slider triangles all the way to the top maximizes red to its highest possible value (255), and dragging it to the bottom lowers it to its lowest possible value (0). Moving the circular marker vertically and horizontally varies the Green (G) and Blue (B) settings, respectively, whereas Red (R) remains constant (see Figure 4.8). When you select a new color, it displays in the top half of the small box to the right of the color slider. Your previously chosen color appears in the bottom half of the box.

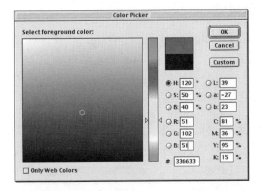

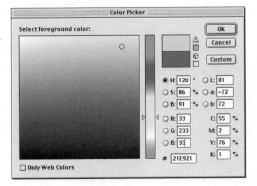

Figure 4.8

Changing colors with the Color Picker's slider.

••

tip   **Using Arrow Keys with the Color Picker's Slider**

When you're in the Color Picker dialog box, holding down the arrow keys on your keyboard increases or decreases the value of the color component of the field that's highlighted or the field in which you've placed your cursor. The longer you press the up or down arrow key, the more you'll see the slider triangles rise or fall.

••

- 👁 **Alert symbol**. Because the RGB color gamut (over 16.7 million colors) is wider than CMYK's, at times you may select and work with colors in RGB mode that can't be printed in CMYK. When you select one of these *out-of-gamut* colors, Photoshop displays an Alert symbol (⚠) as a warning to you. When this happens, you can click the color swatch underneath the Alert symbol to choose the nearest printable color instead. If you plan to use your images only for multimedia formats or other onscreen uses, you don't have to worry about colors that are out-of-gamut for commercial printing.

- 👁 **"Not Web safe" warning**. When you introduce colors not included on the 216-color palette common to Mac and Windows systems into your Web graphics, you run a risk that these colors may not look equally attractive to all visitors to your Web site. To that end, the Color Picker displays a "Not Web safe" indicator (🎲) when you choose a color outside of this set. A small swatch of the nearest Web-safe color value appears beneath this warning; clicking this swatch selects the Web-safe color.

- 👁 **Custom button**. Lets you choose from a number of third-party custom color inks supported by Photoshop. Most of these custom-mixed inks let you consistently print colors that are hard or impossible to reproduce with CMYK colors. After you click the Custom button, you can choose the color family you want from the Book pop-up menu (see Figure 4.9). If you have a swatch book from the third-party manufacturer, it will be useful to consider the colors you want ahead of time and just type in the swatch key numbers to select them. Pantone and Trumatch are probably the best-known color systems on this list, which also includes

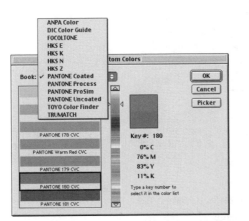

Figure 4.9
Selecting custom colors.

ANPA (now NAA, which stands for Newspaper Association of America), DIC, Focoltone, and Toyo. I use the Custom option in two-color print jobs, where I can select a spot color and create duotones. When you select a custom color, the closest corresponding CMYK values for that color are also displayed. (For more detail on custom colors, see the section "Third-Party Commercial Inks" later in this chapter.)

Using the Color and Swatches Palettes

Photoshop lets you choose colors in a number of ways. You can use the Eyedropper tool to sample existing colors from an image, or you can use the Color Picker as described. The next few sections include brief descriptions of Photoshop's Color and Swatches palettes, which offer a few other ways to choose colors in Photoshop. You might have overlooked these palettes to date, but exploring them here can help you decide whether they will make your Photoshop work easier. If you spend much time searching for and toying with new colors, they'll probably help.

The Color Palette

The Color palette (see Figure 4.10) lets you see more of the available color spectrum at once than you can in the Color Picker dialog box. You can access the Color palette by selecting Show Color from the Window menu.

Figure 4.10
The Color palette and its pop-up menu.

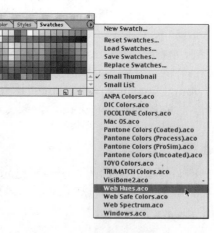

To change the current foreground and background colors, you can click one of the two large, overlapping boxes on the left side of the palette. A pop-up menu at the right of the palette lets you select a color model (Grayscale, RGB, HSB, CMYK, or Lab) and specify the spectrum for the color bar that appears at the bottom of the palette. In the RGB model, for example, you can set values for the red, green, and blue components by dragging the triangles under each of the three color sliders, or by entering a numerical value in the field. Double-clicking the foreground or background swatches launches the Color Picker dialog box.

The Swatches Palette

The Swatches palette (see Figure 4.11) is handy for organizing combinations of colors you use frequently. The pop-up menu on this palette has options for loading, saving, and appending custom swatch sets.

Figure 4.11
The Swatches palette.

tip

Editing Your Swatches Palette

No matter what tool you have selected, your cursor will turn into a paint bucket when you move it over an empty swatch on the Swatches palette. Clicking an empty swatch then adds your currently selected foreground color to the Swatches palette—a quick way to put it aside for future use if you want to select a different color right away. By the same token, you can delete colors on the Swatches palette by [Cmd]-clicking them (for Mac users) or [Ctrl]-clicking (for Windows users); your cursor turns into a scissors icon. You can replace any color on the Swatches palette with your foreground color by [Shift]-clicking the swatch you want to lose. If the order of your swatches is important, you can insert a new color between two others instead of adding it to the end of the list. On Mac OS-based computers, pressing [Shift]+[Option] while you click does the job; on Windows machines, press [Shift]+[Alt] while you click to place your new swatch in its custom position.

The premixed commercial colors that you can access via the Custom button in the Color Picker are all available as custom color palettes that you can load in the Swatches palette. Just click the pop-up menu in the Swatches palette and choose Load Swatches. The Color Palettes folder in your main Photoshop directory contains palettes for Pantone, Trumatch, and other custom commercial sets (see Figure 4.12).

Predefined and Custom Color Sets

At times you might need to restrict the colors you use in your images to a limited set. Say you want to add a special metallic or fluorescent ink; you can't whip those up out of process colors—you have to use a custom commercial ink as a spot color. Or perhaps you're working on a series of graphics for a Web site and you're under strict orders from the client to use Netscape 216, the set of colors common to both the Mac and Windows system palettes discussed previously. In that case you can load a custom indexed color palette—also called a color lookup table (CLUT)—and save your file in Indexed Color mode.

If neither of these scenarios applies to you, feel free to skip this section. If you're looking to expand on the kinds of design assignments you can handle, though, it will be useful to have this information at your fingertips.

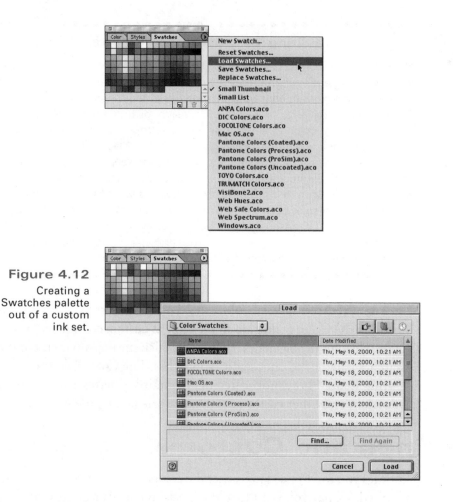

Figure 4.12

Creating a Swatches palette out of a custom ink set.

Third-Party Commercial Inks

Photoshop supports a number of commercial inking systems popular both in the United States and abroad. They are essentially computerized versions of the companies' color swatch books used by designers and printers to match colors for print publications and on press. If you're just beginning to use custom color sets, make sure you check with your printer's customer service representative and find out which color systems it supports.

As mentioned earlier in this chapter, you can access single colors in one of these sets through the Color Picker, or you can load an entire set as a custom Swatches palette. You can also append colors from one of these sets to an existing Swatches palette you have open. Here's

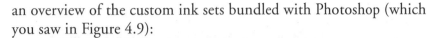

an overview of the custom ink sets bundled with Photoshop (which you saw in Figure 4.9):

- 👁 **ANPA Color**. Formerly the American Newspaper Publishers' Association, this group is now known as NAA (Newspaper Association of America). The color set developed by this group consists of inks that reproduce best on newsprint stock.

- 👁 **DIC Color Guide**. A color system widely used in Japan, but not a leading standard in the United States.

- 👁 **Focoltone**. This color system, which was developed in England, includes 763 inks; it's not a leading standard in the United States.

- 👁 **Pantone Coated, Pantone Process, Pantone ProSim, and Pantone Uncoated**. These components of the Pantone Matching System (PMS), the primary desktop industry standard, cover a range of printing needs. A longtime producer of spot color standards, Pantone also makes available Pantone Process, which is a process-color swatch set with 3,006 CMYK combinations. Pantone ProSim emulates spot colors in process inks. Pantone Coated and Uncoated include Pantone's spot color ranges designed for use on either coated (the inks will appear glossier) or uncoated (the inks will appear somewhat duller) paper stocks.

- 👁 **Toyo Color Finder**. This Japanese color system includes 1,050 inks; although widely used in Japan, it is not a leading standard in the United States.

- 👁 **Trumatch**. Specifically designed for desktop publishers, this set of over 2,000 process colors (all are reproducible in CMYK) is organized according to hue, brightness, and saturation.

The Pantone and Trumatch systems are the most widely supported by other software programs you are likely to use with Photoshop, including QuarkXPress, Adobe PageMaker, Macromedia Freehand, and Adobe Illustrator.

To gain a better understanding of how you can use custom colors in your print production work, follow the steps in Exercise 4.1 to create a duotone. Here, you'll use black ink and a custom ink to create a rich halftone image for a two-color print job.

EXERCISE 4.1

Creating a Duotone with a Custom Commercial Ink

1. Open any existing image from your hard drive. If you don't have a graphic of your own that you want to play with, open one of the samples from Photoshop's Tutorial folder and choose Save As from the File menu to save a test version on your hard drive under a different name. If the sample image is in Indexed Color, RGB, or CMYK mode, you need to change it to grayscale. Select Mode from the Image menu, and then choose Grayscale. Your image must be saved in grayscale mode before you can convert it to a duotone.

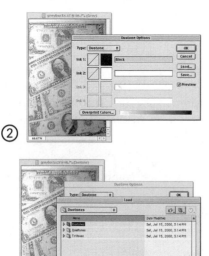

2. Next, select Mode from the Image menu again, and choose Duotone. The Duotone Options dialog box appears, as shown in the following figure.

3. Make sure Duotone is selected in the Type drop-down menu. You'll be able to choose colors for two inks, Ink 1 and Ink 2, by clicking the color box to the left of the color name. Clicking one of the color boxes launches the Custom Color dialog box. You can also load a preset duotone ink included with Photoshop by clicking the Load button in the Duotone Options dialog box. After you click the Load button, you can toggle through your directories to locate duotone settings; a number are included with Photoshop.

   Photoshop includes many color files you can load for duotone options in its Duotones directory; if you're running Photoshop in Windows, you'll see that these duotone files end with an .ADO extension.

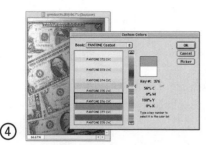

4. Although you can choose any two colors from the Color Picker for your duotone, most duotones consist of black and one commercial ink. Make sure Ink 1 is defined as Black. You should define your darkest ink as Ink 1, because it reproduces the most shadows; Ink 2 will colorize the image. Click in the name field for Ink 2, and then click the Load button. Because Photoshop's preset duotone Pantone Matching System (PMS) color files are named by PMS value, you should either know the number for the color you want or have a PMS swatch book handy. You can also press the Custom button in the Color Picker dialog box to browse or choose a specific color. Click OK when you finish choosing your color.

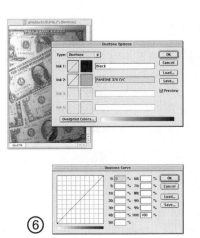

⑤

⑥

⑦

5. The name of Ink 2 automatically changes to the name of the color you chose. If you change your mind and want to name another color value, enter the Color Picker again— don't just type in the name of the new ink.

6. The curve box to the left of each ink's color swatch (and to the right of the ink color's name) lets you modify how much of that ink is actually printed for each color plate. Because you're replacing a single grayscale level with two tints of ink here, you might want to adjust the amounts of ink used to avoid having your image appear too dark and muddy. Clicking it will launch the Duotone Curve dialog box, but you don't need to change any of those settings if you just load one of the preset duotone curve sets.

Click OK in the Duotone Options dialog box. If you've loaded one of Photoshop's present duotones, note how the curve shown in the curve box has changed from the default curve.

7. Save the file in Photoshop EPS format if you want to import the duotone into a page layout program. Make sure the Include Halftone Screen check box in the EPS Options dialog box is checked.

note

Photoshop can identify Pantone inks by short name (such as 199 CV) or by long name (such as 199 CVC). If the final files you submit to your service bureau are printed from other page layout or illustration applications, it's very important that those programs recognize the name of the custom inks you specify in Photoshop. You need to determine whether your page layout software uses long or short Pantone names, and set Photoshop's preferences accordingly. If your page layout software can't recognize the name of the custom ink, your files cannot color separate correctly. To set short Pantone names, choose Preferences from the Edit menu, and then choose General; click the check box labeled Short Pantone Names. To set long Pantone names, leave the Short Pantone Names check box unchecked.

Using Indexed Color Palettes

Indexed color palettes limit the colors you can choose for editing a given image. If your work includes creating graphics for Web sites, you will find yourself using an indexed color palette every time you save an image in GIF format. You can save a file in indexed color format with up to 256 colors (the maximum for 8 bits), but you can also use indexed color palettes with many fewer colors. Doing so will reduce your final file sizes and cause files to appear more quickly, and that's always helpful for good Web design or any onscreen application.

As mentioned earlier, Photoshop has a prominent, built-in indexed color palette called Web that is already optimized for designing Web graphics. The Web palette contains the 216 colors that are common to the standard Macintosh and Windows 8-bit color system palette. As you stray from using these *Web-safe colors*, as they're known, you increase the likelihood that the colors on your Web pages may not be equally appealing to all users. For example, the snappy forest green background you see on a Web site viewed with your Mac's 24-bit color display can appear as a sickly hue the color of pea soup on your neighbor's PC laptop. Some areas of solid color in your original graphics might *dither* as they appear on a different computer platform—which means they have a speckled or moiré effect.

As a designer, you probably use a large-screen monitor configured with thousands or millions of colors. If so, viewing 24-bit JPEGs is not a problem for you—but a significant number of Web visitors use monitors that are limited to 256 colors at most. The way your Web pages look can vary greatly on different computer platforms and Web browser versions, but using a Web-savvy color palette helps ensure that your graphics will largely look the way you intended them to.

In theory, most graphical Web browsers should be able to display the same 24-bit color spectrum available to the RGB color model. In practice, though, if a user only has a 256-color monitor, the browser will display additional colors by dithering, as I mentioned earlier. The user's browser will mix some pixels of one color with others, for an effect that might look okay from a distance but will have a speckled appearance when viewed up close—which is how your visitors, sitting in front of their computers, are going to see them.

Photoshop's Web palette of 216 colors includes all combinations of six specific numeric values—0, 51, 102, 153, 204, or 255—in the red, green, and blue channels. Because there are six possible values in each of three channels, this is how you get 6×6×6 = 216 possibilities altogether. Table 4.1 makes this a bit clearer; it shows some of the RGB colors and their equivalent respective hexadecimal values. The nondithering RGB values, then, include all those in Table 4.1 plus any other combination using these six values—(255, 51, 102) or (153, 0, 204), for example.

Table 4.2 shows the hexadecimal values for these six key numbers. Using Table 4.2, you can see that the hexadecimal values for colors such as (255, 51, 102) or (153, 0, 204) are FF3366 and 9900CC, respectively.

If you load, say, a 24-bit image and then index it using Photoshop's Web color palette, all colors in that image are converted to the nearest Web-safe value. For fun, you can see this happen before your very eyes—first, open the Color Picker and click the Only Web Colors check box. Now try entering various values in the RGB fields; as you tab to the

Table 4.1 Some RGB Colors and Their Hexadecimal Equivalents

COLOR	RGB VALUE	HEXADECIMAL VALUE
Red	(255, 0, 0)	FF0000
Green	(0, 0, 255)	0000FF
Blue	(0, 255, 0)	00FF00
Cyan	(0, 255, 255)	00FFFF
Magenta	(255, 0, 255)	FF00FF
Yellow	(255, 255, 0)	FFFF00
Black	(0, 0, 0)	000000
White	(255, 255, 255)	FFFFFF

Table 4.2 Nondithering Web Colors: RGB Values and Their Hexadecimal Equivalents

RGB VALUE	HEXADECIMAL VALUE
0	00
51	33
102	66
153	99
204	CC
255	FF

next field, the value you entered automatically changes to the nearest nondithering RGB value. For example, in Figure 4.13, I launched the Color Picker, clicked the Only Web Colors check box, and entered RGB values of (172, 60, 145). These were converted on the fly to (153, 51, 255)—the closest Web-safe color.

As mentioned in Chapter 2, using the Save for Web function in the File menu lets you preview multiple versions of your image using various compression schemes before you commit to converting your

Figure 4.13
Clicking the Only Web Colors check box limits the RGB values you can use.

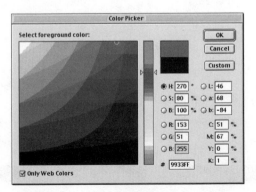

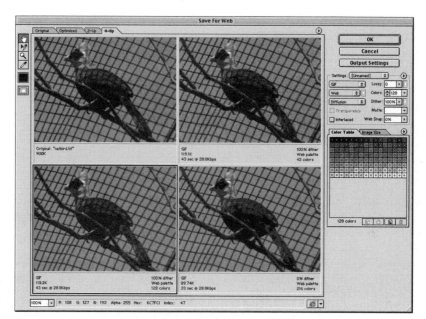

Figure 4.14
The Save for Web interface.

Photoshop files to a Web format (see Figure 4.14). Each preview lists the new file format, file size, typical download times, and number of colors used. This aims to help you balance exactly what you would sacrifice in terms of color or image quality in order to reduce your file sizes for faster display.

The Optimize section of the Save for Web interface (along the right column) lets you try an established compression scheme or tinker with creating your own. The factors you can experiment with here include file format (GIF, JPEG, or PNG), number of potential colors (because reducing the numbers of colors reduces bit depth, which reduces file size), the type of color palette, and the amount of dithering that Photoshop may produce. See Figure 4.15.

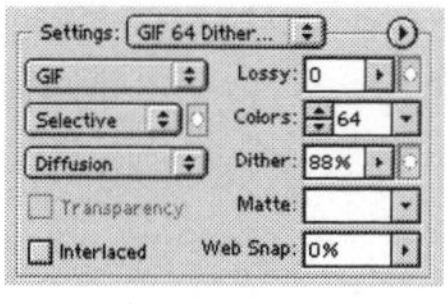

Figure 4.15
Optimizing settings in the Save for Web dialog box.

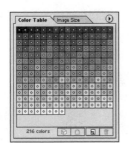

Figure 4.16
The Color Table
palette within the
Save for Web
interface.

You can assess your previewed image's colors using the Color Table palette within the Save for Web interface (see Figure 4.16). You can also edit individual colors one at a time using this palette. If you want to ensure a color isn't changed in the process of resampling to reduce file size—perhaps a color that your marketing team insists be used for your company's logo, example—you can lock it in place. Colors represented in this Color Table palette that are Web-safe have a small white diamond in their center. A small square in the lower right indicates when a color is locked. More extensive details about the operation of the Save for Web function is ahead in Chapter 12, "Web Graphics Essentials."

Color Options in Painting and Editing Modes

Chapter 3, "Toolbox and Palette Essentials," touched briefly on the way the Options palette for Photoshop's painting and editing tools offered Mode settings that could change colors drastically and create a number of special effects. I held off describing these painting and editing modes until this chapter, however, because they largely deal with color. You'll want to understand how each setting determines which colors it will affect. Otherwise, using these modes can largely consist of trial and error. Here is a brief explanation of each setting:

👁 **Normal.** With Opacity set to 100%, this option lets you paint or edit fully with the foreground color in the effect you're applying, knocking out all underlying colors. If the Opacity is set to a lower number, the value of the color you're applying is averaged with the color value of the underlying pixels, so the underlying color will show through the effect you're applying.

- 👁 **Threshold**. Images in Bitmap or Indexed Color mode use this option instead of Normal. Because both these modes use limited color palettes, painting or editing in this mode applies the closest available color value.

- 👁 **Dissolve**. The color you're painting with will replace random pixels that you paint or edit over. The collective effect is that of your image dissolving into the color you're painting with. It works with all the painting tools but not the editing tools. You can create some dramatic effects using this mode with the Airbrush or the Paint tool set and with a large brush from the Brushes palette.

- 👁 **Behind**. This mode works only in images with multiple layers and transparent backgrounds (covered in Chapter 5, "Layering Essentials"). It lets you edit transparent parts of a layer—where no other color has been placed—but not the independent images or objects previously placed on that layer.

- 👁 **Clear**. Available only to certain tools, such as the Line and Paint Bucket. This mode works only in images with multiple layers where transparency is available. When applied, it changes pixel transparency.

- 👁 **Multiply**. Combines your foreground color with the underlying pixel colors, effectively deepening the color values the way you'd get deeper colors by coloring with felt tip markers on top of one another. The more you use a tool in Multiply mode, the darker the affected pixels become.

- 👁 **Screen**. Creates the opposite effect of Multiply mode by whitening affected pixels. The effect is something like using an ink eraser on a colored drawing. The more you use a tool in Screen mode, the lighter the affected pixels become.

- 👁 **Overlay**. A combination of the Multiply and Screen modes that can be used to produce visually pleasing effects—it enhances contrast and enriches color saturation.

- 👁 **Soft Light**. Designed to produce a muted spotlight effect on the areas you're painting or editing.

- **Hard Light**. Designed to produce a rather harsh lighting effect on the areas you're painting or editing.

- **Color Dodge**. Applying this mode is similar to using the Dodge tool. Dodging with lighter colors results in more intense changes, whereas darker colors produce a subtler effect.

- **Color Burn**. Applying this mode is similar to using the Burn tool. Burning with darker colors produces stronger effects, whereas lighter hues have less dramatic results.

- **Darken**. Pixels that are lighter than the color you're applying get filled with the new color; darker pixels remain untouched.

- **Lighten**. Pixels that are darker than the color you're applying get filled with the new color; darker pixels remain untouched.

- **Difference**. Inverts the colors in your image to the difference between your foreground color and the color of the underlying pixels.

- **Exclusion**. Produces an effect similar to Difference, but usually contains more neutral grays.

- **Hue**. Painting and editing in this mode affects only the hue—the pure color—of any pixel you touch, not the saturation or luminosity. Any solid black or solid white pixels are unaffected.

- **Saturation**. Painting and editing in this mode affects only the saturation—how much gray is mixed in each pixel you touch; the hue and luminosity are untouched. Any solid black or solid white pixels are unaffected.

- **Color**. A combination of painting with the Hue and Saturation modes; both hue and saturation are affected, but not luminosity (brightness). The most useful application for this editing mode is in colorizing grayscale images.

- **Luminosity**. This mode is effectively the opposite of the Color mode; it influences the luminosity—or brightness—of the pixels you edit, but not the hue or saturation.

Exercise 4.2 takes a look at how painting with one or more of these modes can create different effects, especially producing the look of a hand-tinted photograph. First, though, you can warm up by applying an overall tinted effect to an image—this can be useful for applying a sepia effect to "age" a photograph, for example.

tip

● ●

Sneak Peek: Adjustment Layers

In Exercise 4.2, you modified your original image extensively to produce several tinted effects—and may not have retained the original unless you saved a backup copy. With Adjustment Layers, a feature of the Layers menu you'll explore in Chapter 5, you can vary the Hue, Saturation, and Lightness settings using the same dialog box you saw here—but your changes take place in a new layer. Your original image is retained on its own layer. For now, suffice it to say that you would add a new Adjustment layer right after opening your graphic. To do so, choose New Adjustment Layer from the Layer menu, and then click Hue/Saturation in the New Adjustment Layer submenu.

● ●

Managing Color Consistency

If you use computer equipment manufactured by different companies—say, a color monitor from one vendor, a printer from another, and a scanner from a third—you might have experienced firsthand how colors produced on one device can differ from those produced on another. As described earlier, computer monitors, which use the RGB color gamut, can display certain bright, fully saturated hues that aren't impossible to reproduce on press because they have no counterpart in the CMYK color range. This makes it difficult—if not impossible—to ensure that the colors you see on your monitor can be reproduced in print. However, calibrating your monitor and using Photoshop's built-in controls for color management go a long way toward helping you achieve predictable final colors.

EXERCISE 4.2

Colorizing an Image with Overall and Hand-Tinted Effects

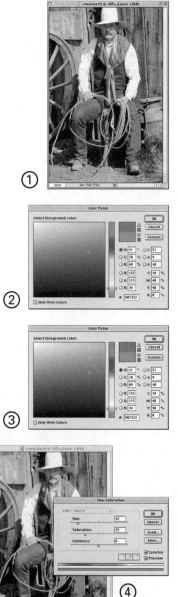

1. Open an existing detailed image from your hard drive. You should use a grayscale image that's been converted to RGB mode (by choosing Mode from the Image menu). Alternatively, you can colorize an RGB image that has been desaturated; to do so, choose Adjust from the Image menu, and then Desaturate from the Adjust submenu. Here, I'm using an image of a cowboy.

2. First you'll apply a subtle, sepia tinting effect to the entire image. Click the Color Picker's foreground color and choose a warm tone to infuse your image with. Click OK when you're done.

3. Now you'll apply the tint using this color to the entire image. Choose Adjust from the Image menu, and then Hue/Saturation from the Adjust submenu.

4. The Hue/Saturation dialog box pops up. Make sure you click in the Colorize box—you will see your image infused with the color you selected as the foreground color in step 3. If you like what you see here, you're close to done!

   Note the values entered in the Hue, Saturation, and Lightness fields. These were derived from the foreground color you selected. Try moving the Hue and Saturation sliders to see how your changes can drastically affect your image's overall color. Click OK when you're happy with how your image looks.

5. You're ready to move on to hand-tinting. Just as in step 1, you'll need either a grayscale image that's been converted to RGB mode, or a desaturated RGB image. Here, I've reverted my modified image to its original state.

6. Use the Magic Wand tool to select distinct areas of your image that you want to add a single color to. Select the Paintbrush or Paint Bucket tool to quickly add dabs of color to your selected areas. Make sure that the mode for the tool is set to Color or another of the color modes besides Normal. Note how the choice of mode can affect where color is applied to your selections.

In this example, I have selected each item of clothing separately and applied a different bright color to each. This can lend a flat, posterized effect to your image. You can also make one or more small parts of your image stand out by tinting just that section, whereas the rest of your image remains desaturated. When you're done experimenting, click OK to save or Cancel to ignore your changes. Here, I've hand-tinted the scarf separately from the shirt; the image to the left shows how I've selected just the pants to apply a bright tint to them as well.

⑥

A color-management system is a tool for your computer's operating system that attempts to reconcile the color relationships between various computer publishing devices such as scanners, monitors, printers, and imagesetters. The leading standard for color-management systems is developed by the International Color Consortium (ICC). Most likely, your color-publishing devices have an ICC device profile that describes the color space used by that peripheral.

When you install Photoshop, you automatically install an Adobe Gamma utility (see Figure 4.17) that lets you interactively calibrate your monitor and then output an ICC-based profile for your monitor's color space. The utility has a step-by-step wizard, or assistant, for entering your configurations.

This calibration acts to remove any color cast from your monitor, as well as ensure that your monitor grays remain as neutral as possible.

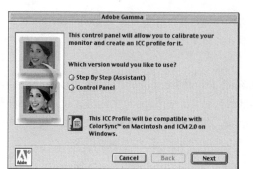

Figure 4.17
The Adobe Gamma utility.

You can access Adobe Gamma from the Control Panels menu. Windows users can also find the utility in the Program Files\Common Files\Adobe\Calibration folder.

Photoshop has its own set of predefined color-management settings, each of which has a corresponding color profile and various options for ensuring color consistency. By and large, you should never need to change these settings. One situation where you might want to choose a predefined color-management setting is when you need to use the same images across different media. For example, you might be designing full-color print brochures and need to send the files to an overseas publisher to print a foreign-language edition—and then reuse that imagery for a Web site. If you do decide to use color management with Photoshop, though, be sure to check with your service bureau or print vendor to see whether they have recommendations for ensuring your color-management settings continue to work well with their systems.

You specify color-management settings by choosing Color Settings from the Edit menu (see Figure 4.18). The available choices are as follows:

👁 Color Management Off uses minimal color-management tweaking to suit applications that can't handle these kinds of settings.

👁 Emulate Photoshop 4 returns Photoshop's behavior to the days of Photoshop 4, before the program extended its color-management capabilities so extensively.

Figure 4.18

The Color Settings interface.

👁 Three default prepress settings are arranged by region:

👁 U.S. Prepress Defaults

👁 Europe Prepress Defaults

👁 Japan Prepress Defaults

👁 Web Graphics Defaults aims to optimize colors for images designed for Web sites.

👁 ColorSync Workflow is designed to work only with the ColorSync 3.0 content management system on the Mac, using profiles chosen in the ColorSync control panel.

Summary

The information covered in this chapter serves as a good basis for the discussions later in the book about how to color-correct images and anticipate other color issues in print production. Learning how to work with custom color palettes will help you create images for applications and systems that have their own internal color models. Gaining an awareness of Web color issues will help you develop coordinated image sets and explore other avenues for improving the display time and appearance of your graphics.

Up next, Chapter 5 covers Photoshop's Layers feature—and from here on, you get to see how powerful Photoshop's image editing truly is.

5

Layering Essentials

IN THIS CHAPTER

Creating and Manipulating Layers

👁

Creating Fill Layers and Translucent Overlays

👁

Using Adjustment Layers

👁

Combining Layers

👁

Creating Layer Masks

Using Photoshop's Layers feature is analogous to overlaying several sheets of acetate on a presentation board, where you can see through the transparent part to images and text on other layers. Or if you're a Toys-R-Us kid, it's a little like playing with Colorforms; you can see the composite effect, but still rearrange parts at any time if you want to. Photoshop's Layers feature gives the program some of the functionality of a vector-based illustration program, whereby objects can be manipulated independently of the remainder of the image. It provides an extremely versatile way to combine images and preview the resulting photocompositions before committing to the changes.

Some of the most breathtaking Photoshop effects come from the judicious use of layers. You can import rendered images from another software package in one layer, add shadows in another layer, and manipulate a background texture in a third. With layers, it's easy to create mask effects—letter or object outlines through which you can see other images. These techniques enable you to create many popular photo effects used on book covers and in advertising and magazine graphics.

Adding layers can require a whopping amount of additional memory, though, so it's important to understand when and how to use layers to create additional effects and retain flexibility in image editing. Here are the major topics to be covered in this chapter:

- 👁 Manipulating layers: creating, deleting, and editing them
- 👁 Moving layers between documents
- 👁 Using the Photoshop Layer Style feature to add drop shadows, glows, bevels, and embossing effects in one quick step
- 👁 Making color adjustments to layers
- 👁 Using layers to fill an outline with another image
- 👁 Blending layers and creating layer masks

Creating New Layers

The Layers palette controls the arrangement of layers in your document. Here's where you specify what parts of your image you want to

Figure 5.1
The Layers
palette.

be opaque and cover up what's below, and what parts should be transparent. You can introduce new layers into your documents so you can edit new content without permanently affecting your existing images. You can merge layers when you finish editing or delete layers altogether. You can display the Layers palette by choosing Show Layers from the Window menu (see Figure 5.1).

When you create a new file, the document contains a single layer that's named Background if you clicked the White or Background Color radio button in the Contents section of the New dialog box. However, as Figure 5.2 shows, if you click the Transparent radio button for Contents, your initial base layer is just labeled Layer 1. As you'll see further ahead in this chapter, you can rename your document's layers however you please.

Figure 5.2
Each new
Photoshop
document begins
with a base layer.
By default,
transparent areas
are displayed in a
gray-and-white
checkerboard
pattern.

> *note*
>
> You might think that if you create a single-layer image with a transparent background, you can import it into a page layout program and retain the transparency. This isn't the case, however. If you want to drop out the background in a Photoshop document, you have to outline an object in the document with a *clipping path*, which is covered in Chapter 6, "Path Essentials."

New Layer Options

When you're ready to create a new layer, you first need to choose Show Layers from the Window menu; this will let you see the current layers in your document. There are several ways you can create a new layer. For starters, you can choose New from the Layer menu, and then choose Layer from the New submenu. Or you can choose New Layer from the pop-up menu on the Layers palette (see Figure 5.3).

Either of these actions causes the New Layer dialog box to appear (see Figure 5.4). The resulting dialog box contains options for the opacity and mode for the new layer, plus whether it should be grouped with other layers. When you create a new layer, it becomes your current active layer.

A third way to create a new layer is to click the Create New Layer icon (▣) on the Layers palette. This method bypasses the New Layer dialog

Figure 5.3

You can create a new layer using the Layer menu or the Layers palette.

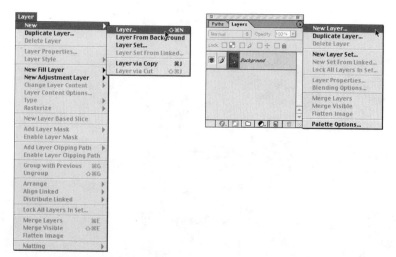

Figure 5.4
The New Layer
dialog box.

box unless you hold down Option (for Mac users) or Alt (for Windows users) when you click it. If you change your mind about what to name your new layer, you can rename it at any time by highlighting that row in the Layers palette and then choosing the Layer Properties command from the Layers palette pop-up menu. If you're working with the background layer, you need to double-click its row in the Layers palette in order to rename it.

After you start adding multiple layers in a Photoshop document, you can save it only in native Photoshop format. When you're done editing individual layers and want to save your file in another format, you need to *flatten* your image first. To do so, choose Flatten Image from the Layer menu—or, if the Layers palette is readily at hand, choose Flatten Image from the Layers palette pop-up menu—before choosing Save or Save As. See the "Merging and Flattening Layers" section later in this chapter.

Establishing What Layer to Work On

If you were editing a composite image made up of several images on transparent acetate and wanted to reposition a certain object, you might have to flip through several sheets to find the one you want. Photoshop's Layers feature works the same way; if you want to edit a black oval on Layer 3, you have to make Layer 3 active before you can select the black oval—you can't touch the oval from another layer. This section covers how to find the right layer when you want to edit part of your image as well as how to tell what layer you're in at any given time.

Using the Layer Thumbnails

One way to keep track of what's on each layer is to look at the thumbnail sketches that appear by default on the Layers palette (see Figure 5.5). You can also adjust this to view a larger thumbnail sketch or to

Figure 5.5

You can see at a glance which images are on each layer.

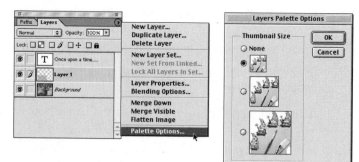

Figure 5.6

Choose Palette Options from the Layers palette's pop-up menu to view the Layers Palette Options dialog box.

hide the thumbnail altogether. Click the Layers palette pop-up menu and choose Palette Options; this causes the Layers Palette Options dialog box to appear (see Figure 5.6). However, the default setting is what usually works best—hiding the thumbnail defeats the purpose of seeing what's on the separate layers, and the larger views take up more screen real estate and take longer to redraw.

Watching the Title Bar

Once you get caught up in manipulating parts of an image you might forget the name of the layer you're working on. With the Layers palette open, you can tell at a glance—that row appears highlighted and bordered in black. Two icons should appear to the left of the thumbnail image on your active layer. The first is an eye icon (👁), which indicates that this layer is visible. The second icon, which should appear between the eye icon and your layer's thumbnail, shows either a paintbrush (✏) or a mask icon (▣). The mask icon indicates that a layer mask is selected in this active layer. (Layer masks, which let you control

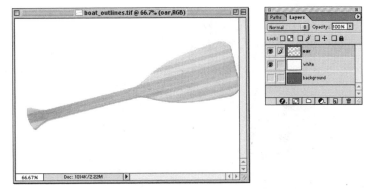

Figure 5.7

If your document has at least two layers, the title bar displays which layer you're working in. The image in this example contains three layers; as the title bar shows, the layer labeled "oar" is the active one.

how much of an image on a given layer actually appears, are discussed later in this chapter.)

Your active layer is also known as the *target layer*. You can also tell which layer you're working in, even if the Layers palette is closed, by looking at your document's title bar (see Figure 5.7).

tip

Photoshop has context-sensitive menus that pop up for various palettes, tools, and screens—and these can save you some time when you're applying a lot of layer commands. To access the drop-down menu for layer, mask, or selection commands, Mac users Ctrl-click, whereas Windows users right-click, on any row in the Layers palette, or on the document window itself (see Figure 5.8). Just select an item on the menu and release the mouse button to apply it.

Figure 5.8

Press the Ctrl key as you click— or right-click, if you have a two-button mouse—in your image to see the layer, mask, or selection options.

Figure 5.9
Options for
deleting a layer.

Deleting Layers

You've added a funny mustache and devil's horns to that annual report
photo of your company's CEO; now you've got to delete that layer and
get back to color-correcting his pasty complexion. You need to start by
making the about-to-be-cut layer your active layer. Now you can either
drag the layer's row to the Trash icon in the lower-right corner of the
Layers palette (🗑), or choose Delete Layer from the Layers palette
pop-up menu, as shown in Figure 5.9. As long as you have the correct
layer highlighted in the Layers palette, you can also just click the Trash
icon in the lower-right corner of the Layers palette to delete it.

You can even remove your image's background, leaving a transparent
background in its place. Make the background layer active, click the
layer's name in the Layers palette, and drag it to the Trash icon. The
background layer will disappear from the Layers palette and Photoshop's
checkerboard pattern, which denotes transparency, will fill the background parts of your image.

Manipulating Layers

This section covers how to move whole layers around at a time as well
as how to link them so that you can move several layers at once. It also
includes some quick tips for toggling between layers.

Moving Layers

You can move a whole layer with the Move tool (![Move tool icon]) or edit objects in a single layer with the usual choices you have in your toolbox. You can use the arrow keys with the Move tool to move a layer in any of the four major directions one pixel at a time; holding down (Shift) will move the layer ten pixels at a time.

Linking Layers Together

It's also possible to link several layers in order to move or edit their content together. You can see how useful this is if you want to reposition, say, a photo of an angel with a halo added in a separate layer—you wouldn't want to have to move them one at a time and hope to maintain the same spatial relationship using guesswork. To link two layers together, first make sure that one of the two is set as your active layer. After you've chosen your active layer, click the empty column to the left of an inactive layer to link it to the active layer. The layer remains inactive and a link icon (![link icon]), which looks like links in a vertical chain, appears next to the layer on the Layers palette (see Figure 5.10). You can click the box again to remove the link. When you choose the Move tool and reposition one layer, the second layer moves with it.

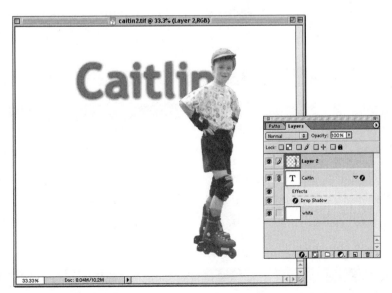

Figure 5.10

Linking an object in one layer with its partner in another.

Figure 5.11

The eye icon indicates which layers are visible in an image.

Viewing and Hiding Layers

As you edit objects on a single layer, you may find it distracting to view the elements on other layers. You can hide the layers other than your active layer by clicking the eye icon next to their names in each row of the Layers palette. You can click the eye icon again to make the layer visible once more. You can click and drag your cursor all the way up or down a long list of layers to make them all visible or invisible (see Figure 5.11).

Scrolling through Layers via Keystrokes

It's also possible to move among layers without calling up the Layers palette. Table 5.1 shows the relevant keystrokes you need to know.

Table 5.1 Using Key Commands to Move between Layers

ACTION	KEY COMMAND (MAC)	KEY COMMAND (WINDOWS)
Move up one layer	Option + [ ]	Alt + [ ]
Move down one layer	Option + [ ]	Alt + [ ]
Jump to topmost layer	Shift + Option + [ ]	Shift + Alt + [ ]
Jump to bottom layer	Shift + Option + [ ]	Shift + Alt + [ ]

If you want to view one layer at a time as you use key commands to jump from layer to layer, just set your active layer to be the only visible layer before you start scrolling from layer to layer.

Copying Layers between Documents

If you want to copy one layer from your image to a different document, Photoshop has an easy built-in way to do so. Select the layer you want to copy as your active layer, and then choose Duplicate Layer from the Layers palette pop-up menu. You'll then see a dialog box that lets you select the open (or new) document into which you want to copy the layer. You can also accomplish this duplicating effect by using the Move tool to drag one layer physically to another document's window.

A third way to duplicate a layer to another file is to click the layer's name in the Layers palette and drag it onto the destination document. This makes your second document active. Your duplicated layer will also be active and appear above the previous active layer.

note

All these duplication methods are more efficient than copying and pasting an entire layer—which can really put a strain on Photoshop's memory and slow the program's operations to a crawl.

Rearranging Your Layers' Order

Sometimes you may need to rearrange the order of the layers in a Photoshop document. Much like shuffling a deck of cards, you can rearrange the order in which layers in a Photoshop document stack one atop the other.

Dragging Layers

To bring a layer to the forefront, display the Layers palette and position your cursor over the name of the layer you want to move up. Click and drag the outline of the row over and above the name of the layer you want it to overlap. The line that separates the rows in the Layers palette will turn darker as you move a layer selection over it, which indicates that this is a spot where you can reposition your selection between two other layers (see Figure 5.12).

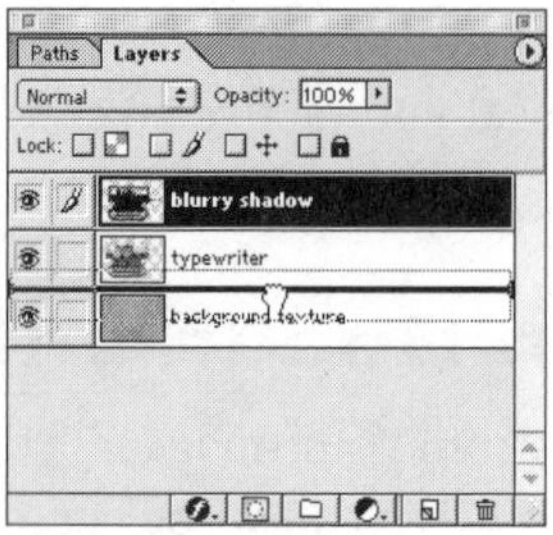

Figure 5.12

Rearranging layers. Here, the blurry shadow layer is being placed in between the typewriter and background texture layers.

The order of the layers in the Layers palette reflects the top-to-bottom order of the layers in your Photoshop document. The background layer is the only one that you cannot reposition elsewhere in your document—by virtue of its name—but you can easily work around this restriction by giving the layer a different name.

Using the Arrange Commands

You can also rearrange your layers' order by choosing Arrange from the Layer menu. The Arrange options let you move an active layer to the front (Bring to Front), move an active layer up one level in the Layers palette (Bring Forward), move the active layer down one level in the Layers palette (Send Backward), and move the active layer to the bottom

Table 5.2 Using Key Commands to Rearrange the Order of Layers in an Image		
ACTION	**KEY COMMAND (MAC)**	**KEY COMMAND (WINDOWS)**
Bring to Front	Cmd + Shift +]	Ctrl + Shift +]
Bring Forward	Cmd +]	Ctrl +]
Send Backward	Cmd + [	Ctrl + [
Send to Back	Cmd + Shift + [	Ctrl + Shift + [

of all the other layers, save for the background layers (Send to Back). Table 5.2 shows the keyboard equivalents for the Arrange options.

Creating Layer Sets

As you create complex Photoshop documents, you may find you're creating more layers than you can readily keep track of. That's where a Photoshop feature called *layer sets* can help—you can organize layers you want to keep together in a single group. Each layer set appears in the Layers palette with a folder icon. You can then click the folder icon to expand it, displaying the layers contained therein, or collapse it to reduce the number of layers shown (see Figure 5.13).

You can create a new layer set in one of several ways:

- Choose New from the Layer menu, and then Layer Set from the New submenu.

- Click the New Layer Set icon (□) in the Layers palette.

- Choose New Layer Set from the Layers palette's pop-up menu.

To put a layer into a layer set, you can just drag that layer's row to the layer set folder (if it's collapsed) or the layer set name. Once the layer set folder and name are highlighted, release the mouse button. The layer is placed at the bottom of the layer set. If the destination layer set is expanded, you'll be able to specify where it should fall in relation to the other layers in that layer set. Just drag the layer to the desired location within the layer set. When the highlighted line appears where you want it to, release the mouse button.

Figure 5.13

A layer set can be collapsed or expanded to hide or display the layers it contains.

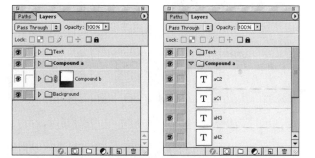

Figure 5.14

The Layers
Properties
dialog box.

Figure 5.14

The Layers
Properties
dialog box.

Layer sets operate just like layers themselves: you can view, select, duplicate, move, or rearrange the order of layer sets the same way you do with layers. You can use the Layers palette to drag layers in and out of layer sets, or create new layers inside an existing layer set.

tip

● ●

Identify Layers or Layer Sets by Color

You can use the Layer Properties dialog box, as shown in Figure 5.14, to assign a color to a layer or layer set to better distinguish them in the Layers palette. Choose Layer Properties from the Layer menu or from the Layers palette's pop-up menu.

● ●

Locking Layers

You can lock a layer or layer set to avoid accidentally making changes or deleting it. When a layer is locked, a lock icon appears to the right of the layer name. The lock is solid when no properties can be changed and is hollow when you specify that only the transparency and layer masks are locked. When you lock a layer, you can even choose to prevent it from being repositioned with the Move tool. You can rearrange where locked layers fall within the order of layers in your document, but they cannot be deleted. See Figure 5.15.

Figure 5.15

The Lock options
in the Layers
palette.

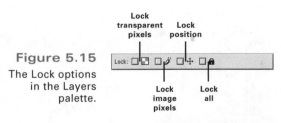

You have several options for locking a layer or layer set. With the layer or layer set selected, you have these choices:

Lock transparent pixels locks the layer's opacity and blending mode setting.

Lock image pixels still lets you adjust the opacity and blending modes.

Lock position disables the Move tool and prevents you from moving the layer.

Lock all acts as if you checked off the previous three options.

To lock a layer set, choose Lock All Layers in Set from the Layer menu. Alternatively, you can choose Lock All Layers in Set from the Layers palette's pop-up menu.

Editing and Manipulating Layer Styles

You'll find that a number of common graphic effects—including several kinds of shadows and glows—can be generated quite easily using the Photoshop's layer styles. You can apply them to objects in any layer, but they look especially good when applied to type. After you apply a layer style, you can continue to edit them—for example, you can lengthen a drop shadow if it does not appear prominently enough when first applied.

To apply layer styles, you need to first activate the layer you want to apply these effects to, and then choose Layer Style from the Layer menu. Alternatively, you can click the layer style icon that looks like a cursive lowercase "f" (🅕) at the bottom of the Layers palette. If you change your mind about any layer style you've applied, you can remove it by choosing Layer Style from the Layer menu, and then selecting Clear Layer Style.

The choices for Layer Styles include the following:

Drop shadows. You can automatically add shadows that fall behind the layer contents.

- **Inner shadows**. This creates a recessed effect by adding shadows within your layer's contents. It works especially well for creating recessed, chiseled lettering.

- **Glows**. You can add glows that emanate from the inside or outside edges of the layer contents.

- **Beveling and embossing**. These can give your layer's objects, especially type, a cool raised 3-D effect.

- **Satin**. This adds a glossy finish to the object or type on your layer.

- **Overlay**. These effects enable you to apply a color, gradient, or pattern to a layer.

- **Stroke**. This outlines the object on the current layer using a color, gradient, or pattern.

Figure 5.16 shows a quick sample of the results of applied layer styles—appropriately, the wording for each layer style listed identifies the effect.

Exercise 5.1 walks through the steps for applying the layer styles shown in Figure 5.16.

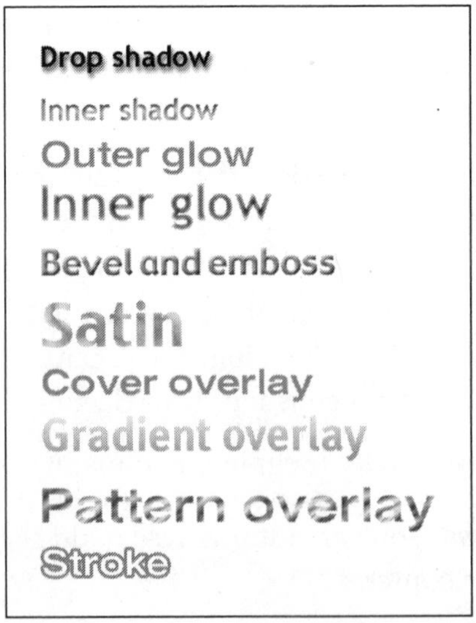

Drop shadow
Inner shadow
Outer glow
Inner glow
Bevel and emboss
Satin
Cover overlay
Gradient overlay
Pattern overlay
Stroke

Figure 5.16

Layer styles are particularly effective for decorating text in type layers.

EXERCISE 5.1

Creating Drop Shadows and Pattern Fills with Layer Styles

1. Open a new Photoshop file. If you prefer, you can open an existing image to which you want to add some type.

②

2. Choose the Type tool and position your cursor where you want the type to display. Click in your document and enter a small amount of new text. This will create a new type layer, which you can see by choosing Show Layers from the Window menu.

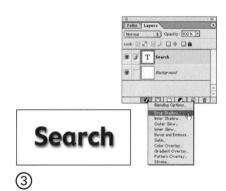
③

3. With your new type layer active, choose the Layer Styles icon in the bottom of the Layer palette and then choose Drop Shadow. Alternatively, you can choose Layer Styles from the Layer menu, and then pick Drop Shadow from the Layer Styles submenu. The Layer Styles dialog box opens; you can modify your Drop Shadow in many ways. Experiment with changing the shadow's angle, opacity, and mode, among other factors. Make sure the preview box is checked so you can see how your effect looks. Click OK when you're happy with the effect.

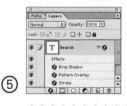
④

4. Consider whether you want to add additional layer styles. In this example, I chose to add both a Pattern Overlay and Stroke layer style. Notice that your type layer shows the special layer style icon (🅕) on its row in the Layers palette, which indicates a layer style.

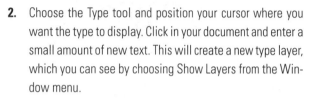
⑤

5. You can turn the effects on and off in the Effects dialog box by clicking the eye icons next to their names in each row of the Layers palette. If you want to turn off all the effects at once, choose Layer Style from the Layer menu, and then select Clear Layer Style.

tip When you apply layer styles to a layer, any object you then add to that layer will have that effect applied to it as well. For example, if you applied a Bevel and Emboss layer style to a layer, and then created a rectangular selection and filled it with a bright color, your rectangle would automatically adopt a beveled and embossed 3-D button layer style.

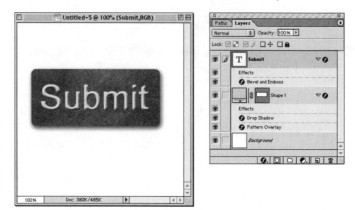

Figure 5.17
Click the triangle next to the layer style icon to expand the list of effects that it contains.

When you apply a layer style, the layer style icon appears to the right of the layer's name in the Layers palette. Next to it is a triangle that can be clicked to collapse or expand each action or effect that was applied to produce the overall layer style (see Figure 5.17).

If you look carefully at how some layer styles are created, you'll see that some effects comprise two other layer styles, applied one after the other. Layer styles become part of the overall layer, so you don't have to worry about the effects becoming separated from the layer. For example, you wouldn't want to leave an object's shadow behind when the object's layer is moved. If desired, though, it is possible to separate layer effects from the layer they modify and put them on their own layer.

From the Layers palette, make sure the layer containing the layer style is selected. Choose Layer Style from the Layer menu, and then Create Layer from the Layer Style submenu. The effects will move to their own layer and appear above the affected layer in the Layers palette. An arrow indicates that this layer modifies the one beneath it, as Figure 5.18 shows.

Remember the impressive patterns that you could load and apply to objects created with the Custom Shape tool, back in Chapter 3? You can look at those patterns as a series of layer styles applied in a certain order. You can see how the Ancient Stone pattern shown in Figure 5.19, for example, was originally constructed from a number of layer styles. Creating variations of the patterns that come packaged with Photoshop is a great way to experiment with creating your own layer styles.

Figure 5.18

Use the Create Layer command to move layer styles onto their own layers.

Figure 5.19

The patterns that come loaded with Photoshop can be analyzed as a series of layer styles applied one after the other.

Creating Fill Layers

If you are upgrading to Photoshop 6.0 from version 5.5, you might recall another kind of layer effect—Color Fill—that no longer appears in the list of layer styles. Photoshop has expanded this feature to an entirely new type of layer. This way, you can experiment extensively with textures, colors, and special effects without altering your original image data.

Fill layers color in the elements on either the layer immediately underneath or on all underlying layers. They tint your underlying elements using either a solid color, gradient, or pattern. Fill layers also blend in the Mode and Opacity settings that you select.

To create a fill layer, just choose New Fill Layer from the Layer menu. From the New Fill Layer submenu, you must first choose whether you want to apply a color, gradient fill, or a predefined pattern. Alternatively, you can click the appropriate icon in the bottom of the Layers palette ( ). The New Layer dialog box then appears with a suggested name for your layer; here, you can define the Mode and Opacity settings you want to use.

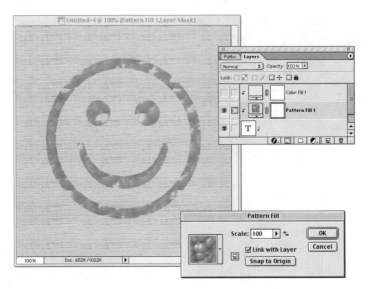

Figure 5.20
Creating a new
fill layer.

After you click OK, you see a dialog box appropriate for the type of fill you chose. For example, if you pick Solid Color, you are presented with the Color Picker so you can enter the color's value. Figure 5.20 shows the Pattern Fill dialog box that displays after creating a new fill layer with Pattern Fill as the fill layer type. Because you control the mode and opacity, you have great flexibility in adding realistic textures and in controlling which parts of your image are affected.

Creating Translucent Overlays

Remember the Opacity setting in the New Layer dialog box? It's particularly useful for blending several layers to produce the effect of a shaded overlay on an image. Say you want to lower the opacity of a rectangular selection (shown behind the text area) on its own layer in the image shown in Figure 5.21. Here, I made the layer with the rectangular selection my active layer, and then lowered the Opacity slider to create a lighter-colored box so the overlying text would be more readable.

Designers frequently use a translucent effect in magazines or on book covers to set apart a section of an image that contains type. The effect helps to draw attention to the type and make that area of the image more prominent.

Figure 5.21

Lowering the opacity of the rectangular selection behind the text is accomplished by using the Opacity slider in the Layers palette.

Using Adjustment Layers

By now you've seen how you can modify parts of an image on one layer independently of the other layers in the same image. But what if you want to apply color or tonal corrections to all your layers at once? You can use adjustment layers, which apply many of the color-correction commands found by choosing Adjust from Image menu to a kind of preview layer. Adjustment layers let you see the effects of color changes on your image without permanently altering any pixels or merging your layers. If you decide you don't like the changes at any point, you can always toss the adjustment layer and start over.

You can create a new adjustment layer by choosing New Adjustment Layer from the Layer menu. The New Adjustment Layer submenu appears with a variety of layer choices, all of which correspond to color-adjustment commands found by choosing Adjust from the Image menu (such as Brightness/Contrast or Hue/Saturation). The New Layer dialog box appears after you make a selection. As an alternative, you can click the icon in the bottom of the Layers palette for creating a new fill layer or adjustment layer (see Figure 5.22). By default, the name of the new adjustment layer you create matches the type you choose (for example, Levels), but you can change its name the same way you can change the name of any layer.

You'll then see a dialog box corresponding to the type of adjustment layer selected. For example, if you chose Levels as the type, you see the

Figure 5.22
Creating a new
adjustment layer.

Levels dialog box. You can begin your edits in this dialog box right away, or click OK and return to it later.

The Layers palette lists adjustment layers much as it displays fill layers, with two small layer thumbnails separated by a link icon. By clicking an adjustment layer's eye icon on and off, you can toggle easily between your image with the color corrections and without—see Figure 5.23.

You can also edit the contents of an adjustment layer (or a fill layer) to indicate areas of your image that should not be affected by the adjustment layer's effects (see Figure 5.24). You do this by using the Paintbrush tool to paint in black, white, or shades of gray as the foreground or background color. Areas painted black are not affected by the layer's color-correcting effects, just as if you were editing a Quick Mask (see Chapter 7, "Channel and Mask Essentials"). Painting with varying shades of gray partially reduces the adjustment layer's effects (or fill layer's effects) and has the same effect as lowering its opacity.

Figure 5.23
Viewing
adjustment layers
in the Layers
palette.

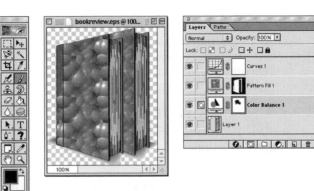

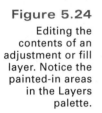

Figure 5.24

Editing the contents of an adjustment or fill layer. Notice the painted-in areas in the Layers palette.

It can be very difficult to tell what areas you're painting in an adjustment layer with the Paint tool. You can see these black and gray brushstrokes if you hold down [Option] (Windows users press [Alt]) as you click the adjustment layer thumbnail in the Layers palette. This displays a view of the adjustment layer mask, which you can edit up close if you want. Mac users [Option]-click (Windows users [Alt]-click again) to go back to the normal editing mode.

Changing Mode Settings to Create Special Effects

Chapter 4, "Color Essentials," talked about the Mode settings that appear in the Options palette for most of the painting and editing tools—including Multiply, Screen, Overlay, Soft Light, Hard Light, and others. These same Mode settings show up when you define the characteristics of a new layer and are pretty versatile here too. When you use these modes as you create and stack layers, the colors of the active layer and the layers beneath them are affected.

note

The only Mode setting from the painting and editing tools that's missing here is the Behind mode—it paints just the transparent parts of a layer and doesn't have an equivalent in this instance.

Here's a brief description of how each of these Mode settings can be used when adding layers to an image:

👁 **Normal**. With Opacity set to 100%, here's where the Colorforms analogy for describing layers works best; objects on your active layer overlap pixels on underlying layers and knock them out. As you lower the opacity, more of the pixels in underlying layers show through.

👁 **Dissolve**. Random pixels in your active layer drop out to reveal the underlying layers. As you reduce the active layer's opacity, more and more of the underlying layers show through.

👁 **Multiply**. Adding a layer with this mode has the effect of creating a darker composite of the image in your active layer with the underlying layers, much as if you were covering an image with felt-tip markings.

👁 **Screen**. Just like the painting and editing tools' version of Screen, this mode is the opposite of Multiply mode; the pixels in underlying layers beneath objects in your active layers are bleached to a lighter composite of the two color values.

👁 **Overlay**. This mode lets you see the highlights and shadows of the underlying layer but uses the color values in the active layer.

👁 **Soft Light**. This mode adds a softened lighting effect over the underlying layers; the effect is often very subtle.

👁 **Hard Light**. This mode adds a much stronger lighting effect than Soft Light.

👁 **Color Dodge**. This mode lightens the base colors in relation to the blend color. Lighter blend colors cause brighter results, whereas darker blend colors have a less noticeable effect, and black has no effect.

👁 **Color Burn**. This mode darkens the base colors in relation to the blend color. Darker blend colors cause more intense results, whereas lighter blend colors have a less noticeable effect, and white has no effect.

👁 **Darken**. Pixels in underlying layers that are lighter than the corresponding colors in your active layer are replaced; pixels in underlying layers that are darker than the corresponding colors in your active layer remain untouched.

👁 **Lighten**. Pixels in underlying layers that are darker than the corresponding colors in your active layer are replaced; pixels in underlying layers that are lighter than the corresponding colors in your layer remain untouched.

👁 **Difference**. With this mode, you subtract the color values in your active layer from the underlying colors and change colors to their RGB complements.

👁 **Exclusion**. The effects of this mode are similar to difference; the brightness value of each color determines whether the blend or base color is subtracted from the other. If your blend color is white, the base color inverts; if the blend color is medium gray, it replaces the base color; if the blend color is black, the mode has no effect.

👁 **Hue**. This layer mode creates a blend of your active layer's color values with the underlying layers' saturation and luminosity. To showcase the mode better, I placed the lobster image on a layer in Hue mode over a bright green background.

👁 **Saturation**. This layer mode creates a blend of your active layer's levels of grays with the underlying layers' hue and luminosity. To showcase the mode better, I placed the lobster image on a layer in Saturation mode over a bright green background.

👁 **Color**. This mode blends the Hue and Saturation values of pixels in your active layer with those in underlying layers; Luminosity values remain untouched, so the underlying layers are colorized but remain just as bright as they were before you added your current target layer. To showcase the mode better, I placed the lobster image on a layer in Color mode over a bright green background.

👁 **Luminosity**. This layer mode creates a blend of your target layer's brightness with the underlying layers' hue and saturation.

Combining Layers

Now that you've seen how a layer's Mode settings can influence a composite effect, it's time to look at a couple of ways you can enact your own version of the movie *The Fly* and blend two disparate images on different layers.

Cutting and Pasting into Layers

You can edit any layer or layer mask using cut-and-paste techniques. One especially easy way to create masked effects is by choosing the Paste Into command from the Edit menu. This kind of masked effect is similar to that described in the section on clipping groups a little earlier—but here, you fill the outline of an object in one layer with a single image or texture from one other layer.

Clipping Groups

You can use layers to create *clipping groups*—a number of layers that are grouped together in such a way that the outline of an object in one layer is filled with an image or texture from another image. (See Figure 5.25.)

There are several ways you can create a clipping group:

- 👁 From the Layers palette, [Option]-click (for Mac users) or [Alt]-click (for Windows users) on the horizontal line between two adjacent layers. You'll see your cursor turn into an icon showing two overlapping circles with a counterclockwise-pointing arrow.

- 👁 Choose a layer in the Layers palette, and then select Group with Previous from the Layer menu.

- 👁 If you have two layers you've already linked together (see "Linking Layers Together" earlier in this chapter), you can choose Group Linked from the Layer menu.

In Exercise 5.2, you'll learn, step by step, how this effect is created using the Custom Shape tool to create the outline shape that contains another image.

Figure 5.25
Use clipping groups to mask an image with an outlined shape.

EXERCISE 5.2

Containing an Image within Another Object's Outline

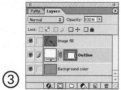

1. You'll first need to decide on an outline shape—such as the letterforms for a single word, or one of the shapes created with the Custom Shape tool (✱). You'll then need to find an image or texture pattern to use as the image with which you'll fill the outline. I refer to these as your outline image and your fill image, respectively. I also suggest creating a separate background layer underneath your outline image, filled with a solid color or appropriate texture, to further dramatize the masking effect.

2. Create a new layer underneath the outline image to hold your background color or texture. Here I've named these two layers **Image fill** and **Background color**. Fill the background layer with the solid color or pattern you want. At this point, the background color or pattern should be completely hidden by your Image fill layer.

3. Now create a new layer that sits between the Image fill layer and the background layer. This is where you'll place the outline shape. Make sure this layer is activated, and then switch to the Custom Shape tool and choose the outline shape you want to use. Click and drag in your image to frame your image just right.

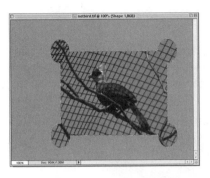

④

4. Now you'll create the clipping group between the Image fill and the outline shape layer. Hold down the Option key (for Mac users) or Alt key (for Windows users) as you click the horizontal line between the Image fill layer and the layer containing your outline. You'll see your cursor turn into an icon showing two overlapping circles with a counterclockwise-pointing arrow before you click. The area outside of your outline shape should fill with your background color or pattern.

5. The path showing your custom shape's outline may still be visible; if so, you can choose Dismiss Path from the Select menu to remove it. You can also apply effects from the Layer Style menu such as drop shadows or glows. Figure 5.26 shows the final effect.

6. Save your file if you want to retain it for future use. Because your file contains multiple Photoshop layers, which aren't supported by other graphics formats, you should save this image in Photoshop's native format.

From a design perspective, filling type with an image works best if the image has easily discernible details. If you're filling the type with a pattern, make sure it's easy to see. For a more unified effect, use a bold, sans-serif typeface.

Figure 5.26
Your completed effect: a masked image.

Editing More than One Layer at Once

You can apply some of Photoshop's tools to work on just one layer, or to affect the pixels in all underlying layers too. The Magic Wand, Paint Bucket, Rubber Stamp, and Smudge tools all function this way. These options produce the kind of color effects you'd get if all your objects were on a single layer. This way, you retain control over whether your background layer (or other layers) feels the effects of the editing you apply in your target layer.

Blending Options

When you double-click any layer besides the background layer, you'll see that you have options for blending colors in your target layer with those in underlying layers (see Figure 5.27). The Blend If section of the Layer Style dialog box lets you set options for how colors in your target layer and underlying layer blend together.

The General Blending options let you choose a Mode setting—such as Dissolve, Multiply, or Color Dodge, which you saw earlier in this chapter—and set the opacity.

The Advanced Blending section contains sliders for your target and underlying layer. You can manipulate these sliders to determine how the pixels of your target layer will be pasted onto the underlying background. Both layers' slider controls let you select color values in

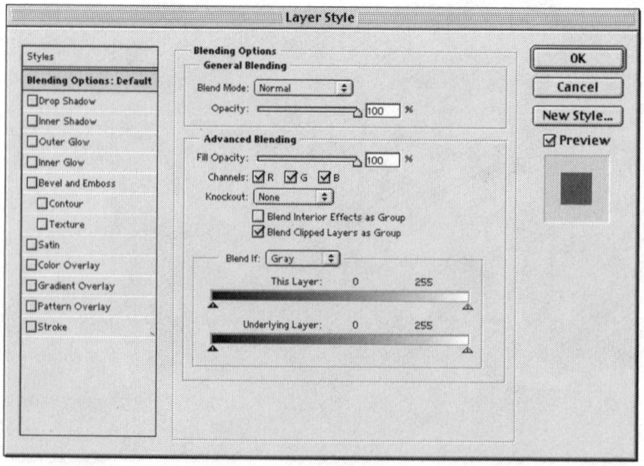

Figure 5.27

Options for blending layers in the Layer Style dialog box.

individual RGB channels or overall values (gray). Both layers' sliders range from 0 to 255, covering the gamut of possible RGB values.

If you look at the controls carefully, you'll see that each layer has a white slider and a black slider. These sliders let you exclude ranges of color from each layer when you blend them. In the This Layer settings, for example, the more you drag each slider toward the opposite side, the more colors you exclude from the composite image. All pixel color values that fall in the range between the two sliders are included in the composite image. In the Underlying layer settings, the more you drag each slider toward the opposite side, the more areas of the underlying image are forced to appear in the composite image.

Blending two layers in this way can sometimes force some harsh composite effects. You can create smoother composites by splitting up the two-part black and white sliders—a trick that involves pressing Option on a Mac, (or Alt for Windows users) while dragging the arrow halves. The pixel values that fall in each split range will only be partially colored in the composite image. Gaining mastery of this feature requires a lot of experimenting on your part.

Creating Layer Masks

For each layer you create in Photoshop, you have the opportunity to add a layer mask, which lets you vary the transparency of objects in your target layer. This mask only affects a preview of your target layer, so you can experiment without actually committing your changes to the pixels in your target layer. When you're done working with a layer mask, you can either put your changes into effect or discard the mask.

To add a layer mask, choose Add Layer Mask from the Layer menu or click the New Layer Mask icon (▣) at the bottom of the Layers palette. A second thumbnail sketch, which represents the layer mask, appears next to the thumbnail sketch of your layer in its row on the Layers palette (see Figure 5.28).

When you create a new layer mask, you can opt for a mask that will reveal all (letting the image show through) or hide all (completely hiding the layer image). You can then click the mask thumbnail and selectively paint to conceal or reveal parts of the image you want to

Figure 5.28
Using layer masks to hide and edit parts of an image.

mask. If you've selected part of your image when you choose to add a new layer mask, you'll have two additional options available to you: Reveal Selection and Hide Selection. These options create a layer mask of the current selection. Depending on which option you choose, you either mask everything but the selected area (Reveal Selection) or mask everything inside the selected area (Hide Selection).

You can edit your layer mask the same way you can edit the contents of an adjustment layer (see Figure 5.29). First, click the layer mask

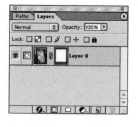

Figure 5.29
Editing a layer mask.

thumbnail in the Layers palette to make it active. Mac users (Option)-
click (Windows users (Alt)-click) on the layer mask thumbnail in the
Layers palette, and use the Paintbrush tool to paint black, white, or
gray pixels to affect the area selected by the mask.

tip You can turn off your layer mask to see the full image without the effects
of the mask, and then turn it back on to compare the two. To do so, hold
down Shift as you click the layer mask thumbnail in the Layers palette. A
red X appears over the layer mask thumbnail; click the thumbnail to activate the layer mask again.

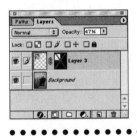

When you finish working with a layer mask, you can either permanently apply it to your image or discard it by choosing Remove Layer
Mask from the Layer menu. If you choose this option, Photoshop gives
you a chance to reconsider and cancel the instruction or apply the mask
after all; click Discard to get rid of the mask.

Merging and Flattening Layers

Once you've decided you're done editing individual layers, you can
collapse your current layer with one or more layers. The Merge Down
command—available in both the Layer menu and the Layers palette
pop-up menu—merges a layer with the layer beneath it. You can collapse all separate visible layers into a single composite layer by choosing
Merge Visible from the Layer menu or Layers palette pop-up menu.
Any hidden layers remain separate, though. Objects in previously transparent layers retain their old transparency settings. You can still save
this file only in native Photoshop format. You can merge sets of linked
layers by choosing Merge Linked from the Layer menu or Layers palette pop-up menu.

If you want to create a single-layer image and discard any hidden layers at the same time, you can choose Flatten Image from the Layers palette pop-up menu. This will get rid of the image's transparent background, too, if it has one. You should choose this setting if you need to save your image in a file format other than native Photoshop.

Both these methods will reduce your file's size. Maintaining separate layers really adds to file size and memory requirements for Photoshop images.

tip If you try to apply painting effects to a type layer or a custom shape layer, you will see the error message shown in this dialog box.

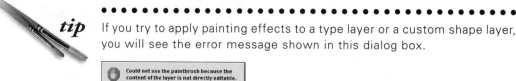

In order to use the paintbrush on the pixels that make up your letterforms or custom shapes, you need to rasterize your type layer first so that it is no longer a vector shape. To do so, choose Rasterize from the Layer menu and choose Type or Layer from the Rasterize submenu.

Summary

With layers, you've got an enormous range of opportunities for combining and blending images. I've touched on some of their most versatile features, but you'll have an even better understanding of their potential after you gain some familiarity with paths—up ahead in Chapter 6—and channels and masks in Chapter 7, "Channel and Mask Essentials."

Path Essentials

6

IN THIS CHAPTER

Saving and Deleting Paths

👁

Importing and Exporting Paths

👁

Converting Paths to Selections

👁

Filling and Stroking Paths

In the last chapter you saw that although Photoshop is a pixel-based program for working with bitmapped images, its layers feature—which lets you move objects in an image independently of one another—gives you some of the versatility of a drawing program. This chapter focuses on a very useful Photoshop feature called *paths*, which supports even more drawing program capabilities.

The paths feature lets you create selections made up of precise lines and curves, just like those you might draw in Adobe Illustrator or Macromedia Freehand. With the Paths palette and Photoshop's Pen tools, you can have much more control over your image editing than you probably thought you could. For example, if you want to export a silhouetted Photoshop image to a page layout program and have text run around its outline—which is no problem for an Illustrator graphic but doesn't happen automatically with Photoshop images imported into a page layout program—you have to use the Paths palette to create what's called a *clipping path*.

Paths can be a big help when creating composite images; you can make precise selections with the Pen tools to add a crisp, clean edge with smooth curves and sharp angles. You can also copy and paste paths between Photoshop and Illustrator, so if you're an Illustrator whiz (or have a lot of Illustrator clip art on hand), you can import paths from Illustrator when you've finished working in that program. In this chapter, you'll gain expertise using the Pen tool and its variations and learn how to do the following tasks:

- Draw, save, load, and delete paths using the Paths palette
- Import and export paths between Illustrator and Photoshop
- Convert paths to and from active selections
- Fill and stroke paths using other Photoshop tools
- Add to, subtract from, and intersect paths
- Add a clipping path to a Photoshop image saved in EPS format

Path Fundamentals

A path is an incredible tool for making selections, but in a sense that's really all it is—it's not part of the image itself. It's a geometric representation of a shape that floats above your bitmapped image, as if on its own layer—although you can only see this layer in the Paths palette, not the Layers palette. You must turn a path into a selection before you can capture the underlying pixels, and it won't show up in your finished image unless you apply a stroke to it.

If you're using a Mac, you can save a path with an image in any available format other than GIF89a. If you're using Windows, JPEG, DCS, EPS, PDF, TIFF, and native Photoshop formats support paths. Saving a path lets you recapture a given area at any time, even if you save and reopen the file. To display the Paths palette (see Figure 6.1), select Show Paths from the Window menu.

● ●

Hiding a Path from View

tip

Unlike the Layers palette, the Paths palette does not have options to hide or display a given path. To hide a path from view, choose Delesect Path (if it's active) or Dismiss Path from the Select menu. To restore a path, just go to the Paths palette and click the row containing the path's name.

● ●

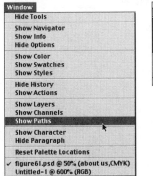

Figure 6.1

The Paths palette.

If you're familiar with Illustrator or Freehand, you'll be able to relate well to the paths interface with its pen-based tools for creating lines and Bézier (pronounced "bay-zee-ay") curves, and understand how to edit their points and segments. Don't worry if object-oriented drawing is new to you; it can take a while to get the hang of drawing with the Pen tool, but it'll get easier with practice.

Figure 6.2 shows an example of an object created in Illustrator and a path that traces the same shape in Photoshop; note that both have similar interface features, with points and handles that determine the shape of the path segments.

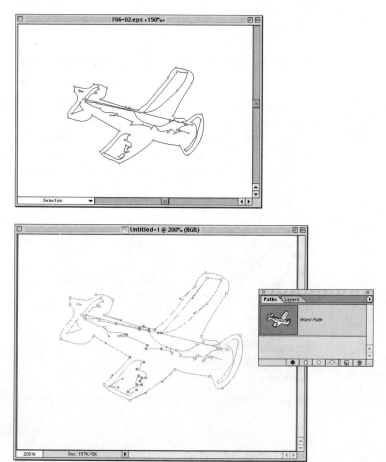

Figure 6.2

Anchor points, lines, and curves in an Illustrator path (above) and a Photoshop path (below).

Path Tools

When you create paths, you can use the Pen tool and a number of other tools to manipulate individual points on a path. There are seven such tools (see Figure 6.3). I'll briefly mention what they do here, and get back to them in more detail later in the chapter.

There are two tools—the Pen tool and Freeform Pen tool—that you can use to create points in a path:

- **Pen tool**. Use this tool to create anchor points connected by straight lines. If you drag your cursor after clicking, your current line segment will create a curved path depending on which way you move the cursor.

- **Freeform Pen tool**. With this tool, you can sketch a Bézier path as you click and drag your cursor; the Freeform Pen tool automatically places the path's points for you. Anyone who's comfortable sketching freehand with Illustrator will get a lot of mileage out of Photoshop's Freeform Pen tool. You can check off a Magnetic Pen option in the Freeform Pen's option bar that frees you from being extremely precise in tracing the edges of your object. In Photoshop 5 and 5.5, the Magnetic Pen tool had its own place in the toolbox—now, though, it's a useful option of the Freeform Pen if you're tracing an object that contrasts highly against the background.

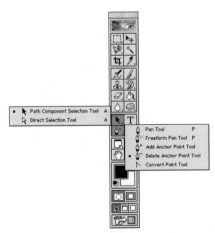

Figure 6.3

Photoshop's tools for drawing paths.

The other tools that share the Pen tool's space in the toolbox—as well as the selection tools (which look like arrows) in the space above the pen tools in the toolbox—are used to modify paths once they're created. Here's a brief description of each:

Add Anchor Point tool. Clicking over a path segment with this tool adds an anchor point. Holding your cursor over an existing anchor point will change your cursor to the Direct Selection tool, so clicking and dragging will move that point.

Delete Anchor Point tool. Clicking an anchor point with this tool removes it and redefines your path accordingly. Holding your cursor over any part of a path that's not an anchor point changes your cursor to the Arrow tool, so clicking and dragging moves that segment.

Convert Point tool. As you add points to a path, you're creating corners—sharp ones if you click from point to point; curved ones if you drag the cursor after you click. You can use the Convert Point tool to convert your sharp corners to rounded ones and vice versa. By clicking and dragging with this tool on a sharply angled corner, you can add direction handles that you can use to manipulate the new curve point.

Path Component Selection tool. Use this tool to select all the points on a path or subpath at once. This is the easiest way to select and move an entire path or subpath.

Direct Selection tool. With this tool, you can select one or more individual points on a path, or path segments.

You create a *closed path* by linking your path segments back to your original anchor point; your Pen cursor changes to include a tiny circle in the lower-right corner when you're about to click a point that will close a path. Your paths do not always have to be closed shapes, however—you can create a path that has a starting and ending point in two separate places.

Paths Palette Menu Items

You can use the path-management commands in the Paths palette to save and manipulate your paths once you've created them. Click the black triangle in the Paths palette's upper-right corner, as shown in Figure 6.4, to see the Paths palette commands in the resulting pop-up menu.

Besides creating, duplicating, and deleting a path, you have several other Paths palette commands at your disposal. I'll just point out each one here, and return to how they work later in this chapter:

- **Save Path**. This command appears in the Paths palette pop-up menu only when you've created a work path. If you select a pen tool and just start drawing, your work will appear as a temporary, unsaved work path. Choose the Save Path command to save a work path and rename it.

- **Make Work Path**. Transforms any active selection into a new, unsaved path. Similarly, the Make Selection command turns a path into an active selection, which you can then save or manipulate.

- **Make Selection**. Defines any closed path as a selection border. When a closed path overlaps a selected area, you can add it to, subtract it from, or combine it with the current selection.

- **Fill Path (or Fill Subpath)**. Applies a colored fill to the area contained in your current path.

- **Stroke Path (or Stroke Subpath)**. Lets you trace the path's outline with a border—and the fun part is that you can use any of Photoshop's paint tools to paint this border.

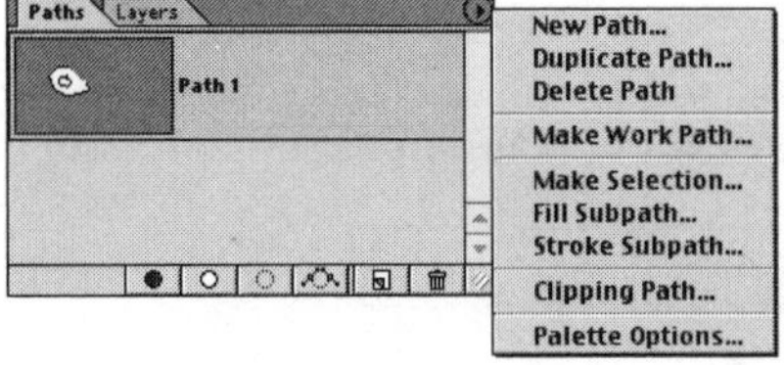

Figure 6.4

Menu items in the Paths palette pop-up menu.

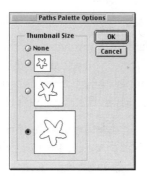

Figure 6.5

The Paths
Palette Options
dialog box.

👁 **Clipping Path**. Lets you trace a silhouetted image that you can export to a page layout program such as QuarkXPress. You can apply clipping paths only to paths you have saved and renamed, not to work paths.

👁 **Palette Options**. Generates a dialog box that should look familiar to you—it's just like the one in the Layers palette (see Figure 6.5). Here you can set the size of the thumbnail sketch that will appear in the Paths palette to preview your path's shape. Just as in the Layers palette, you also can turn off the thumbnail preview. It's most useful, though, to leave the thumbnail settings at the default, which makes the sketch visible at the smallest sized option.

Icons in the Paths Palette

Some of the options in the Paths palette pop-up menu are also located along the bottom of the Paths palette (see Figure 6.6). Most of the commands represented by icons—Fill, Stroke, Load, Make Work Path, and Create New Path—have dialog boxes that automatically appear

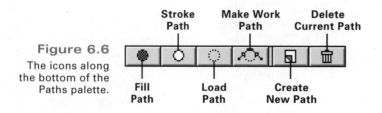

Figure 6.6

The icons along
the bottom of the
Paths palette.

when you select these options from the Paths palette pop-up menu, but the dialog boxes won't show up if you click or drag a path's row to their icons. To make them appear while using the icons on the bottom of the Paths palette, [Option]+click (for Mac users) or [Alt]+click (for Windows users) on the icons.

Drawing with the Pen Tool

Trying the regular Pen tool comes next. If you're already an accomplished Illustrator or Freehand artist, you should mostly just skim this material for the details of Photoshop's Paths interface before moving on to the Magnetic Pen and Freeform Pen tools.

Taking the Guesswork Out of Drawing Paths

You can always edit a path after you've created it, but there are a couple of good ways to ensure that you draw the exact path you want in the first place. Before you click your first point in a path, it's useful to check your settings in the Pen Options toolbar (see Figure 6.7).

Shape Layers and Work Paths

In Photoshop 6.0, when you first create a new path in a document you can choose whether to place your path selection on a shape layer instead of a standard work path. If you choose a shape layer, you can fill your selection with the custom patterns and other layer effects available to objects on shape layers, such as objects created with the Custom Shape tools. This is a useful path to take—pun intended!—if you want to manually create a custom button shape by placing points on a path, and then applying a unique layer style.

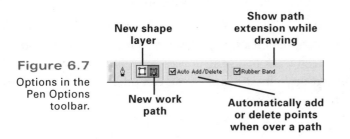

Figure 6.7
Options in the Pen Options toolbar.

New shape layer

Show path extension while drawing

New work path

Automatically add or delete points when over a path

The Pen Tool's Rubber Band Option

The Pen tool has a really great option—called *Rubber Band*—that lets you preview what a path segment will look like before you click to place an anchor point. This helps you see what the segment will look like, so you can correct your positioning of an anchor point as needed before you place it. This saves you from having to click first and then go to lengths to get it right afterward. To turn on the Rubber Band option, click the check box labeled Rubber Band in the Pen tool's options toolbar.

Auto Add/Delete

The Auto Add/Delete option in the Pen tool's options bar lets you automatically add or delete anchor points while you are creating a path.

Using the Info Palette

Another useful way to position your anchor points exactly where you want them is to use the Info palette to track the location of your cursor. Display the Info palette by choosing Show Info on the Window menu.

Among other information, the Info palette lets you see at a glance the horizontal (x) and vertical (y) coordinates of your cursor's location. If you need to create complex geometric paths in Photoshop, it can help to think of your Photoshop document in terms of the Cartesian plane, with your x-coordinate measuring the cursor's horizontal position and your y-coordinate measuring the cursor's vertical position. Make sure you have Show Rulers selected in the View menu. By default, Photoshop places the point of origin (0, 0) in the upper-left corner of your document, although you can change this by repositioning the crosshairs in that corner anywhere else in your document.

If you don't think you'll ever have to be this precise about creating paths, don't worry about measuring where you place your anchor points. If you want to keep track in a general way—say, knowing when you've drawn a line that's two inches long—you can refer to the Info palette.

note

You can change the unit of measurement for tracking your cursor's coordinates to pixels, centimeters, points, or picas. Just click the pop-up menu on the Info palette, select Palette Options, and change your Ruler Units preferences in the resulting Info Options dialog box under Mouse Coordinates.

Straight Lines

Create a new document to begin experimenting with drawing lines with the Pen tool. Now click the Pen icon to select that tool. The first shape you'll draw with the Pen tool will be a triangle. Click in your document window to set your first anchor point, and then release the mouse button. Click a second time some distance away; a straight line will appear between your two points (see Figure 6.8).

Notice how your new anchor point shows up as a dark, filled-in square; that means it's a currently selected point. At the same time, the first point you created changes to a white square, meaning that it's no longer selected. Release the mouse button.

tip

Constraining Lines in a Path

By pressing and holding [Shift], you can constrain the angle at which you place new points to 45 degrees or 90 degrees at a time. Accordingly, this constrains the angles of lines you draw to multiples of 45 degrees or 90 degrees. This can be helpful when you need to create classic geometric shapes.

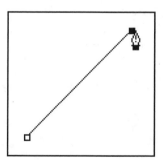

Figure 6.8
Drawing a line with the Pen tool.

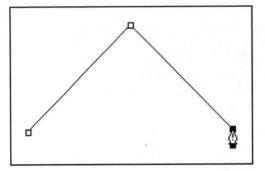

Figure 6.9
Adding a second
line to the path.

Now click and release the cursor to add a third point, which will create the second line in your triangle (see Figure 6.9).

Click your original anchor point to close the path, creating a triangle shape. As you hold the Pen tool over your first anchor point, a small circle appears in the lower-right corner of the Pen icon (see Figure 6.10). This cursor change takes place whenever you move your cursor over a point that will close a path.

After you've drawn a line or a closed path, you can still edit it as much as you like. You just need to select the point or points you want to position with the Direct Selection tool. You can either click the point itself, or—if it's too much work to click so precisely—draw a marquee with the Direct Selection tool around the area that contains the point you want to select. Any points that fall within that marquee area are selected, so make sure you don't select more of your path than you wanted. Once you've selected the point or points you want to move, you can either drag them

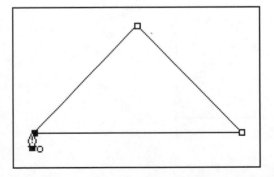

Figure 6.10
The Pen tool's
icon changes
when you're
about to close
a path.

with the Direct Selection tool or use the directional keys on your keyboard to move them one pixel at a time. Using the keyboard keys is useful when the path you drew is just slightly off from the one you wanted, and you want to nudge the path back into line.

Bézier Curves

Sure, drawing lines is intuitive—but drawing curves is where most people get bogged down in object-oriented drawing. Here are some basic maneuvers to give you a feel for curves one step at a time.

Click once in your document window with the Pen tool to create an anchor point, and continue to hold the mouse button down after you've clicked. As you start to drag the cursor, the Pen icon will change to indicate Direct Selection. Two *direction handles* will emerge from your point as you drag; their length and angle determine the height and slope of your curve. Observe that there's a *direction point* at the end of each handle (see Figure 6.11). At any time while you're drawing a curve, you can switch to the Direct Selection tool and reposition these direction points to change the height and angle of a certain part of the curve.

Reposition the Pen tool some distance from your first point, and then click and drag a second time. Keep the mouse button clicked. You'll see a curved line form between the two points you drew (see Figure 6.12).

While you still have the mouse button held down, you can drag the mouse and the curve will slope in the same direction you're dragging. This is crucial to understanding how Bézier curves work. Figure 6.13 shows how dragging the directional handles up, down, and at various angles produces different kinds of curves.

Figure 6.11

The beginning of a curve. Note the direction handles on either side of the anchor point.

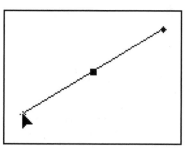

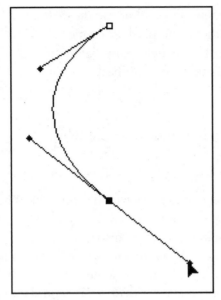

Figure 6.12
Adding a second point draws your first curved line.

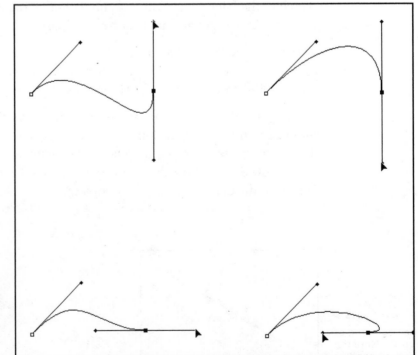

Figure 6.13
Dragging the directional handles in different directions changes the slope of your curve segment.

The following mini-exercises—on drawing a sine wave and curves with corner points, and creating jigsaw puzzle-piece outlines—help demonstrate how dragging the directional handles affects your curves' shapes.

Drawing a Sine Wave

You can create a series of curves—such as those in a sine wave—by alternately dragging up and down as you place a series of anchor points in a horizontal row.

With the Pen tool selected, click to place a new anchor point and drag straight upward. Next, move your cursor to the right and click to place a second anchor point some distance from your first point; note the size and shape of the resulting curve. Continue to hold down the mouse button after you click, and then drag straight downward. This should produce the kind of curved arc shown here:

Continue by adding a third anchor point to the right and dragging straight upward once you've placed it. Note that the direction handles on the first points you created disappear after they're deselected; you can always see them again by switching to the Direct Selection tool and reselecting those points.

After you've created a series of anchor points in a row, alternately dragging upward and downward with each new point, you should have produced a wavy path like this one:

You can experiment with changing the height of an arc by clicking the Direct Selection tool on an individual curve segment and dragging upward or downward. This will select the nearest anchor points and directional handles; you can then move them up or down to accentuate or reduce the arc's depth.

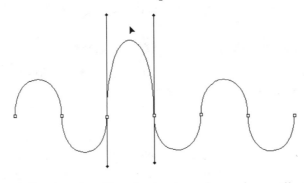

Adjusting the direction points themselves will give you optimal control over the final shape of your curve. Try experimenting with drawing a couple of curved lines. Use the Direct Selection tool to reposition the direction points and see how the shape of the curve changes.

tip

Constraining Lines in a Curve

In the same way you can use ⌈Shift⌉ to constrain the angle of lines, you can constrain the angle of your curves' handles to increments of 45 degrees or 90 degrees when you hold down ⌈Shift⌉.

Drawing Curves with Corner Points

The previous mini-exercise showed how to draw a series of curves in alternating directions. The points in that kind of path are called *smooth points*. Next up is an explanation of how to draw a number of curves connected with *corner points*. The net result is a series of curves that all arc in the same direction, like this:

Create your first two points the way you did in the previous mini-exercise: Select the Pen tool, click to create an anchor point, and then drag upward. Position your cursor to the right and click to create a second anchor point. Drag downward after you click the second time to create the first curve. Release the mouse button. Here's where you'll do something different—you'll need to turn the second anchor point into a corner point.

Hold down Option (for Mac users) or Alt (for Windows users). Position the cursor over the second anchor point, the one you just drew. Click the second anchor point and hold down the mouse button while you drag upward; this removes the downward direction handle and changes the direction of the next curve. Stop clicking and release Option or Alt.

Now move your cursor to the right to create a third anchor point. Click when you're ready to position the point, and drag downward. You should now have two curves side by side, looking something like the McDonald's arches.

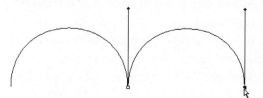

If you like, you can repeat these steps—holding down Option or Alt and reselecting the last anchor point you created, and then dragging upward to establish the corner point and change the curve's direction, and so on—to add to your series of curves with corner points.

Combining Lines and Curves

Of course, the really useful paths contain both straight lines and curves. To create them, you need to create corner points where the path turns from a line into a curve, and vice versa. You'll create corner points where necessary the way you did in the previous exercise.

First, create a straight line made up of two anchor points; click a third anchor point to the right of the other two and drag downward. This creates a curve following the straight line, as shown here:

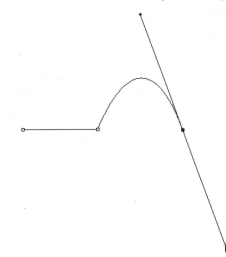

Next, you need to make this third anchor point a corner point. As you did earlier, Option+click (for Mac users) or Alt+click (for Windows users) the third anchor point to convert it to a corner point. Don't hold down the mouse button, though; the next segment you're going to create is a line, not a curve. Now position your cursor farther to the right and click to create a fourth anchor point. Your path should now consist of a line, one arching curve, and another line.

• •

tip **Adjusting an Anchor Point without Leaving the Pen Tool**

While drawing your path with the Pen tool, you can access the pointer tool quickly by pressing and holding down Cmd (for Mac users) or Ctrl (for Windows users). Your Pen tool cursor will change to the pointer, allowing you to make adjustments to your path's anchor points or Bézier curves. Your cursor will change back to the Pen tool when you release.

• •

You should feel free to continue to doodle, create abstract shapes, or practice creating other path outlines. This is a good time to experiment with the Add Anchor Point (✎+), Delete Anchor Point (✎−), Convert Point (⌐), Path Component Selection (▶), and Direct Selection (▷) tools. You can add an anchor point anywhere on one of your lines or curves by selecting the Add Anchor Point tool and clicking the path. To remove an anchor point, use the Delete Anchor Point tool and click an anchor point. You'll get some interesting results from clicking the Convert Point tool on one of your finished paths.

● ●

tip

Repositioning Several Points at Once

If you want to realign two or more points at a time, one easy way to do so is to choose the Direct Selection tool, and then click and drag over a portion of your path to select all the points contained therein. If the two points are not adjacent, you can hold down Shift as you click both points to select them together.

● ●

● ●

tip

Cutting Path Segments in Two

Unlike Illustrator or Freehand, Photoshop has no equivalent for the Scissors tool that can cut a path segment in two, thus adding two new anchor points. You can, however, reasonably duplicate this feature by using the Add Anchor Point tool to add three new points very close together at the point where you want to break the path. Next, select the middle point with the Direct Selection tool and cut it by using Cmd+X (for Mac users) or Ctrl +X (for Windows users).

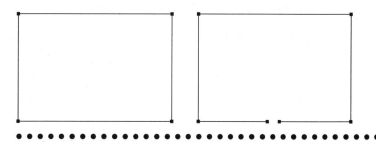

● ●

Drawing Precise Selections

When accuracy counts—such as when creating a very precise clipping path, for example—it can be too painstaking to use the Pen tool. The Freeform Pen can produce more accurate selections in these instances. As you click and drag to outline a shape, Photoshop automatically places points at key intervals and traces curves based on how you draw.

You can specify how closely the paths you create adhere to the outline you've traced. To do so, choose Freeform Pen and enter a low value—for example, 1 or 2 pixels—for Curve Fit in the options bar (see Figure 6.14).

The Freeform Pen is one of the more intuitive path tools in Photoshop. After you finish tracing a shape by clicking and dragging around its outline, you can see the path you've just drawn and the automatically placed points contained within it. If any points are a little off the mark, you can switch back to the Direct Selection tool to nudge individual points into place better.

The Magnetic Pen option in the Freeform Pen tool can give you a boost toward creating more accurate freeform selections by seeking out high-contrast edges between your outlined shape and the background. After you activate the Magnetic Pen feature, you can click its icon in the Freeform Pen's options bar () to edit several options that specify how sensitive the tool is to contrasting image areas (see Figure 6.15). These options include:

- **Width**. This is the radius of the area where the tool seeks the edge to trace. The smaller the width, the more likely the tool will sense the edge correctly (because it has less data to process).

- **Contrast**. This value specifies how much contrast is used in finding the edge. Higher settings work better when there is a strong contrast between the subject and the background.

Figure 6.14
The Freeform Pen options bar.

`Curve Fit: 2 px  ☐Magnetic  ☑Auto Add/Delete`

Figure 6.15
Magnetic Pen options in the Freeform Pen's options bar.

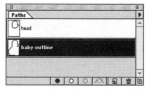

👁 **Frequency**. This specifies how often a fastening point is laid down. As you move the pointer, the active segment regularly snaps to the strongest edge in the image, adding a fastening point to the border each time to anchor previous selections.

With the Magnetic Pen feature on, you can experience brief delays in actually seeing the paths you've created with the Freeform Pen. This is because Photoshop takes time to calculate where the points in those paths are placed. Depending on what you want to do, you might choose one tool over another in creating a path. Take a look at Figure 6.16 to see how I created two separate paths for the baby photo shown there.

I selected the Freeform Pen tool to create a path to outline just the baby's head for future use as a clipping path. I might have chosen the regular Pen tool, but it would take quite a while to place the number of points needed to trace the shape of the head so precisely. Using the

Figure 6.16
The contrast and content of your images helps you decide which Pen tool and options to use in creating paths and selections.

Magnetic Pen feature with the Freeform Pen tool wasn't necessary because there's not enough consistent contrast around the head—for example, see how there's not much strong contrast around the ear region—to easily select just the head.

note

> With the Freeform Pen tool, you can interrupt your tracing at any time. So if you want to reposition your mouse or interrupt your tracing to nudge a point with the Direct Selection tool, that's okay—you can go right back to drawing with the Freeform Pen tool, click again at the last fastening point, and finish your path.

The other path traces an outline of the baby's jumper to prepare this photo for future editing in changing the colors for a seasonal baby-clothing ad. Enabling the Magnetic Pen option in the Freeform Pen tool makes it easier to trace the edges of the jumper because it contrasts so well with the background and with the neckline. If the jumper had been a solid color, I might have used the Magic Wand to make this selection, but in this image, the portion I want to trace consists of many brightly colored stripes.

Saving and Deleting Paths

When you begin clicking in your image with the regular Pen or Freeform Pen tools, you'll automatically create a new row in the Paths palette. Whereas other programs call each individual, closed, object-oriented shape a path, Photoshop really refers to these as subpaths. That's because you can save more than one shape in a row on the Paths palette. Each row in the Paths palette, then, is called a path and can contain multiple subpaths.

You can see this for yourself if you start doodling with the regular Pen tool, close the subpath, and then switch to playing with the Freeform Pen. You'll create a second subpath shape along the same path or work path noted in the Paths palette (see Figure 6.17).

You can also automatically create a new work path whenever you convert an active selection to a new path. A work path is considered an unsaved path; if you want to really manipulate it—say, if you want to use it as a clipping path—you have to save your work path and give it its own name.

Figure 6.17
You can save multiple subpaths in a single Paths palette row.

You do this by double-clicking its row in the Paths palette or by choosing Save Path from the Paths palette pop-up menu. Both actions will launch the Save Path dialog box, where you can enter a new name for the path.

If you create more path segments after you save a new path by name, Photoshop automatically adds them to that path layer; you don't have to save the path again.

You can create a new path by choosing New Path from the Paths palette pop-up menu; this will open the New Path dialog box. You can also click the Create New Path icon ( ), found along the bottom of the Paths palette. However, the New Path dialog box will not appear unless you press Option (or Alt in Windows) as you click the icon.

Double-clicking the name of a saved path in the Paths palette will cause the Rename Path dialog box to appear.

Dragging a path's row down to the Create New Path icon will create a duplicate of your path layer; there's also a menu item in the Paths palette pop-up menu for duplicating a path layer. You can duplicate an individual subpath by pressing Option (or Alt in Windows) as you click and drag that subpath with the Direct Selection tool.

Just as in the Layers palette, you can click a path's name in the Paths palette to work on a different path layer. However, other path layers are hidden from view whenever you're working on a given path layer. If you want to delete a path layer, choose Delete Path from the Paths palette pop-up menu, or drag that path's row in the Paths palette down to the Trash icon.

Importing and Exporting Paths

You may sometimes want to export your path shapes to another graphics program to add certain special effects. You can export a Photoshop path to Illustrator or Freehand, add the change you want, and then import it back into Photoshop.

To do this, you first need to select the whole path in Photoshop and copy it. Switch to your illustration program, and paste the selection into a new document. Now you can impose the changes you want. Note that you can also add all sorts of additional effects to this path, but to bring those changes into Photoshop you have to rasterize the path, thus converting everything to pixels.

Figure 6.18 shows the Paste dialog box you'll see in Photoshop when you begin to paste a path from Illustrator. You can import the full Illustrator path, so you can manipulate it in Photoshop just as easily. You can paste in the selection in pixelated form instead; this way, you retain all blends, stroking, and any other effects you added in Illustrator, but you lose the ability to select the path itself. A new third option in Photoshop 6.0 lets you save the path as a shape layer.

Figure 6.18

This Paste dialog box appears when you paste a path into Photoshop from Illustrator.

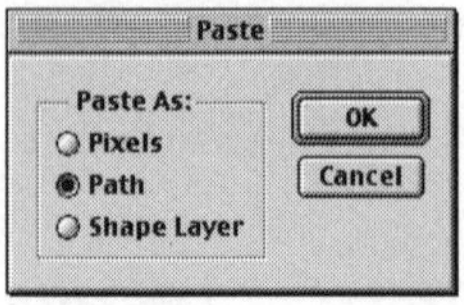

Converting Paths to Selections— and Back Again

Paths are one of Photoshop's more elegant features, but they're most useful after you turn them into selections. Once you've converted a path to a selection—demarcating an area bounded by marching ants— you can access all of Photoshop's tools, filters, and other effects.

Converting Paths to Selections

There are several ways to turn a Photoshop path into a selection. You can choose Make Selection from the Paths palette pop-up menu, which brings up the Make Selection dialog box (shown in Figure 6.19). You can also click the Load Path icon (⬚) on the Paths palette, or drag the path's row down to the icon. However, neither of these last two methods automatically displays the Make Selection dialog box. You can make them do so by holding down (Option) (for Mac users) or (Alt) (for Windows users) when you use these last two methods.

One of the best reasons to use paths to make a selection is if you need to add to—or subtract from—a selection you've already made, and want to be able to do so precisely without taking chances on accidentally deselecting or altering your existing selection. You can leave your selection as is, create a new path and outline the new addition, and then call up the Make Selection dialog box to add, subtract, and intersect your path with your previous selection, as shown in Figure 6.20. After choosing a Make Selection option, choose Dismiss Path from the Select menu to see the kinds of results shown in Figure 6.20.

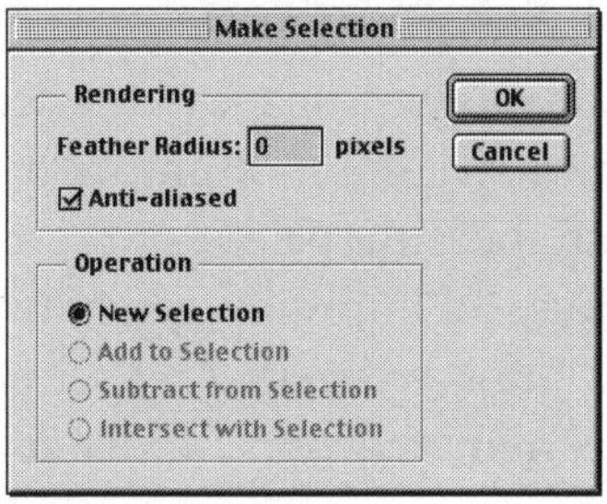

Figure 6.19

The Make Selection dialog box.

> **Make Selection**
>
> **Rendering**
> Feather Radius: [0] pixels
> ☑ Anti-aliased
>
> [OK]
> [Cancel]
>
> **Operation**
> ● New Selection
> ○ Add to Selection
> ○ Subtract from Selection
> ○ Intersect with Selection

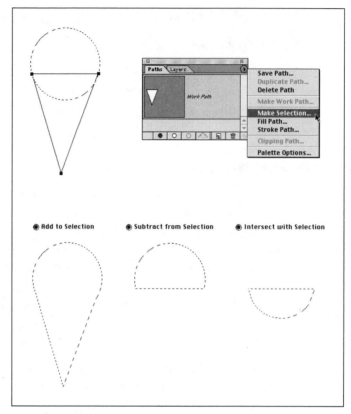

Figure 6.20

Some possibilities for combining paths with a previous selection, with options from the Make Selection dialog box.

You can also launch the Make Selection dialog box to add feathering and toggle anti-aliasing on or off when you make a selection. By default, you get anti-aliasing but no feathering.

Converting Selections to Paths

You don't have to draw all your path shapes from scratch with the Pen tool; you can convert any active selection into a path with the Make Work Path command from the Paths palette pop-up menu. You should experiment, though, because a Photoshop-generated path may not be as close a fit as one you draw yourself. Any selection you make in Photoshop appears with a marching ants border around it; when you convert this to a path, the program has to use a little guesswork in placing anchor points and generating the curves or lines to connect

Figure 6.21
Some different tolerance settings. From left, the selection outlining the rubber ducky image is saved to a path using a tolerance level of .5-pixel, 2 pixels, and 10 pixels.

them. Photoshop uses a setting called *tolerance* when deciding where to place these anchor points.

Deciding what tolerance setting to use can be a tricky call. The higher you make the tolerance setting, the looser the path and the more ill-defined your selection area will be. Lower tolerance settings, however, can create overly complex paths. Using a tolerance range of .5 (the lowest possible value) to 2 pixels works for most situations; you can specify any tolerance setting in .5-pixel increments. The highest possible tolerance setting is 10; a path created with a tolerance of 10 (see Figure 6.21, far right) will probably bear little resemblance to your original selection.

Scaling, Rotating, and Skewing Paths

You have the ability to scale, rotate, and skew selections in Photoshop—by extension, then, you can use a path to load a selection, create the desired transformation, and then save the newly transformed selection as another path.

I usually use these kinds of transformations to create elaborate effects with type or to create custom shadows. Exercise 6.1 takes a look at how you can add a shadow to a silhouetted object so that it no longer appears one-dimensional.

Filling and Stroking Paths

As I've mentioned, the editing effects that you can apply to your paths from within the Paths palette are limited, but the two main ones—filling and stroking—can produce some very colorful effects.

EXERCISE 6.1

Adding a Shadow to an Object Using Paths and Selections

①

1. Begin with a sample silhouetted image for this exercise that is placed on its own transparent layer. Here, I'm using a simple image that appears against an all-white background layer, but this effect works even if you have a colored or patterned background.

2. Make a selection to outline your image as closely as possible. If the object you choose is part of a larger image, you may need to use one of the Pen or Lasso tools to separate the object from its background. Because the object I've chosen here is against a solid-colored background, I just used the Magic Wand tool to select the background, and then chose Inverse from the Select menu to indirectly choose the dog.

③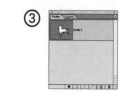

3. Choose Show Paths from the Window menu, and then choose Make Work Path from the Paths palette's pop-up menu. This will store your outline path for future use, should you need it at a later time.

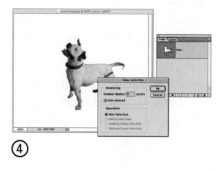

④

4. Now choose Make Selection from the Paths palette's pop-up menu to activate your selection. You need an active selection to perform a transformation effect such as scaling, rotating, or skewing.

⑤

⑥

5. Choose Transform from the Select menu. You will see a bounding box appear around the dog once you choose to create a new selection. Now click and drag the handles to create and lengthen the shadow in the desired direction.

6. Save your new shadow selection as a new path by choosing Make Work Path from the Paths palette's pop-up menu. You can double-click the path's row to give it a name. You can also use the Direct Selection tool or Path Component Selection tool to reposition the shadow to better effect. Now choose Make Selection from the Paths palette's pop-up menu to activate your selection.

7. Click the Layers tab next to the Paths palette or choose Show Layers from the Window menu. Make sure that you have the background layer selected. Make sure that your foreground color is set to a black or gray color. Choose Fill Path from the Paths palette's pop-up menu. It's a good idea to enter a low opacity in the Fill Path dialog box so that your shadow can blend more naturally with the background instead of overlaying that image data entirely.

8. Lastly, choose Blur from the Filter menu, and then choose Gaussian blur to make this shadow very diffuse.

By storing the object's outline in a path, you can return to further skew, lighten, or darken the shadow at any time without affecting the overall image.

⑦

⑧

Figure 6.22
The finished shadow effect created by transforming path selections.

Figure 6.23

The Fill Path dialog box for the Paths palette.

Filling a Path

Choosing Fill Path from the Paths palette pop-up menu causes the Fill Path dialog box to appear (see Figure 6.23). The Fill Path menu item has an icon counterpart that appears at the bottom of the Paths palette (●). Dragging a path's row over the Fill Path icon will fill the path with the current settings in the Fill dialog box; the default setting for the Fill Path icon is 100 percent of the foreground color in Normal mode. Option+click (for Mac users) or Alt+click (for Windows users) on the Fill Path icon to display the Fill Path dialog box.

Your fill options here are basically the same as those available when filling selections using Fill from the Edit menu. You can fill in your path with various colors, a saved pattern, or a snapshot from the History palette. You can apply your fill using a variety of blending modes (just as in the Layers palette), and even feather or anti-alias your path's edges.

If you have several discrete paths on a path layer, you can choose between applying a fill to just one path segment or to every path on the layer. Deselect all points if you want to apply the fill to all paths; otherwise, you should select individual path segments—in which case, the menu item in the Paths palette pop-up menu becomes Fill Subpath.

Stroking a Path

I have to admit, I never tire of playing around with the Stroke effects available via the Paths palette because there are so many cool effects to

Figure 6.24

The Stroke Path dialog box.

create. When you click Stroke Path from the Paths palette pop-up menu, the Stroke Path dialog box that appears gives you a choice of Photoshop tools to use when applying your stroke effects (see Figure 6.24).

Like the Fill Path option, the Stroke Path option appears as an icon at the bottom of the Paths palette (○). Dragging a path's row over the Stroke Path icon will fill the path with the current settings in the Stroke Path dialog box; the default setting for the Stroke Path icon is the Pencil tool (ho hum). Option+click (for Mac users) or Alt+click (for Windows users) the Stroke Path icon to display its dialog box.

You can create some very psychedelic effects by stroking with the Paintbrush tool with one of the more unusual brushes selected in the Brushes palette. Exercise 6.2 walks you through creating one such example.

Making Silhouettes with Clipping Paths

In the last chapter, you learned about using layers to mask out parts of an image. However, a transparent background created in Photoshop won't stay transparent if you import that image into QuarkXPress or PageMaker. In this situation, what you need is a clipping path. A clipping path is a shape or path that creates a silhouette to mask out the background or other parts of your image when combined with other elements—like wrap-around text, shaded backgrounds, or other images—in a page layout or illustration program.

EXERCISE 6.2

Creating Elaborate Borders by Stroking a Path

①

1. You'll need to choose or create a path to use for this exercise. Here, I entered some text with the Type tool. If you use the Type tool for this exercise, make sure you set your options in the Type options toolbar to create text as a mask or selection, rather than as a text layer. Your text will display as a marquee selection. Now click the Make Work Path icon ( ) at the bottom of the Paths palette to turn your selection into a work path.

2. Now, you need to choose a foreground color to use for your stroking effect. The color should be appropriate to the desired end effect—for example, a bright color for a gaudy effect. If your foreground color is too dark, you won't be able to see the effects of the stroke.

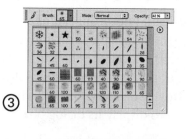

③

3. As mentioned earlier, the Paintbrush can give you the most dramatic effects. You now need to pick a good custom brush for stroking. Click the drop-down menu of brushes in the Paintbrush tool's options bar. If you don't see as wide a selection as you want, remember you can choose Load Brushes from the Brushes palette pop-up menu and select the additional brushes supplied with Photoshop.

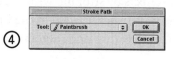

④

4. Open the Stroke Path dialog box by choosing Stroke Path from the Paths palette pop-up menu. Click the Tool pop-up menu; you'll see you can choose from a number of Photoshop tools. Once you've chosen the Paintbrush or another tool you want, click OK.

5. If you want to get rid of your path at this point, you can hide its display by clicking anywhere but the path's row in the Paths palette. You can delete it altogether by dragging the path's row in the Paths palette to the Trash icon.

Figure 6.25
The results of
stroking with the
Paintbrush tool.

A clipping path also ensures that the text on the page will run around your outlined image correctly. You'll also need to save your Photoshop image in EPS format for a clipping path to take effect when you import it into another program. Once you've named a path to use as a clipping path, you can choose Clipping Path from the Paths palette pop-up menu to display its dialog box (see Figure 6.26). Click the pop-up menu in the Clipping Path dialog box to select which path to use.

The only other option you can set in this dialog box is the path's flatness. Flatness determines how exact your printer or imagesetter will be in creating the segments of your path. Lower settings mean greater fineness, and print time will rise accordingly. As the flatness settings increase, curved

Figure 6.26
The Clipping Path
dialog box.

Clipping Path

Path: clippy

Flatness: [   ] device pixels

OK

Cancel

parts of your outline's shape will start to transform into straight line segments. Unless your service bureau tells you to enter a certain value, though, you can leave this blank—the printer or imagesetter will substitute its own settings. If the image generates a PostScript error when your page layout program attempts to print it, though, you'll need to go back and save a flatness setting with the clipping path. The possible values for setting flatness range from .2 to 200 device pixels. Exercise 6.3 walks you through each step in creating a clipping path.

Pat yourself on the back—creating a clipping path can be tricky business, and you've just added a very advanced technique to your Photoshop repertoire. Make sure you run a print test with a sample silhouetted image with your service bureau, and ask if there are any additional steps you should take to ensure your silhouetted images will output well.

Summary

Besides the Magic Wand tool, the various Pen tools provide some of the best ways to make selections in Photoshop. As you've seen, though, it can take a while to get the hang of using the Pen and Freeform Pen tools. You should be very proud of yourself; there are many designers who've used Photoshop for years without putting the Paths palette to use the way you have in this chapter. Look how far you've come—and so fast!—with this very difficult Photoshop concept.

Next I'll cover Photoshop's channels and masking features, including what kinds of effects you can create with alpha channels and Quick Masks.

EXERCISE 6.3

Adding a Clipping Path to an Image

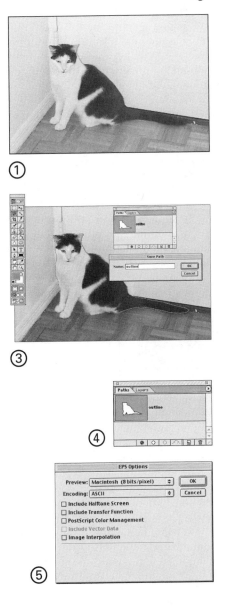

1. You'll first need to pick an image that you want to silhouette and import into a page layout program.

2. Use one of the Pen tools to create a new path, outlining the part of the image you want to include in the clipping path. Make sure you save the path by selecting Save Path from the Paths palette pop-up menu, or by double-clicking its row in the Paths palette and giving it a name.

3. Select Clipping Path from the Paths palette pop-up menu. Choose the name of your saved path. As mentioned earlier, you don't need to enter a specific flatness setting unless your service bureau tells you to. Click OK.

4. Notice that the name of your path is outlined in the Paths palette, although the screen image doesn't change. You'll only see the clipped effect after you import the image into another program.

   Before you save this document as an EPS file, make sure it's in the right color mode for your final output—for example, CMYK instead of RGB.

5. Now you can choose Save or Save As from the File menu to save your image in Photoshop EPS format. The Photoshop EPS Options dialog box will open; double-check with your service bureau to see which of these options, if any, it prefers.

6. Launch your page layout program and import the image into a document (see Figure 6.27). Here, I've imported the image into QuarkXPress. Observe how various page elements affect your silhouetted image differently from images with no clipping paths.

DO IT YOURSELF...DO IT YOURSELF...DO IT YOURSELF...DO IT   LF...DO IT YOURSELF...

Teach your cat to play guitar

By Hutch Mubin

Guitar-playing is not for every cat. Only those who can heel on the leash, all the time, are going to react well to guitar-playing.

Since you may not always be strumming or jamming right next to your cat, you must be absolutely certain that she isn't going to take off at the first sight of a squirrel or race madly under the sofa to chase a mouse. And if you're using an electric guitar, you have to concern yourself with your amps and speakers; you just don't have as much control as you do with an acoustic guitar.

Practice, practice, and more practice is essential if you want to introduce your cat to guitar-playing.

Safe guitar-playing requires a lot of advance planning. You can't just pick up your guitar one day, grab the leash, and expect a pleasant experience. There are certain control elements and safety concerns that must be carefully negotiated before you can begin to play together well.

For several days, or even a week if necessary, walk your pet on a leash

around a guitar. Do this in your basement, where there are no distractions, or in your driveway if it's quiet. If you live in the city, walk your cat and have someone else take the guitar to the park where you can stop at your favorite picnic spot.

Having seen that it's not going to hurt him or play with him, an animal will become bored with the attach or hiding game. It's at this stage that you can let him become accustomed to a little movement. When the guitar is no longer frightening, start to strum a few chords each day. Again, remember not to take the process too fast. The minute your cat starts meowing along with your playing, stop. Take it slowly, easily, and let your pet become relaxed around the guitar. Go forward with it, then backward. If your cat starts reacting badly, go back to a few more days of no movement before proceeding again.

The third stage is a walk alongside the guitar while heeling your pet. Don't pick up the guitar yet—this will only confuse

Tips for getting started

1. **Checking out your guitar.** Your guitar must be in good condition if you want to jam with your pet. If you don't play often, you might want to practice without your cat for a while, until you're completely secure.

2. **Getting your cat used to the guitar.** If your cat's only experience with a bike is watching the noisy neighbor's kids writhing, playing air guitar in the driveway, you'll have a big desensitizing job on your hands. Moving objects often frighten or excite animals.

3. **Going to clubs—how much is enough?** Those animals who have stress-tested in the mild beginner category should start with no more than a minute of guitar-playing before taking a rest. Moderate beginners can go for two to three minutes; those in the medium range can start with three to four; and those in the rigorous group can start with five to seven minutes.

Figure 6.27

A silhouetted image with a clipping path, imported into QuarkXPress.

7

Channel and Mask Essentials

IN THIS CHAPTER

Using Spot-Color Channels

👁

Creating Alpha Channels

👁

Creating Effects with Masked Type

👁

Using Quick Mask Mode

By now, you've had some experience making selections in Photoshop using the Marquee and Magic Wand tools. Another way to think of a Photoshop selection is as a mask, or as a stencil. If you've ever used stenciled lettering to create a poster or a sign ("Post No Bills"), you've seen how a mask works. It lets you create an effect by blocking out (that is, masking) all the parts you don't want changed. Even if you're kind of sloppy, or if you sneeze while you're painting, you won't mess up the part that's covered by the stencil—it's completely protected.

You can save a mask by name in what Photoshop calls an *alpha channel.* This way, you can retrieve your mask and use it again at any time. This eliminates those frustrating situations where you've painstakingly marked out a complicated selection area with one of the Lasso or Marquee tools, only to click inadvertently to the side and lose the selection. An alpha channel is also useful when you need to return to a selected area at a later point in your image editing. You can even use multiple alpha channels to toggle between selection areas in your document with ease.

Add channels and masks to the list of Photoshop features—like layers and paths—that are extremely powerful but not at all intuitive. I found it easier to understand masks once I learned about color channels. To refresh your memory of Chapter 2, "File Format Essentials," when you're working with images in RGB or CMYK mode, each of the colors represented by those acronyms has its own channel in Photoshop. These color channels function the same way that alpha channels do. In other words, you can selectively adjust the Red channel in an RGB image separately from the Green and Blue channels. By fooling around with individual color channels, you can experiment with dramatic color changes in ordinary images for a silk-screened or Andy Warhol painting effect.

Besides the color channels that accompany the color mode you're in, you can now create and save *spot-color channels* with CMYK images in Photoshop. In a spot-color channel, you can specify which parts of the image should be filled with a fifth printing ink—for example, a metallic color that can't be reproduced in CMYK, or a must-have PMS ink used to match a corporate logo.

Understanding how and when to use masks and color channels will lead you to the upper echelons of Photoshop society. These features are among the most difficult concepts to grasp, but with judicious use,

you can create the most sophisticated photocompositions and special effects—not to forget maintain impeccable color control.

In this chapter, you learn how to do the following tasks:

- View and edit an image's individual color channels

- Use spot-color channels to specify fluorescent or metallic inks, or other special print effects in your images

- Create, load, and delete alpha channels

- Use Photoshop's Quick Mask mode to create temporary alpha channels

- Create special effects using alpha channels

Introduction to Channels

If you create a selection using the Marquee or Lasso tool, the boundaries of your selection show up with the border of marching ants you've seen several times by now. Masks are another way of making selections, but they look rather different. Masks trace a silhouette around your selection to show what's covered up and what isn't.

When you create a channel to hold a mask, you see your selection boundaries in black and white. Typically, everything within the area you've defined as selected appears in white, whereas the masked-out part shows up as solid black, as shown in Figure 7.1. Any anti-aliased

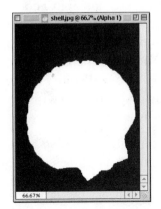

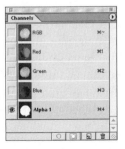

Figure 7.1

The shell's outline represents a mask in an alpha channel.

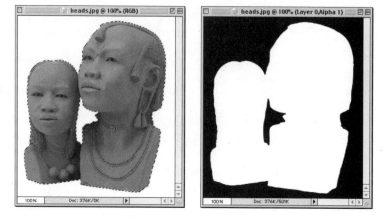

Figure 7.2
A selection drawn with the Marquee tool (left) functions the same as a mask created in a channel (right)—the selection methods just look different onscreen.

or feathered edges appear in various levels of gray. If you like, you can reverse the colors so the masked-out part is white instead of black—I explain how to do this a little later, during the description of the Channel Options dialog box.

Creating a channel in Photoshop to hold a selection mask is functionally the same as using the Marquee tool to make a selection with the same dimensions—it's just that the two selections look different, and you can reselect a masked area at a later time. Figure 7.2 shows how a selection with the Marquee tool still keeps your full image onscreen, whereas a mask delineates the selected area (in white) from the covered-up area (in black) and hides the image itself.

Viewing an Image's Color Channels

Before you begin looking at color channels in a document and creating new alpha channels to hold selection masks, you should open a sample image and display the Channels palette by selecting Show Channels from the Window menu. You'll see the Channels palette appear on your screen, as shown in Figure 7.3. Before exploring the options in this palette for manipulating and adding new channels, take a look at the color channels that already exist in your image.

If necessary, convert your sample image to RGB or CMYK color mode. You'll find that an RGB document has three single-color channels (one each for red, green, and blue color) and a CMYK document has four single-color channels (one each for cyan, magenta, yellow, and black

Show/Hide channel

Load channel

New channel

Save channel

Trash

Figure 7.3
The Channels palette.

color). RGB, Lab, and CMYK documents also have a composite channel, which shows your whole image with all channels displayed and combined. A grayscale image has only one default channel, called Gray; similarly, a graphic in Indexed color mode has a single channel called Index. Figure 7.4 demonstrates how images in different color modes give you different kinds of color channels.

Figure 7.4
The color channels you have in your images depend on what color mode they use. The top image is in CMYK mode, whereas the bottom one is a grayscale image.

Looking at Individual Channels

You need to know how to view and edit a single channel at a time in order to control each color precisely without affecting the other color channels, and—as you'll see a little later in this chapter—to edit a mask in an alpha channel. Notice how each of the channels shown in your Channels palette has an eye icon (👁) next to it. Just as you learned about the Layers and Paths palettes, you can click each of these eye icons in the Channels palette to hide or display a channel.

With an RGB image open on your screen, try clicking the eye icon by the Green channel in the Channels palette to hide that channel from view. When you hide a single color channel in RGB or CMYK mode, you'll see that the eye icon by the composite view also disappears. That makes sense, because if you're only looking at the Red and Blue channels of an RGB image, you can't see the whole graphic any more (see Figure 7.5).

Figure 7.5

Turning off a color channel's eye icon hides that channel from view, and also hides the composite channel. No eye icon appears next to the Green or RGB channel in this case.

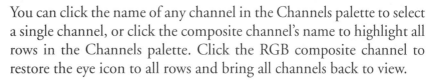
You can click the name of any channel in the Channels palette to select a single channel, or click the composite channel's name to highlight all rows in the Channels palette. Click the RGB composite channel to restore the eye icon to all rows and bring all channels back to view.

Each channel has an automatically assigned key combination for displaying it. These key combinations appear to the right of each channel's row in the Channels palette. Try pressing Cmd+1 (for Mac users) or Ctrl+1 (for Windows users) to display just the Red channel in your document. Notice how the backgrounds change in the Channels palette: now only the Red channel has a gray background and the others appear as white. The eye icon also appears only next to the Red channel, not by any of the others (see Figure 7.6).

You should take note of a couple of other things here. When you've selected a single channel to edit, as you've done here with the Red channel, you're now working with what's called your *target channel*—all changes you make are targeted to just this channel and no others in your image. You can also click the eye icon of any channel to make it viewable, but you'll need to highlight its row on the Channels palette before you can edit it as well. One practical use for this is to click the eye icon next to the composite channel to view how your edits to a single channel affect the entire image. But you should take care to note which channels you're working on at any given time, because you can also edit channels that aren't visible.

Figure 7.6

Key combinations let you select and view a single channel at a time.

Note that, by default, the colors in individual channels show up in their actual colors. If you view just the yellow channel in a CMYK document, you might find it difficult to distinguish what you're seeing because everything displays in yellow. White areas in an individual color channel are like the transparent parts in a piece of film—white means that the color is entirely absent. When you use Photoshop's tools to edit a channel, you might find it easiest to use black as your foreground color to add more of that channel's color to an image.

Painting with white will remove that channel's color from areas of your image—or, looking at it another way, you'll effectively paint with that channel's opposite, or its complementary color. You can also paint with shades of gray or another color to blend in some amount of a channel's color to your image instead of saturating the area with a solid color.

I find it's easiest to stick with percentages of black when editing a single color channel. This helps me remember that the darker the value used, the higher the concentration of that single color. You can always choose to display individual color channels in grayscale (which used to be the Photoshop default) instead of in color (see Figure 7.7). To choose this setting, from the Edit menu choose Preferences and then Display & Cursors. Make sure the Color Channels in Color check box is unchecked and click OK.

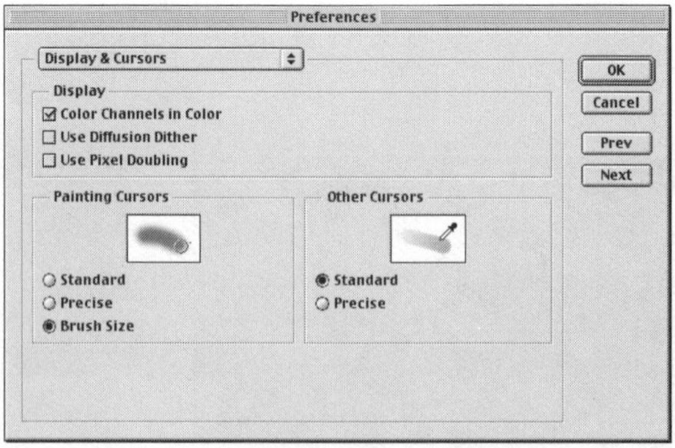

Figure 7.7

If the Color Channels in Color check box in the Display & Cursors Preferences is selected, Photoshop shows colors in individual color channels using those actual colors. If you uncheck the box, you'll see the individual color channel contents in shades of black.

Using Color Channels to Capture Hard-to-Select Areas

If you've ever had an inordinately hard time selecting the right part of an image—too many uneven edges to use the Pen or Lasso tools, and not enough color contrast to use the Magic Wand—you might have an easier time finding color contrast if you look at the image's individual color channels. Very often, at least one channel has greater color contrast than the composite image. After you've made your selection, you can return to your composite image or save your selection to an alpha channel (see Figure 7.8).

Editing Combinations of Channels

Just as you can view and edit two or more layers at the same time (see Chapter 5, "Layering Essentials"), you can view and edit two or more channels at the same time—independently of other channels. I'm going to return now to the photo shown in Figure 7.6, where only the Red channel is displayed. You should follow the same steps with an image on your screen.

With the Red channel still selected as your target channel, hold down (Shift) and click the Blue channel's row in the Channels palette. Now you'll see that both the Red and Blue channel rows have gray backgrounds and eye icons appearing in the Channels palette (see Figure 7.9). Any editing or painting you do here will affect just these two channels; it won't touch the Green channel. To see your image's composite view again, displaying all channels, press (Cmd)+(*) (for Mac users) or (Ctrl)+(*) (for Windows users).

Using the Channel Mixer

As you examine individual color channels in your images, you can see clear-cut proof of any color-balance problems or shortcomings. For instance, if one of your RGB images looks like it needs more red hues, you can bet that the content of the Red channel will be pretty sparse. If another channel in that same image looks more balanced, with good contrast and definition, you can use Photoshop's Channel Mixer feature to use the well-defined channel to boost the weaker one.

 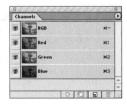

 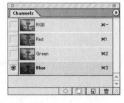

Figure 7.8

Individual color channels often let you select part of an image more easily, or let you see which colors are too dominant.

Figure 7.9

It's easy to view and edit more than one channel at a time.

To do so, first click the composite color channel in the Channels palette. You then access the Channel Mixer dialog box (see Figure 7.10) by choosing Adjust from the Image menu and then selecting Channel Mixer from the Adjust submenu. Next, you indicate in the Output Channel drop-down menu which channel to use to blend one or more of the current channels (known as *source channels*). You can then drag any source channel's slider to the left to decrease its contribution to the output channel, or to the right to increase it. Instead of dragging the slider, you can also enter a value between –200% and +200% in the text box. When you use a negative value, the source channel is inverted before being added to the output channel.

Notice the Constant option and its slider; this option lets you vary the opacity of a channel added to the output channel. If you enter a negative value, this acts as a black channel, whereas positive values act as a white channel. You can click the Monochrome check box to apply the same settings to all the output channels, which creates a color image that contains only gray values.

Figure 7.10

The Channel Mixer dialog box lets you add the contents of one or more channels to another.

Figure 7.11

Click the Monochrome check box in the Channel Mixer dialog box to give your full-color images a grayscale appearance, yet still retain the ability to edit each color channel.

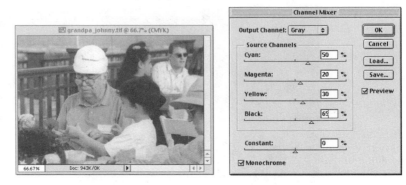

If you plan to convert an image to grayscale, selecting the Monochrome check box in the Channel Mixer dialog box (see Figure 7.11) is a good first step to giving it a hand-tinted appearance. Select and then deselect this option; you then have a number of gray-looking channels that can be edited separately.

The Channel Mixer is just one of many tools at your disposal for tweaking the color balance of your image—you'll find all of them covered at greater length in Chapter 10, "Retouching Essentials."

Using Spot-Color Channels

If you work on four-color print projects, you may sometimes have occasion—that is, if the budget allows it—to add a fifth plate to your print jobs. You might use it for a special metallic ink that can't be created with CMYK colors, or for a PMS ink that you're required to match exactly. Every large corporation I've worked for—from McKinsey & Company to IBM to Merrill Lynch—has extensive logo usage guidelines that include the exact PMS values to use in replicating the company logo. (In Chapter 4, "Color Essentials," you saw how you could find and select such custom colors with the Color Picker.)

You can save and edit such spot colors in their own channel. Click the pop-up menu in the Channels palette and select New Spot Channel. When the New Spot Channel dialog box appears, click the color swatch

Figure 7.12
Use the New
Spot Channel
dialog box to
define a spot
color channel.

it contains to launch the Color Picker and choose your custom color (see Figure 7.12). After you choose a spot color from the Color Picker, the channel is automatically renamed with the name of that color. So don't change those color names—if you do, your page layout program won't recognize the spot color information from your images.

You can save images with spot channels in several file formats, but if you plan to bring these graphics into a page layout program, you should save them in Photoshop DCS 2.0 format—that's the EPS variation that lets you save spot color information. Exercise 7.1 helps you become more comfortable dealing with spot colors and incorporating them into your images.

Creating Alpha Channels

Now that you've seen how color channels and spot-color channels work, the other main use for placing channels in a document—earmarking selections for future use—will make more sense. You can save any selected area to an alpha channel, which preserves the selection's outline although not its contents. You can either first make a selection with the Marquee tool and save it as a mask in a channel, or you can define the channel and then carve out a selection area to place within it.

Saving a Selection in a New Channel

After opening a sample image, use one of the selection tools—such as the Rectangular or Elliptical Marquee, Lasso, or Magic Wand—to choose just a portion of your image. Choose Save Selection from the Select menu. The Save Selection dialog box appears (see Figure 7.13).

EXERCISE 7.1

Adding a Spot-Color Channel to an Image

1. Open a grayscale or CMYK image to which you want to add a spot-color channel. Here, I've chosen a mockup of an event poster for an imaginary client, Royal Blue Racecars. Color is an important part of this company's brand image—it's part of its name, after all—and the corporate logo must be rendered in a specific PMS color in all print ad campaigns, as per the corporate design guidelines.

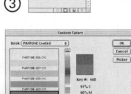

2. Select the portion of the image that you want to fill in with a new spot color. I plan to fill this selection with PMS 660, a vivid shade of blue.

3. If the Channels palette isn't already visible, choose Show Channels from the Window menu. Now choose New Spot Channel from the Channels palette pop-up menu.

4. When the New Spot Channel dialog box appears, click the color swatch it contains to launch the Color Picker. Click the Custom button to open the Custom Colors dialog box and choose the color you want. I selected Pantone Coated from the Book drop-down list, and then scrolled down to find Pantone 660 CVC.

5. Click OK to close each of the dialog boxes. The spot channel automatically fills in your selection, and you can see an approximation of what the spot color will look like in your final image. You'll also see a new spot channel added to the row of channels in the Channels palette.

If you want to experiment further with spot-color channels, try creating the new spot-color channel first, and then using Photoshop's tools to add new content to the color.

Figure 7.13

The Save
Selection
dialog box.

The Document drop-down list shows your document's name, but you can also save this new selection as a channel in another open document or in a new document. To stay with the example, use the defaults as shown to create a new channel in this document. Click OK to create the new channel. You can feel free to deselect your selection at this point if you want, making the marching ants disappear. As you'll see later in this chapter, once you've saved a selection to an alpha channel you can restore that selection at any time.

tip

Using a Shortcut to Create a New Channel

After you've selected a portion of your image, you can just click the Save Channel icon (▨) at the bottom of the Channels palette to convert your selection to a mask in its own channel.

Look in the Channels palette and you'll see that a new row has been added for your new channel (see Figure 7.14). If you don't enter a name for the new channel, the first new alpha channel in your document is called Alpha 1; the second is called Alpha 2, and so on.

So far, you've created a new alpha channel but haven't viewed it onscreen. Look at the thumbnail image next to the new channel's row in the

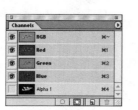

Figure 7.14

An alpha channel
in the Channels
palette.

Figure 7.15

An alpha channel viewed with the other channels in a document. The other channels are covered with a red overlay, a reminder that they cannot be edited when the alpha channel is the target channel.

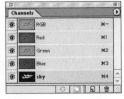

Channels palette. The thumbnail sketch for the alpha channel should look like a black-and-white stencil—the area you selected appears in white, with the rest of the image masked out with solid black.

Click the eye icon in the row for Alpha 1 so that it is visible along with all the color channels. You should see the area outside of your selection covered with a red overlay (see Figure 7.15). If you paint sweeping strokes with one of the painting tools over your image, only areas inside the selection will be affected.

Now take a look at the new alpha channel by itself, which should look like Figure 7.16. Click the eye icon in the RGB composite channel to hide all other channels. You should see a full-screen view of the black-and-white stencil image you saw in the channel's thumbnail sketch.

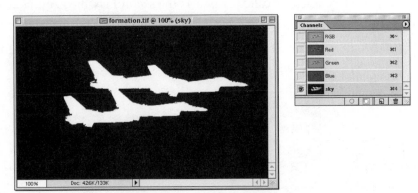

Figure 7.16

Viewing an alpha channel by itself.

You can use the various paint tools in this alpha channel to modify the shape of your saved selection area—but remember you're not yet affecting your actual image per se. For example, you can use the Airbrush or the Paintbrush tools with various brushes selected to soften the edges of your selection area.

• •

tip   Setting Marquee Tool Options before Making Selections

There's an easy way to blur the edges of a selection area evenly when you first save your selection to an alpha channel. If you're making a Rectangular or Elliptical Marquee selection, double-click the tool icon and enter a pixel value in the Feather field in the Marquee Options palette. After you save the selection to an alpha channel, this will blur the edges of your masked selection just as it does any other selection. You'll also have better luck creating masks with smooth edges if you check the Anti-aliased check box in the Options palette for any of the Lasso tools or the Magic Wand and Elliptical Marquee tools.

• •

By now, you've created a selection and used it to create a new alpha channel. You can also create an alpha channel first and then carve out your masked area from scratch using Photoshop's tools.

Try that approach to create a second alpha channel. Choose New Channel from the Channels palette pop-up menu, or just click the Create New Channel icon (⬛) found at the bottom of the Channels palette. You'll see the Channel Options dialog box, as shown in Figure 7.17. Here, you can use Photoshop's defaults for using color to represent masked-out areas and white to show selected areas in your channel, or you can invert this scheme. You can also modify the default color (red)

Figure 7.17
The Channel
Options
dialog box.

and the opacity of the mask that appears over areas outside your alpha channel when you view your composite image and the alpha channel together onscreen. You can also use this dialog box to enter a different name for this channel (Alpha 2). Click OK when you finish.

note

Why is red the default? Because it makes people who started out working on a drafting table, instead of a computer, feel at home. The half-opaque red mask is reminiscent of rubylith—the red film graphic designers have used for years to mask out parts of images on hard copy.

tip

If you want to change the name of the channel you created earlier when you saved an existing selection (Alpha 1), just double-click its row in the Channels palette. The Channel Options dialog box for this channel will appear.

Loading a Selection

It's useful to be able to reload selections once you've saved them. Return to the RGB channel by clicking the eye icon next to the RGB channel, or by pressing Cmd+✱ (for Mac users) or Ctrl+✱ (for Windows users). If either of the alpha channels remains in view, just click the eye icon to hide it.

Choose Load Selection from the Select menu. All spot-color channels as well as alpha channels are included in the list of possible source channels. The selection saved in the alpha channel now appears as an active selection.

If you ever want to load a selection and then choose its opposite, just click the Invert check box in the Load Selection dialog box. This saves you the extra step of choosing Inverse from the Select menu after loading a saved selection. In Figure 7.18, I've chosen the first alpha channel I created earlier, called "sky," and clicked the Invert check box to select the planes' outlines instead of the sky background.

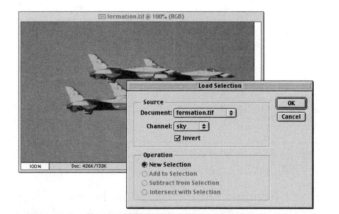

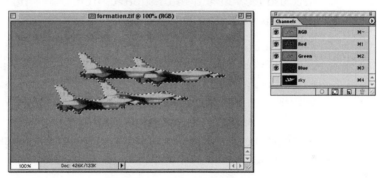

Figure 7.18
Loading a saved
selection.

tip

Shortcuts for Loading Selections

There are a number of quicker ways you can load saved selections:

👁 In an active channel, click the Load Channel icon (⬚) found at the bottom of the Channels palette to create a selection based on it.

👁 Cmd+click (for Mac users) or Ctrl+click (for Windows users) the channel you want from the Channels palette to load it.

👁 You can also drag a channel's row down to the Load Channel icon at the bottom of the Channels palette to load it.

Adding to, Subtracting from, and Intersecting Channels

In Chapter 3, "Toolbox and Palette Essentials," you saw how helpful it can be to add to or subtract from a selection—for example, if your

Figure 7.19

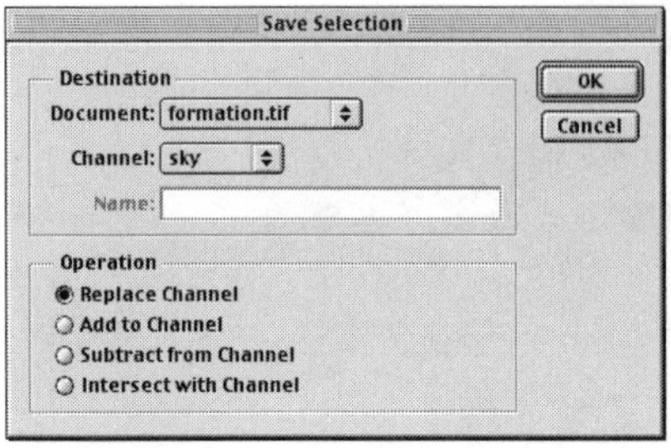

Options for adding to, subtracting from, and intersecting channels when saving a selection.

active selection didn't quite capture the exact area you wanted. Channels also let you add to or subtract from a selection, or intersect two selections to capture the overlapping part.

When you create a second alpha channel in a document, you'll discover you have more options available in the Save Selection dialog box than you did the first time. As Figure 7.19 shows, you can save your selection to an existing channel instead of a new one, and you can choose to add the two selections, subtract from the first selection any overlapping area from the second, or save only the portion that overlaps (or intersects) between the two.

Similarly, you can load a saved selection and add to, subtract from, or intersect it with an active selection. When you choose Load Selection from the Select menu, calling up the Load Selection dialog box, you should see the additional options shown in Figure 7.20. As this example shows, you can even turn to another document (julia3.tif instead of kevin.tif) to find and load a selection. Note, however, that you can load a selection from another image only when the two images have identical pixel dimensions.

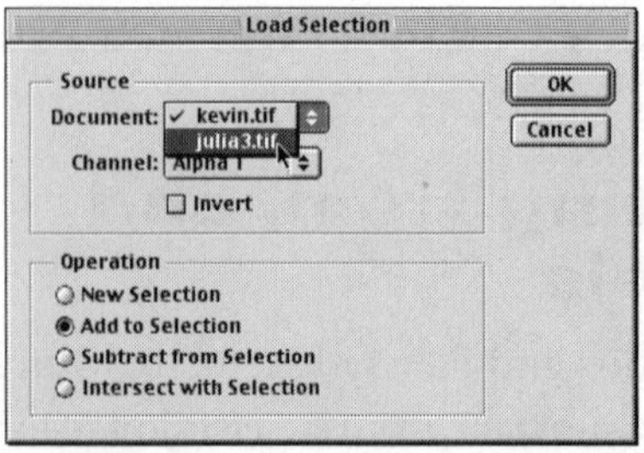

Figure 7.20

The Load Selection dialog box.

tip

Saving Memory When Storing Channels

Storing additional channels in a Photoshop document can really increase file size. If you've created multiple channels so as to add to or intersect them, make sure you delete the original alpha channels when you know you no longer need them.

You can conserve file size if you save your images with channels in native Photoshop format, for example, because Photoshop's built-in compression techniques shrink alpha channels especially well. You can also reduce the size of images with channels if you save them in TIFF format and include LZW compression.

Understanding the Channels Palette Menu

By now you've used several options in the Channels palette pop-up menu, shown in Figure 7.21. It's time to familiarize yourself with the rest of the options. The next sections provide brief descriptions of the options in the Channels palette menu.

New Channel

As you saw earlier, you can use this command to create a new channel without making a selection first. This causes the New Channel dialog box to appear. Alternatively, you can just click the New Channel icon at the bottom of the Channels palette, which lets you bypass the New Channel dialog box.

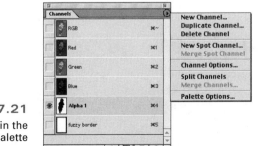

Figure 7.21

Menu items in the Channels palette pop-up menu.

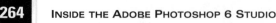

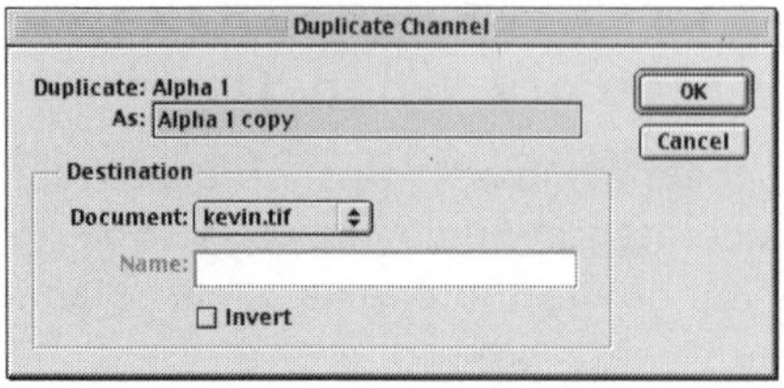

Figure 7.22

The Duplicate
Channel
dialog box.

Duplicate Channel

You can use the Duplicate Channel option to make a copy of a channel to use in the current document or to export to another open Photoshop document with the same dimensions. Choosing Duplicate Channel from the Channels palette pop-up menu opens the Duplicate Channel dialog box, as shown in Figure 7.22. Here you can give the channel copy a new name; you also have the option to create an inverted copy of your image—like a film negative—by clicking the Invert check box.

If you want to duplicate a channel to a separate document, make sure that both documents are open in Photoshop and their pixel dimensions match. After you choose the Duplicate Channel command from the Channels palette pop-up menu, you can click the Document drop-down list and choose the other document's file name. You can also drag a channel's row down to the Create New Channel icon to make a duplicate channel.

Delete Channel

Target a given channel and choose this command to delete it. It's a good idea to delete extra channels whenever it's feasible to do so, because channels hog so much disk space. You can also just drag a channel's row down to the Delete Channel icon (🗑) to get rid of it. If you delete one of your original color channels—say, the Red channel in an RGB document—your color mode automatically converts to Multichannel.

New Spot Channel and Merge Spot Channel

Earlier in this chapter, you learned how to use the New Spot Channel command to add spot-color channels for PMS colors and the like to your documents. If you make a spot-color channel active, you can access the Merge Spot Channel command in the Channels palette pop-up menu. This command converts your spot-color channel's contents to

the nearest CMYK values and removes the spot-color channel. If your document contained layers, choosing the Merge Spot Channel flattens it.

Channel Options

As you saw earlier, the Channel Options command lets you name a channel and control the color and opacity of the mask overlay that appears when you view your composite image along with your alpha channel.

Split Channels

This command lets you save all of a document's channels to separate Photoshop documents. After splitting a graphic's channels into different files, you can apply various filters, and then recombine them into one document—thus creating elaborate, color-specific special effects that might be impossible to achieve otherwise. After you choose Split Channels from the Channels palette pop-up menu, you'll see that each channel will appear on your screen in a separate document window, and the original document will close (see Figure 7.23).

Figure 7.23

After you choose the Split Channels command, the file name of each new image becomes the same as the original file and its channel name, separated by a period.

Merge Channels

This command lets you combine several single-channel documents into one Photoshop document. A typical use is to restore a document after you split up its channels (with the Split Channels command) and applied various filters or other effects to the separate documents. You'll have a chance to try this in Exercise 7.2. But you can also merge channels from different documents, as long as all the channels involved are in grayscale mode and have the same height and width in pixels.

You can merge three single-channel documents into a document with RGB or Lab color mode; you'll need four single-channel documents to merge into one CMYK image.

Palette Options

The Palette Options command controls the size and appearance of your channels' thumbnail previews in the Channels palette. You can change the size of the thumbnail sketch shown in the Channels palette, just as you can with the Layers palette. Just choose Palette Options from the Channels palette pop-up menu, and the Channels Palette Options dialog box appears (see Figure 7.24). You have your choice of three thumbnail sizes—or none. You probably won't have a real need to change the default setting (the smallest size), however.

Figure 7.24

The Channels Palette Options dialog box.

Creating Effects with Masked Type

Creating selections out of type is the first step in fashioning most of Photoshop's snazziest type effects. Choose the Type tool, and then select the masked type option ( ) from the Type options bar to create an active selection in the exact shape of any amount of type. You can also select the Vertical Type option in the Type options bar (↓T) if you want masked type that should be read vertically instead of straight across.

You can then choose Save Selection from the Select menu to save your type selection to an alpha channel, where you can load it at any time. Type selections in Photoshop are frequently used to create the basis for a layer mask; the finished effect is of a type outline filled with another photographic image (see Figure 7.25).

When the masked type option is selected in the Type tool's options bar, the Type tool doesn't create a new type layer when you start typing. Instead, the type outline is a movable selection that appears on whatever layer was active when you chose the Type tool, and the new selection can be manipulated just like any selection drawn manually.

Figure 7.25

After using the Type tool (with the masked type option selected) to create a type selection, you can save and load the selection to let a second image show through the type mask.

EXERCISE 7.2

Creating Mezzotints with Split and Merge Channels

You can add an interesting mezzotint, or engraved, effect to an image by splitting channels, converting each separate channel to Bitmap mode and applying a bitmap pattern, and then converting back to grayscale and merging channels. It's a roundabout procedure, but it will give you lots more options for the type of mezzotint patterns available than you can get from the Mezzotint filter (see Chapter 8, "Filter Essentials"), so your touched-up images will look all the more impressive. This effect is especially nice when your primary photo resources are stock photos and you want to avoid a straightforward cut-and-paste look when using them.

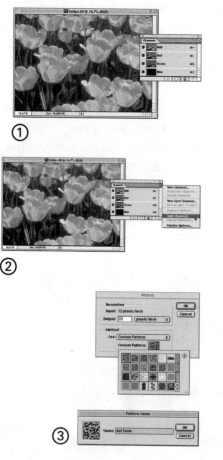

1. Open an RGB or CMYK image. Make sure the Channels palette is visible; if you don't see it, choose Show Channels from the Window menu.

2. Choose Split Channels from the Channels palette pop-up menu to separate your image into separate grayscale documents. You'll wind up with three separate grayscale files for an RGB graphic and four for a CMYK image.

3. Next, convert these new grayscale documents to Bitmap mode. Beginning with the first document, choose Mode from the Image menu, and then choose Bitmap from the submenu that appears. The Bitmap dialog box will display. Click the Use pop-up menu under Method and choose Custom Pattern. Choose from the array of Custom Pattern presets that display; you can also click the black triangle in the upper-right corner of the pattern display to load additional patterns. You can double-click any swatch to see a closer view and the pattern's name in the Pattern Name dialog box. Here, I've chosen the first one on the list, called Ant Farm.

4. Notice how your grayscale document turns into a black-and-white image with your pattern running through it. Repeat for the other grayscale images from your original file.

5. Now that you've applied the custom pattern to all three files (or four, if your original was a CMYK document), it's time to take the steps needed to merge these separate channels again. Convert the mode for the currently selected bitmapped image to Grayscale from the Mode

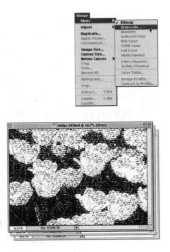

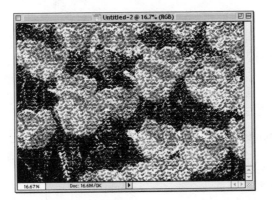

submenu under the Image menu; keep the Size Ratio in the Grayscale dialog box at the default of 1. Repeat for the other bitmapped images.

6. Within any of your grayscale documents, choose Merge Channels from the Channels palette pop-up menu. You'll see one more dialog box, which gives you the option to select other documents to merge. Click OK to accept the default files.

7. Check out the finished effect in Figure 7.26. How about trying this with another pattern selected—or using the pattern in only one channel? You can also experiment with applying various filters from the Filter menu—covered in detail in Chapter 8—to your separated grayscale documents before remerging the channels into a single document.

Figure 7.26

By using Split Channels to apply patterns to separate color channels, followed by Merge Channels, you can achieve many unique effects.

tip

You might want to create a new layer before you create a new type mask. If you use the Move tool to reposition your newly created type outline, you'll move the underlying pixels as well and move them with the selection border. Or, instead of creating a new layer, just choose one of the Marquee tools before you move the type mask selection—the outlined border will move, but not the image underneath, as shown in Figure 7.27.

Exercise 7.3 puts the Type tool's mask option to work so you can see how easy it is to fill type outlines with another image.

Figure 7.27

Use one of the Marquee tools to reposition a masked type selection (top), not the Move tool (bottom).

EXERCISE 7.3

Creating Stenciled Images with Masked Type

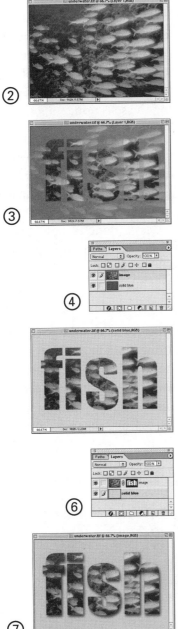

1. Create a new RGB document. Fill the background layer with white or your favorite color.

2. Choose an RGB image that you want to peek through your type outline. Use the Move tool to drag and drop this image into its own layer in your new document.

3. Choose the Type tool and make sure the masked type option is selected. Enter a small amount of type, using any typeface and point size you prefer. A heavy or thick typeface works especially well for type masks. A red overlay will surround the letters you type, indicating which areas of your image are masked.

4. While your type outline is still active, change to one of the Selection tools—for example, the Rectangular Marquee or the Magic Wand. Reposition the type selection as you see fit. When you're happy with the type placement, choose Save Selection from the Select menu. Click OK. Your type selection is saved to the Alpha 1 channel; you can give the channel a different name if you want.

5. Make sure your selection is still active; if you happened to have deselected it, choose Load Selection from the Select menu to restore it. If the Layers palette isn't visible, choose Show Layers from the Window menu. Now click the Add a Mask icon ( ) found on the bottom of the Layers palette.

6. Voilá—the lettering you typed is now filled with your original image!

7. Now you can add any Layer Style effects to your layer mask, such as a drop shadow, to emphasize it further. You can also load this type selection channel in other images—remember how the Load Selection dialog box lets you specify channels from other documents?

Using Quick Mask Mode

If you need to make and edit a selection carefully but know that you'll only need to select that area once, you should use Photoshop's Quick Mask mode to make a temporary mask instead of creating a new channel. A Quick Mask gives you all the versatility of using Photoshop's painting and editing tools to refine a selection that you have in a channel. For single-use effects, though, it spares you the effort of saving a selection, loading it, targeting that channel, and bringing the composite image back into view before editing the selection.

Quick Masks work well as shortcuts once you've already started working with channels and are used to seeing the red overlays—the ones that look like rubylith—that Photoshop uses to represent masked areas when you bring both a saved channel and your composite image into view. After you select an area of your image, click the Quick Mask icon (⬚) in the toolbox to enter Quick Mask mode. When you make a selection and then choose Quick Mask mode, Photoshop automatically puts the red overlay into place (see Figure 7.28).

Editing in Quick Mask Mode

Once you're in Quick Mask mode, you can fine-tune your selection with any of Photoshop's painting or editing tools, including the Airbrush and Paintbrush. This lets you make more refined selections with partially selected pixels. Painting with white as the foreground color will remove the red overlay and add to your selection; painting with black will add more of the overlay and subtract from your selection.

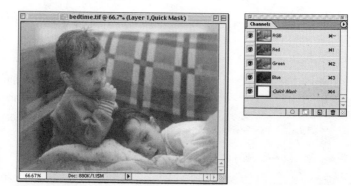

Figure 7.28

Using Quick
Mask mode.

Figure 7.29
The Quick Mask
Options
dialog box.

You can reverse the Quick Mask color preferences if you like, so that painting with white will add to your selection and painting with black will subtract from it, just as you can when you're working with a channel selection. Just double-click the Quick Mask icon to open the Quick Mask Options dialog box (see Figure 7.29); these are the same options you saw earlier in the Channel Options dialog box.

No More Marching Ants

The other bonus to editing your selection in Quick Mask mode is that you won't see the marching ants border around your selection. The hard-edged marching ants border never really represents soft, graduated edges in your selections that well anyway, right? Here, you'll see your partially selected pixels covered with just a lighter shade of the red overlay mask, meaning that those pixels are partially protected and remain partially editable.

Exercise 7.4 gives you some experience working in Quick Mask mode. The effect you'll create is one you saw when you first learned about feathering the edges of a marquee selection in Chapter 3—fading an image into a background for a vignette effect.

● ●
tip   **Reversing Quick Mask Color Preferences in a Hurry**

If you regularly decide to paint your selections in color and use the transparent overlay to indicate the masked area, there's a quicker way to set these options than calling up the Quick Mask Options dialog box. Option+click (for Mac users) or Alt+click (for Windows users) the Quick Mask icon when you're ready to enter Quick Mask mode, and the default color preferences are automatically reversed. Notice that the little Quick Mask icon changes to reflect your preferences.

Whether you decide painting in color should add to or subtract from your Quick Mask selections, you'll probably want your choice to coincide with the Channel Options settings you use. You'll likely get mixed up when you're editing your selections if you do some in channels and some in Quick Mask mode.

● ●

Summary

Go ahead and heave a great sigh of satisfaction—with this chapter's coverage of channels and masks, you've just learned the last of the basic concepts that round out your Photoshop need-to-know arsenal. Coming up: create more embellished effects and learn the situation-specific tips you'll need to optimize your graphics for viewing in print, multimedia, and online applications. The first of these goodies is an in-depth look at how to use filters to dress up your images and alter them dramatically.

EXERCISE 7.4

Creating a Vignette Using Quick Mask Mode

1. Open the image you want to use for this exercise.

   You'll use the Radial Gradient tool for this exercise, so make sure your settings are in order. Here, I've reduced the Opacity to 70% to gain the faded effect I'm looking for.

2. Double-click the Edit in Quick Mask Mode icon in the toolbox to both enter Quick Mask mode and to open the Quick Mask Options dialog box. In the Color Indicates area, make sure the Masked Areas radio button is selected.

3. With the Radial Gradient tool selected, position your crosshair in the center of your image and draw a diagonal line to an outer edge of your image. The Quick Mask red overlay will appear, showing what area of your image is masked.

4. Switch to standard mode by clicking the Edit in Standard Mode icon in the toolbox. Set your background color to the color you want to blend your image into.

5. Now press Delete (or Cmd+X for Mac users; Ctrl+X for Windows users) to subtract the unmasked portion of the image (see Figure 7.30). Congratulations—you've learned another way of making selections without using channels, as well as a second method for creating vignette effects!

Figure 7.30
A completed vignette effect, accomplished using a Quick Mask.

8

Filter Essentials

IN THIS CHAPTER

Artistic, Blur, and Distortion Filters

👁

Noise, Pixelate, and Render Filters

👁

Sharpen, Sketch, and Stylize Filters

👁

Texture and Video Filters

Photoshop's filters give you a fun, fast, one-stop-shopping way to create digital special effects. You can use them to generate the most artistic painting effects, stylized touch-ups, and twisted and twirled distortions. Filters offer a no-hassle way to get many striking effects you'd be hard-pressed to create otherwise.

There are also filters that can help you with every step of photo retouching and color correction. For example, you can use filters to bring blurry edges in a poorly scanned photo into better focus, get rid of moiré patterns on a scanned halftone, or add dramatic lighting effects to a ho-hum image.

In this chapter, you get a chance to see not only what all the filters do but how they differ from one another—for example, the differences between Blur and Gaussian Blur. You also discover what kinds of effects you can produce with combinations of filters, so that you can get more mileage out of Photoshop than you ever dreamed of. In addition, you get to see some real-world applications for which you might want or need to use a certain kind of filter. This might prove to be the most useful part of the chapter for you—it's fun to fool around with each filter one by one to see what kind of effects you can produce, but you may be under the gun. If you have to come up with a stunning design right now, you might not have time to determine by brute force how to achieve the look you want. Here's a broad look at the topics covered in this chapter:

- 👁 How filters work, and how to speed up their operation

- 👁 How to fade a filter for subtler effects

- 👁 How to get the most out of each of the standard filters included with Photoshop 6.0

- 👁 How to extend the effects of filters by using them in channels and layers

Putting Filters to Work

The name is an allusion to photographic filters, but in a way a Photoshop filter is more like a coffee filter or an air filter—it can perform its own processing operation to produce an entirely new product. You can apply

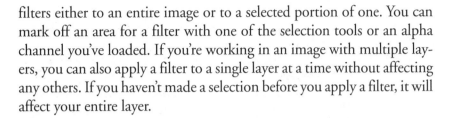

filters either to an entire image or to a selected portion of one. You can mark off an area for a filter with one of the selection tools or an alpha channel you've loaded. If you're working in an image with multiple layers, you can also apply a filter to a single layer at a time without affecting any others. If you haven't made a selection before you apply a filter, it will affect your entire layer.

note

You can apply filters in RGB, CMYK, Grayscale, or Lab color modes—or only in some of them, depending on the filter's capabilities. In addition, Photoshop doesn't allow you to apply filters to images in Bitmap or Indexed Color modes, or to 16-bit-per-channel images.

You can select filters in Photoshop by choosing any menu item from the Filter menu. The standard set that comes with Photoshop 6.0 gives you the Artistic, Blur, Brush Strokes, Distort, Noise, Pixelate, Render, Sharpen, Sketch, Stylize, Texture, Video, Other, and Digimarc filters. (I'll get to these categories in a minute.) Some of these filters are built right into your Photoshop application; but you'll find others included as plug-ins. Vendors of other graphics software packages have created filter plug-ins that work with Photoshop as well as with their own programs; these include Kai's Power Tools from Metacreations and the Auto/FX series of filters. Appendix C, "Vendor Directory," includes information on third-party vendors and their products, including filters.

You can add freeware filters like those you might find on Photoshop-focused Web sites (see Appendix B, "Sources for Further Information," for a sampling of such sites) by placing their files in the Plug-Ins folder inside your Photoshop folder. As you'll see later in this chapter, you can even create your own filters in Photoshop and add them to your Plug-Ins folder.

There's a Filters folder inside your Plug-Ins folder where you can store all your filters for safekeeping, but Photoshop will recognize your filters even if you leave them scattered elsewhere in the Plug-Ins folder. The Filters folder just helps you keep your filters organized by placing them all in one spot, away from other kinds of plug-ins.

note
You can move your Plug-Ins folder—for example, if you use other applications like Adobe Premiere that share some common plug-ins—but you need to tell Photoshop where to find the new directory. To do so, choose Preferences from the Edit menu, and then choose General. Click the drop-down menu at the top of the resulting preferences dialog box and then choose Plug-Ins & Scratch Disks (see Figure 8.1). Toggle through the directories on your hard drive to identify the new location for your plug-ins.

note
If you install filters in Photoshop while the program is still running, you'll have to quit and relaunch Photoshop before you can access the new options.

Depending on which filter you apply, it may go into effect right away or it may prompt you with a dialog box where you supply specific parameters. When you see a filter dialog box, you'll have a chance to preview the results you'll get for the values you enter—as in Figure 8.2.

If you pass your cursor over the dialog box's preview image, it'll turn to a hand icon you can use to click and drag the image to preview different portions of the image. If it's tedious to click and drag to the part of the image you want to see, you can just click your cursor on that portion of the image, and the dialog box's preview will apply the filter to that portion of the image. You can click the Zoom buttons under the preview box to increase or reduce the size of the preview image you see.

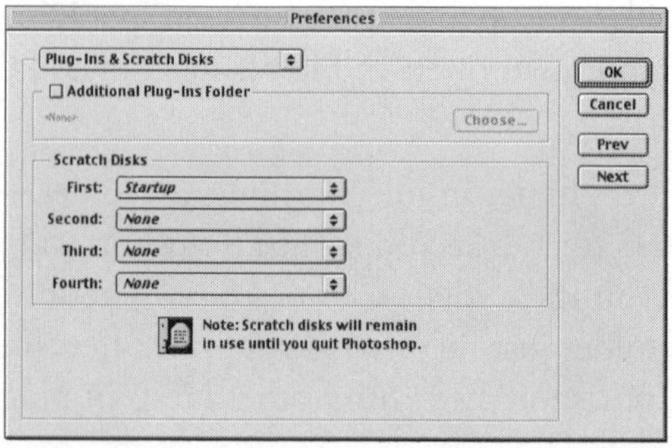

Figure 8.1
The Plug-Ins & Scratch Disks Preferences dialog box.

Figure 8.2
Using a filter's dialog box to preview the results.

tip

• •

Bringing Up a Filter's Dialog Box More than Once

After you apply a filter, you can reapply it by choosing the first menu item under the Filter menu or by pressing ⌘+F (for Mac users) or Ctrl+F (for Windows users)—but you don't see the filter's dialog box a second time. If you want to see the dialog box again and perhaps change the filter's settings, press ⌘+Option+F (for Mac users) or Ctrl+Alt+F (for Windows users) instead.

• •

Applying Filters at Partial Strength

After you apply a filter, you can reduce its intensity—for example, you can choose to apply it at only 50 percent or 70 percent of its full strength—by choosing the Fade command under the Edit menu. This opens a Fade dialog box that lets you lower the filter's intensity by lowering its opacity. The wording of the Fade command under the Edit menu changes depending upon what filter or other image adjustment command was most recently applied. After applying the Crosshatched filter, for example, you can choose Fade Crosshatched from the Edit menu (see Figure 8.3). Check the Preview check box in the Fade dialog box to preview the results as you experiment with the Fade dialog box's Opacity slider control.

Figure 8.4 shows an example to illustrate this. I applied the Find Edges filter (you'll find it under the Stylize submenu) to this image of a sphinx. This overpowers the structure's outlines and makes it seem less realism,

Edit

Undo Crosshatch	⌘Z
Step Forward	⇧⌘Z
Step Backward	⌥⌘Z
Fade Crosshatch...	⇧⌘F
Cut	⌘X
Copy	⌘C
Copy Merged	⇧⌘C
Paste	⌘V
Paste Into	⇧⌘V
Clear	
Fill...	
Stroke...	
Free Transform	⌘T
Transform	▶
Define Brush...	
Define Pattern...	
Define Custom Shape...	
Purge	▶
Color Settings...	⇧⌘K
Preset Manager...	
Preferences	▶

Fade

Opacity: 100 %   OK

Mode: Normal   Cancel

☑ Preview

Figure 8.3

The context-sensitive Fade command under the Edit menu, and the Fade dialog box.

though, as you can see by the image in the middle of Figure 8.4. After applying the Find Edges filter, I chose Fade Find Edges from the Edit menu and lowered the Opacity slider control to 32% to produce the subtle highlights shown in the image at the bottom.

Why Are Filters So Slow?

Some filters function by examining every pixel in an image before transforming each of them in some way. Other filters sample larger areas of your image to make broader determinations about brightness and hue before effecting their changes. Either way, it can be a time-consuming process.

For Mac users, the progress bar is a partial consolation—it lets you judge how quickly (or slowly) your filter is working. Windows users see a progress indicator in the status bar instead of a separate progress bar. If you're experimenting with different filters and settings, you can save time by relying on the preview images in your filters' dialog boxes to judge results before committing to a filter.

Here are a couple of tips for speeding up your filtering:

👁 Try applying your filter to a small selection first instead of your whole image to better judge the effects.

Use the Purge command under the Edit menu to free up more memory before applying the filter.

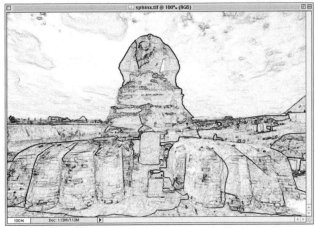

Figure 8.4
Choose Fade from the Filter menu after you apply a too-strong filter to lower the opacity of the filter's effect. Here, I chose Fade to lower the opacity to 32% after applying the Find Edges filter and produced the effect at the bottom, thus improving on the overpowering results of the filter at full strength (middle).

- If you change your mind while waiting for your filter to be applied, you can cancel the operation by pressing Esc. If you're using a Mac, pressing [Cmd]+. has the same effect.

- The more RAM and free hard disk space available to your filters, the better. Allocate more RAM to Photoshop or quit out of other open applications.

- Follow the tips in Chapter 1, "System Essentials," for optimizing memory and performance on your machine.

Artistic Filters

Photoshop's Artistic filters are each designed to stylize your image to emulate a specific traditional style of drawing or painting. The filters in this category work only on RGB or grayscale images. Figure 8.5 showcases the effects of each of the Artistic filters.

Colored Pencil

The Colored Pencil filter edits your image so it looks like you applied cross-hatching over the original with a pencil in the same shade as your background color. With this filter, you can adjust these settings:

- **Pencil Width** affects the heaviness of the cross-hatching, measured on a scale of 1 to 24; lower values produce finer hatch marks, whereas higher values produce large areas of solid color and fewer hatch marks.

- **Stroke Pressure** controls how many hatch marks are created in total, measured on a scale of 0 to 15. Lower values create so many hatch marks that it darkens your image using the background color. A Stroke Pressure of 0 fills in solidly with your background color, whereas higher values retain the brightness of your original.

- **Paper Brightness** darkens or brightens what purports to be the color of the "paper" background on a scale of 0 to 50. Setting Paper Brightness to 50 makes the "paper" background the same color as the background color you've chosen in the toolbox.

Original

Colored Pencil

Cutout

Dry Brush

Film Grain

Fresco

Neon Glow

Paint Daubs

Palette Knife

Plastic Wrap

Poster Edges

Rough Pastels

Smudge Stick

Sponge

Underpainting

Figure 8.5
Compare the
effects of applying
the various
Artistic filters to a
single image.

Water Color

Cutout

The Cutout filter reduces the number of colors in your image to a level you set. This is similar to the Posterize command available when you choose Adjust from the Image menu, but it creates anti-aliased edges wherever colors meet. These edges tend to resemble torn pieces of paper; you can generate the most dramatic effects with high-contrast images. The Edge Simplicity setting ascertains the number of edges found by the filter. The Edge Fidelity setting determines how closely the edges of the solid colors used will match those of the original image. This can be a very time-consuming filter to apply, because it creates such elaborate edges where colors meet.

Dry Brush

Traditionally, the dry brush technique of painting involves dipping a brush in paint without wetting it first with water, and then applying it to the design until it runs dry. This produces large areas of solid, bright color with fractured, hard edges. The Dry Brush filter recreates this effect by repainting your image with small areas of dense, solid colors with well-defined edges. It produces a much more detailed image than most of the other Artistic filters.

Use lower values in the Brush Size setting to create many small areas of color, and larger values to define fewer but larger areas. The Brush Detail setting determines how many edges are found; higher values depict the most detail. The Texture setting shows how colored areas are lightened or darkened compared to their original values. A value of 1 retains the original averaged color values; the highest setting (3) results in a number of stray black and white pixels sprinkled across the image.

Film Grain

This filter adds noise (single, randomly colored pixels) throughout your image—much like the effect of Photoshop's own Noise filters, described a little later—but it doesn't have the destructive potential of those other filters. No matter how heavily you apply this filter, it still largely retains the look of the original. It gets its name from a distorted quality found in photographs shot using high-speed film—although its effects bear little resemblance to actual film grain. (You can obtain much more realistic film grain effects using the Add Noise filter from the Noise submenu or the Grain filter from the Texture submenu.) You can choose to apply grain (or noise) on a scale ranging from 0 to 20. You can also specify settings for highlight area and intensity on a scale from 0 to 10.

Fresco

Even if you have no formal art training, you've probably heard of frescos. This traditional art technique involves painting with watercolors on freshly spread, drying plaster—but the Fresco filter is something of a misnomer because its effects do not recall traditional frescos very well. Instead, it defines areas of your image based on similar colors, and then averages those color values and fills in the defined areas solidly with the averaged color. These defined areas are then outlined heavily with dark, thick borders. Its options are the same as those for the Dry Brush filter.

Neon Glow

The Neon Glow filter infuses your images with an other-worldly duotone or tritone appearance. When you apply the filter, any shadows in your image are replaced with whatever color is selected as your foreground color. All midtones in your image are replaced by the background color, and highlights are replaced with the third color selected within the Neon Glow dialog box. You'll see the most dramatic results when your foreground color, background color, and dialog box color are highly contrasting.

Paint Daubs

Here's another filter that doesn't live up to its name; instead of generating anything remotely resembling blotches of paint, this filter defines areas of color similarity in your image and then blurs them into highly stylized, abstract patches. All the fine detail gets lost in the blurred results, but any highly contrasting edges stay in place and get even sharper. Your options for this filter include changing the brush size and how much sharpening is conducted after the blurring takes place. From the Paint Daubs dialog box shown in Figure 8.6, you can choose from

Figure 8.6
The Paint Daubs
dialog box.

a number of brush types—which bear no resemblance to the brushes you can load for any of the standard Photoshop painting tools:

- **Simple Brush**. No additional effects are added.

- **Light Rough**. Lightens and sharpens the images after it is first blurred.

- **Dark Rough**. Darkens and sharpens the images after it is first blurred.

- **Wide Sharp**. Simply sharpens the image after it is first blurred.

- **Wide Blurry**. Blurs the image further.

- **Sparkle**. This choice seeks out the lightest highlight values and further lightens them to an extreme.

Palette Knife

The traditional technique of painting with a palette knife results in heavy strokes of solid pigment on a canvas. This filter does a reasonable job of re-creating the effect, except that there's no sense of depth; the color appears to lie completely flat, not piled up in globs like you'd get from a real palette knife. This filter can be used to good purpose with simple line art or before applying the Crystallize filter. Your options here include stroke size (the thickness of each stroke), stroke detail (the roughness of the stroke's edges), and softness (the level of blurring).

You can apply warp styling to your type selections to align the text along the shape of a wave, arc, or another path. The type remains editable even after warp effects are applied.

Here, I grouped a gradient fill layer with each of the two type layers to create the gradated disappearing and reappearing type.

Color Plate 2

You can create interesting cutout borders for your images by applying a filter to a selection in a layer mask.

Layers

Normal ▼ Opacity: 100% ▶

Lock: □ ▨ □ ⌀ □ ✛ □ 🔒

👁 ▣ 🖼 ⑂ ⬜ Layer 0

👁 ⬜ Layer 1

Color 3 Plate

By carefully applying the Clone Stamp tool, you can eliminate distractions in the background of your images. Here, for example, I've blocked out the white metal fencing. The stamped-in portion doesn't have to match the original landscape; what's important is that it blends in well with the rest of the background.

Color 4 Plate

When creating a navigation bar for a Web site, you can use Photoshop 6 to create and slice all states of this collection of grouped-together button graphics. You can then use ImageReady to assign the rest, rollover, and mouse-down states in ImageReady's Rollover palette.

Color 5 Plate

To incorporate a key message or navigation in your image, you can use Photoshop 6's Warp Text feature to inscribe its words parallel to the perimeter of a shape within the picture. Here, the words lead to subsections within a resort's Web site.

Color Plate 6

Gradient fills are the key to creating realistic-looking chrome lettering. Add a glint or gleam to your text by applying one of the sparkling brush patterns with the Airbrush tool.

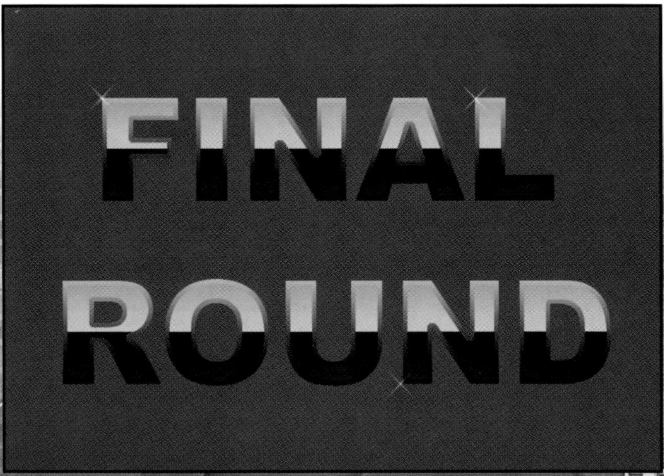

Color Plate 7

One way to draw attention to your subjects is to desaturate their surroundings. For this birthday-party snapshot, I duplicated the state using the History palette, then used the Channel Mixer to turn the full-color picture into a monochrome one. I then used the History Brush to repaint selected portions.

Color **8** Plate

The new vector-based shapes in Photoshop 6 can be used as shape layers, as vector masks, or for painting pixels. After choosing my subject photos, I created a new layer in each using the Custom Shape tool. I rasterized the shapes, chose Copy Merged from the Edit menu, and placed the masked outlines in a new file.

Color **9** Plate

You can easily create translucent effects with type by lowering the type layer's opacity. Here, I also added a layer style for a Drop Shadow and Bevel & Emboss effect.

Color Plate 10

To blend several images in a collage, drag each image into a composite file where each will have its own layer. Add a layer mask and choose the Hide All option. Now you can paint in as much or as little of each individual image to construct the overall effect.

'twas the night before Christmas...

A

Color Plate 11

Bright sunlight can cause extreme highlights and shadows in your images. In Figure 11B, I used the Curves dialog box to lighten the extreme tonal values while leaving the midtones virtually untouched.

B

Color Plate 12

The Angled Strokes filter adds a painterly impression to an image while maintaining the clarity of the original well. For more sophisticated effects, remember to experiment with combinations of filters.

Color Plate 13

When you use the Extract command under the Image menu, your subject is placed on its own layer. Here I've blurred the original background to make the subject stand out more.

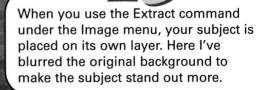

Color Plate 14

You can create translucent, 3D text by applying the Bevel & Emboss effect. You can also fine-tune your text layer's mode and opacity for highlights and shadows.

Color Plate 15

Using Photoshop's preset duotone curves in the Duotone Options dialog box is the easiest way to ensure that the screen angles in each color are set properly. You should always set the darkest color in your images as Ink 1 to reproduce shadows in fullest detail.

Color Plate 16

With the Art History brush, you can paint stylized strokes on an image much as you would brush paint onto a canvas. You then tweak the look you're creating by adjusting the size, fidelity, tolerance, and paint style controls.

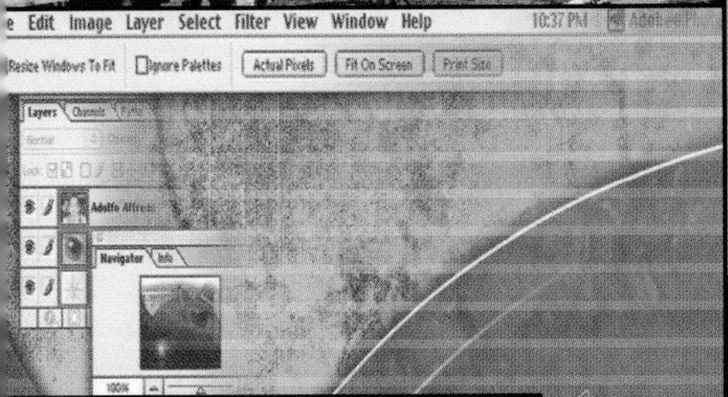

Color Plate 17

You can add feathery-edged vignettes to any image by choosing one of the Marquee tools, entering a Feather value in the contextual options bar, designating your selection area on the original image, inverting it, then deleted the inverted selection. You can also accomplish this effect with the Quick Mask feature.

Color Plate 18

Button templates distributed at online archives, like these layered Photoshop files from ScreamDesign.com, can help save you time in your Web design projects. Study the ones that most intrigue you to learn how they were put together, and you'll have a head start in creating your own variations.

Color Plate 19

To create this masked effect, I created the lettering in a Type layer and rendered the selection. I then loaded the selection in a new type layer, inverted it, and filled the inversion with a shade of blue.

Color Plate 20

To create an image that appears as if it were displayed on a television screen, you simply need to add a low-opacity horizontally striped pattern across your image. Framing your subjects within a TV set image adds to the illusion.

To restore this old photo, I made liberal use of the Dust & Scratches filter, then used the Clone Stamp tool to fill in other degraded areas. I chose Color Balance under the Adjust submenu of the Image menu to brighten the colors in the baby clothes, as well as imbue the background with an overall purplish hue.

This sample Web interface shows how you can combine buttons and animated GIFs created in Photoshop for a stunning interactive effect. This freely distributed interface from the NavWorks Interface Vault shows six buttons and a large center sphere. The wording on each button lights up when the mouse is moved over one of the buttons, and a large spiral animation appears in the center.

Color Plate 23

Retouching the "red-eye" syndrome produced by camera flashes involves more than filling in the reflections or area with a solid color—that would look as unnatural as the red eye itself. Here, the pupil was stroked using the Paintbrush set to a 60 percent opacity and a blending mode of Luminosity. This retains the natural reflections and specular highlights. You can also reduce red eye by applying the Sponge tool, setting it to Desaturate, and using a medium pressure such as 50 percent.

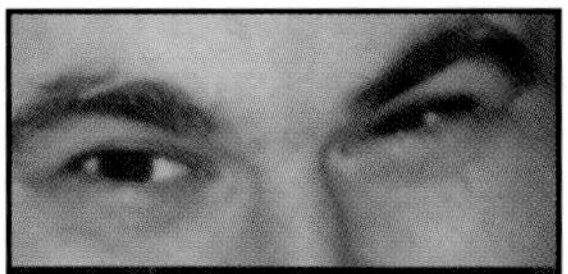

Color Plate 24

You can create a jigsaw-puzzle effect using the Displace filter. This filter moves pixels in your original image according to the brightness values in your displacement map, which, in Color Plate 24B, is a jigsaw outline.

Color Plate 25

With the Replace Color option in the Adjust sub-menu of the Image menu, you can give any subject an instant makeover: select hair, eye color, or lip color, and adjust all corresponding shades of the overall color for a natural change effect.

Color Plate 26

In less time than it takes for ice cream to melt, you can put the new Liquify command in Photoshop 6 to work to distort, twist, and shrink various parts of an image. It's especially fun to use to add fun-house effects to images of people.

Color Plate 27

Although it won't replace your page layout program, Photoshop 6 has finally added real typographic capabilities. You can create text boxes, use word-wrapping, assign color on a per-character basis, vary the justification among paragraphs, and use hanging punctuation.

Construction of the Statue began in France in the year 1875, by sculptor Auguste Bartholdi. The final completion date of the individual sections was in June of 1884, and it stood in Paris until it was dismantled in early 1885 for shipping to the US. Engineering of the structure's assembly was done by Gustave Eiffel.

The French frigate "Isere" transported the Statue from France to the United States. In transit the Statue was reduced to 350 individual pieces and packed in 214 crates.

(The pedestal was designed by architect Richard M.Hunt in 1877. Construction of the pedestal began in 1883 and was completed in 1884, and final assembly of the statue & pedestal was completed in 1886)

Color Plate 28

You can apply a number of effects, like the rainbow and chrome effects shown here, in a single step by specifying a layer style whenever you build a custom shape using a vector layer.

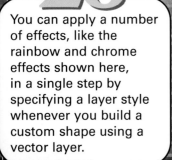

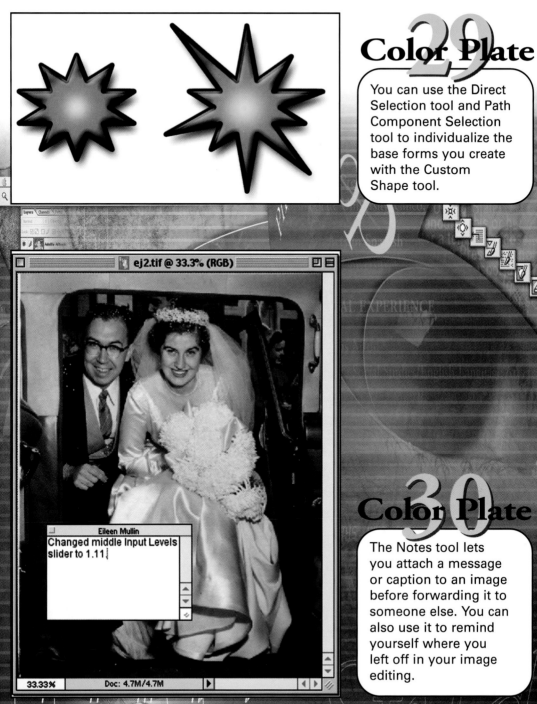

Color Plate 29

You can use the Direct Selection tool and Path Component Selection tool to individualize the base forms you create with the Custom Shape tool.

Color Plate 30

The Notes tool lets you attach a message or caption to an image before forwarding it to someone else. You can also use it to remind yourself where you left off in your image editing.

ej2.tif @ 33.3% (RGB)

Eileen Mullin

Changed middle Input Levels slider to 1.11

33.33%   Doc: 4.7M/4.7M

Color Plate 31

This grained-wood effect in beveled and embossed letters looks difficult and time-consuming to create, but it is an example of an effect that can be generated quickly using Photoshop actions — macros or shortcuts that other Photoshop fans have figured out and made free for distribution and download over the Web.

Color Plate 32

Because Photoshop 6 is tightly integrated with ImageReady version 3.0, you can toggle transparently from one program or the other to work on the same files, whether it's to add multi-state JavaScript rollovers or apply layer effects.

Plastic Wrap

This filter adds shine and dimension to the objects in your image by enveloping them with the look of heat-shrink plastic. This filter can greatly enhance simple line art or text in your graphics. The options in the Plastic Wrap dialog box control highlight strength (the intensity of the reflected light), detail (how closely the plastic wrap seems to cling to the edges of objects), and smoothness (the glossiness of the plastic wrap).

Poster Edges

Like the Cutout filter, this filter works rather similarly to the Posterize command available when you choose Adjust from the Image menu. The differences are that Poster Edges is more faithful to the original colors in the image, anti-aliases the image edges better, and traces a black border around the edges of similarly colored areas. You can produce a woodcut or stained-glass type of effect using Poster Edges. The filter does have a couple of shortcomings—you can't eliminate the black border detail or control the number of levels of color used in posterizing the image.

Rough Pastels

Rough Pastels adds a bumpy canvas texture to your image, stroked with smears of highly saturated colors sampled from your original image. This filter works well on text in an image and also produces good effects with any simple line art images. You can set a number of options for controlling the texture with this complex filter (see Figure 8.7). For example, you can invert the stroke of the texture, choose different textures or images as textures, or change the lighting direction.

Smudge Stick

The Smudge Stick filter gently smears and smudges dark-colored pixels in your image at a diagonal angle. You can control the stroke length (higher settings produce longer smudges), or how long a trail each smudge leaves, as well as highlight area and intensity, which lightens pixels before smudging them. One good use for this filter is in generating textures. To accomplish this, create a blank image, run the Add Noise filter to generate some noise, and then apply Smudge Stick.

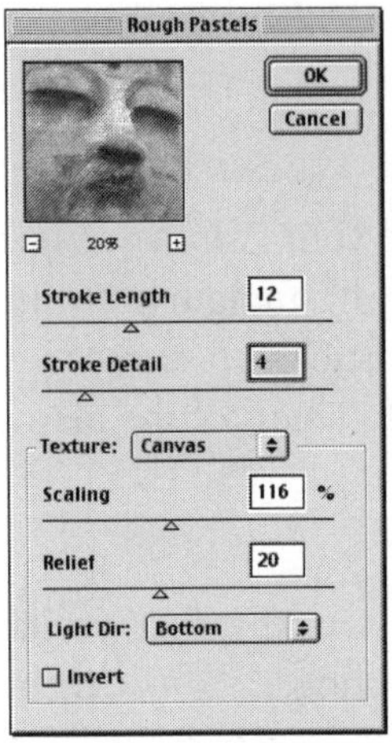

Figure 8.7
The Rough
Pastels
dialog box.

Sponge

The Sponge filter lives up to its name; it produces the effects of dabbing a damp sponge filled with paint on an image. It works well in generating textures. Its dialog box options include Brush Size, which should really be called Sponge Size. You can also control Definition, which controls the value difference between the sponge and the underlying image. The Smoothness option controls how anti-aliased the edges of the sponge are; higher values introduce greater smoothness and anti-aliasing.

Underpainting

Traditional fine artists use underpainting to map out the general colors and shapes in an image before painting in the details. This filter re-creates this technique remarkably well, giving the impression of a very sketchy, blurred image with only the faintest of detail painted in. Given the nature of this filter, you can do a lot with your image after applying it as a first step—don't just consider it an end result. You can achieve good results by using the History Brush tool to paint parts of your original image back in at a low opacity after applying the Underpainting filter.

Watercolor

The Watercolor filter is another in the Artistic category that doesn't quite live up to the promise of its name—what's up with that? It produces results similar to those generated by the Fresco filter. The Watercolor filter defines similarly colored areas, averages the colors, and fills the area with the new averaged value. The border edges of these areas appear darker than the color contained in that area, which is reminiscent of a watercolor, but overall the filter produces very intense colors and dark shadow areas and not the slightly dreamy effect often found in water-color paintings.

Blur Filters

Blur filters reduce the contrast between pixels and their surrounding neighbors, so you can use them to soften hard edges in your images where there's too much contrast.

Blur and Blur More

The Blur filter produces a straightforward blurring effect, as if your glasses had slipped down your nose. It softens contrasting edges and can reduce noise—that is, individual pixels that sharply contrast with surrounding ones. The Blur More filter just produces a more exagger-ated blur effect.

Figure 8.8 shows one really useful application of the Blur filters— namely, blurring background objects so as to highlight objects or figures in the foreground. The picture at left in Figure 8.8 shows a quirky little statue that my husband spotted outside a storefront in the Ginza dis-trict in Tokyo. To emphasize the statue over the other bright colors and surroundings in the photo, I made a copy of the layer and used the Extract command under the Image menu tool to outline the statue of the girl. I ran the Motion Blur filter over the background imagery to obscure the detail. In the image on the right in Figure 8.8, the statue is the only discernible object in the photo. This effect can, of course, be toned down to only slightly blur the focus of the background scenery, thus subtly drawing attention to the foreground subject.

Gaussian Blur

With Gaussian Blur, named for the bell-shaped Gaussian distribution curve, you have greater control over the blurring effect. (The Gaussian

Figure 8.8
Using Blur filters to make a foreground object stand out.

distribution curve, by the way, slopes gradually at first, and then quite drastically in the middle, before tapering off gradually at the end again.) You can enter a value between 0.1 and 250 to cause a certain amount of change between contrasting pixels; higher values indicate more extreme blurring. This is a good filter to use for exaggerating shadows when they're on their own layer.

Figure 8.9 demonstrates how Gaussian Blur enhances a shadow effect. In the image at top, I created a cast shadow for the type layer, which is filled with gray and distorted as if the sun is setting behind the letterforms. In the image at bottom, I applied a Gaussian Blur to the shadow layer and reduced the opacity a little further, which made the shadow much more realistic-looking. (You can replicate this cast shadow effect, by the way, using a prerecorded set of steps that Photoshop calls an *action*; this action is one of a number of shortcuts for creating quick effects that's included with Photoshop 6.0. You'll find out much more about actions in Chapter 15, "Automation and Batch Processing Essentials.")

Motion Blur

As the name implies, this filter helps produce the illusion of capturing an object in motion, as shown in the before-and-after pictures you saw previously in Figure 8.8. The filter's dialog box lets you control the

Figure 8.9
Using Gaussian
Blur to enhance a
shadow.

angle and intensity (through the distance that pixels are blurred) of the
motion effect.

Radial Blur

There are two kinds of blurring effects you can produce with this filter.
The *spin* method whirls the edges of your image with a circular motion;
the *zoom* method produces blurred lines from all edges focusing in on
the center of your image. The Radial Blur dialog box includes a wireframe
preview instead of an image preview to indicate the intensity of the effect. You can enter values between 1 and 100 or drag the slider control in
the dialog box to control the level of the blur (see Figure 8.10).

You can also choose one of three quality levels in generating a Radial
Blur—called draft, good, and best. Figure 8.11 shows the Radial Blur
filter in action.

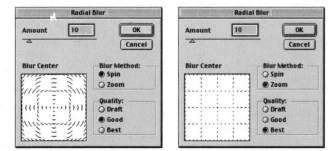

Figure 8.10
The two Radial
Blur options:
spin and zoom.

Figure 8.11

Three kitties: The original is on the left. The middle image uses the Radial Blur filter's Spin option at a level of 10. At right, the image uses the Radial Blur filter's Zoom option at a level of 35.

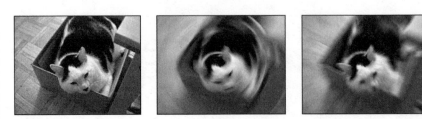

Smart Blur

Smart Blur identifies highly contrasting edges in an image and blurs only the area contained within. That's what makes this Blur filter "smart"—it can be used to eliminate noise in areas such as skin tones without adversely affecting the larger image's details (see Figure 8.12). The dialog box for Smart Blur lets you set the blurring Radius, Threshold, and Quality. You can also use the Mode option to apply Smart Blur to the image normally or trace the edges and fill the remaining areas with black (the Edge Only option). You also can fill the traced edges with white and apply this border over the original image (the Overlay Edge option).

Figure 8.12

The Smart Blur dialog box.

Brush Strokes

The filters in the Brush Strokes category all apply striking texture effects to any image. They're also useful for creating textures from scratch; you can try this by opening a new image, applying the Add Noise filter at a high setting, and then applying one of the Brush Strokes filters to the whole image. In Figure 8.13, I opened an image of a rather bumpy textured stucco effect before applying the Brush Strokes filters.

Figure 8.14 showcases the effects of each of the Brush Strokes filters on a single image.

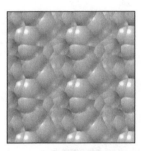

Original

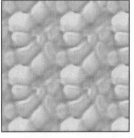

Accented Edges

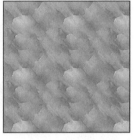

Angled Strokes

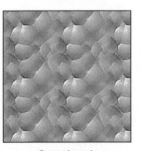

Crosshatch

Dark Strokes

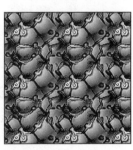

Ink Outlines

Spatter

Sprayed Strokes

Sumi-e

Figure 8.13
Embellishing
textures using
the Brush Strokes
filters.

Original

Accented Edges

Angled Strokes

Crosshatch

Dark Strokes

Ink Outlines

Figure 8.14
Compare the effects of applying the various Brush Strokes filters to a single image.

Spatter

Sprayed Strokes

Sumi-e

Accented Edges

The Accented Edges filter traces the edges of highly contrasting areas on an image, and then emphasizes those edges by stroking them with either a dark or a brightly glowing color, depending on what settings you enter. The Edge Width option determines how thick the traced edges are; lower values are more effective, whereas higher values can completely distort your image. The Edge Brightness setting determines the amount that the traced edges are lightened or darkened. Values for Edge Brightness can range from 0 to 50: 25 is the neutral setting; higher values turn the edges closer to solid white, whereas lower values turn the edges closer to solid black.

Angled Strokes

This filter gives the painterly impression of long, diagonal streaks of color applied to a canvas, while maintaining the overall contrasts in your image. All strokes are placed at a left or right diagonal and you can mix the two through the Direction Balance setting, although you can't control the angle of the stroke.

The value you enter for Direction Balance is difficult to interpret. The dialog box accepts values between 0 and 100. If you enter 0, the strokes are all applied diagonally from the left; if you enter 100, the strokes are all applied diagonally from the right. Any values you add in between apply a mix of the two angles. The other two options that you can set in the Angled Strokes dialog box—Stroke Length and Sharpness—affect the distance of the blurring and how much the image is sharpened after blurring.

Crosshatch

The Crosshatch filter is very close in function to the Angled Strokes filter. Here, the brush strokes can overlap, and you don't need to set the directional balance. In the Crosshatch dialog box you can choose settings for Stroke Length and Sharpness, just like the Angled Strokes filter. You can also specify a setting for Strength, which controls an embossing effect applied to your strokes.

Dark Strokes

Dark Strokes is also similar to the Angled Strokes filter, but here it's much harder to differentiate the actual strokes as it darkens your overall image. You can control how many strokes are angled from the left or right through a non-intuitive setting called Balance, which has a range of 0 through 10. At 0, all strokes are angled from the right, whereas at 10, all strokes are angled from the left.

Ink Outlines

Ink Outlines is almost identical to Dark Strokes, but you have control over the length of each stroke rather than the direction of the strokes'

angles. All stroking with Ink Outlines is crosshatched, but if you choose a low value for Stroke Length, this fact might not be apparent.

Spatter

Use the Spatter filter to produce an effect reminiscent of a rough spray of paint from an airbrush. This creates pleasing border effects for simple line art, image edges, or text in your graphics. You can control the heaviness and distortion of the spray with the Spray Radius and Smoothness settings in the Spatter dialog box.

Sprayed Strokes

The Sprayed Strokes filter is one of the few in this collection that lets you explicitly specify a stroking angle (Right Diagonal, Horizontal, Left Diagonal, or Vertical). It functions much like the Spatter filter, although here you can constrain the length of the strokes.

Sumi-e

This filter takes its name from a Japanese art of painting with black ink. It applies dark strokes and heavy blotches spread from a right diagonal angle over your entire image. Experiment with the Stroke Pressure setting, which controls the darkness of the strokes, to get the most interesting results. You can also adjust the stroke width and contrast in the filtered effect.

Distortion Filters

These filters produce a variety of real funhouse-mirror effects, reshaping an image rather than altering the colors of pixels. You might have few everyday uses for them, but they're always an option for striking or unusual effects. One notable exception to the weird-and-warped flavor of most of the distortion filters is Displace, so I cover that one last, after all the other distortion filters.

Diffuse Glow

Diffuse Glow is an exception to the other Distort filters because it really doesn't distort pixels—rather, it creates a glow around selected

Figure 8.15
The Diffuse
Glow filter.

areas in your image, using your background color as the basis for the glow color (see Figure 8.15). If you choose a light background color, you'll see a glowing effect; choose a dark color and it will infuse your image with a gritty soap-scum feel.

Glass

The Glass filter emulates the impression of looking at an image through a pane of textured glass (see Figure 8.16). Much like the Displace filter, covered at the end of this section, the Glass filter uses information from a second image to map pixels in your original to a new location. However, unlike the Displace command, you have very little control over the distance and direction the pixels in your image move. You can control the level of distortion, how much noise can be introduced, which file to use as a displacement map, and whether you want to scale the texture to another size.

Figure 8.16
The Glass filter
and its options.

Figure 8.17
The Ocean Ripple filter dialog box.

Ocean Ripple

As the name implies, the Ocean Ripple filter is designed to produce the effect of seeing your image through rippling water (see Figure 8.17). It functions much like the Glass filter you just saw, but you cannot choose the displacement map used for the rippling effect. You can control the ripple size (which really means the frequency) and magnitude.

Pinch

The Pinch filter distorts an image by squeezing it inward or outward. You can enter values between –100% (which bloats your image in a complete outward pinch) and 100% (for a complete inward pinch). Figure 8.18 shows an image of pennies pinched inward in the dialog box's preview image.

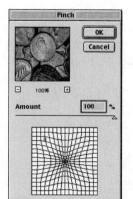

Figure 8.18
The Pinch filter does what its name implies.

Figure 8.19

The Polar
Coordinates filter.
Original images
are shown at left,
with the results
of applying the
Rectangular to
Polar (center) and
Polar to
Rectangular
(right) options.

Polar Coordinates

The Polar Coordinates filter converts rectangular objects into circular shapes, and vice versa. Probably the only popular visual representation of this filter in action is the Mercator projection of the globe. I use Polar Coordinates sometimes for generating unusual or hard-to-draw shapes for logos or background patterns. Figure 8.19 shows the original images on the left, with the results of applying the Rectangular to Polar option in the center, and the Polar to Rectangular options on the right.

Ripple

This filter creates a rippled, wavelike effect. In the example shown in Figure 8.20, I've applied the Ripple filter to an image used to make a tiling background for a Web page. (You'll see Web graphics covered in more detail in Chapter 12, "Web Graphics Essentials.")

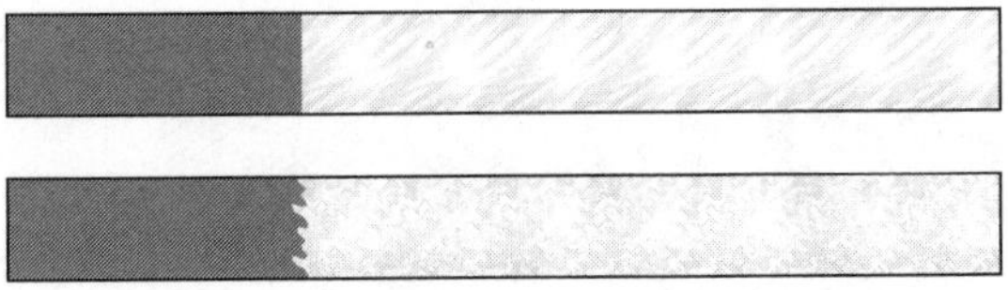

Figure 8.20

The effects of the
Ripple filter.

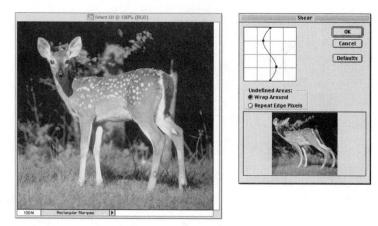

Figure 8.21
The Shear filter
in action.

Shear

This filter can create effects that really do look like funhouse-mirror distortions. It twists your image according to a curve that you specify in the Shear dialog box (see Figure 8.21). To define the curve, click the vertical band that appears in the grid. You can click on the band multiple times, adding a new control point each time for editing the curve. You can click the Reset button to restore the band to its default settings. You also need to choose one of two settings for distorting pixels in areas undefined by the curve: Wrap Around or Repeat Edge Pixels.

Spherize

This filter lets you create an easy-to-produce ray-tracing effect—mapping an image onto a spherical shape. One use for this filter is to make caricatures of people—for some reason (as Figure 8.22 illustrates), it's always funny to mess with the size of someone's head.

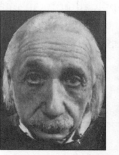 

Figure 8.22
Two spherized
Einsteins, at
100% (left) and
−100% (right).

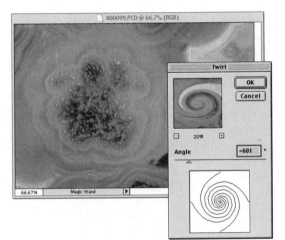

Figure 8.23

The Twirl
dialog box.

Twirl

This whirling effect makes your image look like you dropped it in a blender or washing machine. You can set the angle in the Twirl dialog box. Using higher angles is akin to using the Liquefy setting on your blender, as opposed to Stir. As Figure 8.23 shows, it's also nice to use the Twirl filter on a gridded pattern because the effect is most clear.

Wave

The Wave filter, like Shear, is good for creating funhouse-mirror effects—but you have much more control with this filter. In the Wave dialog box, you can control how many waves you get, from 1 to 999. You can specify minimum and maximum values for the distance (*wavelength*) and height (*amplitude*) of each wave. In addition, you can choose from one of three wave types (Sine, Triangle, and Square) and percentages for horizontal and vertical scaling distortions.

Too many choices? You can always just click the Randomize button in the Wave dialog box to have Photoshop generate its own wave for you. Just as with the Shear filter, you'll need to tell Photoshop what to do with areas containing undefined pixels—wrap the image from one end of the screen to the other with Wrap Around, or tile the image using the Repeat Edge Pixels option.

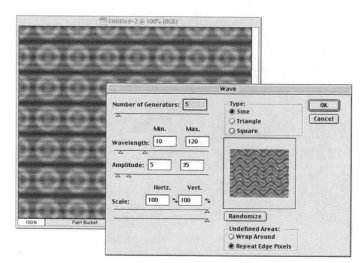

Figure 8.24
The effects of the
Wave filter.

Although you can do all sorts of goofy things to pictures of your friends with the Wave filter or use it to make "flaming" text, the most practical use I have for it is to create interesting textures or background patterns like the one in Figure 8.24. It works especially well when the patterns you start off with have horizontal lines running through them.

ZigZag

With the ZigZag filter, you can create all kinds of realistic water splashes and dropping-pebbles-in-a-pond type effects (see Figure 8.25). It's a natural filter for framing or enhancing any kind of nautical image.

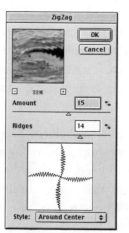

Figure 8.25
The ZigZag
dialog box.

Displace

The Displace filter is by far the most sophisticated of the distortion filters, offering a unique way to add texture and dimension to an image. You'll really have to put your thinking cap on to use this filter effectively and, over time, intuitively.

When you apply the Displace filter, Photoshop asks you to supply the direction and distance you want to move the pixels. The filter can potentially shift each pixel in your image—either horizontally or vertically, and to the left or to the right. The directional instructions the Displace filter uses are determined by a second image you specify, called a *displacement map* (also called a *dmap*).

The Displace filter looks at the brightness of each pixel in your displacement map and uses the color value it assigns to determine which pixels in your original image to move and how far it should move them. (You might want to refer back to the discussion of color and brightness in Chapter 4, "Color Essentials.") The important part to remember is that brightness represents a color's intensity; a brightness value of 0 translates into solid black, and the highest brightness value—100—represents solid white. Here's how the Displace filter assesses each pixel:

- Black pixels have the lowest value. They are displaced down and to the right. Values in between medium gray and black are displaced in the same direction (down, to the right, or both), but to a lesser amount than that specified in the Displace dialog box.

- White pixels have the highest value. They are displaced up and to the left. Values in between medium gray and white are displaced in the same direction (up, to the left, or both), but to a lesser amount than that specified in the Displace dialog box.

- Neutral or medium gray pixels remain static; they are not displaced.

You can use any file saved in native Photoshop format (as long as it's not in Bitmap mode) as a displacement map, but you'll get the most predictable results from seamless tiles or plain geometric designs, preferably in grayscale mode, for reasons I'll go into a little later. A number of displacement map files come packaged with Photoshop; you can also search on the Web or commercial online services for tried-and-true displacement maps that other Photoshop users have created and made available to the public. Figure 8.26 shows a very simple demonstration of the Displace filter at work.

In the Displace dialog box, you can enter values for horizontal and vertical displacement, as shown at the top of Figure 8.26. These values are actually percentages, not pixel amounts. The highest value you can enter, 100, will displace areas in your image an absolute value of 128 pixels when they correspond to solid black or white areas of the displacement map.

After you use the Displace dialog box to specify an amount to shift pixels horizontally and vertically, Photoshop prompts you to choose a file as your displacement map (dmap). As you experiment with dmaps, you'll be better able to predict from looking at them what your displaced results will look like. Once you've selected a dmap file, the Displace filter will shift pixels in your image according to the color values of pixels in the dmap.

note

From here I can hear Barbie saying, "Math is hard!" Well, that might be, but I've long contended that graphic designers and Photoshop users in general already know and can understand more math than they give themselves credit for. The best way to get a handle on displacement maps is to roll up your sleeves and try mapping a sample image or two to see what kind of results you get.

Figure 8.26
The Displace filter moves pixels in an image (left) according to the brightness values in a second image that you specify, called a displacement map (center). The results are shown at right.

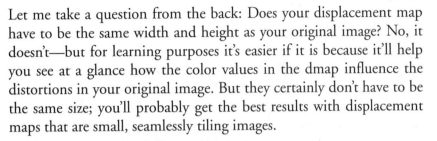

Let me take a question from the back: Does your displacement map have to be the same width and height as your original image? No, it doesn't—but for learning purposes it's easier if it is because it'll help you see at a glance how the color values in the dmap influence the distortions in your original image. But they certainly don't have to be the same size; you'll probably get the best results with displacement maps that are small, seamlessly tiling images.

Photoshop has two ways of handling differences in size between images and their dmaps. You can click the radio button Stretch To Fit in the Displace dialog box, which forces the dmap to stretch to match the proportions of your original. Alternatively, you can click the radio button marked Tile, which treats the dmap as a repeating tile pattern. Figure 8.27 shows the results of clicking the Tile radio button when displacing an image. This is the only setting changed from Figure 8.26, when I displaced the same image using the same displacement map, stretched to fit. Most of the dmaps included with Photoshop work well as repeating tile patterns—which is good to remember when you're in a rush to whip up some new backgrounds.

Here's one last point I feel obliged to make before you turn to Exercise 8.1 and try using your own displacement map. A lot of the calculations involved in determining the way the dmap works depend on how many channels are in that image. It's simplest to imagine using a grayscale dmap, which has only one channel. Pixels are displaced according to the x- and y-axes in this channel, as described a little earlier: white (or high) values are displaced upward according to the specified Vertical Scale value, and to the left as defined by the Horizontal Scale value. Black (or low) values

Figure 8.27

Clicking the Tile radio button instead of Stretch to Fit in the Displace dialog box can produce very different—and dramatic—results.

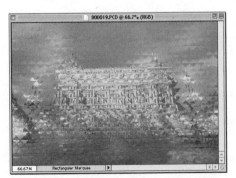

use the Vertical Scale and Horizontal Scale values to displace pixels down and to the right, respectively. But when a displacement map has two or more color channels—remember, RGB and Lab images have three channels, and CMYK images have four—the filter displaces according to the first two channels. It uses the first channel to set horizontal displacement, and the second channel to determine vertical displacement. As a result, it gets much harder to predict how your image will be displaced when you've got to think about color range differences in individual channels rather than the map as a whole. At first, anyway, better you should stick with grayscale displacement maps!

note

If you take a look at the dmaps packaged with Photoshop, you'll notice that although they are RGB images, the Blue channel in each is empty. This makes sense, because there's no reason for an RGB displacement map to contain any information in the third channel when the Displacement filter uses only the first two channels.

Noise Filters

The filters in this category help you clear up graininess in images—or actively add it. I cover adding graininess first.

Add Noise

This filter can give your images a gritty look, one that you can almost feel (see Figure 8.28). Because the Add Noise filter introduces randomly colored pixels into an image, it also has a lot of potential for creating textured backgrounds.

Figure 8.28

Use the Add Noise filter at a high setting as a basis for creating textures from scratch.

EXERCISE 8.1

Using a Displacement Map

1. Open your image for mapping, and then determine which displacement map you plan to use. A number of displacement maps are included with Photoshop in the Plug-Ins folder, in a subfolder called Displacement maps. Here, I'm using a picture of a windsurfer as my base image and a displacement map from Adobe called Crumbles.

   You don't actually have to open your displacement map file within Photoshop—you'll be prompted to select the displacement map after you apply the Displace filter command—but I tend to open the one I'm using to remind myself of the effect I'm going after.

①

2. Make sure your original image is your active document. Select Distort from the Filter menu and then choose Displace from the Distort submenu.

②

3. In the Displace dialog box, you'll need to make some decisions about how many pixels to displace, how to map the differently sized images to one another, and what to display in undefined areas. Here, I've chosen the Tile option to tile the displacement map, and the Repeat Edge Pixels option to fill any gaps left by the mapping algorithm.

③

4. Next, you'll be prompted to select a displacement map. Scroll through your directory structure to select the file you want to use. Click OK.

④

5. You've done it! Stand back and assess the results of your displacement mapping.

How about trying a different displacement map and seeing what that one looks like? Or what kind of results can you get when you change the number of pixels to displace? The more you experiment with the Displace filter, the more you'll be convinced you can add any and every kind of texture imaginable to your images.

⑤

You can type a value between 1 and 999 in the Add Noise dialog box or drag the slider control; higher values add more noise, which provides a very grainy effect. When you specify a value for adding noise—say, 20—Photoshop can then replace each pixel with a color up to 20 values greater or less than your original color. As a result, the greater the amount of noise you use, the more pronounced and colorful the effect you'll see in your image. If you click the Monochromatic check box, though, Photoshop adds noise in all channels, so that the filtered effect depends on differences in luminance, not hue—thus producing noise that is gray in color.

In the Add Noise dialog box, you'll see two radio buttons for the distribution method, Uniform and Gaussian. The Uniform method picks colors at random to replace the original pixels, using the range you specified. The Gaussian method for picking colors uses the Gaussian bell curve, so you'll get a much more extreme distribution with many more light and dark pixels.

Despeckle

This filter under the Noise submenu helps to reduce noise or blur oversharpened areas. It can also remove imperfections from a dusty scan or interference from video stills. Unfortunately, the Despeckle filter doesn't have its own dialog box—so there's no way to tweak its options directly.

Dust & Scratches

This filter targets small areas in an image that contrast strongly with surrounding pixels and helps blend them in for a continuous effect. In the Dust & Scratches dialog box, you can enter a Threshold value between 0 and 255 to tell Photoshop which pixels to change when it analyzes them (see Figure 8.29). Photoshop treats the value you enter as a tolerance setting; it finds and changes contrasting pixels within an otherwise continuously toned area if those pixels have brightness values that fall outside that tolerance level. In the Dust & Scratches dialog box you can also enter a Radius value (between 1 and 16 pixels) to tell Photoshop how wide an area it should search at a time.

Figure 8.29

The Dust & Scratches filter in action.

Median

This filter has an interesting approach to reducing noise. After you specify a radius (between 1 and 16 pixels) for Photoshop to search, the program determines the median brightness of all pixels in each area and replaces the center pixel with that value.

One of the single most useful functions for the Median and Dust & Scratches filters—in conjunction with one or more of the Blur filters—is to obliterate moiré patterns on images scanned from a printed copy. (Remember—you don't notice the dots in a halftone, but your scanner always does!)

I should say up front that most newer scanners now have plug-ins for fixing this kind of common problem, but not all do. If your scanner doesn't have a descreening plug-in, you should experiment with using combinations of the Median, Dust & Scratches, and Gaussian Blur filters. If the scanned photos are in color, try converting your scanned image to CMYK color mode and applying these blurring filters on each separate channel to get the best results.

Pixelate Filters

These filters introduce some cool painterly effects, making your images look like they were created from large dabs of color, patterns, or

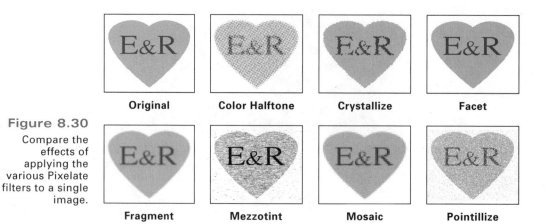

| Original | Color Halftone | Crystallize | Facet |
| Fragment | Mezzotint | Mosaic | Pointillize |

Figure 8.30
Compare the effects of applying the various Pixelate filters to a single image.

tiles. The only problem is, you might have trouble finding practical uses for them. As Figure 8.30 shows, text effects are always a good bet.

Color Halftone

This filter will transform your image to a colorful half-toned jumble, a grid of large halftone dots reminiscent of Roy Lichtenstein's comic-book paintings. The effect is a cute one, although if the dots are too big it can be hard for your viewers to determine what they're looking at.

Crystallize

Crystallize overlays your image with a grid of polygon-shaped cells, kind of like a honeycomb. You can enter a cell size between 3 and 300 to control how big the polygon shapes are. The colors of the pixels in your original image influence the colors used to fill the cell shapes, but much of your original image's detail can be lost—more detail disappears the larger the cell size you choose.

Facet

This filter gives your image a hand-painted look. It searches out larger areas of continuously toned color in your image and fills odd pixels out to create broader similarly colored areas. As a result, you can lose a lot of detail from your original image.

Fragment

This filter produces a somewhat blurry effect, as though the image was in motion. It copies the pixels in your image four times, averages them, and lowers their opacity. The effect is more obvious in line art images; you might find some use for it in blurred background layers just to emphasize an object in a foreground layer.

Mezzotint

The Mezzotint filter uses a pattern of lines, dots, or strokes in one of several weights to simulate your image. If you mezzotint a grayscale image, the result is a two-toned, black-and-white reproduction. For color modes—RGB, CMYK, or Lab—the Mezzotint filter will go to work on each channel in the image.

I like the idea of this filter but think its options for patterns are just too limited; I almost always lean toward using the more roundabout but more controllable method of mezzotinting described in Exercise 7.2, "Creating Mezzotints with Split and Merge Channels."

Mosaic

A little like Crystallize, this filter blends pixels into larger monotone squares. You can specify the size of the squares in the dialog box's Cell Size option box.

Pointillize

If Georges Seurat were alive today, would he just use the Pointillize filter instead of going to all that work in his paintings? Well, maybe not… But this filter is reminiscent of the pointillist style of painting, breaking up the colors in an image into random dots. You can control the size of the dots used by specifying a value between 3 and 300.

Render Filters

The filters in the Render category produce a variety of transformation and lighting effects.

3D Transform

Using the 3D Transform filter, you can manipulate flat images of three-dimensional objects as if you were rotating them with a 3D rendering tool.

This filter works best with simple boxes, spheres, and cylinders—and with smaller rotations that don't compel Photoshop to render much new content. Its real value lies in aligning objects to better match the perspective of other objects in photo montages.

I've saved the step-by-step discussion of how the 3D Transform filter works for Chapter 11, "3D Rendering Essentials," which focuses entirely on creating 3D effects. See Exercise 11.6, "Moving a 3D Object to View from Another Angle."

Clouds

Apply this filter to create a cloud-filled pattern in your image. It uses random pixel values in the range between your foreground and background colors. Just use a light or bright blue color for your foreground color and white for the background, and voilá—instant sky pattern!

If you hold down (Shift) as you apply the Clouds filter, you'll get fewer in-between shades—so your clouds appear fluffier and your sky more vivid.

Difference Clouds

Essentially, this filter runs the Clouds filter and then subtracts the returned pixel values from the existing color values in your image, as if you were working in Difference mode. This filter can produce some pretty ominous storm clouds (see Figure 8.31).

Figure 8.31
You can apply the Clouds or Difference Clouds filters to create an instant sky (left) or cloud-filled pattern (right).

Lens Flare

Most photographers go to great lengths to avoid lens flare effects, but if you want you can use this filter to reproduce the effect of a bright light (like the sun) shining directly into a camera lens, as shown in Figure 8.32. The dialog box asks you to set the type of lens to simulate, and you can also choose a brightness percentage (between 10 and 300) by typing in a value or using the slider control. You'll also need to click in the preview of your image to indicate the center of the bright light source.

Texture Fill

You use this filter in conjunction with the Lighting Effects filter, which is covered just ahead. Use Texture Fill to load an image—grayscale only—into an alpha channel to overlay as a custom texture. Once you've placed a texture in an alpha channel, it can be used as a Texture Channel in the Lighting Effects filter.

Lighting Effects

The Lighting Effects filter is a powerful one. It lets you shine as many as 16 light sources on your image for a variety of shadowy and reflective effects. It can also serve as a primitive method of ray-tracing because you can combine these light sources with texture fills as mentioned earlier.

note

The Lighting Effects filter only works with RGB images—but remember that any texture channel you want to load must be a grayscale image.

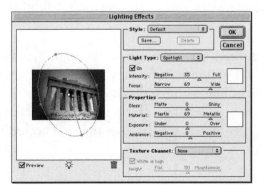

Figure 8.32
The Lighting Effects dialog box.

Lighting Effects has a very complicated dialog box. Following is a list of the properties you'll need to set.

Style

If you've ever set the lighting for a school play or amateur production, you're already familiar with the variety of light sources at your disposal here. Otherwise, take a few minutes to experiment with the Preview check box checked. You can click and move the ellipse (or its handles) on the preview image to reposition the spotlight and the lighting angle. Widen the ellipse to see your image grow brighter. If you click the white center spot, you can move the whole light around.

You can create multiple light sources by dragging additional Light Bulb icons ( ) from beneath the preview image into the preview area. If you change your mind about a light bulb you've added, just drag it to the Trash can icon ( ).

Light Type

Here you can click a check box to turn the light on. You can choose from one of three light types:

- **Spotlight**. Casts the light just like a spotlight on a theater stage or in a circus ring. You can drag the slider controls to adjust the intensity and focus of the spotlight.

- **Omni**. Radiates the light in all directions from the center point, as if the light is sitting directly above your image. If you drag out one of the handles on this ellipse in the preview image, the light becomes more diffuse; dragging the handle inward makes the light more concentrated.

- **Directional**. Aims the light in a straight line from the angle you specify. The directional light you see in the Preview area looks like a straight line with handles, not an ellipse with handles. As with the other two settings, dragging the handles toward or away from the center increases or diffuses the light accordingly.

Properties

For each light source you add, you can set the following properties:

- 👁 **Gloss**. A range of finishes from dull (matte) to shiny (glossy), and percentages thereof.

- 👁 **Material**. The color of the reflected light on your image. Options range from plastic on one extreme to metallic on the other.

- 👁 **Exposure**. The amount of light used.

- 👁 **Ambiance**. The other light present in the image. This lets you combine light from the light source with the general lighting. You can also specify a color in the adjacent color swatch to color the ambient light, and use the slider control to specify the amount of ambient light used.

Texture Channel

Here, you can specify a grayscale image for the Lighting Effects filter to apply as a texture map to the image. You can use this setting to create embossed effects and other surface texture patterns. To use this setting, you must take a few steps before you open the Lighting Effects dialog box.

You must first create an alpha channel and load your desired texture into it. When you open the Lighting Effects dialog box, you must choose the alpha channel containing that texture from the Texture Channel pop-up menu. You can add an embossed effect to the texture by clicking the White Is High check box. The Height slider controls the bumpiness of your texture; you can drag the slider control to select a value from Flat on the low end to Mountainous on the high end.

Great, great—but what can you use all this for? In Exercise 8.2, you'll see how you can use these two filters to add 3D textures and sophisticated lighting to a flat image.

EXERCISE 8.2

Using the Lighting Effects Filter with a Texture Channel

1. For this exercise, you need to open or create a file with two layers—a colored or textured background layer and a layer with some type on it. In separate steps, you're going to emboss the type—with better results than you can get with the Emboss filter—and then add a rocky surface to the background layer.

2. At this point, you need to save your letterforms to an alpha channel—you'll use this alpha channel, not the type layer, to build the embossed or carved effect. Choose Load Selection from the Select menu. In the Channel drop-down menu, you should see an option named after the wording in your type layer, followed by the word Transparency. Click OK. You'll then see a series of marching ants tracing your letterforms.

3. Now choose Save Selection from the Select menu. Give your new channel any name you want and click OK. You can deselect the marquee too.

④

4. Display the Layers palette and uncheck the eye icon next to the type layer—you won't be needing this layer any more. Click the background layer's name to target it.

5. Choose Lighting Effects from the Render submenu of the Filter menu. Here, I set the light source to about 45 degrees, so that it appears to be coming from the upper-right corner of the image. I toyed with the Light Type and Properties settings until I was happy with those effects as well.

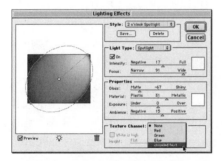

6. Now for the most important part—click the drop-down menu next to the Texture Channel label near the bottom of the dialog box and choose the text channel you saved earlier. I've also unchecked the White is High box to make the effect look chiseled—if I left the box checked, the type would look raised and embossed.

After you've fussed with Lighting Effects settings to your satisfaction, you can click the Save button to save them for future use. This is a good idea if you're going to create a number of textured effects for the same project, so they can all enjoy the same light source settings. Click OK when you're finished.

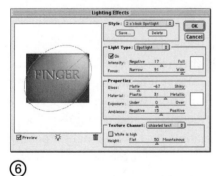

⑥

7. Here's a look at the composite effect (see Figure 8.33). At this point you can create new layers with textured patterns—a fill layer is the easiest way to do so—and apply this Lighting Effects filter again to see these letterforms chiseled against a different background. You've now seen how one filter can create two very different kinds of textured effects—and its potential to create a great many more.

Figure 8.33
Check the White is High box in the Lighting Effects dialog box to create embossed text (top). You uncheck it to create chiseled, recessed text (bottom).

Sharpen Filters

Sharpen filters help draw distinct edges from blurry objects. They're especially useful after you've scaled or distorted images using the Effects submenu from the Image menu.

Sharpen and Sharpen More

The Sharpen filter increases the contrast between neighboring pixels throughout an image. Sharpen More is just a more intense application of the Sharpen filter.

Sharpen Edges

Like the Sharpen filter, Sharpen Edges increases contrast, but only affects the edges of each object in your image. It doesn't touch continuously toned areas. Any of these first three Sharpen filters are useful to apply after you've scaled an image or a selection to a smaller size, or executed another distortion or skew effect.

Unsharp Mask

As shown in Figure 8.34, this filter emphasizes the sharpness of the edges of each object in your image. The real advantage of this filter over the other Sharpen filters is its dialog box, which lets you specify a percentage (up to 500%) for how much the image should be sharpened. You can also specify in pixels a radius for how far the sharpening should extend beyond contrasting edges. The Threshold field is useful

Figure 3.34

The Unsharp Mask filter dialog box.

when you want to specify sharpening only when the contrast between edges is a significant amount; this lets you selectively sharpen edges only when they'd stand out the most. A good use for applying Unsharp Mask is after you've converted an image's color mode from RGB to CMYK or made any other conversion involving interpolation.

Sketch Filters

The filters in the Sketch category represent a variety of drawing techniques. On the whole, they simplify your image to rough outlines and replace many of the original hues in your image with your chosen foreground and background colors or sometimes include shades of both. Most of these filters work best when you use black and white as your foreground and background colors. Let me also point out that the Sketch filters work only with grayscale and RGB images. Figure 8.35 showcases the effects of each of the Sketch filters.

Bas Relief

The Bas Relief filter tries to emulate a three-dimensional embossment of your image using the foreground color for the highlights and the background color for your shadows. All colors in your image are reduced to shades of the foreground or background color, depending on their lightness values and the setting you specify for light direction.

Chalk & Charcoal

This filter treats your image as a mixed media composition. The charcoal strokes tend to appear rather broad and rough, whereas the chalk strokes are heavy and powdery. The filter uses your foreground color as the basis for the charcoal strokes and uses your background color as the basis of the chalk strokes. The two media are drawn from opposing diagonal angles, so they appear crosshatched wherever they smudge up against one another.

Charcoal

This filter varies a little from the previous filter, Chalk & Charcoal. The Charcoal filter uses your foreground color as the basis for the charcoal

Original

Bas Relief

Chalk & Charcoal

Charcoal

Chrome

Conté Crayon

Graphic Pen

Halftone Pattern

Note Paper

Photocopy

Plaster

Reticulation

Figure 8.35
Compare the
effects of
applying the
various Sketch
filters to a single
image.

Stamp

Torn Edges

Water Paper

strokes and uses your background color as the color of the paper this sketch is sitting on.

Chrome

The Chrome filter creates some impressive text effects by applying a highly reflective, metallic sheen to any image. Its options are straightforward; you can specify Detail, which controls how many reflective surfaces are created, and Smoothness, which tracks the smoothness and

number of edges. The higher you raise the smoothness level, the fewer edges you'll see.

Conté Crayon

The Conté crayons found at art supply stores are very hard, waxy crayons you can buy in basic colors like black and white. When you apply this filter, you can create highly contrasting images with hard edges, but also a soft, shaded texture effect at blend points—almost as if your image were drawn on textured paper, similar to the effect you'd get by drawing with Conté crayons. You can use one of the texture selections or specify your own file to use as the basis for the texture.

Graphic Pen

I really like using this filter for mimicking the style of sketching in ink with a Rapidograph pen. It uses your foreground color as a scratchy, solid ink color over any dark or shadowed area of your original. The rest of your image is solidly replaced by your background color. Use black and white—or any dark hue paired with white—as your foreground and background color for best results. The options you can set here include stroke length, the light/dark balance (which affects which colors get filled in with your foreground color and which with the background color), and stroke direction.

Halftone Pattern

This filter lets you apply dots, lines, or circular strokes in one of several patterns to simulate a halftone pattern over your image. You can create some very dramatic effects by experimenting with this filter; if you apply this filter to line art portraits, you can create filtered images similar to the drawings of people found as illustrations in *The Wall Street Journal* or used in Barnes & Noble's advertising.

The Halftone Pattern filter lets you control the size of the pattern, contrast, and pattern type (circle, dot, or line)—but you can't reposition the center of the circular halftone pattern, so that one tends to work best when the subject of your image is well-positioned in the center of your graphic.

Note Paper

This filter applies a soft, papery texture to your image, as if your image were printed on tissue paper. You can control the Image Balance settings on a scale of 0 to 50 (which controls the contrast between light and dark areas), Graininess (or paper roughness), and Relief (or how much 3D embossing is applied).

Photocopy

The Photocopy filter infuses your image with the look of a second- or third-generation printed Xerox copy. The filter greatly reduces the number of colors in your image and loses much of the image's detail. It fills in any shadow or midtone areas with your foreground color and highlights areas with your background color, so choosing the default black and white as your foreground and background colors will net you the most predictable results.

Plaster

If you've ever made impressions of your handprints in wet plaster or scratched your initials in freshly laid sidewalk concrete, you've seen the general application for how the Plaster filter works. This filter simplifies complex images by applying a Threshold setting, and then fills in most shadowed areas with your foreground color and the remainder with the background color. It produces strong highlights and shadows in the edge borders to form wet-looking 3D contours, and blends a gradient from the background to foreground color across the image.

Reticulation

This filter renders your image as if it were a dark pen-and-ink drawing in black and gray shades on a textured canvas. Your foreground color is used to fill in shadow areas, and highlights and midtones are filled with your background colors. The dialog box options let you adjust Density on a scale of 0 to 50, which controls contour mapping and the density of rendered pixels. The Black level controls how much image detail is retained; lower levels maintain more original detail, whereas higher values produce more abstract ink washings. The higher the White level, the more the image highlights and midtones are filled solidly with the background color.

Stamp

This filter makes your image look as if it had been imprinted by a giant rubber stamp. It converts your image to a two-color one with no shading in between, using your foreground color as the ink color and the background color as the paper color.

Torn Edges

This is another filter that converts your image to two colors, using the foreground color to fill in all shadows and dark areas and the background color for highlights and midtones. Here, though, the border edges between contrasting areas are made to appear as if they have been generated by torn bits of paper; the overall effect blurs all detail from photographs, but can be used effectively on text or in generating edges for a layer mask.

Water Paper

The Water Paper filter makes the colors in your image start to run and bleed into a lightly textured background, as if it were a pen-and-ink drawing soaked in a puddle of water. Options for this filter's dialog box include fiber length, which controls the wetness of the effect, and the length of each painted stroke. You can also adjust the image's brightness and contrast here.

Stylize Filters

These filters can produce dramatic changes to the color of pixels in an image, often with artistic results. Figure 8.36 showcases the effects of each of the Stylize filters.

Diffuse

This filter creates a blurred effect as if you were viewing the image through a pane of frosted glass. You can use this filter to add eroded or weathered edges to objects and type. Using the Lighten Only option in the dialog box will make your objects appear to dissolve into nothingness, whereas the Darken Only option makes it look like the borders are spreading—*bleeding*, in design speak—into surrounding areas.

Original

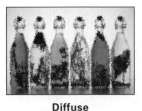

Diffuse

Emboss

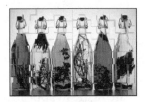

Extrude

Find Edges

Glowing Edges

Solarize

Tiles

Trace Contour

Figure 8.36
Compare the
effects of
applying the
various Stylize
filters to a single
image.

Wind

Emboss

This filter provides an easy way to create all kinds of raised lettering and embossed edge effects. You control the degree of the embossing by entering the angle for the direction of the light source, ranging from 0 to 360 degrees. You can also enter negative values from 0 to –360 degrees, which are automatically converted. You can also specify the depth in pixels of the embossing and a percentage (up to 500%) for applying color.

Exercise 8.3 creates a good all-purpose textured effect—perfect for Web background graphics or in building 3D objects—that looks more complicated to create than it really is.

EXERCISE 8.3

Creating All-Purpose Stucco

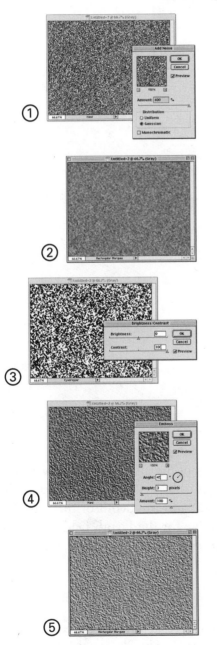

1. Create a new grayscale document for your texture pattern. Choose Add Noise from the Noise submenu of the Filter menu. Click the Gaussian Distribution radio button and set the amount to 400%.

2. Choose Gaussian Blur from the Blur submenu of the Filter menu. Set the radius to a low number, say between 0.5 and 2.0. The larger the Gaussian Blur radius setting, the coarser your stucco pattern. Here, I've set the radius setting to 1.5.

3. Then set an extreme level of contrast by using the Brightness/Contrast dialog box. Choose Adjust from the Image menu, and then choose Brightness/Contrast from the Adjust submenu. Crank the contrast all the way up to 100.

4. Applying the Emboss filter is the next crucial step. Set the angle to 135 degrees to keep the light source coming from the upper-left corner, or at 45 degrees to direct the light source from the upper-right corner.

5. If the stucco effect is a little harsh for your taste, use the Blur or Blur More filters to weather the edges of the pattern.

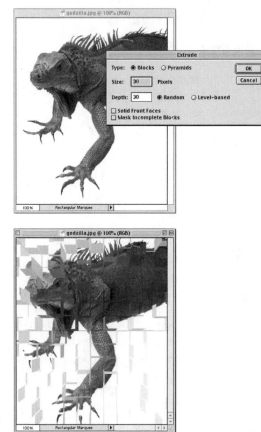

Figure 8.37
The Extrude
dialog box.

Extrude

With this filter, you can map your image onto a set of 3D blocks or pyramids that will seem to burst out of the image directly toward you. You can set the size of the pyramids or blocks by entering a value (between 2 and 255) in the Size field, and the depth of the extruding pyramid or block by entering a value for the Depth field (see Figure 8.37). There is also a Random setting that will generate random depths for the extruding objects.

Find Edges

You can use this effect to produce images that look like traced outlines of your originals drawn in charcoal or pencil. The filter works by searching

out areas of major color contrast and then enhancing the pixels along the contrasting edges.

Solarize

This filter reproduces the photographic effect of *solarization*, in which film is exposed to light part way through the development process. After you apply the Solarize filter, some of the tones in your image will be reversed—as if you had combined the negative version of your image with the positive version. The net result is that some of the tones are reversed for an interesting (if less-than-practical) effect.

Tiles

The Tiles filter divides areas of your image into square checks and offsets them slightly from their original positions. From the Tiles dialog box, you can specify the minimum number of tiles to appear in each row and column, as well as the maximum percentage each tile can be offset. You can choose to fill the gaps between the tiles with the foreground or background color. Alternatively, you can fill gaps between the tiles with a reverse color image of your original picture by clicking the Inverse Image radio button, or with the original image by clicking the Unaltered Image radio button. The filter can be useful for creating background patterns.

Trace Contour

This filter produces effects similar to Find Edges. Here, though, you can enter a value between 0 and 255 in the Level field to determine at what level of contrast you want to trace the image's contours. You can also use the Upper and Lower options to specify whether the value you've entered is the point above or below which contours should be traced.

Wind

This filter helps add the effect of motion to an image by adding small horizontal lines to object borders with transitional areas of color in your image. You can choose the intensity of the windblown effect in the Wind dialog box by choosing among the Wind, Blast, and Stagger settings. The dialog box also lets you choose which side—left or right—to simulate the wind's direction.

Texture Filters

Photoshop's Texture filters apply a texture-mapping algorithm over your image to create the impression that it's lying on a textured or contoured surface. Figure 8.38 shows how each of the Texture filters makes its presence felt.

Craquelure

The Craquelure filter is designed to give the effect of a very old painting that has begun to crack. This can create dramatic effects when used on simple line graphics or in creating distressed type, but it's tough to use it to enhance full-color photographic imagery.

Grain

The Grain filter offers a variety of techniques for adding noise to an image. Like Add Noise, it's useful as a first step in creating a lot of textures from scratch. The Grain dialog box lets you control Intensity (which affects how heavily the grain effect appears) and Contrast (which balances light and dark values). You can choose your Grain Type from a drop-down list and select Regular, Soft, Sprinkles, Clumps, Contrast, Enlarged, Stippled, Horizontal, Vertical, or Speckled.

Mosaic Tiles

If you experiment with the Texture filters one after another, you'll see that Mosaic Tiles produces almost the same effect as the Craquelure filter. The main difference is that Mosaic Tiles imposes cracks in the image in a repeating grid pattern—living up to the Tiles part of its name, but not acting much like a mosaic. In the Mosaic Tiles dialog box, you can choose options for Tile Size, Grout Width, and how much to lighten the grout to set off the tiles. This is a good filter to use on a brightly colored or lightly textured image to make it suitable for a background or desktop pattern.

Patchwork

Patchwork can create a brightly colored tiled version of your image. Like Mosaic, it overlays a grid pattern on your image, but it then averages the

Original

Craquelure

Grain

Mosaic Tiles

Patchwork

Figure 8.38
Compare the
effects of
applying the
various Texture
filters to a single
image.

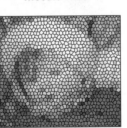
Stained Glass

Texturizer

colors of the pixels within each individual grid square and replaces the contents with that color value. The filter then applies shadows and highlights to each square to add a 3D, beveled effect to their appearance.

Stained Glass

Turn your image into a model for a Tiffany lamp with the Stained Glass filter—it overlays irregularly shaped, interlocking hexagons over your image, borders each shape using your foreground color, and then averages the colors of the pixels within each individual grid square and replaces the contents with that color value. You'll get the most predictable results if you set your foreground color to black. Use the filter's dialog box to control the cell size of each hexagon; the smallest cell size

settings are the only ones that will keep your original image recognizable, but don't be afraid to experiment—you can create some beautiful background patterns by accident with this filter.

Texturizer

This filter emphasizes the creation of a textured surface that seems to lie beneath your image. You can choose textures from the dialog box's Texture drop-down list or load any native Photoshop file you choose as the basis for your texture. The Texturizer dialog box lets you scale the texture before you apply it, so you can better preserve the appearance of your original image if the texture is so large that there's a danger of obliterating the overall look. The filter's options also include a Relief setting for specifying a value for how beveled the texture should appear, and a setting for specifying the light direction.

Video Filters

These filters help you edit images that you get from or plan to output to videotape.

De-Interlace

You can use this filter to remove the interlaced scan lines that accidentally become captured on still video frames.

NTSC Colors

This filter converts colors in your image to the range used in standard television settings.

Other Filters

This Filter menu item is really an odds-and-ends collection of leftovers. It includes a few general filters for changing contrast, as well as the useful Offset filter and, for the truly inspired, the Custom setting for experimenting with creating your own filters.

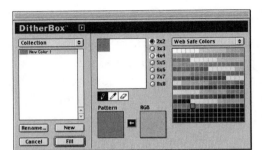

Figure 8.39
The DitherBox
dialog box.

DitherBox

You can use the DitherBox filter to create customized dither patterns for specific RGB colors, for when you convert from RGB colors to Web colors. You can load another color palette, but if you're creating Web graphics you should use the default shown, called Web-safe colors.

To pick a color to dither, click the RGB color square in the DitherBox dialog box (see Figure 8.39). This will spawn the Color Picker dialog box. After you choose a color and close the Color Picker, click the arrow to the left of the RGB color square in the DitherBox dialog box. The filter automatically generates a dither pattern that will substitute for that RGB color. You can edit the pattern by choosing one of the pattern sizes—these square sizes range from 2×2 pixels to 8×8 pixels—and using the pencil and eraser tools to color in the sample.

High Pass

This filter functions similarly to the Sharpen filters by removing gradual tonal changes in your images while preserving highlights. The only option you have in the High Pass dialog box is setting the radius for judging contrast in the image, in a range from 0.1 to 250. The higher the settings you use for High Pass, the more you can distinguish high-contrast from low-contrast areas in your image. Low values tend to strip out the color in your images. You can produce some interesting color-enhancing results with this filter, though, if you apply it to individual color channels only.

Minimum and Maximum Filters

The Minimum and Maximum filters are the digital equivalents of the traditional printing concept of spreading and choking. The Minimum filter can enhance dark areas in your image, swelling them outward and giving them more oomph. The Maximum filter does exactly the opposite with light areas of your image.

Offset

Buried as it is at the bottom of the "Other" filters, I wouldn't be surprised if you haven't experimented much with Offset. But it's a wonderfully versatile function for moving your image or portions of your image over a specified number of pixels (see Figure 8.40). Photoshop doesn't have a "step and repeat" function, but many Photoshop designers accomplish such things by replicating a layer and using the Offset filter to offset the repeated part a certain distance, such as for shadows.

Custom

Do you harbor dreams of becoming the next Kai Krause? It's just a first step, but you'll want to try the Custom setting from the Other submenu under the Filter menu (see Figure 8.41). With its controls, you can create algorithms for generating your own sharpening, blurring, and embossing filters.

Keep an eye out for *custom kernels* that Photoshop devotees make available on the commercial online services and on their Web sites for public use; these already-tested settings are a nice way to discover new filter variations without a lot of legwork.

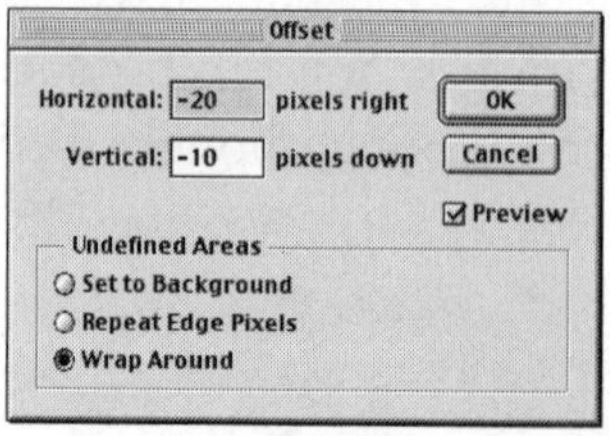

Figure 8.40

The Offset
dialog box.

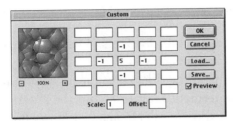

Figure 8.41

The Custom dialog box.

Digital Watermarking

Adobe licensed the Digimarc watermarking filters for inclusion in Photoshop as a way to prevent unauthorized use of copyrighted images. To take full advantage of this service, though, you have to register with Digimarc and pay a fee to obtain your own identifier pattern to use as an electronic watermark.

Embed Watermark

This filter embeds identifying information into an image as background noise (see Figure 8.42). These digital watermarks are not visible to the untrained eye; once embedded, they're impossible to shake—the watermark can still be read even if the image has been printed, rescanned, filtered, and manipulated in all kinds of ways. Your identifying information includes your Digimarc Locator Service ID Number (assigned to you by Digimarc when you register), a content rating to specify if the material is unsuitable for children, and an URL for the Digimarc Locator Service.

Figure 8.42

The Embed Watermark dialog box.

Read Watermark

This filter decodes an embedded digital watermark in an image. If you open a watermarked image, you'll see a copyright symbol appear next to the artist's name in the title bar of the image window. You can then use the Read Watermark filter to obtain the artist's creator ID. After you know the ID, you can call Digimarc's toll-free 800 number—which appears in the filter's dialog box—or check Digimarc's Web site to find out how to get in touch with the artist to ask for permission or to purchase rights to use the image.

Summary

There are a great many third-party filters available as Photoshop plug-ins—both the commercial and shareware or freeware variety. In Appendixes B and C, I include contact information of the makers of the major commercial filter collections and those created and made publicly available by individuals.

As you've seen, you can use Photoshop's filters across a wide spectrum of image editing, from subtle changes to earthquake-level distortions. I want you to leave with an appreciation for the subtler ways to invoke filtering changes—for example, at partial opacity on a layer—as opposed to the sweeping changes you get from applying a filter from the menu command.

Next up in Chapter 9, "Scanning Essentials," is an overview of how to create good-looking scans. If you aren't using a scanner to snag images, feel free to skip ahead to the discussion of image retouching in Chapter 10, "Retouching Essentials."

9 Scanning Essentials

IN THIS CHAPTER

Scanner Specifications

◉

Resolution Issues

◉

Halftone Scanning

◉

Adjusting Brightness/Contrast

Just as you'd expect better results from high-end cameras (and film) than you would from lower-priced consumer models, you can expect the quality of your scans to vary widely depending on the device you use to digitize your images. If quality is the most crucial factor in your projects, you're far better off outsourcing your photo and slide scanning work to a professional service bureau for drum scanning or high-end flatbed scanning. Many publishing companies reserve their in-house scanners almost exclusively for *FPO* scans—creating "for position only" images that the service bureau replaces with its own high-resolution scans just before final film output.

But if you have a small production budget or have more artistic uses for a scanner—such as capturing textures from or reproducing images of real-life objects—it'll be worth it to learn techniques for optimizing your desktop scans for final output. Many designers are of two minds about desktop scanners. Although such flatbed scanners are deceptively simple to operate, it can be very difficult to cajole them into producing high-quality scans.

If you're in a shopping mood, "Which scanner should I buy?" is always a popular query on Usenet newsgroups such as **comp.graphics.apps. photoshop** or **rec.photo.digital**—you'll get a large focus-group sample, and you'll usually hear about newer models than those profiled in any book. If you're unfamiliar with Usenet, the easiest way to see which newsgroups are discussing the topics of interest to you is using a keyword search of the Usenet discussions section of Deja.com (**http:// www.deja.com/**).

Chapter 1, "System Essentials," touched on basic hardware questions about the kinds of scanners available and how they work. This chapter focuses on how to get the most from desktop scanners on an everyday basis, as well as covers the following topics related to scanning images in Photoshop:

- 👁 Criteria to look for in images to be scanned

- 👁 Getting the most out of your scanning interface's options

- 👁 Resolution issues, including special requirements for scanning slides and line art

- 👁 Adjusting brightness and contrast in your scanned images

Scanner Specifications

If you're considering purchasing a new scanner, the following are features you'll want to bear in mind as you evaluate one model against another. The most important differences among scanners have to do with how they register light (or how they produce pixels), how many pixels they can see per inch (resolution), and how they register shadows.

- 👁 **Registering light**. High-end drum scanners like the ones at service bureaus use *photomultiplier tubes* (PMTs). The flatbed scanner on your desktop uses *charge-coupled devices* (CCDs), which are faster than PMTs but not as sensitive about picking up low levels of light.

- 👁 **Resolution**. The more CCDs across the scanner bed, the greater the resolution; 300ppi or 600ppi are common. Most scanners also offer interpolation, which attains higher resolution by making guesses about image data. Because interpolation doesn't add any true detail to your scans, you should find out a scanner's maximum optical resolution when evaluating models—this will avoid confusion with interpolated performance. Photoshop can interpolate data better than most scanners, so if you need to simulate higher levels of resolution than your scanner can accommodate, you're probably better off scanning at your scanner's maximum optical resolution. You'll find tips for Photoshop interpolation later in this chapter.

- 👁 **Dynamic range**. This term refers to the range of density the scanner can see—that is, how wide a range of light and dark tones it can distinguish. Dynamic range is measured on a scale from 0.0 (solid white) to 4.0 (solid black). A scanner's dynamic range is given as a number within this range and indicates how much of this range it can distinguish. An average desktop scanner might have a dynamic range of about 2.4; higher-end color flatbed scanners range from 2.8 to 3.2 or so. Drum scanners have the highest performance when it comes to dynamic range; these units frequently have a dynamic range of 3.0 and up. This is an important setting to look for if you scan many transparencies.

- 👁 **Bit depth**. As you saw in Chapter 2's discussion of file formats, images that store information at high bit depths (such as 24-bit images) capture more information and can capture more colors than images with lower bit depths. As a result, the higher the bit depth of your scanned images, the better their potential quality is likely to be. Many manufacturers now offer 30-bit, 36-bit, and 42-bit scanners that capture more detail from an image than a 24-bit scanner can. Photoshop can use the extra information because it can handle high bit depths (up to 64-bit). The extra detail is most noticeable when you're scanning film—slides and negatives—rather than color prints.

- **Color scanning method**. Color flatbed scanners filter red, green, and blue separately, either in three passes—where values for each color are captured for the entire image one at a time—or in a single all-in-one pass. Three-pass scanning is simpler from a machine-design standpoint, but it takes three times as long as one-pass scanning, and color misalignment problems can occur when the three separate scans are combined. As a result, three-pass scanning is considered out of date these days. When shopping for a scanner, you should consider only single-pass models.

- **Scanning area**. On a practical level, you want to make sure that your scanner can handle the largest images you want to scan. This is what limits the usefulness of handheld scanners—they're wonderfully portable, but have a scanning area only about 4 inches wide. With flatbed scanners, you can usually choose from letter size (8.5 inches by 11 inches) and legal size (8.5 inches by 14 inches). If you need to scan a document that's larger than the size of the scanner bed, you can scan different parts of the image in separate files and then use Photoshop to stitch them together.

Choosing Good Scanning Material

Is it too obvious to say that the scans you'll get are only as good as the originals you use? Successful reproduction has much more to do with the quality of your original image than with any tweaking you do later in Photoshop. This is especially important when you're making your own scans with a low- or midrange desktop scanner, because you'll be limited in terms of what corrections you can make during the scanning

process. Following is a straightforward checklist of good-to-have features in your raw material:

- 👁 **Sharp, focused images with good contrast**. What constitutes good contrast? Look for easily discerned white and black elements with a wide range of tones between.

- 👁 **Lots of detail throughout the image**. You want a good range of highlights, midtones, and shadowed areas.

- 👁 **Good color balance without an overcast of a single color**. Even if you plan to emphasize a single color in your final image, better you should add it later in Photoshop, if possible.

- 👁 **Clean originals**. Make sure your scanning materials are free of dust, smudges, and fingerprints before you put them on the scanner.

If you have a choice between very similar images when you're making a scan, look for greater detail in terms of highlights, midtones, and shadows.

note

Here's one situation where this whole checklist will matter little. When you're planning to do a great deal of photocompositing and image editing and just need to scan an image to capture an object's outline, it doesn't matter much if the overall lighting or quality of the image is poor.

Installing Scanning Software

Most scanner manufacturers create plug-in modules that can replace the scanner's stand-alone software and allow scanning from within Photoshop. After you use a Photoshop plug-in to make a scan, a new untitled document containing the scanned image opens in Photoshop.

Like the third-party Photoshop filters you saw in the last chapter, scanner plug-ins can be copied to the Plug-Ins folder within your Photoshop folder. On both Mac and Windows machines, the best place to keep scanner plug-ins is in the Import/Export folder within Photoshop's Plug-Ins folder. After you've installed your scanner's plug-in, it should appear as a menu item in the Import submenu under the File menu (see Figure 9.1).

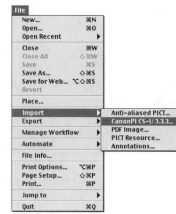

Figure 9.1

You can use plug-ins provided by your scanner manufacturer or a TWAIN module to scan images into Photoshop.

Your scanner should come with its own Photoshop plug-in or a TWAIN (Technology Without An Interesting Name) module that you can use to scan directly into Photoshop or another graphics or page layout program. Instead of launching a separate scanning program, you need only select Import from Photoshop's File menu, select the scanner plug-in (or the TWAIN source if your scanner doesn't have its own plug-in), and the scanning interface will appear, letting you make adjustments and proceed with scanning. Other scanning software options available to you include third-party commercial packages such as Agfa FotoLook or OmniPage Pro.

Scanning Options

Most scanner software packages have settings for correcting brightness, contrast, and color, among other options (see Figure 9.2). The first

Figure 9.2

The interface for a scanner's Photoshop plug-in.

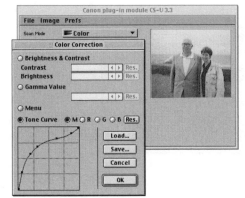

Figure 9.3

Many scanner plug-ins let you correct brightness, contrast, and other options.

step in getting oriented to your scanner is to take a look at some of the settings you can adjust in your scanner interface's window (see Figure 9.3). Until you know what they do, you'll never use them!

note

Before you slide your artwork into your scanner and click the Scan button in the interface's dialog box, you should know how you plan to use the final image. Your end use helps determine the right resolution and color mode for scanning.

Preview

Position your material in the scanner and click the Preview button to get a preview of how your image will look when digitized. If you need to rotate the original, you'll usually get better results by scanning squarely and letting Photoshop perform the rotation rather than scanning the original at an angle. Some scanning software lets you specify the size of the preview scan, along with color mode preferences. If you're scanning a number of large color originals, you may want to preview in grayscale mode—grayscale previews show up onscreen much more quickly than color ones.

Color Mode

Your choices should include line art (black and white), grayscale (8-bit, or 256 shades of gray), and color modes (see Figure 9.4). If your scanner

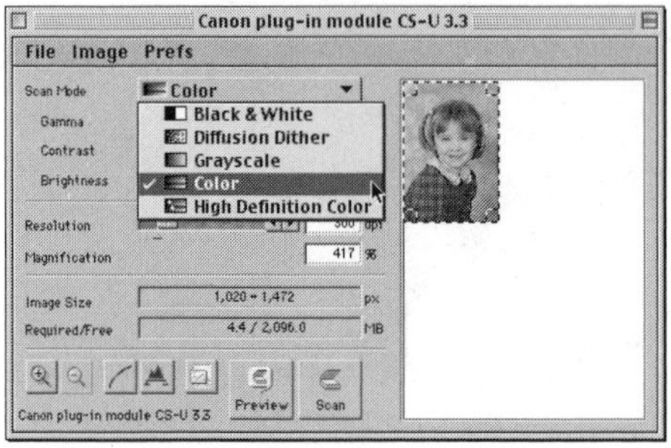

Figure 9.4

Before you preview, you need to decide whether your image will be scanned in grayscale, color, line art, or a halftone mode.

has an option for specifying CMYK mode, ignore it—all scanners scan in RGB, so any CMYK color conversion is generated by the scanner software. If you need to convert your images to CMYK, you are better off letting Photoshop take care of that step.

Cropping

After you preview your scan, you'll be able to see where to reposition the cropping rectangles to select only the portion you want scanned. This will save time in the scanning process and keep the file size smaller.

Sharpening

The scanning process tends to blur the edges of images, so you might be inclined to use your scanning software's options to resharpen them. Unless the blurring is extremely severe, though, you're better off scanning first and then sharpening later in Photoshop, after you've made all your tonal and color adjustments.

Descreening

This option lets you obtain better results when you scan previously printed materials—such as a photo taken from a book or magazine (see Figure 9.5). As a rule, you should go to lengths to avoid scanning prescreened images like these because it produces screen conflicts called moirés that will interfere with the scanned image. If you can't avoid scanning prescreened images, though, descreening is one of a few steps that will help (see "Halftone Scanning" later in this chapter).

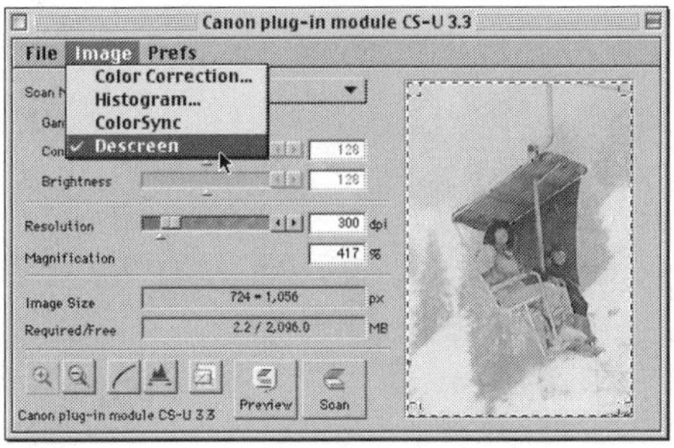

Figure 9.5

Your scanning software might include options for descreening previously halftoned images. If you need to scan an image from a printed publication— such as a magazine, book, or newspaper— make sure you apply your scanner's descreening function first.

Black Point and White Point

Setting the black point and white point defines the high and low ends for the overall tonal range in your scans (see Figure 9.6). By changing these values from the scanner's default, you can automatically give yourself some leverage for later tonal adjustments. I'll cover the usefulness of this trick a little later in this chapter (see "Adjusting Brightness and Contrast"), but for now, a good general rule for improvement is to set the black point at 95 percent (this equals a target black value of 13) and to set the white point at 5 percent (this equals a target white value of 243).

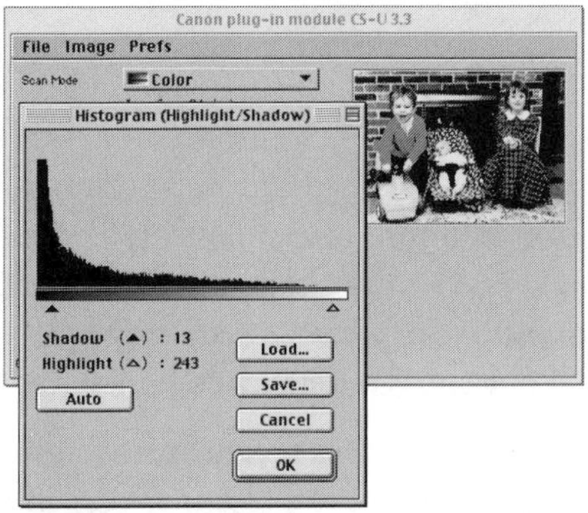

Figure 9.6

Setting the black point and white point within a scanner's interface.

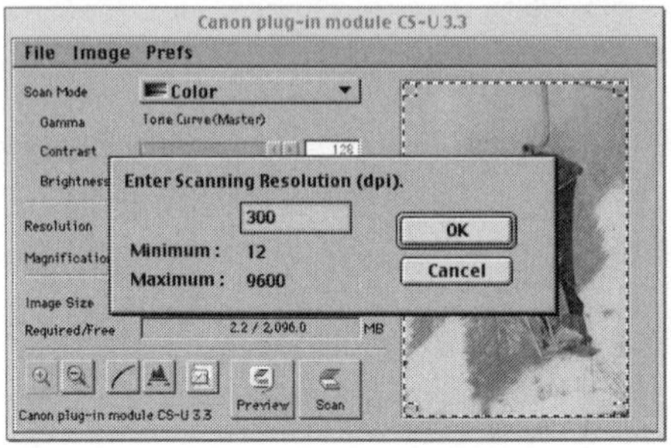

Figure 9.7

Changing resolution within a scanner's Settings dialog box.

Resolution

Your scanner's resolution, which directly affects the optimum resolution of your final scanned image, is the final setting you should consider. Any advertising or promotion you see for a desktop scanner should include details about its optimum resolution capabilities. As a result, changing your scanning resolution is usually one of the easier scanner settings to locate and customize within your Settings dialog box (see Figure 9.7). Even though your settings will probably vary from those pictured here, you can see that changing your scanning resolution involves entering a numeric value for the target scanning resolution.

Because resolution requires more attention than the other options in this section, it's a good idea to step back a second to examine how it works and how it relates to file size—and that warrants a section of its own.

Considering Resolution Issues in Depth

In Chapter 2, I mentioned that image resolution is a measure of how many pixels—that is, how much information—can fit in a given unit of measurement. An image's resolution is commonly measured in pixels per inch (ppi); the more pixels there are per inch in an image, the more detail you'll see. If you scan at too low a resolution, you'll immediately see the results in the scanned image—a blurry or pixelated appearance with not enough detail in the image as a whole.

You might conclude from the previous paragraph that you should always scan at the upper end of your scanner's capabilities, whatever that

might be—say, 300 or 600ppi. But this will lead to a Catch-22 situation—file size is directly tied to your image's resolution, so you wind up with staggeringly huge file sizes.

Scanning for Print Production

So what's the best resolution to use when you're scanning images? If you're scanning images for print production, start by doubling your printing resolution, or line screen frequency, which is measured in lines per inch (lpi). If you don't know at what line screen your job will be printed, your printer can tell you. Your projects will almost certainly use one of the standard line screen settings, such as 85lpi for newspaper printing; 120, 133, or 150lpi for most book and magazine printing; or 200 to 300lpi for coffee-table-quality books.

After you know your line screen—say, 133lpi—you can plan to scan all your photos at twice that number—in this case, 266ppi. If you can't determine the line screen frequency before you start your scanning work, take a conservative approach—scanning at 300ppi (doubling a 150 line screen) might turn out to be overkill, but you won't need to redo your efforts.

You might need a much higher scanning resolution if your image's dimensions in print are greater than the originals. For example, let's assume you're scanning a 2×3-inch image that will appear in print as a final size of 6×9 inches. If your line screen frequency is 120, you first multiply this by 2 to get 240. Then, multiply 240 by 3 (because the final print dimensions are three times larger than the original dimensions). Your scan resolution in this case should be 720ppi.

Scanning for Web or Onscreen Production

What if you're scanning images for use as Web graphics or onscreen multimedia presentations? Although in this case you might never send your images to print to a service bureau's imagesetter, don't dismiss it from the realm of possibility. Thus, as a safeguard, you should still begin by scanning at twice the line screen settings you use for your print work and then downsize to a standard screen resolution using Photoshop. The standard screen resolution for PCs is 96ppi and the Mac standard is 72ppi; optimizing at the higher of the two will give you the best results for the widest onscreen viewing audience.

Interpolation Issues

When you resize an image either up or down—also called *resampling* or *interpolating*—you're bound to lose some information because Photoshop has to make guesses about how to fill in missing pixels (if you're enlarging) or which information it can sacrifice (if you're reducing the image). For example, if you reduce an image and then enlarge it to the original size, the final image will not be as good as the one you started with because Photoshop interpolates—it can't just restore the pixels you cut earlier.

Although Photoshop also interpolates as it scales down (or *downsamples*), its best method for doing so is still better than anything you get with the scanner software. This is another good reason to scan at higher-than-screen-resolution settings. You can always delete information from your image file to reduce its size, but you can't restore the same data easily.

note

Photoshop has several interpolation methods, which you can view and change by choosing Preferences from the File menu, and then choosing General. Of the three, *Bicubic* is the most accurate interpolation method; it analyzes contrast and is the best choice for continuous tone images and just about all other resizing situations in Photoshop. The other two are *Nearest Neighbor*, which is the fastest but least accurate, and *Bilinear*, which falls between Bicubic and Nearest Neighbor in terms of quality.

Changing Resolution and File Size

Doubling the resolution of an image will actually quadruple its file size and produce four times as much information. When you double the number of pixels per inch, you're doubling the dimensions both across and down, for four times as much square pixelage.

Photoshop tracks your image's file size and automatically updates it whenever you change the resolution or color mode. An easy way to illustrate this is to create a new file in Photoshop. For example, a grayscale document measuring 1 inch by 1 inch with a resolution of 150ppi will take up 22KB.

If you choose Image Size from the Image menu and enter 300 as a new value for the resolution, you'll notice that the file size jumps to 88KB, or four times 22KB.

If you then change the mode from Grayscale to RGB using the Mode submenu from the Image menu, you'll discover that the file size has tripled—because you're going from an 8-bit mode to a 24-bit one—the next time you call up the Image Size dialog box.

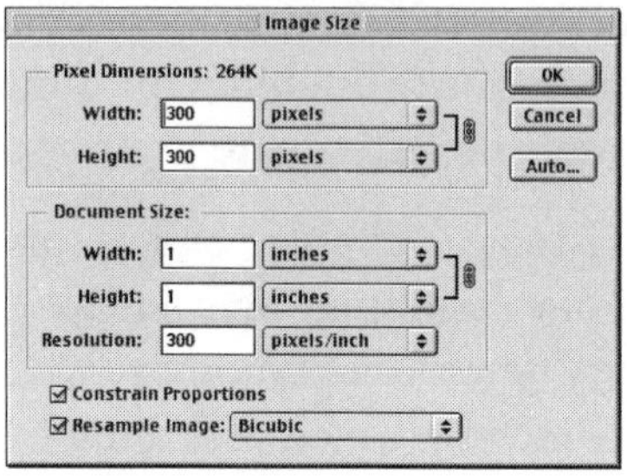

Photoshop also has an Auto Resolution feature for computing your resolution if you just enter the line screen. You can see it in action by clicking the Auto button in the Image Size dialog box. It's interesting to see because it offers three settings for determining what your image resolution should be (see Figure 9.8). The double-your-line-screen formula I mentioned earlier is the same that Photoshop uses for its Best setting. Its Good setting multiplies the line screen by 1.5 to determine the resolution. The Draft setting is set to 72ppi unless you entered an even lower resolution for the image earlier.

For some images, the differences between scanning at 1.5 (Good) versus 2 (Best) times the line screen frequency might be negligible, but why take chances? The Auto Resolution dialog box seems designed for users who don't know about the relationship between line screen and resolution, and I wish it were used to inform rather than offer these questionable Draft-Good-Best choices.

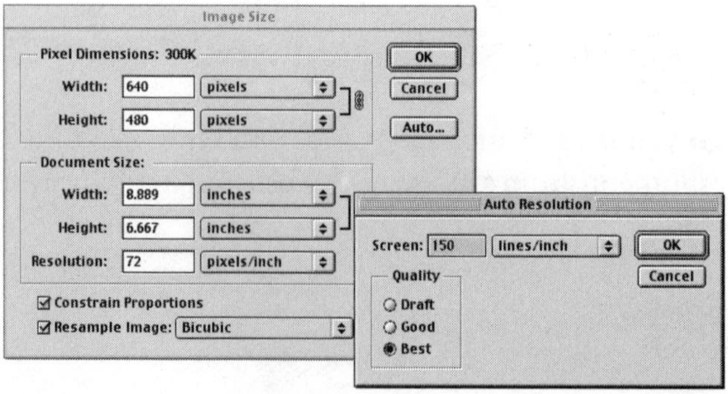

Figure 9.8

Clicking the Auto button in the Image Size dialog box will open the Auto Resolution dialog box.

The Resample Image Check Box

After you create a new image in Photoshop you can resize it at any time using the Image Size dialog box from the Image menu. Experimenting with values in this dialog box should help you understand the relationship between file size, image height and width, and resolution in your graphics.

As you've seen by now, resampling has its uses if you need to reduce an image's physical size, but resampling as you increase your image's dimensions can be detrimental to its quality. You can prevent resampling in your image when resizing an existing image by unchecking the Resample Image check box in the Image Size dialog box.

For example, I frequently take screen shots (also called screen grabs) of what's on my computer screen; these come with the standard Macintosh screen resolution of 72ppi. I send them to be printed in a magazine that calls for a 133-line screen. Along with converting the mode from RGB to CMYK, the other change I always need to make is to convert the resolution from 72 to 266. By keeping the Resample Image check box unchecked, I make Photoshop automatically recalculate the width and height and keep the file size the same (see Figure 9.9). This nets better results than letting the page layout program access the 72ppi image and calculating the size percentage based on the lower resolution. If I need to reduce an image's dimensions, though—for example, when creating small, fast-loading Web graphics—I usually check the Resample Image check box. This way, I can reduce the image's height or width in pixels to the desired specifications, maintain the image's resolution, and reduce the file size to boot.

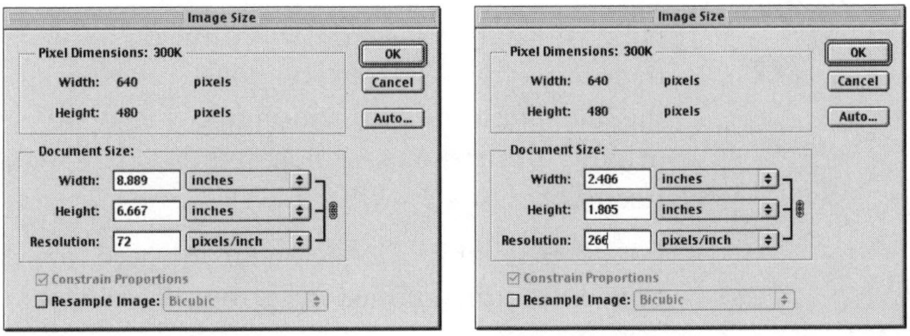

Figure 9.9

If you leave the Resample Image check box unchecked in the Image Size dialog box and then change the resolution, you will see your file's height and width dimensions change.

Take the time to understand the dependencies between resolution and file size, especially if you create graphics for use in more than one medium—say, for both print and Web site production. This will help you understand why you typically want to reduce the dimensions of images originally used in print when you're ready to put them online. Because many visitors to your Web site have 640×480-pixel or 800×600-pixel monitors, for example, you'll frequently want to restrict the size of the images you post there to avoid compelling users to scroll horizontally.

Similarly, if you work in print production, you'll need to remember that because screen shots are low-resolution (72ppi or 96ppi). Converting the resolution to twice the line screen will reduce the document's height and width, and remind you that you'll need to display these images at a smaller size in print than they appear onscreen to retain the image quality.

Enlarging Images

If your artwork is going to be enlarged when you scan it—for example, when you're scanning slides—for best results, you need to increase the resolution before you scan. If the original scan is given the chance to generate plenty of file information early on, you are more likely to avoid a blocky, pixelated appearance later.

To determine what resolution to use for a graphic that will be enlarged, just multiply the product of the previously mentioned formula (twice the line screen) by the ratio of the final image dimensions to the scanned image dimensions. For example, say you have an image that measures 1×1 inches, and you want your final image to be three times larger, for a final size of 3×3 inches. That image's ratio is 3:1, or, after you treat that colon like a division sign, just 3.

Now say your final image will print on an imagesetter with a line frequency of 120. To find your ideal scanning resolution, first double the line screen (to 240) and multiply it by the ratio of the final-to-original-dimensions, which was 3. That makes your scanning resolution $240 \times 3 = 720$ppi.

It's easy to use this ratio method if you need to match a certain height or width for the finished image but don't know what the other final

dimension will be. For example, if the artwork needs to fit a hole on a page that's 5.5 inches wide, and you have an original slide that measures 1.375 inches by .75 inch, you can do the math (go right ahead and whip out that calculator) and see that the ratio of the final to the original width is 4:1. Thus, the final height will be .75 × 4 = 3 inches. If your line screen frequency in this example is 150lpi, you can just plug these numbers into the formula. Scan this slide at twice the line screen times the ratio of the final size to the original, or 2 × 150 × 4 = 1,200ppi.

Scanning Line Art

When you scan line art you're using 1-bit scanning, with no colors other than black or white. Because line art scans can't take advantage of anti-aliasing to make smooth transitions between black and white, they are highly prone to *jaggies*—jagged edges around curves—when you scan at anything lower than your scanner's native resolution.

Unlike photos, line art requires high scan resolution for optimal results. Ideally, you should scan line art at the same resolution as the final output device that will print your job. For example, say you have a line art logo measuring 7×2 inches that you want to appear at the same size in your newsletter, which you're going to have printed on your service bureau's 1,270dpi imagesetter. Optimally, you should scan it at 1,270dpi for the best appearance.

But what if you have only a 300dpi or 600dpi scanner and can't afford to send the logo to a service bureau for scanning? After you scan at the highest possible resolution, choose Image Size from the Image menu, and change the resolution to the desired final resolution—and make sure that the Resample Image box is checked. You'll immediately see the image quality degrade as both the file size and viewing ratio grow significantly.

Don't worry—now you can use one of two processes (or a combination of the two) to sharpen the image a great deal. The first method involves achieving tonal correction by using either the Levels command or the Curves command, accessed by choosing Adjust from the Image menu. The second and more flexible approach is to use the Unsharp Mask filter. All scanned images can afford some sharpening, and the Unsharp Mask filter is better suited than Sharpen or Sharpen More for improving scans.

tip

If your scanned line art is a fairly simple sketch, you can also get good results by using Photoshop's pen tools or selection tools to trace the scan's outlines and save as a path. Then, you can fine-tune the vector-based path as necessary and save the image as an EPS file.

Halftone Scanning

Printing presses can't produce continuous tones—that is, pixels in varying shades of gray—the way cameras and scanners can. As a result, most commercial printers translate the continuous tones of photographs and other images into rows of dots in screening patterns called *halftones*. The size, shape, and angle of these halftone dots simulate the continuous effect. Pick up any newspaper or magazine, turn to a page with a printed photo, and hold it right up to your face—the photo that looks like a solid, continuous image at arm's length will reveal row after row of halftone dots.

Halftone dots are a measure of the number of dots you see on the printed page, not the pixels in your document. Your commercial printer's line screen, which I've talked about a lot in this chapter without really defining so far, measures the number of halftone dots per inch.

note

As mentioned earlier, for best printing results, the resolution of your Photoshop images should be set to twice your line screen—and please remember to uncheck the Resample Image check box in the Image Size dialog box when you change your image's resolution to match this number.

Full-color print jobs combine four halftone screens, one for each of the CMYK plates. Each of these screens is set at a different angle to help produce consistent color (see Figure 9.10). Traditionally, the plates are set in order of lightest to darkest at the following angles:

Yellow=90°

Cyan=105°

Magenta=75°

Black=45°

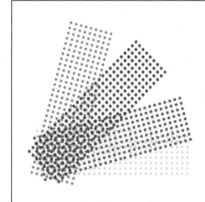

Figure 9.10
Halftone screens
are combined—
each color at a
different angle—
to produce
photorealistic
effects in print.

You can see a rough enactment of this effect with the Color Halftone filter under Pixelate in the Filter menu; experimenting with this filter can also demonstrate how the greater the number of dots in an image, the more realistic (that is, continuous) the halftone effect looks (see Figure 9.11).

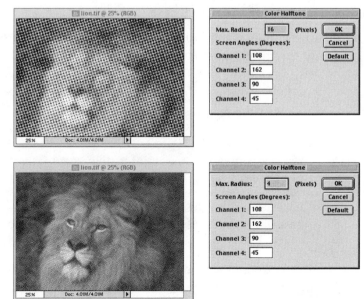

Figure 9.11
The Color
Halftone filter
simulates the
effect of halftone
printing.

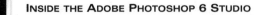

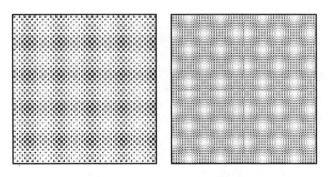

Figure 9.12
Examples of
moiré patterns.

If the screen angle of one color plate is not quite right, the halftone dots can clash to create blotchy, funny-looking patterns called moirés. And if you happen to scan an image from a print publication, you'll also unwittingly generate moiré patterns that will interfere with the scanned image. This happens because your printed originals already have dot patterns generated in the halftone screen for each color plate before printing—and those patterns are virtually certain to be different from the ones Photoshop generates this time. Moirés are produced where these patterns reinforce and interfere with each other (see Figure 9.12).

Eliminate Moirés Using Your Scanning Software and Photoshop Filters

Most scanners now offer descreening filters in their software and plug-ins specifically geared to moiré problems. For example, all Agfa scanners have a scanning program called FotoLook that offers a Descreen option for removing moiré patterns. Check your scanner's documentation or contact the manufacturer directly to make sure.

note

Several times in this chapter, I've recommended you choose Photoshop over your scanning software for obtaining certain results. For descreening, though, you should always start by using your scanner's options—this is usually a good one-step solution. This filtering process can take several steps in Photoshop.

Be sure to use the word *moiré* when inquiring about options for scanning halftones. Some scanners offer settings for creating your own

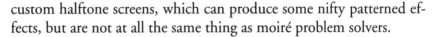

custom halftone screens, which can produce some nifty patterned effects, but are not at all the same thing as moiré problem solvers.

Exercise 9.1 looks at how to remove the crosshatched or dotted patterns that appear when you scan previously printed images, such as those in a magazine or newspaper page. At this point, let me remind you that scanning images from printed material presents copyright issues—make sure you have obtained permission to reprint or reuse previously published material if it is copyrighted.

If you're really ambitious—or if you have a lot of high-quality printed images to scan—another thing that can help is to try scanning at a multiple of the line screen of the printed piece. You can find out what that line screen is by obtaining a screen gauge (try asking at art supply stores) to read the screen level, and then setting your scanning resolution to two or four times that number.

Adjusting Brightness and Contrast

Besides moirés, other common scanning problems include images that scan too dark (poor contrast) or look dull (not enough brightness, or reflected light from your image). The scanning process can mute a lot of fine details in your image, especially when your scanner interpolates to attain higher resolution levels.

This section covers a few options for making tonal improvements before you even create the scan—and afterward as well.

Setting Black Point and White Point Values

No matter how careful you are in choosing high-quality images with a broad range of tonal values, you'll see poor contrast when you scan if your scanner can't handle the full gamut of light and dark colors in your image. That's where black point and white point settings come in—these settings rein in the boundaries of your image's tonal range, turning all dark values lower than the black point to solid black, and all bright highlight values greater than the white point to solid white. In this way, your scanner can focus on a narrower visual range, resulting in better differentiated grays that draw out more details. Your service bureau or printer can tell you what the highlight and shadow dot percentages should be.

EXERCISE 9.1

Cleaning Up Images Scanned from Magazines, Books, or Newspapers

①

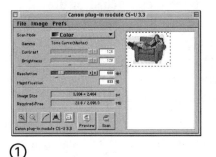

②

③

1. Cut out and scan your image from a magazine or newspaper. Scan in color mode at twice the desired scan resolution; later, you will resample back to half this size. I scanned my picture from a catalog at 600dpi. If your scanner comes with a descreen filter, ensure that this option is used.

2. If you use a descreen filter with your scanner software, you should be able to eliminate most of the moiré patterns in your scanned images. Because most scanners add a slight color cast to any image you scan, you will probably have some color touch-ups to fix as well. In my example, I can still see some of the halftone pattern in the face area. I also have to clean up the lines from where I cut the image out of the catalog.

3. Next, you're going to apply a filter to remove any remaining halftone effects. You'll get the best results with either the Despeckle filter (from the Noise submenu under the Filter menu) or a Gaussian Blur filter (from the Blur submenu under the Filter menu). If you choose Despeckle, the effect is applied automatically; you might need to apply it several times to see all of the halftone artifacts eradicated. Two other good choices to try under the Noise menu include Dust & Scratches and Median. If you choose Gaussian Blur, you can enter a value for Radius and preview how your choice affects a target area of your image.

4. Now you're ready to resample the image to the intended resolution. This will throw out some unnecessary file information and, ideally, lose any lingering unwanted halftone screening effects as well. This resampling will halve your image's dimensions and reduce the file size to one-fourth.

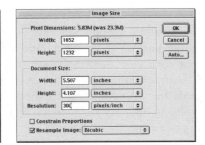

④

⑤

5. To compensate for any fine detail you might have lost when you applied the Gaussian Blur filter or resampled down, use the Unsharp Mask filter (from the Sharpen submenu under the Filter menu). You can enter several values for this filter: the amount to apply, the radius, and threshold. This is a good last step whenever you're editing a scanned image.

6. If you still need to correct the color cast, saturation, or tone, use the options in the Adjust submenu under the Image menu (covered in the next section). Your moiré elimination work is done! See Figure 9.13.

Figure 9.13

Use your scanner's Descreen filter, if available, when scanning previously printed images. Resampling, as well as the Despeckle or Gaussian Blur filters, can help eliminate any remaining moiré effects.

> **note**
>
> Are you still wondering how your service bureau or printer's customer service reps could possibly advise you on what settings to use with your desktop scanner? Consider this: only they can tell you how variables such as the ink, paper stock, the printing press used for your job, and anticipated dot gain affect the size of the halftone dots in your scanned images. You'll learn about these printing concerns in Chapter 14, "Print Production Essentials."

Setting Brightness and Contrast

Some scanner interfaces include options for modifying brightness and contrast in an image, but you can exert greater control over these settings using the Adjust submenu of the Image menu (see Figure 9.14).

The simplest way to adjust brightness and contrast is through the Brightness/Contrast dialog box (see Figure 9.15). Be sure to click the Preview box so you can see the changes you make. This dialog box includes two straightforward sliders. Dragging the Brightness slider to the right lightens the image; dragging it to the left darkens the image. Dragging the Contrast slider to the right adds detail by making the whites whiter and the dark portions even darker, and dragging the Contrast slider to the left reduces extremes in light and dark areas, as if a gray smog has drifted in front of the image.

Another very intuitive method for adjusting brightness and color is through the Variations command, the last item under the Adjust

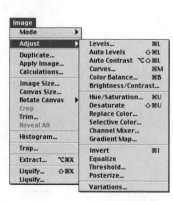

Figure 9.14
Adjust options under the Image menu.

Figure 9.15
The Brightness/
Contrast
dialog box.

submenu of the Image menu (see Figure 9.16). By displaying a number of variations on your original, Photoshop lets you adjust the image based on the visual results you like instead of compelling you to master the formulas yourself. That's also the main drawback with the Variations command—you don't have the precise control here that you do with some of the other Adjust submenu commands.

Another way to increase brightness in your image is to try using the Levels command. When you select Levels from the Adjust submenu under Image, you'll see a *histogram*, which is a graphical representation of your image's brightness values. Darker pixel values are shown on the left side of the histogram, whereas lighter ones appear on the right. You can adjust the gamma of the image—the middle slider under the histogram or the middle number above the histogram—to a higher number to add more contrast to the middle tones. You'll find more information about the Levels command in Chapter 10, "Retouching Essentials."

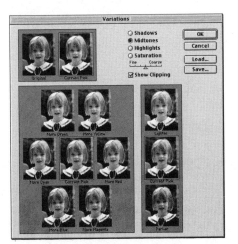

Figure 9.16
The Variations
dialog box.

For more finicky adjustments, the Curves command lets you adjust the contrast of the image as a whole or in each individual color channel. If you raise one of the color curves in a region, you increase the contrast there. By sampling the colors in various parts of the image, you might find that one channel doesn't cover its entire range, and you can then adjust its curve to use more contrast for the colors that are actually present. You'll find more information about the Curves command in Chapter 10.

note

> **Some designers recommend doing curve corrections in Lab Color mode, especially if your scanned image is going to be converted to CMYK for print use.**

Sharpening with the Unsharp Mask Filter

After you adjust levels or curves, you might want to try the Unsharp Mask filter, under Sharpen in the Filter menu. As you saw in Exercise 9.1, this filter is great for emphasizing the edges of your scanned images, making the image appear sharper to the eye.

There are three settings to consider in using Photoshop's Unsharp Mask filter: Amount, Radius, and Threshold. Amount sets the intensity of the filter's edge enhancement. Experiment with values between 200 and 400 and work down from there; make sure you preview your results to see what effect different values have.

The wider the Radius, the more obvious the sharpening will be; depending on the image's dimensions, experiment with Radius values between .6 and 2.4.

The Threshold setting indicates how far apart the tonal values of two adjacent pixels should be before sharpening kicks in; you should always start with a very low Threshold setting.

Removing a Color Cast

I mentioned earlier that just about any desktop scanner adds a color cast—that is, color information that wasn't in your original—to your scanned images. Exercise 9.2 shows you how you can methodically identify just what color effects your scanner's idiosyncrasies are adding to your images, and how to then establish a color-cast correction that you can apply to any images scanned using that machine.

Photo CD—An Alternative to Straightforward Scanning

With Kodak's Photo CD technology, you can easily—and fairly inexpensively—store images from slides or 35mm film negatives onto a compact disc. You take your film or slides to a local photofinishing service that offers Photo CD capabilities and have someone else do the scanning for you. You can have your images stored on a Photo CD just as you would order finished prints or slides.

You can then retrieve your files at one of several file sizes and bit depths (see Figure 9.17). They maintain all the fine detail and tonal quality of the originals, because none of the original scan is sacrificed to save space. This can give you a lot of flexibility with images—for example, you can place a low-resolution version in your layout documents but later link to the high-resolution version when you go to press. Many CDs containing royalty-free photos use the Photo CD format too.

If your local photofinisher doesn't offer Photo CD services, a number of mail order photo labs will create Photo CDs for you.

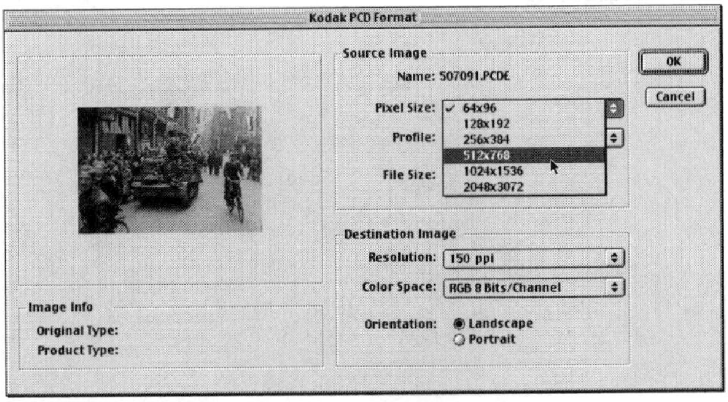

Figure 9.17

When you open a Photo CD, you can choose the file size and resolution you want.

EXERCISE 9.2

Identifying and Correcting a Color Cast Added by a Scanner

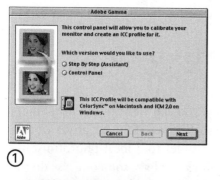

①

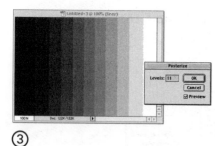

②

③

1. For this exercise, you need to ensure that your monitor has been calibrated. You can use the Adobe Gamma utility (described in Chapter 1, "System Essentials") to make sure this is done.

2. Create a new Photoshop file; make sure you choose the default foreground and background colors. Choose the Gradient tool ( ) and select the Linear Gradient in the options bar. Now drag from left to right in your image to create a blend from solid black to solid white.

3. Choose Posterize from the Adjust submenu under the Image menu; enter 11 in the Levels field. You'll see the gradiated image transform into a number of gray swatches, colored from solid black all the way to white.

4. Print the page of 11 black, gray, and white swatches on a black-and-white printer. Scan this page into Photoshop. Be sure to scan using your scanner's color mode, not grayscale.

5. Choose Show Info from the Window menu to display the Info palette. Read the RGB values for each of the gray levels. If the R, G, and B values are uneven, this indicates what kind of a color cast your scanner is introducing.

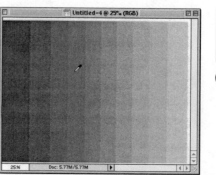

④

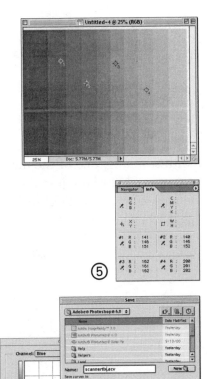

⑤

⑥

6. You can now use the Color Sampler tool ( ) to take sample readings from several points in your image, so you can better track how the color value numbers change when you apply tonal corrections. (I specified a 3×3-pixel average in the tool's options bar, and then clicked four points in the image that I plan to use for tracking tonal changes.) Use Levels or Curves to correct the color cast. Save the dialog box settings. In correcting the values that are uneven, be sure you're not adversely affecting other parts of the image where the values are well coordinated.

7. Save the Levels or Curves dialog box settings when you're done.

8. Open an image you've scanned that has a color cast. Now reopen the dialog box you used to correct the cast in the previous step and load the saved settings. See Figure 9.18.

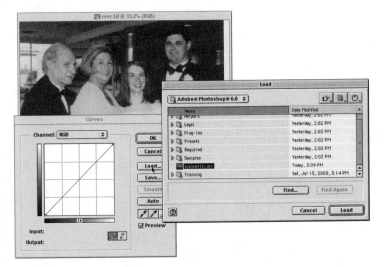

Figure 9.18
Load the Levels or Curves settings that correct your scanner's color cast immediately upon scanning subsequent images—this will correct the color cast.

> *note* **Although you can open Photo CD files (named with a .PCD file extension) in Photoshop, you cannot save files in Photo CD format from within Photoshop.**

Summary

In this chapter, you became familiar with scanning, one of the most common ways to obtain images for editing in Photoshop. Just ahead, Chapter 10 goes further in showing you more sophisticated techniques for polishing your images.

The 10 Retouching Essentials

IN THIS CHAPTER

Making Tonal Corrections

👁

Making Color Corrections

👁

Removing Dust Spots and Blemishes

👁

Making Facial Corrections

Like a makeup artist or an auto mechanic, a Photoshop designer might be called upon to make defects disappear. In the world of image editing, that includes removing dust spots, eradicating skin blemishes in portraits, or changing a distracting background. You might need to tweak poor lighting or enhance washed-out colors in photographs.

Whether your retouching efforts are going to be an everyday event for you at an advertising job or a once-in-a-while need for salvaging a less-than-perfect photo shoot, you need to know how you can retouch and color-correct images in Photoshop.

This chapter takes a good look at the more advanced techniques that you can use to remove defects from photos while maintaining a convincing overall appearance. In this chapter, you learn the following techniques:

- Assess an image to determine the best way to correct flaws
- Use the Levels and Curves commands to correct poor lighting
- Use the Clone Stamp tool and feathering to eliminate dust spots and blemishes
- Use the Dodge and Burn tools to adjust shadows
- Replace objects in an image background—or the entire background—to focus attention better on the subject

Taking Stock

As you saw in the previous chapter, the best predictor for getting good results in your digitized images is using the highest-possible-quality originals. All too often, though, that can be beyond your control. For example, you might wind up with only one blurry or funny-looking head shot that has to run with a magazine profile, or a limited, time-worn selection from a historical archive to illustrate an article that requires artwork.

Once you have a digitized version of your original photo, examine it in Photoshop at a high magnification to identify any scratches or spots visible onscreen that might not have been apparent in the print. If your photos were digitized on a low-end scanner, look for dust spots or other blotches generated during the scanning process.

Now take a step back and assess your image with an objective eye—you're doing a makeover here, much as if you were a makeup artist or a beauty consultant. Identify which areas are less than perfect, and—more importantly—what needs changing to suit the context in which you'll use the image. For example, does the photo give the subject's skin a yellowish cast? If you're working on a beautiful-baby photo spread, you'd better retouch that jaundiced look. For any kind of portrait, you want to make sure that your subject is in tight focus and in good lighting; you might also want to remove distracting details in the background.

Checking Color Values in the Info Palette

No matter how objectively you search your image for hidden flaws, your eyes can be somewhat limited when you're assessing images for print. Why? You're seeing your image's colors and shadings onscreen in RGB mode instead of how they'll really appear printed in full color. As a result, rely on readings you get from the Info palette as a guide to the colors in your image (see Figure 10.1). When you select either the Eyedropper or Color Sampler tool and move your cursor over an image, the Info palette reports the exact color values of the pixels beneath the cursor. As the bottom half of Figure 10.1 shows, the sample points you place using the Color Sampler tool give you before-and-after information about color values when you apply color adjustment commands such as Curves (available when you choose Adjust from the Image menu).

note

As you saw in Exercise 9.2, "Identifying and Correcting a Color Cast Added by a Scanner," the Color Sampler tool lets you take sample readings from up to four points in an image. Here are a couple of quick pointers for manipulating your color samplers once you've placed these points in an image. To reposition a color sampler, just place your cursor on it and click and drag it to a new location. To delete a color sampler, [Alt]-click (for Windows users) or [Option]-click (for Mac users) on the color sampler.

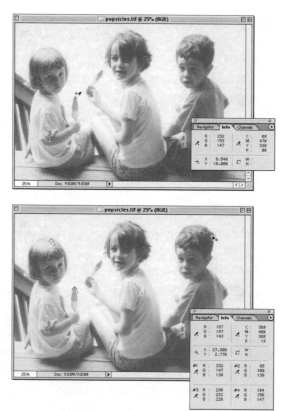

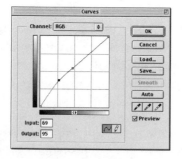

Figure 10.1

Use the Info palette to check color values in your image at a glance. To compare the before-and-after effects of color adjustment commands, use the Color Sampler tool with the Info palette.

You can change the sample size of either the Eyedropper or Color Sampler tools, too. The default is the Point Sample, which takes readings from one pixel at a time, but it's a good idea to change it to a 3×3-pixel sample or even a 5×5-pixel sample. The benefit to this is avoiding being thrown off by chance readings from stray, odd-colored pixels. When

you choose the Eyedropper or Color Sampler tool, you can update this setting in the options bar.

As you'll see later in this chapter, you'll also find Eyedropper tools in the Levels and Curves dialog boxes. You saw these options briefly in Chapter 9, "Scanning Essentials," but here you'll see how you can really put them to work for you in radically retouching your images.

Keeping Backups Close By

Most graphic designers quickly learn to be compulsive savers, storing copies of scanned images before embarking on any major retouching, lest they need to return images to a much earlier state. There are a lot of pluses to this strategy; if you change your mind about what parts of the image you want to edit, it's much easier to restore an archived image than to haul out the original again for rescanning. The downside is the cost in terms of file size—you can quickly overload your hard drive with multiple versions of graphics waiting in limbo.

If you do a lot of experimenting during your image editing, you can avoid creating so many memory-hogging backup files—your insurance policies, really, against wrong moves—during an editing session if you take advantage of the History palette. This feature is the mechanism by which Photoshop lets you go back to a previous state of the image during your current editing session. You can return at once to an earlier state of your image editing, or you can use the History Brush or Art History Brush to daub in parts of your earlier image one brushstroke at a time.

In other words, you can of course undo the last boneheaded filter or other editing change you just made—that's what Cmd+Z (or Ctrl+Z) has always been there for—as well as view a list of the most recent changes you've made to an image during that session and return to any stage in that process. To withdraw or retrace your steps one action at a time—essentially, to use multiple levels of undo or redo—you choose Step Forward or Step Backward from either the History palette menu or the Edit menu to move to the next or previous state.

You can see how the History palette works after you edit any image on your hard drive; after you make a few changes, choose Show History from the Window menu. You'll see each of your actions listed in the palette, starting with opening the file and ending with the last command you issued (see Figure 10.2). By clicking any of these steps in the History palette, you can revert to that point in your edits.

Any given stage in your image-editing process is called an *image state*. If you choose to undo several steps—for example, undoing steps where you cropped an image too closely or applied a filter too heavily—what you're doing is reverting to an earlier image state. The number of actions the History palette can track is limited by how much memory is available; as a result, older actions are dropped from the History palette when memory is tight. You can guard against losing this information by taking temporary snapshots of different image states to preserve them throughout your editing session.

This History palette works independently of the Undo command ([Cmd]+[Z] or [Ctrl]+[Z]), so you can actually do things like revert to an early stage in your image editing—undoing a dozen steps in the editing

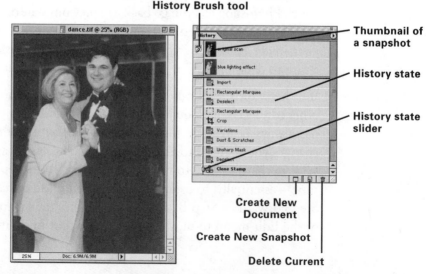

Figure 10.2

The History palette shows recent actions taken in your current editing session.

Click the left column next to a snapshot to set the source for the History Brush tool

Thumbnail of a snapshot

History state

History state slider

Create New Document

Create New Snapshot

Delete Current

process, say—and then change your mind and undo that reverting step. Click the image state's name in the History palette—or click and drag the history slider—to reach any given state as quickly as possible—this lets you immediately undo a number of intermediary steps. The "un-done" steps still appear in a grayed-out state following the step you returned to. You can click any of these undone steps to return to the later stage. This instantly reinstates the steps you eliminated.

To create a new snapshot, click the black triangle in the upper-right corner of the History palette, and choose New Snapshot from the re-sulting pop-up menu. This will open the New Snapshot dialog box (see Figure 10.3). You can also just click the New Snapshot icon (⬛) located on the bottom of the History palette to create a new snapshot without displaying the dialog box.

One good way you can use such snapshots is if you're really not sure what final effect you're striving for. You can experiment with filters or rearrange layers to discover new effects and take snapshots of the re-sults you like best. At that point, you can compare several snapshots before you make your final decision—all without having to save mul-tiple versions of your image.

Snapshots are available only during your current image-editing session—they disappear once you close the file. As a result, to retain a snapshot or image state for later use, you need to save each in a separate file. To do so,

Figure 10.3
The New Snapshot dialog box.

New Snapshot

Name: Snapshot 1   OK

From: ✓ Full Document   Cancel
        Merged Layers
        Current Layer

choose New Document from the History palette pop-up menu, or drag the snapshot's row down to the New Document icon (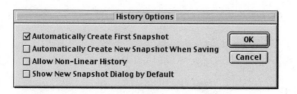).

If you want to continue to work with multiple snapshots from the same file at a later date, you can save each to a separate file, and then reopen all when you're ready to work on the image again. You can drag each snapshot file's initial snapshot to your original image, thus re-creating the multiple snapshots you had originally created in your first image-editing session.

Linear vs. Non-Linear History

I've described how ordinarily the History palette operates in a *linear* fashion—it tracks step-by-step all the developments or changes that have been made. When you select a given snapshot, all the changes made since that state disappear from the image and the commands carried out since that point are grayed out in the History palette.

Photoshop gives you another way to rewrite history with its Allow Non-Linear History mode. You can activate this mode through the History Options dialog box reached through the History palette's fly-out menu (see Figure 10.4). Allow Non-Linear History lets you make changes to a selected state without deleting the states that follow. Your changes are appended at the end of the history list, instead of just eliminating the rows of the commands you effectively undid. In this way, the non-linear mode records everything that has happened in your document, even the parts that were undone. If you refer to the History palette to track where and how certain changes were made, you will probably find this non-linear history mode extremely confusing.

You might have noticed that there's both a Purge Histories command (from the Purge submenu under the Edit menu—see Figure 10.5) and a Clear History command in the History palette. Although both delete

Figure 10.4

The History Options dialog box lets you opt to change the linear recording of changes made to your images.

Figure 10.5

Purge Histories wipes out the history for all open documents.

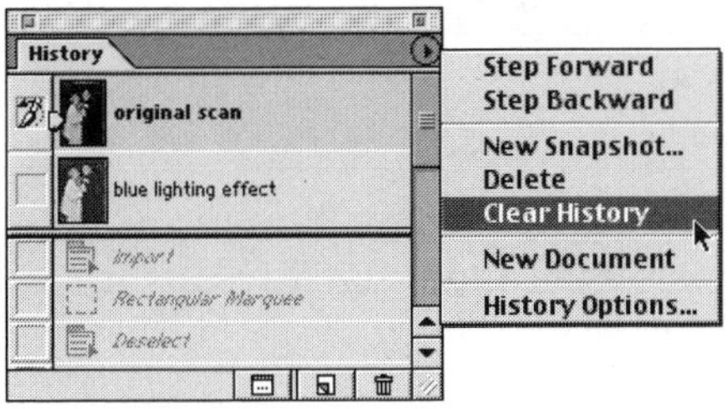

Figure 10.6

The Clear History command in the History palette affects just the history of the current document.

the snapshots and image states in memory—thus freeing up more RAM for Photoshop's operations—it's important to know that these two commands have very different purposes. Purge Histories affects all open Photoshop documents, whereas the Clear History command affects only the document you're currently working on (see Figure 10.6).

A Brush (or Two) with History

Another creative use for snapshots is integrating selected parts of a saved snapshot into your current image using the History Brush tool ( ). After selecting the History Brush tool, you click in the left column next to the specific snapshot in the History palette you want to restore to your image. I find it very useful to apply filters to an entire image, take snapshots of the finished effect, and then revert to the original and

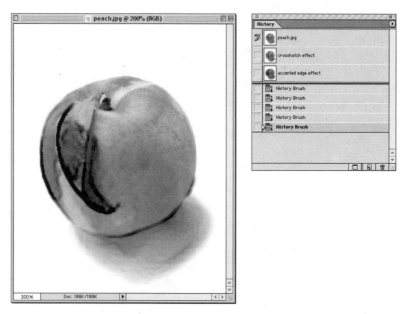

Figure 10.7

You can use the History Brush tool to restore specific parts of a saved snapshot to an image.

paint in only portions of the filtered results using the History Brush tool (see Figure 10.7).

The cool part about using these options is the control you have over making your image restoration look natural. In the options bar for the History Brush tool, you can choose the thickness and edges of the brush used for painting the snapshot. You can also control the opacity and mode (for example, Overlay, Darken) through the History Brush tool's options bar. By tweaking the opacity and brush settings, you wield great control over parts of your image, making the restored bits look realistic, not just pasted in digitally.

You'll have even greater artistic license with the Art History Brush tool (see Figure 10.8). Like the History Brush, the Art History Brush starts with a snapshot or image state you select as its source. But whereas the History Brush relies entirely on previously stored data for painting, the Art History Brush incorporates that data with the stylizing options you set to create new artistic effects with each stroke. You can specify one of a number of paint styles (such as Dab or Tight Curl), fidelity, brush size, and tolerance options.

Figure 10.8

Options for the Art History Brush tool.

	Brush: 21	Mode: Normal	Opacity: 100%	Style: • Tight Short	Fidelity: 100%	Area: 50 px	Spacing: 0%	

Tight Short
Tight Medium
Tight Long
Loose Medium
Loose Long
Dab
Tight Curl
Tight Curl Long
Loose Curl
Loose Curl Long

Can This Photo Be Saved?

Your life may be full of Kodak moments, as the ads promise, but they don't mention the near-misses that get captured on film all too often. Poor lighting, closed eyes, and bad hair days can result in photos you'd sooner toss out than consider for a page one layout. Here's a brief run-down on some of the kinds of corrections you might find yourself making:

- **Tonal corrections**. These include setting the lightest and darkest points in your image and adjusting midtone areas and highlights.

- **Removing dust spots**. Scanners capture any dust on the scanning area along with your artwork, and you need to get rid of the spots for a professional-quality image.

- **Facial fixes**. You might find yourself critiquing portrait shots the way you'd scrutinize your own appearance before going out. Things to check for here include dark shadows under the eyes or blemishes on the skin. If you're doing a more radical makeover, you can even remove the subject's glasses or trim facial hair. Another common problem with digitizing photos of people is the evil, red-eyed look that crops up when they catch the camera flash wrong—Photoshop makes it easy to restore the proper color.

- **Fixing a distracting background**. Bystanders, passing cars, or other objects in your image's background can distract from the subject. Often you can blur the background or remove intrusive objects from the scene.

This chapter tackles these problems one by one, starting with strategies for grayscale tone and color correction. Following that are tips for removing blemishes and fixing backgrounds. I've included these in the general order in which you'd want to fix your image—it's easier to take care of the smaller problems, such as dust spots, after you have a handle on adjusting contrast and other tonal corrections.

Making Tonal Corrections in Grayscale Images

In making tonal corrections to your grayscale images, you'll draw out hidden details in the shadows, midtones, and highlights. You'll improve the tonal range so that the lighter tones don't turn completely white when printed. The most intuitive way to learn how to do tonal corrections is by example, so open a grayscale image of your own in Photoshop or follow along with the one shown here (see Figure 10.9). The example I'm using here is an extremely dark scan—it's difficult to see the girls' facial features.

The first step on the path to tonal correction is to open the Info palette—choose Show Info from the Window menu—and use the Eyedropper or Color Sampler tool to take some readings. Notice that the Info palette gives you readouts in two modes; this can be very useful when you're working in RGB and want to keep tabs on values for

Figure 10.9

A grayscale image in great need of tonal correction.

Figure 10.10

The Info Options dialog box. For grayscale images, your first color readout should be set to either Actual Color or Grayscale.

CMYK output or percentages for total ink values. Click the Info palette pop-up menu to choose the Palette Options command. Click the First Color Readout mode drop-down list and select either Actual Color or Grayscale (see Figure 10.10).

What should the second color readout show? If you've managed to wrap your mind around thinking in terms of the 0-255 gray value range, you should choose the RGB values for the second color readout; you'll see identical values for the R, G, and B values.

note

> If you set the second color readout to CMYK, you might wonder why the Info palette shows values for the cyan, magenta, and yellow channels when you're working with a Grayscale image. After all, why isn't black the only channel that registers, because it's just a grayscale image? Photoshop is displaying the values it would use if you did convert the mode from Grayscale to CMYK—the program doesn't just translate your grays over to the black channel. It translates them to values in all four channels that would yield a similar gray.

The third drop-down list in the Info Options dialog box controls the mouse coordinates; you can choose your preferred unit of measurement. I usually use pixels.

Your next task is to take readings of the lightest and darkest points in your image. Bear in mind that your printer might display much less tonal variation than your monitor does; it will not distinguish between, say, 10 percent black and 13 percent black in a noticeable way. Any values you have in the 1–8 percent black range will likely print entirely as white. Similarly, any black values over 90 percent might print completely in black because of *dot gain*, or the tendency of a printing dot to spread during the halftone process that produces its final printed version on paper.

Dot gain, which you'll see again in more detail in Chapter 12, "Web Graphics Essentials," is most prevalent in offset printing on lower-quality paper such as newsprint. For major projects such as book production or a magazine redesign, it's essential to arrange a press test with your printer. You supply a sample of all the kinds of graphics destined for your print job and see how they look on paper. If, for example, your original photo scans turn out so dark that little detail is distinguishable, you can correct the problem ahead of time without wasting money or time on press.

In my example photo, the lightest reading is 9 percent black and the darkest point is 96 percent black. Later, when you start making tonal corrections, you'll find more interesting information here that shows your before-and-after pixel values—so you can see exactly how much you've lightened or darkened sample areas.

For now, the readings of the midtone areas are more telling because just from looking at the image it's apparent that the midtones are too dark and need to be lightened. You can generate readings of your midtone values by analyzing a histogram of the image, which is a graph showing the distribution of gray tones in an image. Histograms are always a good first step after you scan an image. You can see this graph by choosing Histogram from the Image menu.

If you have an active selection in your image, the histogram includes only the values in your selected area. Here's a sample histogram dialog box, showing the sort of well-balanced chart you'd want to see for your images.

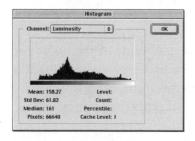

Instead of measuring gray values in percentages of black, the histogram shows how many occurrences there are of each of the 256 possible values in a grayscale image. Running along the x-axis of this chart you'll see a color bar blending from black to white. Each point along this chart shows one of the gray values between 0 (black) and 255 (white).

This chart can tell you at a glance which direction to go in to correct your image's tones. A high frequency of 0 or 255 values might indicate that your scanner wasn't able to handle the full tonal range of your image and has clipped, or converted to 100 percent black or white, some extreme dark and light values. A histogram with values bunched toward the right side indicates the image is way too light, whereas a bell-curved histogram (high in the middle) has too many midlevel grays and needs more contrast. A well-balanced histogram should contain values spread in fairly equal amounts across the length of the chart.

Beneath the graph in the Histogram dialog box you'll find some additional information. You probably won't need to refer to most of it, but it's useful to know what it's telling you.

- 👁 **Mean**. Shows the average brightness value.

- 👁 **Std Dev**. Shows how much the brightness values vary. The term is short for standard deviation.

- 👁 **Median**. Gives the middle brightness value in the image—half the pixels are darker than this point and half are lighter. It's a different value from the average (mean).

- 👁 **Pixels**. Tells you the total number of pixels in the image—which you can also determine by multiplying the image's height and width in pixels—or in the active selection.

The next four values change as you move your cursor (a crosshair) across the histogram.

- 👁 **Level**. Shows the gray value of the point your cursor is passing over. Although it's easy to tell where 0 (black) and 255 (white) fall at the ends of the spectrum, using the crosshair is the best way to see the frequency of other gray values.

- 👁 **Count**. Gives the exact number of occurrences of the gray value the cursor is passing over, which you see represented graphically on the chart.

- 👁 **Percentile**. Tracks the percentage of the grays in the image that are less than or equal to a given value. For example, if you put the crosshair on the median value, the Percentile reading should be equivalent to 50.00; if you put the crosshair at the 255 level, Percentile should read 100.00.

- 👁 **Cache Level**. Relates to the Cache Levels setting that appears under Memory & Image Cache after you choose Preferences from the File menu, which is where you can set how many low-res previews Photoshop holds in short-term memory. You can click the Use Cache for Histograms check box in the Memory & Image Cache Preferences dialog box to reserve one of the cache levels. This allows you to generate the histograms in the Histogram and Levels dialog boxes.

If you're working with a grayscale image, the histogram you see in the Histogram dialog box matches the one you see in the Levels dialog box. If you have an RGB or CMYK document, though, the Histogram dialog box gives a histogram for luminosity and individual channels; to see a histogram of the overview channel, you have to look at the Levels dialog box. As you make tonal changes to your images, it's a good idea to frequently check the changes to your image's histogram. Gaps in the histogram indicate *posterization,* that is, areas where there are sudden jumps in tonal variation.

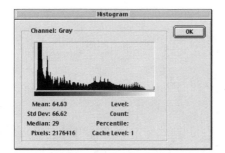

Figure 10.11

The histogram for the image shown in Figure 10.9, before tonal correction, shows that it's too dark.

The histogram for Figure 10.9 (shown in Figure 10.11) shows a chart heavily weighted toward the left, indicating that the image has too many shadows and not enough detail in the lighter midtones and highlights.

There are several ways to correct this image using one or more of the Adjust subcommands under the Image menu for making tonal corrections. I'll start with some of the primary methods for making these kinds of tonal corrections, starting with the easiest to use first—these include Variations, Levels, and Curves.

Variations

As you saw in Chapter 9, Variations offers the most intuitive interface for tonal correction. Although this is the last option in the Adjust submenu, I've listed it first because it's not a bad place to begin when you're just starting out (see Figure 10.12). Like an interactive kiosk, this option offers you pictures you can click to apply a new variation on your image. You get new options based on your past decisions. You can see your original image next to your current pick in a convenient before-and-after view.

The Fine/Coarse slider offers the only control you have here for increasing or decreasing the level of change that takes place as you increase or decrease brightness or contrast. The Variations dialog box doesn't let you sample pixels in your image the way you can with the Levels or Curves commands.

The Show Clipping check box effectively warns you when your variations will produce areas of flat color—extremes at the 0 (black) or 255 (white) ends of the tonal range. Avoid applying variations that produce

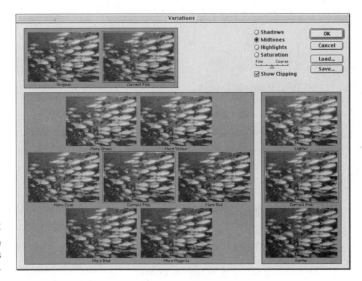

Figure 10.12
Using the
Variations
command.

these results, because these are areas where detail has been destroyed and where your variations have exceeded the tonal range.

This easy-to-use interface prevents you from exerting precise control over changes. In a general way, you can boost contrast by darkening shadows and lightening highlights, and reduce contrast by doing the opposite. If, however, you decide you've overuse the Variations, you can apply some measure of control by choosing Fade Variations from the Edit menu.

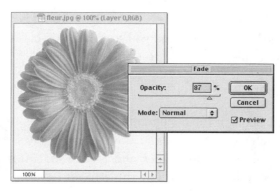

Figure 10.13

The Fade command under the Edit menu lets you temper your image-editing effects once they're applied.

The Fade dialog box will appear. You can now tweak your Variations effect by changing opacity and altering the color mode. You also can use this Fade command with other editing effects through the Adjust submenu under the Image menu—you can Fade Levels, Fade Curves, and so on, depending upon which effect you've most recently applied (see Figure 10.13).

Levels

You can also alter an image by using the Levels command, which lets you drag sliders or enter specific values to alter the shadows, highlights, and gamma (midtone) settings. For making tonal corrections in grayscale images, Levels is usually the best choice. Choose Adjust from the Image menu, and then select Levels to display the Levels dialog box. In Figure 10.14, I've displayed the Levels dialog box for my uncorrected example image.

Figure 10.14

You can use the Levels command to manually remap the tonal values for an image.

The main part of the Levels dialog box should be familiar—it shows the same kind of histogram you see when you choose Histogram from the Image menu.

Input Levels

Directly beneath the histogram are three slider controls: a black slider (on the left) for controlling shadow values, a gray slider (in the middle) for controlling gamma values, and a white slider (on the right) for controlling highlight values. The three Input Levels boxes correspond to the black, gray, and white sliders respectively—so you can enter specific values instead of dragging the sliders.

The values for the black (shadows) and white (highlights) sliders use the 0-255 range for measuring levels of gray. You can move the black and white sliders in toward the center to increase the overall contrast; in doing so, you'll change the tonal range in a couple of significant ways. For example, if you move the black slider from its default of 0 up to 15, you'll clip all the pixels in the range of 0 to 15 to level 0, or solid black. All the levels to the right of the black slider will be remapped between 0 and 255. Similarly, if you move the white slider from its default of 255 down to 240, all the pixels in the range of 240 to 255 will be clipped, or converted, to solid white at level 255, and all values to the left of the white slider will be remapped between 0 and 255. Figure 10.15 illustrates how this works.

The gray slider lets you change the midtones without affecting either the shadows or highlights. It lets you determine where you want the

Figure 10.15

Moving the black and white sliders in the Levels dialog box turns all values beyond a specified point to solid black or white, and remaps all tones in between.

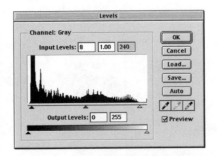

Figure 10.16
Moving the gray slider in the Levels dialog box lightens your image by reducing the number of pixels with values in the darker half of the tonal range.

midtone gray—that is, level 128—to fall. If you move the gray slider to the left, you're lightening the image by reducing the number of pixels that fall between 0 and 128 in value. If you move the gray slider to the right, your image will become much darker because you're remapping a much lighter gray value down to 128, and increasing the number of pixels between 0 and 128 (see Figure 10.16).

Output Levels

Beneath the three Input Levels slider bars is the Output Levels option, which is designed solely to reduce contrast. You can enter values or drag a black or white slider toward the center to control just how much you reduce the contrast. When you drag the black slider to the right, you lighten the image by reducing shadows; move the white slider toward the center to darken the image by removing highlights.

How does this differ from the way the Input Levels sliders function? Here's an example: as you just saw, if you move the Input Levels black slider to 50, you'll turn all the pixels that had been in the range of 0 to 50 to level 0, or solid black. With the black Output Levels slider, setting it to 50 tells the program to take all those pixels that had been in the range of 0 to 50 and make 50 the lowest possible value; those darkest values are remapped to lighter ones. As a result, the image brightens but there's less overall contrast in the range between light and dark.

I'll save the other options in the Levels dialog box—including the Load and Save buttons, the Auto button, and the Eyedropper tools—for the "Making Color Corrections" section a little later in this chapter.

Curves

The Curves dialog box has a somewhat different metaphor for making tonal corrections than the one in Levels; ultimately it's more powerful, but it's certainly less intuitive for the uninitiated.

With Curves, you won't see a histogram of the gray values in your image the way you do with the Levels command. Instead, you get a graph that represents the relationship between the values you're starting off with (or input levels) and the values that you'll alter (your output levels). You can also think of input and output levels as the before and after values in your picture, the way the Info palette shows your starting and ending values when you edit an image using the Levels command. You can modify curves by typing in the output level you want for a given input (see Figure 10.17).

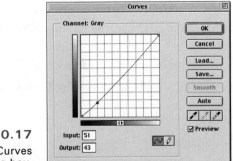

Figure 10.17

The Curves dialog box.

The input levels are mapped along the x-axis and the output levels along the y-axis. When you first open the Curves dialog box, the input levels and the output levels have the same values; as a result, the graph maps the simple equation x = y, which produces a straight diagonal line at 45 degrees.

The default settings for the gradient bar under the Curves graph blend from white to black, representing the percentage values measured by the graph, from 0 percent black (that is, white) to 100 percent black (solid black). The lower part of the graph represents the lighter areas of your image; you can reduce highlights by clicking and dragging up along the lower part of this curve. Likewise, the upper part of the graph represents the darker areas of the image, and you can lighten these shadows by clicking and dragging down at points along the upper part of the curve. Clicking and dragging along the middle part of the curve affects the image's midtones.

note

> **You can reverse the gradient bar under the Curves graph; this will let Curves use the model of 256 levels of gray for measuring input and output levels. The lower end of the curve will measure shadows and the upper end of the curve will measure highlights. It doesn't matter which model you use for editing in Curves—just use whichever one you're more comfortable with, percentages of black or the model using 256 levels of gray.**

If you move your cursor over different parts of the graph, you'll see the input values increase as you move the cursor to the right, and the output values increase as you move the cursor up. You can also track at what point on the graph any pixel in your image falls by selecting the Eyedropper tool and moving it across your image while the Curves dialog box is open. A circle appears at the point on the curve that represents the percentage of black for that pixel.

The Curves dialog box gives you a great deal of control over the tonal range as a whole, allowing you to make very precise adjustments to one part of the curve. When you add a new control point, creating an output level that has either more or less black than the input level at that point, you're actually affecting the slope of the entire curve. If your output level is very different from the input level, you'll see a dramatic shift in the curve as other points move to new output levels along the curve. You can add multiple control points at any part of the curve to gain further control over the changes you make on the graph in the Curves dialog box.

Any tonal changes you can make with the Levels dialog box you can reproduce in Curves, and then some. For example, to clip all values over a certain value—say, solid black—in Curves, you just need to move the uppermost point on the curve straight to the left, so the highest values are mapped in a straight line. Figure 10.18 shows what a highly posterized curve would look like; as you can see, many output level values in this graph are identical.

After lightening my example image so much with the Levels command to bring out the details, I know that the contrast needs to be boosted again. I can practice achieving contrast by creating a slight S curve. Here, I'm increasing the highlights by clicking and dragging down a new control point along the lower part of this curve, and increasing the shadows slightly by clicking and dragging a new control up point along the upper part of this curve (see Figure 10.19).

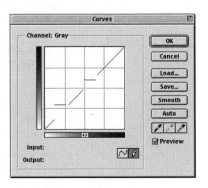

Figure 10.18

Posterizing an image with the Curves dialog box.

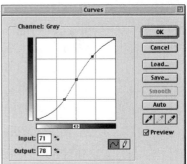

Figure 10.19
Making tonal corrections using the Curves dialog box.

Near the bottom of the Curves dialog box, you'll see a curve icon and a pencil icon; these represent the mode you're working in.

In curve mode, you can add, move, and delete the control points as I just discussed. If you switch to the pencil—in what is called arbitrary mode—you can use the pencil to draw new lines in the graph. Switching to arbitrary mode helped me create the posterized mode in Figure 10.19; I just drew several straight lines across to map numerous values to the same output level value. If you change the mapping function in this way, you can create your own unusual effects just by doodling. You can then click the Smooth button to convert a manually drawn curve to one based on points. If you continue to click the Smooth button repeatedly, you will eventually wind up straightening the curve completely.

Making Color Corrections

You'll need to attend to fine-tuning the shadows, highlights, and midtones in your color images just as you've done in grayscale images. Furthermore, you have additional color correction issues to face before you can produce images that look good in print.

For starters, you might need to correct color casts that the scanning process generated. There might also be color casts in your original transparency or print that you'll want to try to correct. Just as you tackled tonal corrections in editing a grayscale image before touching up the more nit-picky problems, you should color-correct your image here before worrying about smaller issues.

In anticipating problems that can arise on press, you might need to correct for dot gain the same way you did for grayscale images. Later in this chapter, you'll learn about techniques for reducing the overall ink density to compensate for poor trapping during printing, which refers to the ink's ability to adhere to another layer of ink as well as it does to paper. When your job has poor trapping, some of the inks will fail to adhere, resulting in color and tonal changes in your final output.

Here, I've opened a clip art color photo of a telephone repair person (see Figure 10.20). There are a few dust spots or blemishes to change, but I'll walk through making some tonal corrections here.

There are two main ways I'm hoping to manipulate the color for this image. First, I want to tone down some of the highlights; some of the lightest

Figure 10.20

A sample RGB image in need of some tonal corrections.

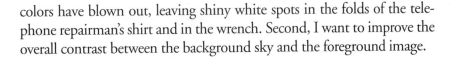

colors have blown out, leaving shiny white spots in the folds of the telephone repairman's shirt and in the wrench. Second, I want to improve the overall contrast between the background sky and the foreground image.

Taking Eyedropper and Color Sampler Readings

Now is a good time for you to switch your Info palette's first and second color readouts to show both RBG and CMYK values, because the colors you see onscreen might not match their print counterparts very well. (Pssst—have you calibrated your monitor yet? If not, consult Chapter 1, "System Essentials.") If you're working on images for print publication, you'll want to have your future CMYK values available at a glance so you can guard against *out-of-gamut colors* (RGB colors that have no CMYK equivalent) and too-heavy total inking.

Another good reason for keeping both the RGB and CMYK values at the ready in your Info palette is to help you add or subtract colors to produce their complementary colors. Remember in Chapter 4, "Color Essentials," you learned that opposite color pairs (such as cyan and its opposite color, red) are called complementary colors. For example, an image with little cyan in it has a high percentage of red and vice versa. You might want to get hold of a color wheel or refer to the color model charts in Chapter 4 when you're doing your color correcting, to help keep these relationships in mind.

By selecting the Eyedropper tool and passing the cursor over the image to take some readings, I was able to make some initial suppositions about what colors I needed to add and subtract. For example, the overall image is very dark but also suffers from lack of contrast; there are few highlights or shadows. The image is so blue—because of the deep sky tones—that the denim-clad worker doesn't pop out enough as the subject; the focus moves to the hat and the ladder.

The Color Balance Command

The Color Balance command gives you a quick-and-dirty solution for removing a color cast from an image. You can display the dialog box by choosing the Color Balance command from the Adjust submenu under the Image menu (see Figure 10.21).

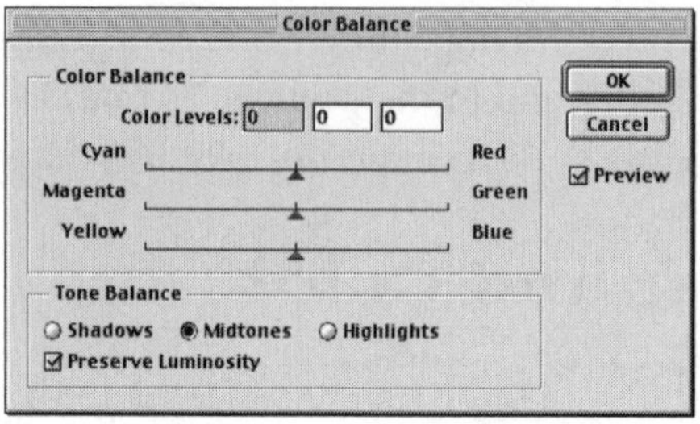

Figure 10.21

The Color Balance dialog box.

The Color Balance dialog box reflects the relationship between adding and subtracting the primary colors (red, green, and blue) and the secondary colors (cyan, magenta, and yellow). You can use it to affect color casts in one of three ways:

- Add more of one color by dragging its slider closer to the color name. For example, you can add more green to an image by dragging the bottom slider toward Green.

- Reduce a color cast by dragging its slider away from the color name. For instance, dragging the top slider toward Cyan reduces the amount of red in your image.

- Indirectly add or subtract a color by adjusting its two components. In this way, you can reduce the blue cast in an image by adding cyan and magenta.

Although the Color Balance dialog box is easy to use, its adjustments aren't very precise. The effects you produce by moving the sliders can usually be reproduced just as easily—and with more precision—through judicious use of the Curves dialog box.

The Hue/Saturation Command

When you choose Hue/Saturation from the Adjust submenu under the Image menu, you can edit colors based on the HSB (hue, saturation, brightness) color model described in Chapter 4 (see Figure 10.22). This technique is especially useful for colorizing black-and-white images, because clicking the Colorize check box in the Hue/Saturation

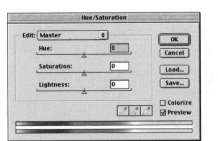

Figure 10.22

The Hue/
Saturation
dialog box.

dialog box makes it easy to infuse a selection or a whole image with any single color. If you need to edit tones, though, you should opt for the Levels or Curves commands instead.

With the Hue/Saturation dialog box, you can select any color in your image and shift its hue, saturation, and lightness. This lets you selectively adjust colors in particular areas of an image, so you can perform radical color shifts more easily.

The next step is to turn to the same tools for color correction that you used earlier with tonal correction in grayscale images: histograms and the Variations, Levels, and Curves dialog boxes. Functionally, they work the same but can produce much greater effects in three channels (for RGB mode) or four channels (in CMYK) than they did in just one.

Using the Histogram Command

Just as when you're assessing a grayscale image, you can turn to the Histogram command under the Image menu to assess the tonal range of an RGB or CMYK image. As mentioned earlier, when you look at a histogram for an image in RGB or CMYK mode, you have the option of viewing the histogram for any individual color channel, or for a channel called luminosity that represents the composite brightness values (see Figure 10.23).

In Figure 10.23, I've clicked the Channel drop-down list to view the Red, Green, Blue, and composite luminosity channels for my sample image. In each channel, the histogram is skewed with very high values in the midtones but few in the highlights and shadow areas.

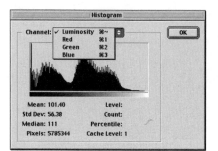

Figure 10.23

Checking the luminosity histogram in a color image.

Setting Black, White, and Neutral Points

When images like the one in Figure 10.20 lack shadows and highlights, it indicates they have compressed tonal ranges. One technique you can use for expanding a compressed tonal range is to set a white point (for the highlight) and a black point (for the shadow).

You can set the white and black points either automatically by using the Auto button in either the Levels or Curves setting (see Figure 10.24), by entering specific numeric values, or by choosing colors for the white and black points with the Eyedropper tool. If you've been wondering how the Auto command works, you can see that it automatically remaps only the lightest and darkest pixels to the white and black point—it doesn't automatically fix a bad histogram.

Setting a neutral point helps you eliminate a color cast. For example, if your photo was shot indoors under fluorescent lighting you might notice a reddish color cast. There are also different kinds of film optimized for indoor versus outdoor work; if you used the wrong kind of film for your photo shoot, a problematic color cast might arise in the prints. With the neutral point, you can identify a neutral gray for Photoshop to use for its midtone, and with luck correct other off-tinted midtones at the same time.

Now that you've seen how the Auto command works, it's time to look at how you can enter specific values for the black and white points. In either the Levels or Curves dialog box, just double-click the black or white eyedropper. This will launch the Color Picker dialog box, where you can enter the value you want. Your printer might be able to supply the optimal values you should use. These values are retained until they

Figure 10.24

The Auto button and icons for manually choosing a white point, black point, and neutral point (from left). These options appear in both the Levels and Curves dialog boxes.

are manually changed. A more intuitive way to select black and white points for your image is to identify and use the darkest and lightest values in your particular image. Exercise 10.1 shows you how to apply these endpoints manually.

Variations

Just as when you edit a grayscale image, you can probably have fairly good success editing the color balance using the Variations command (see Figure 10.25). Note that the Variations dialog box gives you several extra options with a color image; among other things, you can edit the saturation, or vividness, of the colors used.

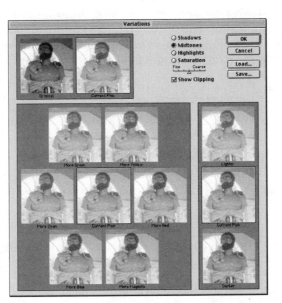

Figure 10.25

Using the Variations command with a color image offers controls over saturation as well as shadows and highlights.

EXERCISE 10.1

Manually Setting the White and Black Points in an Image

1. To select a white or black point manually, move your cursor over your image; notice the cursor changes to an eyedropper. Keep an eye on your Info palette reading to find the highest RGB level to set as the white point, or the lowest RGB level to set as the black point.

2. When you're ready to set those levels, double-click the white point or black point icon in the Levels or Curves dialog box. Move your cursor back to the area you identified for the white point and click; the Color Picker dialog box appears with the words "Select white target color" at the top. You have the option of altering the values in the dialog box if you didn't manually select the exact value you intended to.

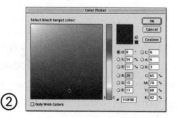

3. Repeat these steps for choosing the black point. Note that if you choose solid white and solid black for your white and black points, it has the same effect as if you pressed the Auto button in Levels or Curves.

> **note**
>
> **You can also use the Auto Levels or Auto Curves command under the Adjust submenu of the Image menu to set the white and black points in an image. These commands have the same effect as pressing the Auto button in the Levels or Curves dialog box.**

Levels

For greater control than the Variations command allows, you can use Levels (see Figure 10.26) to correct a composite color image—or better yet, individual color channels. Here, I used Levels most heavily in the Blue channel, to tone down the highest values while trying to expand the tonal range in the Red and Green channels.

Using the Save and Load buttons in the Levels dialog box, you can retain and then load settings that you plan to use.

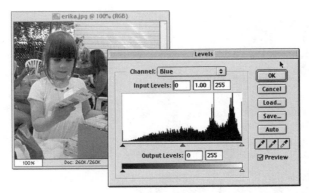

Figure 10.26
You can use the
Levels command
to edit individual
color channels.

Curves

As with the Levels command, you can use Curves to edit individual
color channels for touching up your color images (see Figure 10.27).

Using Adjustment Layers to Preview
Corrections

Besides the History palette, another safe way you can retouch your
image without making irrevocable changes is using Adjustment layers.

Figure 10.27
Using Curves to
increase overall
contrast slightly.

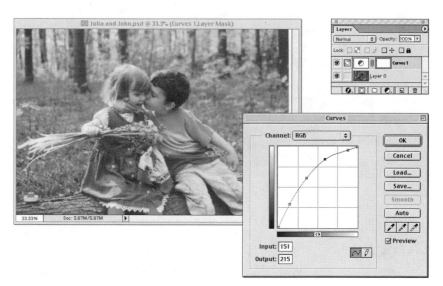

Figure 10.28

With adjustment layers, you can tweak an individual layer's levels, curves, color balance or another measure of the Adjust submenu under the Image menu— without actually touching the original layer's image data.

As you saw in Chapter 5, "Layering Essentials," adjustment layers let you apply many of the Adjust commands found under the Image menu—from Levels and Curves to Color Balance and Hue/Saturation—and affect your image as a whole. You need to create a separate adjustment layer for each of the Adjust commands you use—one for Levels, one for Curves, and so on (see Figure 10.28).

Adjustments layers act as both a preview and a buffer; you can see the results of your color adjustments, but if you want to remove an effect you've created, you need only to hide that layer from view. You can save your adjustments on their individual layers in Photoshop format, or, once you decide you're happy with the color and tonal corrections you've made, choose Flatten Image from the Layers palette pop-up menu and save your file for final output.

Using the Dodge and Burn Tools

After you've made your tonal corrections, you might still have small areas where you need to tweak some shadows. Here's where the Dodge or Burn tools come in handy. As mentioned in Chapter 3, "Toolbox and Palette Essentials," the Dodge and Burn tools (which share a spot

Figure 10.29

Compare the color-corrected image here with its original in Figure 10.20.

in the toolbox with the Sponge tool) derive from photographic techniques for, respectively, lightening and darkening parts of an image. The image that I've tweaked here—Figure 10.29—is in much better shape than when you first saw it in Figure 10.20.

Now that you've seen how to get a handle on some of the big tonal and color correction issues, you're ready to sweat the small stuff: fixing dust spots, scratches, and other minor imperfections.

Removing Dust Spots and Blemishes

It's easy to find dust spots on any scanned image, but scanned slides are especially prone to dust spots—the enlargement process tends to magnify any imperfections on an image. And when you sharpen the scanned image (which most scans need to improve the focus), you'll enhance those dust spots too (see Figure 10.30).

Figure 10.30
This scanned image picked up several dust spots and other blemishes.

Using the Clone Stamp and Pattern Stamp Tools

You can usually eliminate small stray blotches easily with judicious use of the Clone Stamp tool; you can clone another portion of your image and blend it in to replace dust spots or scratches seamlessly.

Although the Clone Stamp tool is more useful for obliterating dust spots and scratches in an image, its counterpart, the Pattern Stamp tool, is a better choice when you need to embellish an image. For example, use the Pattern Stamp tool to fill in a sparse forest or grass background in an image; to do so, you select one sample and define it as a pattern.

The Aligned Check Box

After you check the Aligned check box in the Clone Stamp tool's options bar, click and drag in a different area to duplicate the original area. As you continue to drag the cursor, more of the original area appears. The Pattern Stamp tool also has a setting for aligned cloning. Figure 10.31 illustrates an example of cloning using the Clone Stamp tool with the Aligned check box checked.

If you then move your cursor around to click and drag in a different part of the image—say, an inch to the right—you'll start cloning an

Figure 10.31
When you check the Aligned check box in the Clone Stamp tool's options bar, Photoshop keeps tabs on how wide an area you're cloning.

area an inch to the right of the original source area. Take care not to clone too broad an area—otherwise, you might inadvertently replicate other blotches near the source area or other contrasting pixels that would be out of place.

It's usually a good idea to choose a new source area frequently if you're touching up a wide area; using and reusing the same selection can cause noticeable patterns to emerge, which detracts from the realism of your retouching efforts.

Pattern Stamping

If you want to keep cloning the original source area over and over again, you'll find the Pattern Stamp tool more useful than the Clone Stamp tool. After you identify an originating point, the Pattern Stamp tool lets you replicate your source area anywhere else you click. Figure 10.32 shows the effect most people think of first when they hear about cloning: multiple copies of the same object.

Figure 10.32
Cloning with the Pattern Stamp tool lets you produce multiple copies of the same image area.

If you want your cloned copies to overlap one another, like the cheeseburgers shown in Figure 10.32, your original object should appear on its own transparent layer to get the best results.

• •

Stamping across Layers

tip If you're touching up a scanned photo, your cloning affects a single layer. But what if you've added layers or are working with another Photoshop document with multiple layers? Click the Use All Layers check box in the Clone Stamp tool's options bar to clone pixels from other layers.

• •

Using Feathering to Smooth Transitions

Sometimes you might find it easier to replace parts of your image by duplicating and pasting in a selection from another area. Feathering is a key part of making this kind of switcharound look more realistic.

You can feather a selection either before or after you actually make it. To feather the selection ahead of time, enter a numeric value (in pixels) in the Feather field in the options bar for whichever selection tool you use—for example, the Lasso or Rectangular Marquee tool. Or to feather after you've made a selection, just choose Feather from the Select menu.

When you duplicate the selection by copying and pasting—or as a shortcut, [Cmd]-[Option]-dragging for Mac users; [Ctrl]-[Alt]-dragging for Windows users—the feathered edges help obscure the boundaries of the pasted selection and add to the realistic effect.

In Exercise 10.2, you'll put these techniques described above to work to reduce or remove the dust spots and scratches introduced during scanning—or to correct blemishes on the original photo.

Making Picture-Perfect Facial Corrections

By now you've seen how to remove flaws introduced during the printing or scanning process, but what about touching up real facial characteristics such as wrinkles or freckles? With Photoshop, you can perform a digital facelift or wipe away a faceful of freckles with a few artful moves.

EXERCISE 10.2

Masking Dust Spots and Scratches

Practicing these spot-removal techniques is easiest when your subject matter is a human portrait or a prized possession—in other words, someone or something whose appearance you normally pay attention to.

①

②

1. Choose an image for editing, taking care to identify the spots you want to eliminate. Zoom in to a high magnification, one you can work at on a pixel-by-pixel basis. For example, try a 3:1 or 4:1 ratio.

2. Select the Clone Stamp tool from the toolbox. Make sure that the Aligned check box in the options bar is checked. You can also choose a brush size and set the opacity; here, I'm just using the Photoshop defaults of a small brush size and 100% opacity.

3. Position your cursor over an area of your image that has similar tones as the area you want to replace the first dust spot. To select that area as the point of origin, Option-click if you're a Mac user (or Alt-click if you're a Windows user) on that spot. Notice how your cursor changes while you're selecting a point of origin.

4. Now you're ready to start altering your first dust spot. If it's a large area, work from the outside to blend each pixel with the bordering ones. As mentioned before, you can change the point of origin by Option-clicking (or Alt-clicking) elsewhere as necessary to get a realistic mix of tones.

5. Now move to fixing another spot in your image. You'll almost certainly have to Option-click (or Alt-click) to choose a new source point. When you finish touching up your dust spots manually, the net effect should look clean and fluid, with no obvious digital futzing.

⑥

6. If any blemishes remain that are too small or tedious to eliminate with the Clone Stamp tool, select the area containing the dust spots and then apply the Dust & Scratches or Despeckle filters.

The first step, if the subject of the photo is the one urging you to make these corrections, is to point out reassuringly that physical appearance is no measure of real worth despite society's messages. Most real-life facelifts look a lot scarier than the untouched originals, anyway.

Keeping It Natural

If and when you do pursue improving on a person's looks in Photoshop, remember to emphasize a natural look above all else. A digital facelift doesn't mean removing all facial lines—everyone has some of those—but just blending them into lighter skin tones so they're less prominent.

Just as when you're removing dust spots, the Clone Stamp tool can be most useful in clearing up a complexion. Make sure you change your source point frequently—no one's skin tone is perfectly uniform. For the most realistic blended effects, choose a slightly larger brush size and lower the opacity slightly, so there are no sudden changes between pixels. The Smudge or Airbrush tools are other useful tools to use; just like applying concealer or other cosmetics in real life, you can dot on a perfect skin tone color and Smudge or Airbrush to blend it in.

The Eyes Have It

I also use the Clone Stamp tool to fix a common photo flaw that can afflict your subjects even if they look like Fabio—camera flashes that reflect off their eyes, giving them that demonic, red-eyed look. Similarly, you might have trouble photographing your pets head-on. When camera flashes reflect off your cat's or dog's eyes, they might appear especially glassy or filled with white. Also in the same vein are glares in your photos that reflect off of your subjects' eyeglasses.

For all three cases, you can eliminate the problems by applying the Clone Stamp tool or filling in the selected areas with samples taken from unaffected parts of the eyes.

Making Your Image Pop: Replacing a Background

Editing the background—that is, what's going on behind your image's subject—can help you establish the subject as the main focus. For

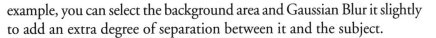

example, you can select the background area and Gaussian Blur it slightly to add an extra degree of separation between it and the subject.

But details can lead the viewer's attention astray, so you might want to wipe out distractions in the background. For example, other people walking behind your subject—especially if they're partially cut off by the photo—can make your otherwise good photo not so good anymore.

You can even drop an entirely new background behind your subject and make it look realistic, but you need a good grasp on how to make selections to do so. The Extract command and background eraser can help you make intelligent selections for isolating a background based on both shape and color.

Extract

Although the Extract command under the Image menu is extremely useful for isolating parts of your image, it does not wrap your subject in a marquee of marching ants like the other selection tools do. Instead, you draw a highlighted border around your subject. You can then preview your extraction and add last-minute touch-ups. The Extract command then isolates your subject by eliminating all background pixels on that layer. The erased image data is replaced by transparency. This command is intended to facilitate replacing a background altogether without producing an obvious colored halo around your subject's edges.

If you want to avoid losing the original image data after the extraction, be sure to duplicate the layer or to take a snapshot of the original image state with the History Palette first. You might want to keep the original background on hand to blur heavily and put back into place, which leaves your subject in the original environment but suddenly appearing in much greater focus. Exercise 10.3 demonstrates how to achieve this effect.

Background Eraser

The Background Eraser works a little bit like an on-the-spot Extract command—it erases all pixels it swipes over, leaving a transparent background behind.

EXERCISE 10.3

Extracting a Subject from the Background

①

②

③

④

1. Choose an image for editing and identify the layer containing your subject. If your subject is on the background layer, this layer becomes a non-background layer after the extraction. As mentioned earlier, you should duplicate this layer if you want to preserve the background image data.

2. Select Extract from the Image menu. The Extract dialog box appears. To focus on just the subject, you can use the Zoom tool in the dialog box's interface to draw a marquee around it, zooming in on just that part of your image.

3. Now, you'll use the Edge Highlighter tool (✐) to outline your selection. In the right side of the Extract dialog box are the settings you can change. You can enter a value for Brush size or just drag the slider to change the width of the highlighter tool. Later, you can use this option for resizing the Eraser, Cleanup, and Edge Touchup tools. If your subject's outline has a well-defined edge, click the Smart Highlighting check box under Tool Options in the right side of the Extract dialog box. Use a large brush wherever you have wispy or intricate edges to trace or when the foreground blends into the background—for example, when tracing the hair on a person's head or a leafy tree.

4. You can use the Zoom tool to zoom in or Option-click (or Alt-click) with the Zoom tool if you need to zoom out again. If you make any mistakes as you highlight your image's border, just switch to the Eraser tool (✐) to undo part of your outlining. To erase all of the highlighting you've done, just click Option+Del (on a Mac) or Alt+Backspace (in Windows).

⑤

⑥

5. Once you've finished outlining your subject, you're ready to define the foreground area. Select the Fill tool ( ) in the Extract dialog box. Click inside the subject outline to fill the interior with another color. By default, the highlighter appears in green and the fill color appears as blue, but you can change these in the Tool Options area in the right side of the Extract dialog box.

6. Click Preview to see the extracted subject. You can zoom in to review more closely, or repeat the extraction—going back to step 2—to improve the results. Or, you can eliminate stray background traces with the Cleanup tool ( ). To fill in gaps in the extracted subject, just hold down (Option) (on a Mac) or (Alt) (in Windows) as you drag with the Cleanup tool. To edit the edge of your subject's outline, use the Edge Cleanup tool ( ).

7. Click OK when you're ready to apply the final extraction. All pixels on the layer outside your extracted object are erased to transparency. See Figure 10.33.

Figure 10.33
After extracting, you can place your subject's layer on a new background or blur the original to make your subject stand out more.

Figure 10.34

The Background Eraser tool's options bar.

It samples the color in the center of the brush as a hot spot, and then deletes that color wherever it appears inside the brush. The Background Eraser (see Figure 10.34) also extracts color at the edges of your foreground objects, which helps eliminate the color halos that can appear when objects are later pasted over another background image.

The options you can set with the Background Eraser tool include the following:

- **Limits**. The Discontiguous choice erases the sampled color wherever it occurs under the brush. Contiguous erases areas with the sampled color only when they're connected to one another. Find Edges erases connected areas that use the sampled color, while helping preserve the sharpness of the shape's edges.

- **Tolerance**. The higher you set the tolerance, the broader the range of color that's erased. When this is set to 0, pixels of just a single color are erased under the hot spot.

- **Protect Foreground Color**. When this is checked, any pixels that use the current foreground color swatch are not erased.

- **Sampling**. Choose Continuous to erase every color the hot spot is dragged over, so the erasable color is constantly changing. The Once option erases only the color that was under the hot spot when you first clicked using the Background Eraser tool. The Background Swatch option erases only areas containing the current background color.

Selective Magnetism

If your background is truly a distracting one, you might want to outline your subject with the Magnetic Lasso or the pen tool with the Magnetic Pen option selected in the options bar. As you loosely trace your subject's edge, these tools automatically follow the color contrast and snap to place, thus fastening points accordingly. Remember that if

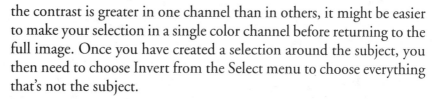

the contrast is greater in one channel than in others, it might be easier to make your selection in a single color channel before returning to the full image. Once you have created a selection around the subject, you then need to choose Invert from the Select menu to choose everything that's not the subject.

Don't forget to feather your selection before you blur or otherwise distort it. Because you'll probably go to some lengths to get the exact selection you want, it makes more sense to feather afterward instead of before. When you've made your selection, just choose Feather from the Select menu and add a value for the number of pixels for feathering.

Distorting Effects

In Chapter 8, "Filter Essentials," you saw how several Photoshop filters—such as Wave and Shear—can add funhouse-mirror effects to your image. The new Liquify tool in Photoshop 6.0 has a broad interface for adding even more of those effects, with some sophisticated controls for "freezing" parts of your images that should not be affected as well as one-step processes for reverting to or reconstructing your original image. Its interface is similar to Kai's Power Goo—you can pull on, twist, melt, and shrink different parts of an image. It's especially enthralling when used to edit images of people's faces—you can make eyes bulge or shrink to piggish orbs, for example, or stretch a nose into Pinocchio's. The fun factor on this one definitely outweighs its practical uses, but it has potential for moving parts of an image that would otherwise require painstaking manual efforts with the Clone Stamp tool or Transform commands—and, of course, you can create instant and painless nose jobs.

Choose Liquify from the Image menu to display the Liquify dialog box (see Figure 10.35). If you want to change only part of the current layer, select the area or areas to be changed. (You can also create an alpha channel to use as a mask that defines frozen areas.)

You can use a selection to zoom in on an area to be displayed in the preview image, but you can't zoom within the Liquify preview. Just as with the Extract interface, your tools are at the left and options for adjusting the tools are at the far right side of the interface.

Figure 10.35
The Liquify
interface.

You have the following tools at your disposal for creating distortions:

The Warp tool moves pixels forward as you drag.

The Twirl Clockwise tool rotates pixels clockwise while you click and hold the mouse or drag.

The Twirl Counterclockwise tool turns pixels counterclockwise while you click and hold the mouse or drag.

With the Pucker tool, you move pixels inward toward the center of the brush area while you click and hold the mouse or drag.

The Bloat tool pushes pixels away from the center of the brush area while you click and hold the mouse or drag.

The Shift Pixels tool moves pixels in the direction you move the mouse as you click and [Option]-drag (for Mac users) or [Alt]-drag (in Windows).

Figure 10.36
Before and after effects with the Liquify interface. Although gross distortions are the most fun part of this tool, you can apply subtle digital plastic surgery effects as well.

 The Reflection tool copies pixels to the brush area and then reflects them perpendicularly to the direction in which you then stroke with the mouse. When you click and drag with overlapping strokes, you can create an effect similar to a reflection in water.

You can also define any areas in the preview image that should remain fully or partially unchanged using the Freeze tool ( ). If you change your mind about freezing that part of the image, use the Thaw tool ( ) to put that image data up for grabs again. Then select the Reconstruct tool ( ), and hold down the mouse button or drag over the areas. Figure 10.36 shows some of the effects you can achieve using Liquify.

Summary

In this chapter, you've learned some advanced techniques for retouching flaws and correcting color casts in images using the Clone Stamp tool and the various Map and Adjust subcommands. With the information covered here, you'll be well-equipped to optimize your images for print—the topic of Chapter 14, "Print Production Essentials." Up ahead in Chapter 11, "3D Rendering Essentials," you'll learn methods for creating 3D shapes and text, and other special geometric effects.

11

3D Rendering Essentials

IN THIS CHAPTER

Creating Geometric Shapes

Using the 3D Transform Plug-In

Using Layer Styles to Create 3D Effects

Adding Shadows

From plain geometric shapes to raised plastic or metallic effects, there are many three-dimensional effects you can create within Photoshop. Three-dimensional shapes let you dress up bullets and icons or add depth when embellishing print pieces. They're also great for creating the kinds of clickable buttons and polished-looking interfaces seen on so many Web sites. The new textures in Photoshop 6.0's Layer Style options and Gradient and Pattern overlays go a long way toward helping you achieve these effects quickly.

Now suppose you want to manipulate the position of a three-dimensional object in one of your images, whether it's part of a photograph or a gradated shape you've created yourself. You can use the 3D Transform filter to rotate it slightly or adjust its size and position realistically—even though the object was photographed from a different angle or orientation. This capability for rotating and manipulating three-dimensional objects in your flat images lets you control perspective and image depth so you can edit your photocompositions more flexibly and realistically. In this chapter, you learn the basic techniques and some jumping-off points for creating the following effects:

- 👁 Spheres, cubes, and cones

- 👁 Textured surfaces on 3D shapes

- 👁 Shadows and gradients to enhance 3D effects

- 👁 Rotation of three-dimensional objects in your image

- 👁 Plastic effects and raised buttons for Web sites

- 👁 Beveled edges on objects and type using layers for a clickable button effect

Gaining Perspective

When you reposition or combine photorealistic objects in your images, you need to maintain a perspective that helps reproduce that 3D effect in two dimensions. To do so, you use *perspective projection*, which makes objects appear larger when they are closer and smaller when they are further away.

To understand how this works, think back to a long car ride or train trip. Remember how road signs or telephone poles would whiz right by as you stared out the window, but it seemed to take forever to reach the mountains or the city outskirts you could see at the horizon? That's because objects that are close to you appear larger and move by you much more quickly, whereas objects at a distance seem to appear smaller and move more slowly. As you work with graphics that contain a number of objects, you'll see that the relative sizes of the objects provide important visual clues about how far each seems from the viewer.

Transformed is a key word for describing Photoshop manipulations that affect how objects appear to someone viewing your image. As you see in this chapter, you can use many of the Transform subcommands under the Edit menu—such as Scale, Rotate, Skew, or Perspective (see Figure 11.1)—to create 3D geometric shapes from scratch or add realistic-looking shadows to objects in your images. The Free Transform command, directly under the Edit menu, gives you access to all these dynamic transformations simultaneously.

Geometric Shapes

I'll start with something simple—the basic kinds of geometric shapes that even "people who can't draw" can draw. The next set of exercises lets you practice creating spheres, cubes, cones, and rods with gradient fills, followed by a section on adding textures and mapping images to these kinds of shapes.

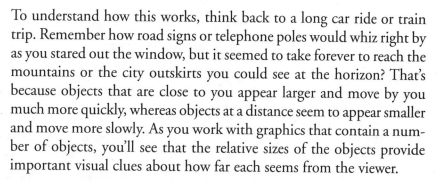

Figure 11.1

The Transform subcommands under the Edit menu help create the illusion of depth for 3D geometric shapes.

EXERCISE 11.1

Creating Spheres

Photoshop 6.0's new Fill Layers feature lets you apply gradients and fill colors without touching one of the Gradient tools. In this exercise, you'll apply a radial gradient in a fill layer in combination with channels and filters to create a sphere whose color and shadow can be edited easily.

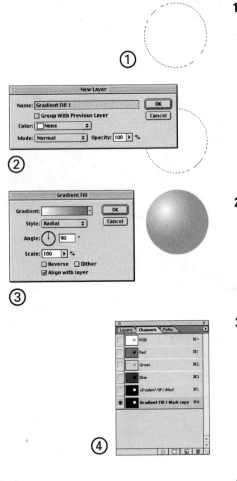

1. Launch Photoshop and create a new document. Be sure to select the RGB Color mode. It's a good idea to either use a transparent background or create a new layer for your sphere—this makes it easy to place your completed sphere in other images without copying over a solid background. Now choose the Elliptical Marquee tool and hold down (Shift) as you click and drag to form a perfect circle. Remember that if you want, you can draw a circle from the center outward by also holding down (Option) (for Mac users) or (Alt) (for Windows users) while you're pressing (Shift).

2. Set the foreground color to white for the highlights on the finished sphere, and make the background color bright. Choose New Fill Layer from the Layer menu, then select Gradient from the submenu. By default, this channel is named Gradient Fill 1 Mask; you can rename it if desired. Click OK when you're done.

3. The Gradient Fill dialog box appears. Click the gradient swatch to make sure the Foreground to Background option is selected. Pick Radial from the Style drop-down menu. At this point, you can click within your sphere to indicate where the light (your white starting point) should shine. Notice how you can use the mouse to move the center of the gradient by clicking and dragging in the image window. Once you're satisfied with the gradient's display, click OK.

4. Now choose Show Channels from the Window menu. The Fill Layer you applied to the spherical selection has created a layer mask; as a result, you should see a new channel named after your fill layer with the word "Mask" appended to the end. Next, you'll create a duplicate of the sphere mask to use in adding a realistic-looking shadow. Drag the

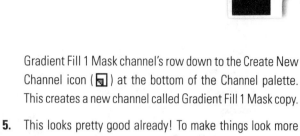

Gradient Fill 1 Mask channel's row down to the Create New Channel icon ( ) at the bottom of the Channel palette. This creates a new channel called Gradient Fill 1 Mask copy.

5. This looks pretty good already! To make things look more realistic, blur and offset this channel so as to create a shadowy selection for the composite image. Choose Blur from the Filter menu, and then choose Gaussian Blur. Enter a value to generate a fairly pronounced shadow effect. The exact value you enter depends on how big your original sphere is and how deep you want the shadow effect to be. The higher the value, the more pronounced the offset effect looks.

Next, choose Other from the Filter menu, and then choose Offset from the Other submenu. Here, the idea is to get the blurry shadow edge to move a little upward and to the left, so you need to enter negative horizontal and vertical values in the Offset dialog box. There is one basic rule to remember: offset your shadow in the opposite way you created your gradient. Earlier, you added a gradient fill by dragging to the right and down, so you need to move this shadow area to the left and up. In this example, I entered values of −20 and −10 pixels.

6. The next step is to carve out the little half-moon of shadow you need from this blurry channel. Essentially, you want to load your original gradient fill mask selection (the basic sphere shape) into the copy you made of that channel (with the Gaussian Blur and offset effects) and subtract the overlapping parts. Choose Load Selection from the Select menu and pick the Gradient Fill 1 Mask alpha channel. Once again, choose Load Selection from the Select menu and pick Gradient Fill 1 Mask copy—and this time, be sure to click the Subtract from Selection radio button.

Next, pick Save Selection from the Select menu to send the results to a new channel. Here, I've named the new channel Half Moon.

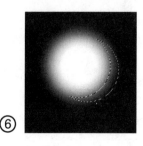

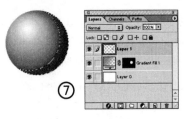

⑦

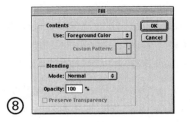

⑧

7. You're almost done now; you just want to save this channel in its own layer so you can edit it independently of the sphere. Click the RGB channel's row in the Channels palette to return to the composite view. Create a new layer by clicking the Create New Layer icon in the Layers palette.

   With the new layer targeted, choose Load Selection from the Select menu and load the Half Moon channel.

8. Fill the shadow selection with any color you like. Here, I've added a dark gray shadow to my bright green sphere. Because the sphere and its shadow are on different layers, you can change the colors or the opacity any time you like without having to redraw your sphere (see Figure 11.2).

9. Save your newly created sphere image to disk; it will be used in a later exercise in this chapter.

Figure 11.2
A sphere with its shading on a separate layer to facilitate future editing.

EXERCISE 11.2

Creating Cubes

Cubes are an especially useful design element; for example, you can map a different photo image to each face. Here's one way to create a cube that you can edit later. In the following steps, you place each side in a separate layer for future use.

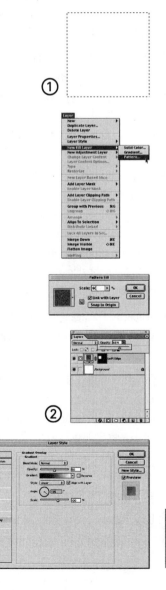

1. Create a new document. Just as in the sphere exercise, it's a good idea to either use a transparent background or create a new layer for your cube. Here, I've created a new layer called Left Edge. Now choose the Rectangular Marquee tool and hold down [Shift] as you click and drag to form a perfect square. Remember that if you want, you can draw a square from the center outward by also holding down [Option] (for Mac users) or [Alt] (for Windows users) while you're pressing [Shift].

2. Now you'll add a pattern or gradient fill to this first square via a fill layer. Choose New Fill Layer from the Layer menu, then select Pattern from the submenu. In this example, I've picked a pattern called Stucco.

   Because you can control the opacity of your fill layer, you might want to reduce the opacity of the pattern fill so that the shadows you add next are visible.

3. Next, you add the shadows to this cube's left edge by choosing Layer Style from the Layer menu, and then Gradient Overlay from the Layer Style submenu. Here, you can set many options at once to determine the gradient's style, opacity, and colors used. Choose Linear from the Style pop-up menu. You can click the gradient color swatch if needed to choose a new starting and ending color. Click in the Angle diagram to alter the angle of the gradient; here, I've selected –35 °.

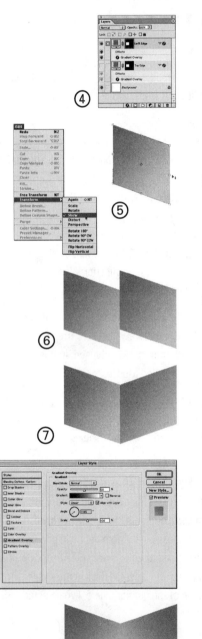

4. Now, you need to create a duplicate of this layer; this lets you keep a copy of your square in reserve while you assemble the left and right sides of the cube. Drag the Left Edge layer down to the New Layer icon or choose Duplicate Layer from the Layers palette pop-up menu. I've renamed the new layer Top Edge. Hide this duplicate layer by turning off its eye icon in the Layers palette; you'll use the Top Edge layer later to create the top edge of the cube.

5. Make sure that the Left Edge layer is the active layer. Now choose Transform from the Edit menu and then choose Skew. Small square handles appear at all four corners of your selection and in the center of all four sides; drag the one in the middle of the right edge down to create a skewed shape. Click the check mark in the options bar to make the change.

6. Now you need a duplicate of this selection for the right edge of the cube. Drag the Left Edge layer down to the New Layer icon or choose Duplicate Layer from the Layers palette pop-up menu. I've renamed the new layer Right Edge. Select the Move tool. Hold (Shift) as you click and drag the selection to the right; drag until the right side of the selection is aligned with the original skewed shape's left edge, as shown.

7. Select Transform from the Edit menu, and then choose Flip Horizontal. The skewed right edge selection is horizontally flipped to create a wide V-shape with the skewed left edge selection.

8. The shape of these two edges is fine, but the gradation in the right edge selection is a little off because you flipped it. Double-click the Right Edge layer's row in the Layers palette to bring up the Layer Style dialog box. Highlight Gradient Overlay in the left side to display the layer's gradient fill options. Click in the Angle diagram to change the angle of the gradient; here, I've selected –145 °.

Now that the base looks more realistic, you can bring the Top Edge layer back into view and place the top edge on the cube.

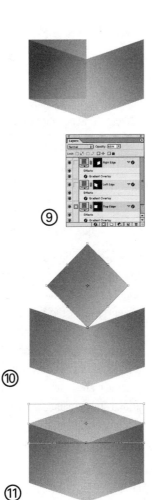

9. Click the eye icon next to the Top Edge layer and target that layer. Use the Move tool to position the square over the other two sides in the cube.

10. Select Transform from the Edit menu, and then choose Rotate. In the options bar, set the angle of rotation to 45°. Use the Move tool to reposition the square's bottom corner to the junction where the other two sides meet. As in Step 8, you can alter the Top Edge layer's gradient angle through the Layer Style dialog box.

11. Choose Transform from the Edit menu, and then choose Scale. You need to drag the square handles on all four sides so that the lower two diagonal edges align perfectly with the top edges of the other two cube sides. Click inside the selection to make the change.

When your top edge selection is perfectly in place, save it to an alpha channel so you can reselect it whenever you like. As Figure 11.3 shows, your cube is now complete!

Figure 11.3

A cube with each side available for further editing using alpha channels.

EXERCISE 11.3

Creating Cones

Now you can move on to creating a more interesting 3D geometric shape. This exercise shows how to create a shiny, metallic-textured cone. Because this is a real quick-and-dirty effect, I'll demonstrate this one with the Gradient tool instead of creating a fill layer with a gradient fill.

1. Create a new Photoshop document with a white background. The exact dimensions aren't important, but it should be square. For this example, I created a document measuring 400×400 pixels.

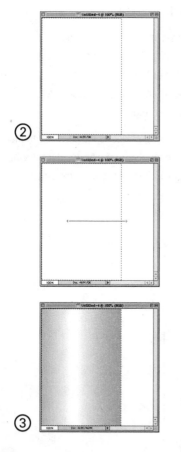

2. Choose the Rectangular Marquee tool, and then click and drag to select about three-quarters of your image.

3. You're going to add a gradient fill from the middle of your selection out to the right by using the Gradient tool with the Reflected Gradient selected, which will reflect the gradient from the middle back to the left as well. Set the foreground and background colors to white and black, or any two other contrasting colors, with the lighter color in the foreground. Check the gradient swatch in the option bar to make sure that the blend is set to Foreground to Background. Press (Shift) and drag straight across from the middle of the selection to the right selection edge.

4. You've now created the blend that will appear on the front and left sides of your cone. Now you're ready to make your second and final gradation. Begin by choosing Inverse from the Select menu to select the remaining portion of your image. This time, you need to apply a dark-to-light linear fill going from left to right. Because you don't need to reflect this second gradation, switch to the Linear Gradient option in the Gradient tool's option bar. Here, I've also reversed my foreground and background colors so the lighter color is in the background. Press (Shift) and drag across your selection from left to right.

   From here on, make sure that your background color is set to white; you're going to start reshaping this image into the cone, so you don't want any strange colors filling in the background.

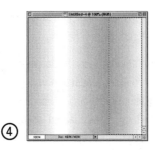

④

5. Select your entire image by pressing Cmd+A (for Mac users) or Ctrl+A (for Windows users). You can also use the Rectangular Marquee tool to select the entire document. Select Transform from the Edit menu, and then choose Perspective from the Transform submenu. Small square handles should appear at each corner of the image. Click one of the upper handles and drag straight across to the center of the image; this will create the pointy head of your cone. You can also drag downward if you want the cone to squat lower. You can make the cone narrower by clicking one of the lower handles and dragging straight across to the center of the image. When you finish shaping your cone, click the check mark in the Options menu to make the change.

⑤

⑥

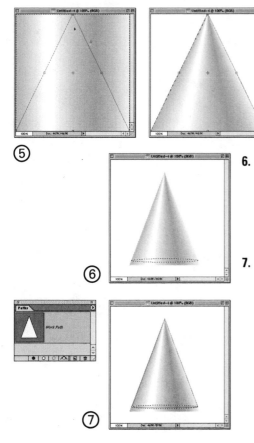

⑦

6. Now to give the cone a rounded edge at the bottom, choose the Elliptical Marquee tool and create a long oval ellipse near the bottom of the cone, extending from edge to edge. The bottom part of this ellipse will form the rounded bottom part of the cone when you're done.

7. To select the sides of the triangle, you can create a path using the Paths palette. First, make sure the Paths palette is visible; if necessary, choose Show Paths from the Window menu. Use the standard Pen tool to draw a triangle that traces from the point of the cone down the left side, straight across the middle of your elliptical selection, and back up the right side.

Magnifying the cone shape with the Zoom tool can help you place your points with the Pen tool more easily.

⑧

8. Now convert the path to a selection by choosing Make Selection from the Paths palette pop-up menu.

    Click the Add to Selection radio button in the Make Selection dialog box. Your new selection will include both the area covered by your ellipse and the converted path. Save your cone outline to an alpha channel for future use as necessary. You can drag the Work Path row in the Paths palette to the palette's Trash icon.

9. Now choose Inverse from the Select menu and press Delete (see Figure 11.4). Congratulations—you're done!

Figure 11.4
Creating a
3D cone.

EXERCISE 11.4

Creating Rods

In the previous exercise, you made use of the Reflected Gradient option in the Gradient tool, which helps create the illusion of depth by creating two opposing lighting effects; I use it whenever I need to create a 3D rod, cone, or can shape.

1. Create a new Photoshop document with a white background. The exact dimensions aren't important, but it should be another square. For this example, I created a document measuring 600×600 pixels.

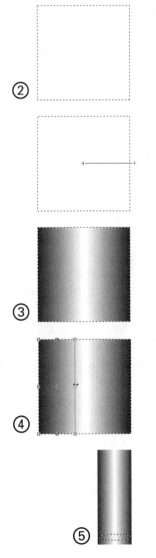

2. With the Rectangular Marquee tool selected, click and drag to make a rectangular selection in your image. Be sure to leave some extra room at the top of your rectangle, since the top of the finished 3D rod will extend above the top of the original rectangle.

3. Just as in Step 3 of Exercise 11.3, the idea is to add a gradient fill from the middle of your selection straight out to the right. Set the foreground and background colors to white and black, or any two other contrasting colors with the lighter color in the foreground. Select the Reflected Gradient tool and make sure that the gradient is set to Foreground to Background. Press (Shift) and drag straight across from the middle of the selection to the right edge.

   From here on, make sure that your background color is set to white. You're going to start reshaping this image's edges, so you don't want any strange colors filling in the background.

4. If you like, you can resize your marquee selection to change the rod shape. To do so, choose Transform from the Edit menu, and then choose Skew. When you finish shaping your rod's width, click the check mark in the Options menu to make the change.

5. Now give the rod a rounded edge at the bottom. Choose the Elliptical Marquee tool and create a long oval ellipse near the bottom of the rod, extending from edge to edge. The bottom part of this ellipse will form the rounded bottom part of the rod when you're done.

Make sure you save the ellipse to an alpha channel; you'll need to load it a little later to create the top edge of the rod.

6. Unlike Exercise 11.3, this one doesn't require you to use the standard Pen tool and the Paths palette to add the main part of this shape to the ellipse selection—because the body of the rod is rectangular, you can use the Rectangular Marquee tool to select it. Make sure you hold down 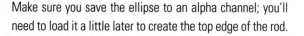 Shift as you make this selection to add it to the ellipse selection.

7. Now choose Inverse from the Select menu and press Delete. This creates the rounded bottom edge of the rod, but you still need to work on the top edge.

Deselect the current selection. Now choose Load Selection from the Select menu and load the alpha channel containing the ellipse. Change to the Move tool. Hold down Option and Shift if you're a Mac user (Windows users choose Alt) to drag a copy of the ellipse up to the top of the rod shape.

8. Your rod shape should now look like a cut section of pipe. Evaluate your image to determine whether the gradient on the top needs adjustment to create a 3D effect. If you want the rod to look like a filled shape, you might want to skew the angle of the top gradient. I want this rod to look like a hollow section of pipe, so to make the effect more realistic, I apply a slightly darker reflected gradient in the top ellipse. Here, I've set my foreground color to a slightly darker shade than my original light foreground color, and kept the background color a dark shade. Choose the Reflected Gradient tool, click in the middle of the elliptical selection, and drag all the way to the right.

Deselect the top elliptical selection, and you're done! Figure 11.5 shows the 3D rod.

Figure 11.5
Creating a
3D rod.

Overlaying Images on 3D Graphics

By now you've seen how to create some geometric shapes with a textured surface by adding a patterned fill as you built the object. But what if you have an image you want to superimpose on a 3D shape after the fact? Photoshop's Transform commands and several filters can help you get the job done—the combination you use depends largely on the effect you want to achieve.

Open the file containing your geometric shape. Always create a new layer for the overlaying photo so that it can be edited separately and—most importantly—so that you can continue to edit the shape's shadows or gradient fill without adversely affecting the quality of your overlaying image.

Say you want to superimpose an image or some text on a spherical shape. Consider the Teletubbies: inside the sun, one can see a gurgling baby peeking out—that's the kind of superimposed spherical effect you'll create next.

When superimposing an image on the side of a cube or block shape, remember the Transform commands you saw in Exercises 11.2 and 11.3. You can use Free Transform under the Edit menu, or Skew in the Transform submenu under the Edit menu to rotate the superimposed image to match the angle of each edge. As in Exercise 11.5, you need to load each side's outline as a selection to trim off unwanted parts of the superimposed image. Figure 11.6 shows the beginnings of a photo cube.

Figure 11.6

Use the Free Transform command to superimpose an image on the side of a cube in perspective. You can use this effect to create your own photo cubes.

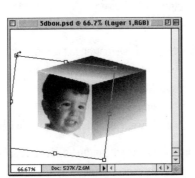

EXERCISE 11.5

Superimposing a Photograph on a Sphere

① ② ③ ④ ⑤

1. Open the image of the 3D sphere you created in Exercise 11.1. The important part to remember here is that you need to load the layer mask as a selection. You should also open the file containing the image to be superimposed. Make sure that the two have comparable dimensions—otherwise, you might need to scale one or the other, or create a new sphere shape.

2. Create a new layer for the image you want to superimpose on the sphere; you might want to make the mode either Overlay or Multiply to let any gradient fill on the left edge show through.

   After you create and target the new layer, drag the photo into the file containing the sphere. Reposition the photo until you're satisfied with how it's framed within the shape's outline.

3. Choose Spherize from the Distort submenu under the Filter menu. Choose a percentage that will create an appropriate rounded effect without cutting off too much of the subject from within the sphere's shape.

4. Open the Channels palette and click the row containing the mask for the sphere. From Exercise 11.1, I had named this Gradient Fill 1 Mask. Make sure that you are still on the layer containing the superimposed photo. Choose Load Selection from the Select menu and load Gradient Fill 1 Mask. The sphere's outline should appear within a row of marching ants.

5. Choose Inverse from the Select menu and press ⌘-X (on a Mac) or Ctrl-X (for Windows users) to delete the extraneous portion of the superimposed photo.

6. Now you can rearrange the order of the layers or experiment with the opacity to determine how much of the sphere's color should show through and how heavy the gradient fill should be. Here, for example, I changed the color of the gradient fill from my original bright green to an infusion of yellow.

Figure 11.7 shows the end result. You can further enhance the button effect by applying a drop shadow or glow using the Layer Style commands from the Layer menu.

Figure 11.7
A do-it-yourself
photo button.

The warp text styles new to Photoshop 6.0 are also a good complement to an image superimposed on a 3D shape, especially spherical ones (see Figure 11.8). These warp text styles include Fisheye, Bulge, Shell Upper, Shell Lower, and a number of other effects that appear to wrap around or over unseen shapes. You can access these warp text styles by clicking the Create warped text button (**T...**) in the Type tool's options bar.

Figure 11.8
You can use
warped text to
further enhance a
3D effect.

EXERCISE 11.6

Moving a 3D Object to View from Another Angle

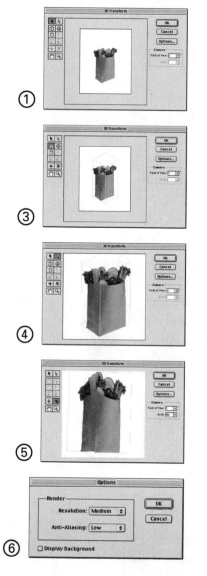

1. Open a Photoshop document containing a 3D image. If you don't have a suitable stock image on hand, use the finished cube from Exercise 11.2. You'll have better results if your 3D object is on its own layer.

2. Choose Render from the Filter menu, and then choose 3D Transform.

3. Choose a geometric shape tool in the 3D Transform dialog box that best matches the shape of your object. Here, I'm using an image of a bag of groceries, so I've selected the cube tool. Position your cursor a little above and to one side of your object, and then click and drag to create a geometric outline on top of your image. If it's difficult to discern whether the shape you've chosen overlays your image properly, use the Magnifying Glass tool to enlarge the image.

4. Now choose the Direct Selection tool ( ) and drag each anchor point one at a time to better align them with your image.

5. Use the Pan Camera tool ( ) and the Trackball tool ( ) to move and rotate the object so that you're viewing it from a different angle.

6. If the background of your image is in the way, click Options and uncheck Display Background.

Using the 3D Transform Plug-In

The 3D Transform plug-in can help if you need to rotate a 3D object in your image to fit better with other objects in place. Imagine, for example, that you need to combine separate product shots in a group collection. Suppose four of the five boxes were photographed head-on, whereas the fifth was shot at three-quarters view. Unless you can change the perspective of that fifth image, it will not look realistic for you to group that object in the picture with the others.

In Exercise 11.6, you rotated a 3D image in a Photoshop document to view it from another perspective.

tip   When you use the 3D Transform filter, you might find it useful to set Photoshop guidelines to visually align the transformed object in your image more precisely with the rest of your image. To lay down these guidelines wherever you need them, first choose Show Rulers from the View menu. This places rules along the top and left edges of your file window. Just click one of these rulers to drag out a horizontal or vertical guideline and release the mouse pointer when you're ready to place the guideline.

Using Layer Styles to Create 3D Edges and Realistic Shadows

As you saw in Chapter 5, "Layering Essentials," you can add one-step drop shadows, glows, raised or recessed lettering, or beveled and embossed effects to any part of your image on its own layer. Just target the layer containing the texture or object you want to embellish, and then choose Layer Style from the Layer menu. The commands under the Layer Style submenu direct you to apply the specific effect you want (see Figure 11.9).

Creating Buttons with Beveled Edges

Beveled edges—whereby each side's highlights blend at the corners instead of making a sharp angle—give clickable buttons in online and onscreen presentations the illusion of depth. Even ATM machines use them for onscreen keypads. For raised buttons, the edges of the top

Figure 11.9

Creating drop shadows and beveled and embossed effects are one-step processes with Photoshop 6.0's Layer Style options.

and left sides have light-colored highlights; the bottom and right sides have dark, shadowed edges. Reverse the colors, and the button looks recessed instead of raised.

Here's a quick look at using layer effects to create 3D buttons. Open the image you want to add beveled edges to, or create a new layer in a document. Here, I've used a plain square of pink granite texture.

Make sure that your button texture is on its own layer. Choose Layer Style from the Layer menu, and then choose Bevel and Emboss. You should see the following dialog box.

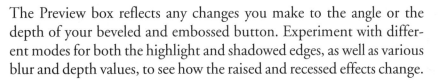

The Preview box reflects any changes you make to the angle or the depth of your beveled and embossed button. Experiment with different modes for both the highlight and shadowed edges, as well as various blur and depth values, to see how the raised and recessed effects change.

By now you've seen how the Layer Style options can automate the process of adding dimension to your image elements through effects like beveling and embossing. You've also seen how the Layer Style options can add shadows through gradient overlays, and embellished textures through pattern overlays. It's now time to revisit the custom shape tools, new in Photoshop 6.0, which can combine a series of layer effects in a single-step process.

Choose the Rectangle or Rounded Rectangle (ideal for Web buttons) custom shape tool. In the options bar, click the Layer Style drop-down menu and select one of the glass button textures (see Figure 11.10). If you don't see these colored glass styles, you need to click the black triangle next to the layer style swatches to display the fly-out menu; choose Load Styles and be sure to select the Glass Buttons.asl file.

You choose the effect to apply by sight in a single step—but you might not realize at first that Photoshop is actually applying several layer styles to achieve that visual effect. You can see the steps you've saved by looking at the effects listed in the Layers palette for your custom shape layer (see Figure 11.11).

Figure 11.10

Use the custom shape tools and layer styles to create textured buttons in a single step.

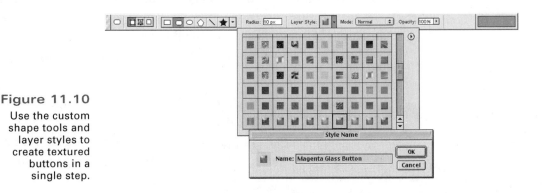

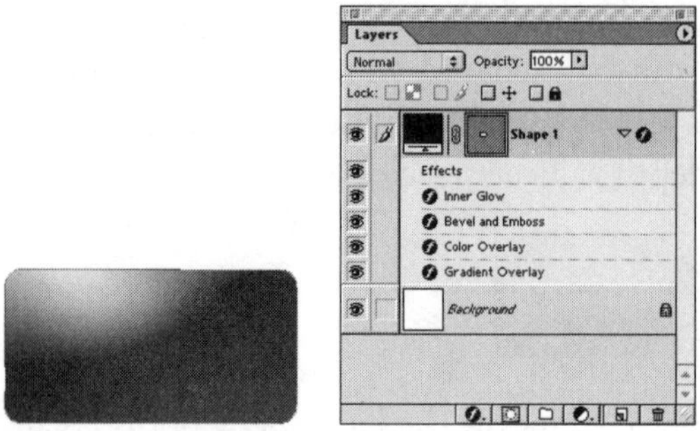

Figure 11.11

The Layers palette shows you how many layer styles were applied when you selected a layer style swatch with a custom shape.

Creating 3D Lettering

Just as the beveled edges on buttons can be concave or convex, you can add such edges to text to create raised or recessed type. In Exercise 11.7, you're going to add raised text to a clickable button.

Adding Shadows

Shadows are an important accessory to 3D objects because they help enhance the illusion of depth. As you've seen in other layer effects covered in this chapter, the drop shadow layer effect is a no-brainer method for adding shadows to type and objects in your images. For more flexibility, you can always create a duplicate of the layer containing your text, and then darken, blur, and offset the shadow text from the original. Here are a few pointers I've collected for enhancing the realism of your shadow effects:

👁 **Vary the shadow's darkness against its width**. Look around at the real world—larger shadows tend to thin out and seem less intense. They're cast when the main light source is at a steep angle or the object is floating above its background, and side light diffuses into them.

👁 **Create more than one shadow**. One way to make more realistic drop shadows is to make the scene look as if it has more than one light source—so that things in it cast more than one shadow. Experiment with creating a darker, shorter shadow combined with a

lighter, longer one. Use the Lighting Effects filter in the Render submenu under the Filter menu to try different effects.

◉ **Keep the direction of all shadows consistent**. The shadow direction from the originating object should always be consistent with the apparent light direction and shadowing in the original image.

◉ **In CMYK mode, keep all shadows in the black channel**. This removes any potential for printing problems—such as poor trapping (described in Chapter 12, "Web Graphics Essentials")—in simple shadows.

Summary

This chapter was very hands-on, with plenty of exercises so you can try the different special effects for yourself. I hope it helped turn some wheels in your head and you now have some ways to use these techniques in your own work!

Next up in Chapter 12 are some need-to-know guidelines for getting started with graphic design on the Web. Take a deep breath and dig in!

EXERCISE 11.7

Adding Raised Text to a Textured Surface

①

1. Open the image you want to use as the background. Select the Type tool. You can complete this exercise using the Type Mask option, but I like to use the standard Type tool because this creates a new type layer, and I might change my mind about what wording to use! Enter the text you want to raise on this textured surface. Reposition the text as necessary. Note that for onscreen use, sans-serif typefaces tend to be more readable, as do the Crisp or Strong anti-aliasing options. Click OK when you're done.

2. This creates a type layer with the same name as the text you entered. Now select your type and save it to an alpha channel—it will come in handy a little later. Choose Load Selection from the Select menu. Choose the transparency mask for your type layer. You should see a marquee of marching ants around your letterforms.

   Now choose Save Selection to save your outlined type to an alpha channel.

3. Click the eye icon next to your type layer to hide it. Create a new layer on top of your texture layer. Load the alpha channel you created in the previous step.

4. Choose Layer Effects from the Layer menu, and then choose Bevel and Emboss. Add values for a Drop Shadow layer effect as well.

5. Experiment with additional layer effect settings to obtain bright highlights along the upper and left sides of your type, and deep, blurred shadows along the right and bottom sides. Figure 11.12 shows the end result.

②

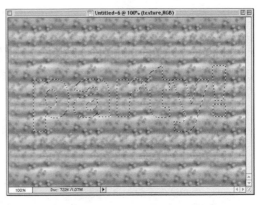

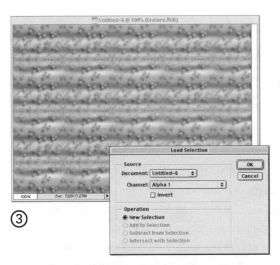

Figure 11.12
Adding
embossed text to
a clickable
button.

EXERCISE 11.8

Adding Recessed Text to a Textured Surface

Creating recessed lettering with layer effects requires steps very similar to the ones for raised lettering. This time you're adding shadows within the letterforms by reversing the light source and thereby reversing the highlights and shadows.

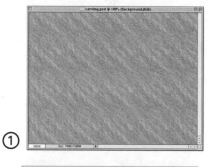

1. Open the image you want to use as the background texture.

   Select the Type tool. You can complete this exercise using the Type Mask option, but I like to use the standard Type tool because this creates a new type layer, and I might change my mind about what wording to use. Enter the text you want to raise on this textured surface. Reposition the text as necessary. Just as in the previous exercise, select your type and save it to an alpha channel—it will come in handy a little later.

2. You can turn off the eye icon next to your type layer; you don't need it for the rest of this exercise. Switch layers to target the background texture pattern, and then choose New Adjustment Layer from the Layer menu. Choose Levels as the type and click OK. In the Levels dialog box, move the white Output Levels slider to the left to darken the background image in the selected areas of your image.

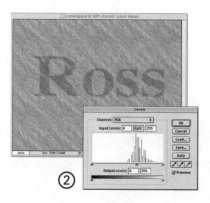

③

3. Choose Layer Style from the Layer menu, and then choose Inner Shadow. Once you've created the shadow, you can choose Bevel and Emboss from the list in the upper-left corner of the Layer Style dialog box. Experiment with the settings to obtain bright highlights along the upper and left sides of your type, and deep, blurred shadows along the right and bottom sides. Here, I've chosen an angle of -120 degrees in applying the Inner Shadow layer effect. You might also want to apply an Inner Glow effect to enhance the carved area.

This recessed text effect is shown in Figure 11.13.

Figure 11.13
Embellishing recessed text with shadows and highlights.

12
Web Graphics Essentials

IN THIS CHAPTER

Design Considerations

👁

Optimizing Web Graphics

👁

Functions of Web Graphics

👁

Using Color Palettes

Whether you're responsible for the look and feel of your company's new Web site or you're digitizing artwork for a personal online gallery or home page, it's easy to get excited about what you can do on the Web. This chapter covers the design considerations of different types of Web graphics, whereas Chapter 13, "Using ImageReady," focuses on using ImageReady to achieve advanced Web graphics effects such as highlighted rollovers.

For your Web graphics to have the greatest impact, you have to take into account—or is that grudgingly accept?—the differences between designing for online viewing and designing for print publication. Some users have monitors that can display thousands or millions of colors—but many see only 256 colors. Will your images look as good to users on other computer platforms as they do to you? You also need to balance the goals of offering great-looking images and keeping file sizes low so users don't have to wait too long for the graphics files to download.

As an artist and information designer, you'll probably find many ways to use graphics on your Web site—from the all-important logo and other highlighted images on your main page to the buttons and icons that help people find their way around. You might also have image maps or other images on a *splash page*—a visually compelling entry point that readers click before they can enter your site. Just as important to consider is how much of a coordinated look your graphics convey as readers jump from page to page within your site.

But unlike print publishing, where you can specify pretty much everything the reader sees, a lot of online presentation factors are difficult—if not impossible—for you to control. You can't anticipate how wide your users' browser windows will be, for example, or make assumptions about their monitors' resolution or bit depth, or be certain their browser will wrap text around graphics or display your table cells just the way you intend. You also need to account for differences in bandwidth; whereas some users zip by on T1 connections, others plod along on 28.8Kbps modems. Because graphics-intensive Web pages can take an achingly long time to load for users with slower modems, you might unintentionally alienate and drive away visitors if you fill your site with the finest and fanciest effects you can get with Photoshop.

That said, Photoshop has many features that are wonderfully handy for developing graphics for the Web. This chapter focuses on the following topics:

- 👁 How designing graphics for the Web differs from creating graphics for print production

- 👁 Choosing file formats for Web graphics, and taking advantage of features such as transparent backgrounds and interlacing

- 👁 Using the Save for Web command under the File menu to optimize your images for faster downloading

- 👁 Creating graphics for specific Web site purposes: background patterns, navigation buttons, bullets and icons, banners, and all-around Web interfaces

- 👁 Slicing and dicing images for faster display

- 👁 Resolving color-management issues, including browser palettes and RGB-to-hexadecimal color conversion

- 👁 Protecting your Web graphics from unauthorized use with digital watermarking

Design Considerations for Web Graphics

How should you approach creating graphics that are intended for Web use versus graphics designed for print publication? Let me offer a few points for you to mull over:

- 👁 **Information design is less intuitive in online settings**. Print conventions such as page numbers, chapters, or an index provide an orderly way of proceeding through information. Because the Web encourages linking from one information source to the next, users can find it difficult to retrace their steps if they get lost. Web visitors can also quickly grow confused about how to find the specific data they need. As a result, ensuring your site's information architecture is straightforward enough for your average user to navigate should be one of your prime design considerations.

- **Web layout and page dimensions are driven by monitor screen size.** In print, designers are always aware of the final dimensions of their printed pieces—and can then design two-page spreads, left- or right-page openers, or images that bleed off the page. As a Web designer, you have no way of knowing what size monitor your visitors will use to view your pages. Accordingly, many designers begin with anticipating the needs of the lowest common denominator. For example, if you assume that users have at minimum a 640×480 pixel monitor resolution, you would design your widest image or row of navigation buttons to measure no more than 600 pixels wide in total (leaving room for the browser window interface and a scroll bar). In this way, users don't ever need to scroll across to find crucial navigational cues. A splash page or all-important links should display well within that initial 640×480 pixel display, so that users don't need to scroll down to find your most important information (such as the company name, or a link to search or find contact info). Many overall Web page interfaces are based on the 4:3 aspect ratio of computer monitors, whereas print pieces come in all shapes and sizes.

- **Color issues and file size.** On one hand, some aspects of designing graphics for the Web are much more liberating than designing for print. For example, you aren't limited to using just a certain number of inks (as for 1-color or 2-color printing), and you don't have to worry about dot gain, ink density, or bad trapping. On the other hand, it's not unusual to create Photoshop images for print publication that are 1MB to 10MB in size—but on the Web, every byte counts. In this medium, even a 70KB file can be unforgivably huge. Fortunately, Photoshop gives you several ways to tweak your graphics especially for Web applications.

- **Onscreen resolution is much lower.** As I've mentioned elsewhere, standard screen resolution measures 72ppi (for Macs) to 96ppi (for PCs), whereas graphics designed for print production usually start at 266 or 300ppi (typically twice your line screen) and go up from there. Accordingly, you need to resize graphics originally destined for print that are being repurposed for online use. You also want to take special care to ensure that type in your graphics is readable onscreen at that resolution.

👁 **Opportunities for interactivity**. Another big plus for Web designers are the opportunities at hand for incorporating interactive elements—from animations to alternative, rollover states for buttons—into your pages. Face it, when was the last time you saw a pop-up in print? Children's books are the only good examples that come to mind.

File Formats Revisited

You can use Photoshop to save your Web graphics in either of the leading Web graphic formats, GIF or JPEG. Deciding whether you should save your Web graphics as GIFs or as JPEGs should largely depend on what kinds of graphics they are.

The JPEG format is the best choice for photographic-quality images or graphics with many color blends. You can choose from a variety of quality levels when you save a JPEG; review Chapter 2's discussion of JPEG's lossy compression scheme. JPEG also has an option for progressive display (in a GIF, it's called *interlacing*), which means you can choose to have your images first appear rather blurred onscreen and then acquire sharper focus.

GIF is the most widely used format on the Web. It's an 8-bit color format, so it can contain only up to 256 colors. Although JPEG is the best choice for high-quality photographic images, GIF should be suitable for almost any other kind of Web graphic—from icons to logos to navigational graphics. GIFs use *lossless compression*, which means that none of your color data gets lost; as a result, it's a better choice for images with type—or any images where replaced colors would especially stand out—than JPEG. When you save a GIF in Photoshop—what the program calls "CompuServe GIF"—you can choose between interlacing (described in the preceding paragraph) or standard format, which displays from top to bottom.

The GIF format also supports background transparency, which knocks out a file's background and replaces it with a transparent one, so your images appear to float on top of the Web page's background color or pattern instead. The JPEG format, on the other hand, does not support transparency.

You can simulate transparency in a JPEG with *background matting*, a feature supported by GIF as well. Background matting fills transparent pixels with a matte color that you choose (using either the Save for Web command under the File menu, or ImageReady) to match the Web page background on which the image will be placed. Background matting works well only if the graphic's Web page background is a solid color, and if you know what that color will be.

note

> In version 6.0, Photoshop has eliminated the GIF89a export option under the Export submenu of the File menu. You are no longer prompted to choose one or more background colors to "knock out" into transparency. Instead, your best bet for retaining transparency is to ensure your silhouetted images are still on a layer with a transparent background when you bring up the Save for Web interface or save in Indexed Color mode. There, any areas of your image with less than 50 percent opacity are treated as transparent.

Photoshop also supports a third Web graphics format called PNG, short for Portable Network Graphics. Pronounced "ping," PNG was once a long-shot contender for taking over as the Web graphic format of choice, and has failed to rally much popularity to date. PNG began to take shape after the patent controversy over the GIF format in the mid-90s seemed likely to threaten GIF's widespread use (see Chapter 2, "File Format Essentials"). Although GIF is still around, PNG format development has continued. PNG has many of the same features as GIF, including indexed color palettes, interlacing, transparency, background matting, and lossless compression. It also has some features that GIF doesn't, such as support for 48-bit color. PNG also automatically adjusts graphics for gamma correction to compensate for cross-platform differences in brightness and contrast—a major bonus for Web graphics, because many Photoshop designers forget that their GIFs will look different to Web visitors running other computer platforms. Despite its impressive list of features, PNG has failed to make it big in mainstream Web design so far—probably because it doesn't have a major corporate booster or a compelling raison d'être anymore.

Now that you have a better sense of when to use GIF or JPEG, I can demystify the dialog boxes you see when you choose Save or Save As from the File menu.

JPEG

The slider in the JPEG Options dialog box (see Figure 12.1) controls how much compression is used in your image—and, by extension, what amount of image quality is preserved. You can also type in a number between 0 (lowest quality, smallest file size) and 10 (highest quality, largest file size) in the Quality field instead of dragging the slider.

note   The compression in the JPEG format creates *artifacts*—such as wavy patterns or blotchy areas of banding, every time you save an image. Because these artifacts accumulate every time you save the image to the same JPEG file, you should always save a JPEG file from the original image, not from a previously saved JPEG file.

You'll also see three radio buttons in the JPEG Options dialog box in the Format Options area. These are your options for choosing whether your JPEG image displays one line at a time (the Baseline "Standard" option), is Baseline Optimized (which uses a slightly different encoding scheme),

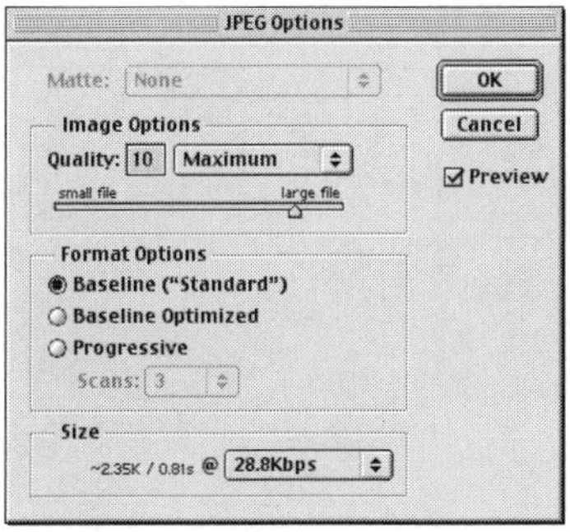

Figure 12.1

The JPEG Options dialog box.

or is Progressive. Progressive (or interlaced) graphics have become commonplace on the Web because they give the illusion of displaying faster (though any difference is negligible). If you choose Progressive, you can then specify how many passes (or Scans, as the JPEG Options dialog box calls them) your image should go through as it gradually appears onscreen. The greater the number of passes, the longer it takes your JPEG to come through completely.

The Size section at the bottom of the JPEG Options dialog box shows the estimated file size and download time needed to display the file at one of three modem speeds (14.4-, 28.8-, or 56.6Kbps).

GIF

Because GIF is an 8-bit (256-color) format, you need to reduce the colors in your image to 256 colors or fewer. The quick way to accomplish this is to choose Mode from the Image menu and then pick Indexed Color, which spawns the Indexed Color dialog box shown in Figure 12.2. To really balance the number of colors (which determines file size) with image quality, though, you should use the Save for Web command under the File menu (discussed just ahead).

When you see the Indexed Color dialog box, you need to make a couple of key decisions about how your image will look. You need to choose what color palette to use, how many colors will be used, and how Photoshop will trick the eye into seeing colors from your original image that have no equivalent in the limited color palette.

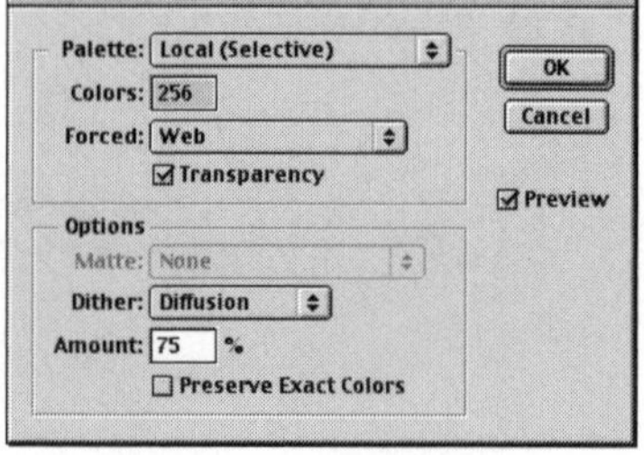

Figure 12.2
The Indexed
Color dialog box.

Palettes

In the Indexed Color dialog box, you can choose from the following choices in the Palette drop-down menu. You'll see that for three options—Perceptual, Selective, and Adaptive—you can choose either a local palette (based on the current image's colors) or a master palette created in ImageReady.

- **Exact** is automatically selected if your original image has fewer than 256 colors.

- **System (Macintosh or Windows)** uses your computer platform's default system palette. The Macintosh and Windows system palettes overlap to a large extent, although not completely. These palettes are useful when you're creating custom desktop icons for one platform or another but have no real use in Web graphics, given the diversity of computer platforms your Web visitors could be using.

- **Web** represents the 216-color palette common to the Macintosh and Windows system palettes. Dubbed the "Netscape 216," this is the safest palette you can use for your Web graphics, because you can be confident that these colors will appear largely as intended to most of your visitors. Its color range is somewhat limited, though, so if your image doesn't look good when mapped to the Web palette, try Uniform or Adaptive instead.

- **Uniform** is a more well-balanced—color-balanced, that is—version of the Web palette. This palette opens with 216 colors, but you can enter your own values for Color Depths (for example, 7-bit color or 4-bit color) or an exact number of colors, down to as few as eight.

- **Perceptual** creates a custom, adaptive palette weighted toward colors for which the human eye has greater sensitivity.

- **Selective** creates an adaptive palette that favors Web colors as well as colors that occur in broader expanses of flat color.

- 👁 **Adaptive** generates a palette based on the most frequently used colors in your image. The less frequently used colors are omitted. If there is a wide diversity of colors in your original image, some original color values might get shortchanged, but you can overcome this by making a selection in your image (containing a good cross-section of colors) before choosing Adaptive. Photoshop generates the new Adaptive palette based on the color values in the selected area, rather than on the image as a whole.

- 👁 **Custom** automatically opens the Color Table dialog box, into which you can load a previously saved color palette, or create one on-the-fly from the colors already present in your image. Before Photoshop included the Web palette in version 4.0, I frequently used Custom to load a Netscape 216 color palette. Now, the best reason I can find for using it is when I want to create a series of graphics for a site that shares the same select color palette.

- 👁 **Previous** applies the most recently used color palette, and is available only after you convert at least one image to Indexed Color mode during your Photoshop session.

Color Inclusion

In the Indexed Color dialog box, you can choose from a variety of color palette options and also specify the exact number of colors by entering a value for Colors. The Colors text box controls only how the indexed color table is created; the Photoshop file is still treated as an 8-bit, 256-color image.

You can force certain colors to be included in one of these palettes as well using the Forced drop-down menu in the Indexed Color dialog box. Black and White ensures that a pure black and a pure white value are included in the color table; Primaries adds red, green, blue, cyan, magenta, yellow, black, and white. The Web choice adds the Netscape 216 color palette. With Custom, you can hand-pick the custom colors to add.

Dealing with Dithering

Through dithering, Photoshop simulates the appearance of colors absent from the indexed color palette by interspersing pixels of the available colors. Dithering produces the best results for large photographic images or any image with a lot of blends or transitions; it's less useful for digitized line art or simple graphics. You can choose from three dithering options from the Dither drop-down menu in the Indexed Color dialog box:

👁 **None** is the setting to use if you want no dithering. Any gradients or subtle shadows in your image will most likely be adversely affected. Images with no dithering result in smaller files because the LZW compression used in the GIF format takes advantage of large areas filled by a single color value.

👁 **Pattern** is used with the System (either Macintosh or Windows) palette or the Uniform palette; it redistributes the colors in your image in a halftone-like manner—usually with mediocre results.

👁 **Diffusion** is the better dithering method; it uses an error-diffusion method that randomizes the dither to simulate the missing color values.

Interlacing

When you save a file in CompuServe GIF format, Photoshop prompts you to choose an option for row order (see Figure 12.3). You can choose from Normal (no interlacing) or Interlaced. Interlaced (or interleaved) graphics begin to appear as blurred, low-resolution shapes and then gradually appear in sharper focus, instead of appearing line by line from top to bottom (see Figure 12.4). As a result, your Web visitors can get a sense of the graphic's content while they wait for the rest of the image to load.

Table 12.1 includes an at-an-glance checklist for analyzing which file format to use for your Web graphics.

Figure 12.3
The GIF Options
dialog box.

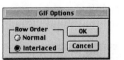

Figure 12.4

An example of an interlaced graphic gradually appearing in sharper focus.

Table 12.1 Choosing a File Format for Your Web Graphics

IF YOUR IMAGE IS CHARACTERIZED BY...	USE THIS FILE FORMAT
A rectangular full-color image with color gradients, and no transparency	JPEG.
A full-color, vignetted image with soft, feathered edges	JPEG can be used if you know what the background color of the Web page will be; otherwise, GIF's transparency features can help preserve the silhouetted image.
Monochromatic images or artwork with few gradations	GIF, but experiment with reducing the number of colors in the Save for Web interface to see whether you can reduce the number of colors without degrading appearance in order to reduce file size.
A native Photoshop file containing Logo artwork or other imagery with a transparent background on its own layers	GIF. Use the Transparency option in the Settings section of the Save for Web interface. The Matte color determines what color will swap in for semi-transparent pixels at the edges.

Optimizing Your Web Graphics and Minimizing Download Time

If your graphics take too long to load on your pages, chances are your visitors will grow tired of waiting and jump somewhere else instead. As a Web designer, you have to work at keeping your graphics small without losing too much image quality. For your images to serve their purpose, they must be clearly discernable with accurate colors (especially for online catalogs) and legible type (wherever letterforms occur).

There are a couple of ways you can actively try to reduce the file size of your graphics—for example, you can reduce the number of colors in your GIFs or increase the compression in your JPEGs. I discuss these techniques next, and then provide some tips for giving your visitors options for viewing low-resolution versions of your complex graphics.

Using Fewer Colors

Reducing the number of colors in a GIF is one way to make a file smaller. (Reducing colors in a JPEG is less important, because its file size depends more on its level of compression.) As Figure 12.2 showed, you can set the number of colors used when you convert a file to Indexed Color mode. Exercise 12.1 shows you how to experiment with reducing the number of colors in an image in order to reduce its file size without reducing its quality too much.

note   You can reduce your graphic's loading time if you save all the images on your Web pages using the same color look-up table—for example, Photoshop's Web palette—or another custom color table you create.

note   By default, the download time shown in the preview window is based on a 28.8Kbps modem. You can see the download times for another modem speed by clicking the black triangle in the upper-right corner of the tab preview windows. This action brings up a preview menu listing a variety of download rates, as shown in Figure 12.6.

EXERCISE 12.1

Reducing the Number of Colors Using the Save for Web Interface

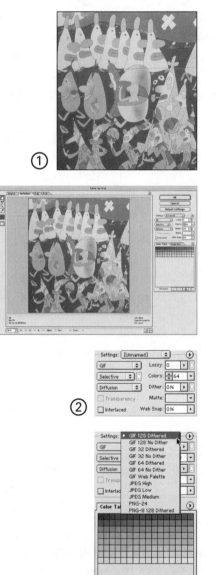

①

②

③

1. Choose the image you want to reduce for Web display. The example I used here is a scanned photo of a section of a wall mural in Kamakura. The original TIFF weighs in at 796KB, but I obviously need this image to be much smaller in its online format.

2. With your image open onscreen, choose Save for Web from the File menu. The Optimized tab displays at the forefront.

   Notice the Optimize panels on the right side of the dialog box, underneath the Output Settings button. Here you choose in a single dialog box the settings for file format, how many colors appear in the image, how much dithering occurs, and any interlacing or transparency options. The current settings are applied to your image; click the Settings drop-down menu to consider another set of color options.

3. Now you need to assess whether your image is better suited to being saved in GIF or JPEG format—Table 12.1 can give you some guidelines. Here, for example, this image of a brightly colored mural contains many areas of flat-color, so I don't need to worry about preserving the color gradations through the additional colors available in a JPEG. On the other hand, there are so many color variations in this image, so I'm not sure yet how well I can reduce the number of colors. Click one or more of the standard settings in the Settings drop-down menu to get started. Conduct some trial-and-error here to see whether your image looks better with dithering or without. You can type in a value for number of colors in the Colors field too. Notice how the swatches in the Color Table palette are updated when you change the number of available colors.

④

```
GIF
78.8K
29 sec @ 28.8Kbps
```

4. You can evaluate the results in real-time as the preview image in the Optimize tab updates. Feel free to experiment as much as you want—you haven't permanently changed any of your image data yet. Here, for example, I realized after reducing the number of colors as much as I judged reasonable, I still wasn't happy with the substantial download time—and that made me reconsider the actual file dimensions. I clicked the Image Size palette (next to the Color Table palette), so that I could reduce the file dimensions and continue to experiment with reducing colors to see how far I could reduce the file size.

Keep an eye on the file size and download time listed in the lower-left corner of the Optimized tab. Here, my main concern was to make sure the image took less than 30 seconds to display in full—now I know what file size and number of colors worked in this particular instance.

Before enacting any of these changes though, I cancelled out of the Save for Web interface. I wanted to reduce the image dimensions using the Image Size command under Photoshop's Image menu, and then sharpen the edges using the Sharpen filters. Only then did I return to the Save for Web interface to save this image as a GIF with a reduced number of colors. You should continue to experiment with your own images to see how far you can reduce the number of colors without adversely affecting image quality. Figure 12.5 shows the wall mural in Kamakura, reduced for the Web.

Figure 12.5

Reducing the number of colors specified in Indexed Color mode reduces the overall file size of your GIF files. If you're adapting images originally used in print, consider reducing the file's dimensions for online display.

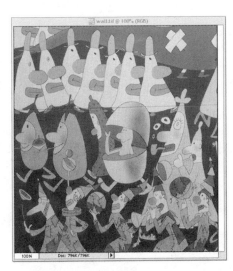

Figure 12.6

Changing the
download rate
shown in the
Save for Web
interface's
preview
windows.

Studying the Save for Web Interface

By now, you've seen a quick real-world use of the Save for Web interface. Here's a more comprehensive rundown of exactly what the tools and options in the Save for Web interface do and what they can be used for.

Tools

The toolbox at the left side of the Save for Web interface (see Figure 12.7) includes the following features:

- 👁 The Hand tool for navigating to different areas of the preview.

- 👁 The Slice Select tool, which is active only when you've sliced your image using the Slice tool. Within the Save for Web interface, you can double-click any slice in a preview window using the Slice Select tool. This launches the Slice Options dialog box. From there, you can edit the URL the slice links to or other Web features affecting that image slice when it's displayed on a Web page.

- 👁 The Zoom tool for zeroing in on a specific part of the image within a preview window.

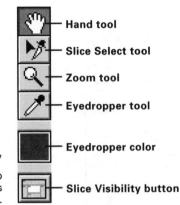

- Hand tool
- Slice Select tool
- Zoom tool
- Eyedropper tool
- Eyedropper color
- Slice Visibility button

Figure 12.7
The Save for Web interface's toolbox.

<ul>
<li>The Eyedropper tool for sampling colors.</li>
<li>The Eyedropper Color swatch, which shows the current foreground color.</li>
<li>The Slice Visibility button, which toggles between showing and hiding slices.</li>
</ul>

note

You can't move and resize user slices in the Photoshop Save for Web dialog box the way you can in Photoshop or ImageReady.

Output Settings

You click the Output Settings button to load and save settings that determine how your HTML code is generated (for example, whether the HTML tags appear in uppercase or lowercase), your Web pages' background images, naming conventions for your graphics in their normal and rollover states, and slices. See Figures 12.8 and 12.9.

2-Up and 4-Up Modes

Click the 2-Up or 4-Up tabs at the top of the Save for Web interface to preview compression options. The 2-Up view (see Figure 12.10) compares your original image and the format and compression you're currently considering (using the settings shown in the right side of the

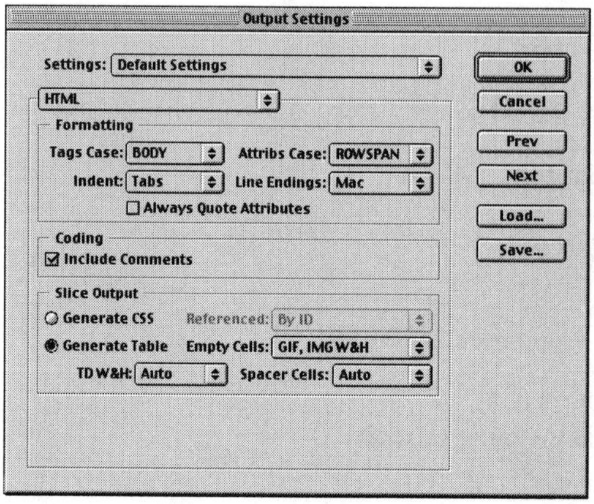

Figure 12.8

Whether you edit your own HTML code later or hand it off to a production team, you can tweak HTML defaults in Save for Web's Output Settings to produce more readable code.

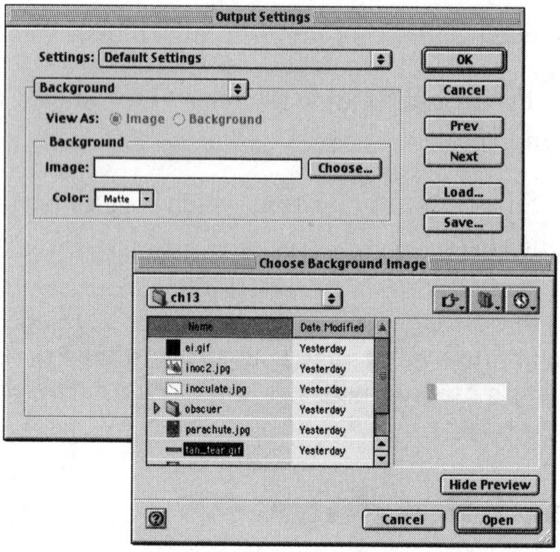

Figure 12.9

When you edit a Background setting, you can browse through the directories on your hard drive to locate the background image to use.

Save for Web interface). The 4-Up view (see Figure 12.11) shows two additional compression options.

Optimizing Settings

Your optimization settings are visible no matter which tab you select in the Save for Web interface. As you saw in Exercise 12.1, you can choose stored settings for GIF, JPEG, or PNG file formats with a variety of image quality settings. You can also further fine-tune your own settings

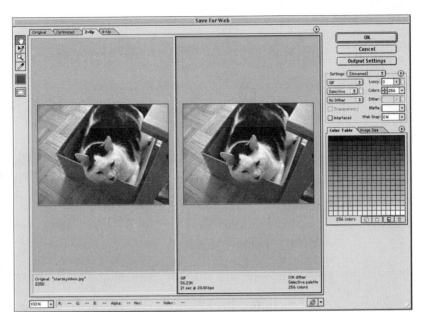

Figure 12.10

The 2-Up tab in the Save for Web interface.

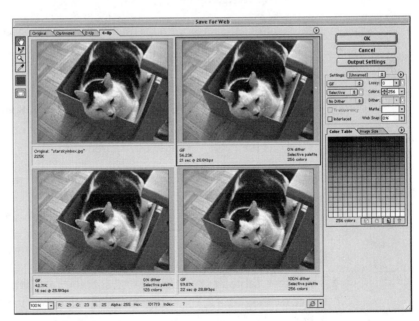

Figure 12.11

The 4-Up tab in the Save for Web interface.

Figure 12.12

Optimization settings for GIF (top) and JPEG (bottom) in the Save for Web interface.

after you choose a file format (see Figure 12.12). For example, when you choose to save the file as a GIF you can then try the settings that you otherwise would choose by trial and error in the Indexed Color dialog box. For a GIF, you can choose:

- The color palette.

- The type and amount (percentage) of diffusion.

- An indication of whether the image has a transparent background or an interlacing effect.

- Whether to sacrifice image quality through lossy compression (not a good idea in general).

- The number of colors in the image.

- The color used for background matting, which should match the background color of the Web page (if you know what that will be). This helps simulate transparency.

- A percentage for *Web snap*—this value determines how close a color in your image needs to be to the nearest Web-safe color before it is automatically changed to the Web-safe one.

Color Table

The Color Table lets you choose and sort the colors that appear in your image (see Figure 12.13). This feature also lets you lock in color values to ensure they're not changed as you continue to reduce colors or introduce dithering.

To indicate a Web-safe color, a small white diamond appears in the center of the color swatch. If you edit a color by hand and it's no longer

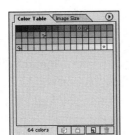

Figure 12.13
The Color Table
in the Save for
Web interface.

Web-safe, you'll see a black dot appear in the center of the color swatch. Any color you edit by hand is automatically locked. If a color is locked, a small square appears in the lower-right corner of its color swatch.

Four icons appear at the bottom of the Color Table space:

🔲 Reassigns colors to the Web palette

🔒 Locks a color in the palette so it cannot be altered as you continue your optimization

🔲 Adds the Eyedropper color to the palette

🗑 Deletes the selected color from the Color Table

Maximizing Image Compression

Both GIF and JPEG have built-in compression schemes for reducing file size, which helps your images download faster. As you read earlier, a JPEG reduces file size by using a lossy algorithm, losing some of the information that the human eye can't necessarily see. This loss of visual detail—usually slight changes in pixel color and brightness values—is virtually unnoticeable. GIF uses a lossless algorithm, so it keeps all the visual data. GIF's compression method takes advantage of large areas of similar color—so you can see how reducing the colors in an image can help with compression too. JPEG can often create smaller files than GIF, but it's still only worth using JPEG on photographic-quality images. Simpler images tend to lose too much detail in the compression process, so any savings in file size doesn't make up for the loss in image quality.

Cropping Your Graphics

As you saw in Exercise 12.1, cropping the dimensions of your graphics can greatly reduce their file sizes. If you originally designed your images for print publication, for example, you might have kept them at a larger-than-necessary size to allow them to *bleed*, that is, to run past the edges of the printed page. You don't have to think about that on the Web, so you can crop your graphics to a smaller size.

Creating Thumbnails

If your graphics are still unavoidably hefty, you might want to consider embedding smaller—and faster-downloading—thumbnail sketches of your images in your pages, and then including a link to the larger images. This way, you let users decide whether they want to see the bigger images. You can use the Web Photo Gallery command in the Automate submenu under the File menu to automatically create a set of thumbnail images for each of your full-size images. This command also generates an HTML page that links each of these thumbnail images to the full-size version. Exercise 12.2 describes the steps to follow to create your own Web photo gallery.

Creating Low-Resolution Versions of Images

It's also possible to let visitors load a small, low-resolution version of your image on a page before they get the full-resolution one. After all the other elements on your page appear, the high-resolution image will load and cover up the low-resolution version. (Visitors to your Web page see this effect only if their browsers support the LOWSRC attribute in the IMG tag.)

Before high-speed Internet connections became so widely available, this effect was considered very considerate because it gives users with lower-speed connections a sense of your page's overall layout as well as some text to read while the larger image loads. Today, though, its real impact is its usefulness as a special effect.

The low-res image you use doesn't need to be black and white—for example, you can load a 256-color image over a 16-color, low-res version—but it should have the same dimensions as your high-res graphic. After your visitors have your page's images cached in browser memory, though—which means the graphics file is saved on the users' hard drives for fast reloading upon return visits—they'll see only the high-res image when they come back to your page again.

To create a low-resolution version of one of your graphics, open the image. You can reduce the number of colors using the Save for Web command under the File menu, as described in the "Using Fewer Colors" section of this chapter. To create a grayscale or black-and-white version of one of your images, just convert the image to Grayscale or Bitmapped by choosing the appropriate menu item under the Mode menu. Choose Save As from the File menu to save the new low-res file with a different name. Figure 12.14 shows how a high-res image appears on a Web page after the low-res version fills in.

tip

Another good way to reduce download time for graphics is to reuse graphics whenever possible. It's much kinder to your visitors to use just one bullet icon instead of five in different colors, for example. A general rule: give some thought to whether the additional graphic adds anything to your page's message.

Figure 12.14
Displaying a low-resolution version of an image, followed by the final, high-resolution one.

EXERCISE 12.2

Creating a Web Photo Gallery Using a Series of Thumbnail Images

1. Place all the images that you want to appear linked in your Web gallery in a single folder on your hard drive. You can include subdirectories contained within this folder if you like.

2. Choose Automate from the File menu, and then pick Web Photo Gallery. The Web Photo Gallery dialog box appears.

3. Before changing any of the display options, you need to choose the source folder. Click the Source button and toggle through the directories on your hard drive to choose the right one. Select Include All Subdirectories to include images inside any subfolders of the selected folder.

4. Now click the Destination button and choose the destination folder that should contain the images and HTML pages for your Web page gallery. Click OK when you're done.

5. Click the Styles drop-down menu to choose one of several gallery styles. You can choose from a horizontally oriented or vertically oriented framed site. A small preview image of the style appears on the right.

6. You can also personalize the information that appears on the resulting Web page through a series of user-friendly dialog boxes. Choose Banner from the Options pop-up menu. Here, you can enter a title under Site Name, a photographer credit, and a date that should appear on each page (the current date is the default). You can also choose options for font and font size.

7. You can set several options for how your gallery pages appear. First, choose Gallery Images from the Options pop-up menu. Under Border Size, you can enter a width in pixels for a border if you want to add one around each mage. If you want to resize the images, check the Resize Images check box and enter a new size either in pixels or an image size from the pop-up menu. You can enter a value for JPEG

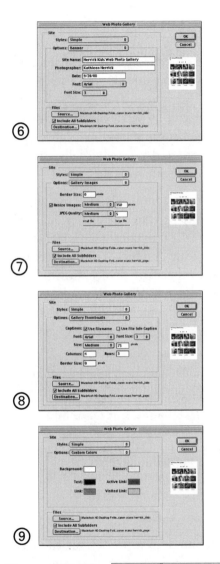

quality between 0 and 12 (where higher values improve quality and increase file size).

8. You can now set options for your gallery's home page. Choose Gallery Thumbnails from the Options pop-up menu. You can choose to display each file's name under each thumbnail, use the caption text from the File Info dialog box under each thumbnail, and pick a font and font size for the text on the page. You can also choose options for the border and thumbnail size by choosing from the Size pop-up menu or entering your own value in pixels. Depending on the gallery style you pick, you might also be prompted to enter the number of columns and rows that should be used to display the thumbnails on the home page.

9. Choose Custom Colors from the Options pop-up menu to set options for the colors of the links in your Web pages. This way, the colors of links can change as they're clicked or after you've visited the page they point to. To change the color of a particular element, click its color swatch, and then select a new color using the Color Picker. The Background option lets you change the background color of each page. The Banner option lets you change the background color of the banner.

10. Click OK you're when done. You'll see Photoshop then open each image and resize it. The program places your resulting JPEG thumbnails, a gallery home page (entitled index.htm), and the HTML pages for each resulting gallery page inside a pages subfolder (see Figure 12.15).

Figure 12.15

Use the Web Photo Gallery command to automatically generate a series of thumbnail images arrayed on an HTML page that then points to gallery pages containing the full-size images.

Functions of Web Graphics

You can use graphics on your Web pages for all kinds of purposes. They can serve as background patterns, logos, navigational aids, hyperlinks, section dividers, icons and bullets, advertisements, or as the content material itself. This section focuses on editing your images with their intended Web purpose in mind. Your challenges here are to create graphics that are small and easy to download, and yet are visually striking and communicate essential information about your site.

Your graphics for print publication often communicate a message as well as—or better than—the accompanying text, but that's not always the case on the Web. You also need to take into consideration that not all visitors to your Web site can see your graphics—some users will have nongraphical browsers whereas others, tired of enduring long download times, turn off automatic image loading. (If you're coding your own pages as well as supplying the graphics, make sure that you enter any text equivalents in your image tag's ALT attribute to let users know what they're missing.)

note

In this chapter, I occasionally refer to the HTML tags you'd use to reference graphics or colors in Web pages, but learning how to use HTML is beyond the scope of this book. For Photoshop designers who are just starting to learn HTML, check out *Learn HTML In a Weekend, 3rd Ed.* (Prima Publishing, 2000).

Splash Pages

Incorporating a splash page as an entry point to your Web site can serve as one way to arrest your readers' attention right off the bat. Some sites also build in such a page to facilitate browser detection—determining which Web browser is being used and what version it is—in order to redirect visitors to a version of the site optimized just for that browser.

It's most important to design the *initial* graphic or graphics that go on your splash page to load quickly, because the initial entry point is when your visitors are most likely to become impatient and leave.

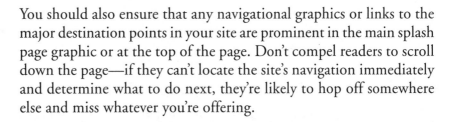

You should also ensure that any navigational graphics or links to the major destination points in your site are prominent in the main splash page graphic or at the top of the page. Don't compel readers to scroll down the page—if they can't locate the site's navigation immediately and determine what to do next, they're likely to hop off somewhere else and miss whatever you're offering.

Background Patterns and Colors

Most Web browsers let Web designers display a background pattern or color on their pages. As you've seen, you can achieve this through the output settings in the Save for Web command under the File menu. These output settings add additional attributes in a document's HTML <BODY> tag: BACKGROUND names a background image, and BGCOLOR lets you specify a background color using either a predefined color name (for example, `BGCOLOR="RED"`) or a hexadecimal color value (for example, `BGCOLOR="#00BF00"`). Your full <BODY> tag might look something like this:

```
<BODY BACKGROUND="/images/redtile.gif" BGCOLOR="#FF0000">
```

note

If you want to change the color of your Web pages' text to complement your image, note that you must specify both a background image and color. If your viewers have turned off automatic image loading, the browser won't change the default text colors unless you've also specified a new BGCOLOR. This is good to know—and logical, to boot—because if your image and specified BGCOLOR require type in a light-colored hue to make your pages readable, you'll want the right colors to appear. So if you want your page's words to be white or yellow, make sure you specify a dark-hued BGCOLOR in addition to serving up your background image.

The design considerations for background images and colors are similar to ones you keep in mind for images in print publications that require type overlays. You want to make sure that the background image isn't so intricate or dark that the overlying text is unreadable. No matter what you use for a background image, reducing its opacity is sure to help with readability. In your Web page, you can specify light-colored type to run over the background, but bear in mind that even though people can read it, it'll strain your readers' eyes after a while.

Background Images and Tiling

You can use any GIF or JPEG graphic for your background image; the user's browser tiles the image repeatedly to fill the browser window. Conduct a little Web browsing of your own to see how other designers use background patterns—you'll probably find many good (and bad) examples.

Many Web designers design tiling patterns to be viewed in one of two ways. The first involves creating a very wide but thin graphic, intended to repeat over and over down the page, but so wide as to prevent any horizontal tiling. Typical dimensions for such graphics might be 1,024 pixels wide by 1 pixel deep. This produces a vertical pattern that winds its way down the page. You can use graphics with this shape to create background designs that run flush against the left side of the browser window (see Figure 12.16).

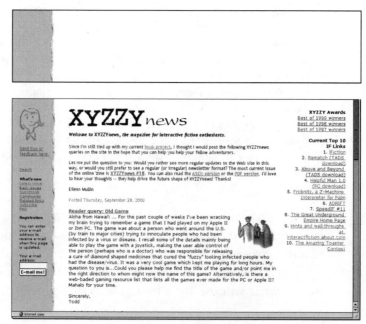

Figure 12.16

Wide but shallow images work well for creating patterns that run down the left side of a browser window.

note

> It's not practical to create patterns that run down the center or flush right with the browser window, because you can't control the width of your users' browser windows—or their monitors, for that matter.

The second—and probably more common—method, involves creating small square graphics (generally, from 16×16 pixels to 96×96 pixels) that tile across and down the user's browser window, as shown in Figure 12.17.

For these kinds of tiling graphics, you'll probably want your tile pattern to appear seamlessly—meaning that viewers won't notice where the image's edges end and where the tiling effect begins. How do you go about doing this? A lot depends on what your background image is going to look like. If you want to use a picture that has a silhouetted outline—say, a floating logo or object—you can create a borderless tile so that all edges use the same solid color. If your image already has its own border—such as a bathroom tile bordered by grout—your image is ready-made to appear as a square tile, as shown in Figure 12.18. Any Web clip art collection you delve into online or pick up on CD-ROM

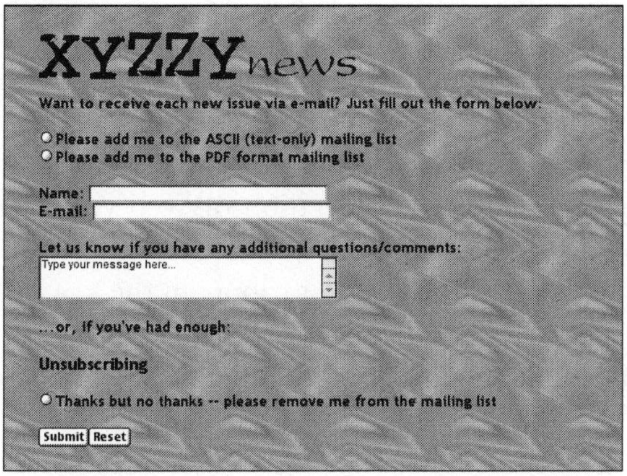

Figure 12.17

Square tiles repeat both horizontally and vertically across the browser window.

XYZZY news

Want to receive each new issue via e-mail? Just fill out the form below:

○ Please add me to the ASCII (text-only) mailing list
○ Please add me to the PDF format mailing list

Name:
E-mail:

Let us know if you have any additional questions/comments:
Type your message here...

...or, if you've had enough:

Unsubscribing

○ Thanks but no thanks -- please remove me from the mailing list

Submit Reset

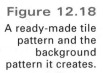

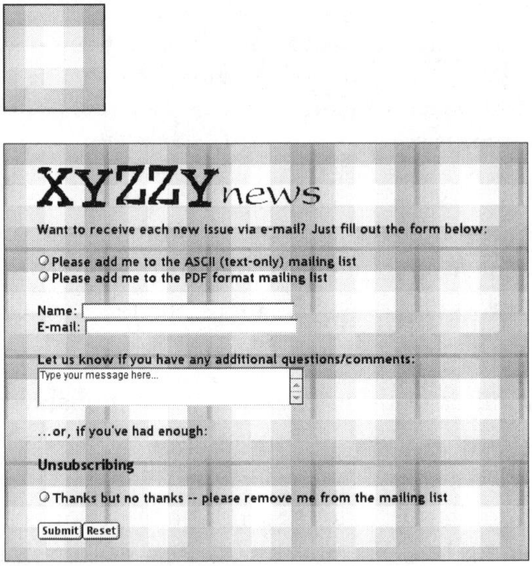

Figure 12.18

A ready-made tile pattern and the background pattern it creates.

includes seamlessly tiling backgrounds. Appendix B, "Sources for Further Information," lists some online resources for them as well.

But suppose you have a cool but nontiling image that you want to transform into a completely blended seamless tile—say, to create a giant abstract pattern, or the overall jumble of a starry night sky or a million M&Ms. As you'll see in Chapter 13, you can jump over to ImageReady and use a filter called Tile Maker, which simplifies blending the edges so that your image will tile as well as possible.

Instead of (or in addition to) using a background pattern, you can specify a hexadecimal color to replace your browser's default background color. It's especially important to do this if you're using a tiling background graphic, in consideration of Web visitors who have disabled automatic image loading. You can add a background color to your Web pages with the BGCOLOR attribute in the <BODY> tag. See "Using Color Palettes Throughout a Site" later in this chapter for more information about choosing background colors.

There are a few other design guidelines you should keep in mind when choosing graphics and colors for your Web page backgrounds:

- **Keep the pattern or design simple and light in color**. Your pages' text appear on top of this image, so you want to maximize readability.

- **Use a small color palette in background graphics**. The more colors that need to load, the longer it takes for your page to appear—and the more likely that impatient users will tire of waiting and go elsewhere.

- **Don't go overboard with dramatic color changes**. White or yellow type on a multicolored background pattern is a striking effect that'll get people's attention, but please keep readability in mind if you have a lot of text on your pages. (Say, more than about five or six words…)

- **Keep an eye out for good and bad backgrounds on other Web pages**. Even through casual Web surfing, you'll find many examples of how other designers have handled this challenge. Observation helps you get a sense of what works and what doesn't.

Navigational Buttons and Icons

Navigational graphics can liven up your Web pages by drawing the reader's eye to important lines of information and links to important content. They are typically very small GIFs, measuring 32×32 pixels or at most 64×64 pixels and containing only a few colors—although there are no hard-and-fast rules. Icons afford great opportunities for getting very creative in a small space. With only a few pixels to work with, for example, how would you represent navigational arrows—say, back to the previous page, go right for the next page—in an interesting way?

As mentioned earlier, you can also create thumbnail images of highly detailed graphics that you can embed in your pages as icons that link to their larger, longer-to-download versions. There are many free, downloadable icon archives available on the Web (see Appendix B).

But they're much like commercial clip art collections: after much searching, you might find a few icons that are perfect for your needs, some that'll inspire you to create better-looking versions, and a whole bunch that you'd never find a use for.

Splitting a Large Web Graphic into Smaller Contiguous Pieces

If you're preparing a large overview graphic, such as for a splash page or a navigation interface, you will probably want to slice it into a number of smaller individual graphics that fit into table cells for faster loading. Similarly, you might want to design a large splash image that contains one animated part—in this instance, you might want most of the pieces of the overall image to be JPEGs, but you can use an animated GIF to handle just the animation part.

In both cases, you can use the Slice tool (✍) to readily dice up your image, and then use the Slice Select tool (▶✍) to generate the HTML to put the pieces together in a table. When you divide an image into slices, each slice is saved as an independent graphic file with its own settings, color palette, links, rollover effects, and animation effects.

You can also accomplish these tasks in ImageReady; Chapter 13 focuses on the steps you take in that program to create rollovers and animations with slices. But first, take a look at how you can create and manipulate slices and add links to them within Photoshop—many of these capabilities are new in version 6.0.

In your slicing-and-dicing maneuvers, you will encounter several different kinds of slices:

- 👁 **User-slices**, which are ones you create with the Slice tool. These are denoted by a solid line.

- 👁 **Layer-based slices**, which are slices you create from a layer. These display with a solid line.

- 👁 **Auto-slices**, which are dynamically generated as the flip side to the user-slices you carve out. These are automatically created to fill in the undefined spaces left around the slices you've manually

Figure 12.19

Check the Show Slices Numbers check box in the Slice tool's options bar to see what slices are denoted in your image. Because no slices have been added to this masthead image, only one auto-slice appears.

created. Whenever you edit slices, auto-slices are regenerated. These display using a dotted line.

👁 **Subslices** are a type of auto-slice generated when you create slices that overlap.

When you select the Slice tool, you need to make sure the Show Slice Numbers check box in the options bar is checked (see Figure 12.19). This allows you to see the slice numbers needed to track your slices. If you haven't carved out any slices, you'll see a single auto-slice, numbered as 01.

Layer-Based Slices

In the sample image shown in Figure 12.19, the various design elements are on separate layers. This section demonstrates one of the easiest ways to create a new slice —that is, through layer-based slices. Target the appropriate layer—here, I'm choosing the layer containing the logo image—and then choose New Layer Based Slice from the Layer menu (see Figure 12.20).

The new layer-based slice is now called 01. As Figure 12.21 shows, the auto-slice reshapes to fit the space not defined by slice 01 and is numbered 02.

If you then reposition or edit the image data on that layer, the slice automatically adjusts to accommodate the changes. This is particularly useful for creating precise slices for rollovers.

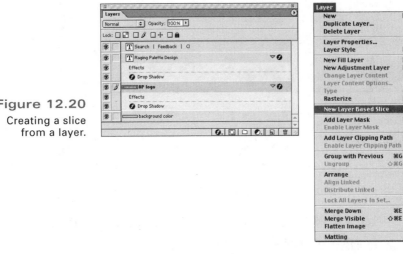

Figure 12.20

Creating a slice
from a layer.

Figure 12.21

A layer-based
slice
(numbered 01)
and an auto-slice
(numbered 02).

User-Slices

You can now put the Select tool to work to create slices for the Search, Feedback, and Client List letterforms.

You have three choices for style settings in the Slice tool's options bar: Normal, Constrained Aspect Ratio for restricting your slice's proportions, and Fixed Size, if you need to match a slice to a particular height and width. Just as when you're drawing a marquee, you can hold down Shift as you drag to constrain the slice's size to a square. Or, you can hold down the Option key (on a Mac) or Alt key (in Windows) to draw from the center out.

When this masthead is placed on a Web page, each of these slices should link to a separate Web page. I've made three adjacent slices for each of these words or phrases. The slices in the masthead now look like what you see in Figure 12.22—there is one layer-based slice (01),

Figure 12.22
The results of adding user-slices.

three user-slices (03, 04, and 05), and two auto-slices (02 and 06). Slices are numbered from top left to bottom right, beginning in the upper-left corner of the image.

By now you might have noticed the various icons and line colors and widths surrounding your slices. As mentioned earlier, solid slice lines indicate that the slice is a user-slice or layer-based slice; dotted lines indicate that the slice is an auto-slice. Color also differentiates user-slices and layer-based slices from auto-slices. By default, user-slices and layer-based slices have blue symbols, whereas auto-slices have gray symbols.

Table 12.2 aims to help you decipher the various icons you might notice next to your slice numbers.

Table 12.2 Slice Icons and Their Meanings

ICON	FUNCTION
⊠	Image slice.
⊠	No Image slice. This contains a solid color or HTML text that will not display in either Photoshop or ImageReady; you need to view with a Web browser to see the overall effect.
⊡	Layer-based slice.
🔗	Linked slice. If users click anywhere in this sliced graphic, they will be delivered to the destination page hyperlinked from this graphic.
⟲	Includes a rollover effect. When a user passes the mouse over this graphic, a different image will display.

Promoting Auto-Slices or Layer-Based Slices to User-Slices

If you want, you can convert one or more auto-slices to user-slices so that they are no longer continually resized. To do so, choose the Slice Select tool and click Promote to User Slice in the options bar. You can also do the same for layer-based slices, because you might want to change the boundaries of a layer-based slice beyond the image data captured on that layer.

Specifying Slice Options with the Slice Select tool

Now that you've sliced up your overview graphic, you're ready to apply each slice's characteristics. To do so, you need to click the Slice Options button in the Slice Select tool's options bar (see Figure 12.23).

Clicking this button causes the Slice Options dialog box to appear (see Figure 12.24). Here, you have an opportunity to generate a great deal of code for how these graphics function within your Web page—all without actually messing with a single HTML tag. Take a look at the different options you can set in the Slice Options dialog box:

- 👁 You can rename the slice to any name you want. In the example shown in Figure 12.24, each slice is named after the original (raging.psd), followed by an underscore, and then the slice number. These default names automatically change after you add rollover states for the buttons. You can change this naming convention in the Save for Web command under the File menu. Click the Output Settings button in the Save for Web interface and choose Saving Files from the settings drop-down menu.

Figure 12.23

The Slice Select tool's options bar.

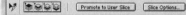

👁 You can enter an URL (Web address) in the URL field. If your Web site uses frames to maintain navigational elements in place on every page, you might need to specify a target attribute here as well. If you are not involved in the HTML production of your site, ask the production team if the site is frame-based and, if so, what target attribute (such as _top or _self) you should use in the anchor tag for these graphic elements.

👁 You can edit the default message that appears in the Web browser's status line (at the bottom of the browser window) when a user rolls the mouse over this slice. By default, the link URL is shown, but you can place message text here instead.

👁 You can also specify the ALT (alternative) text that should display for users who cannot see the images, such as users with nongraphical Web browsers or those who have turned off images. Without ALT text, these users have no way of knowing what information was imparted in these graphics, so it's good form to include ALT text for any images that contain text or other meaningful information.

tip ●

Remember to uncheck the Show Slice Numbers check box in the Slice tool's options bar when you're ready to hide the slice numbers. If you want to hide the slice lines altogether as you go on to other kinds of image editing, choose Show from the View menu. You'll see that the Slices menu option has a checkmark next to it. Chose Slices to deselect this option.

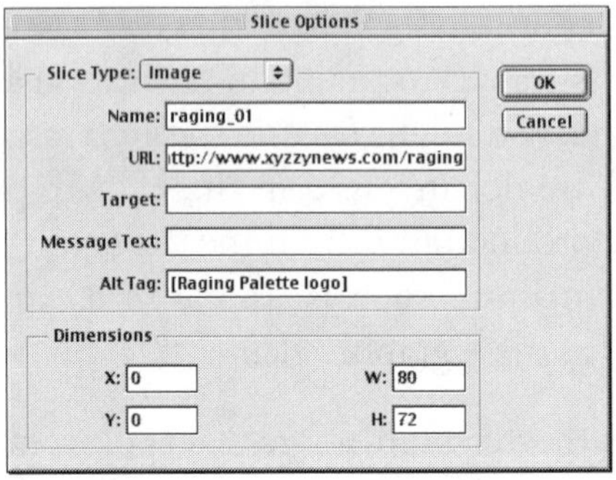

Figure 12.24

The Slice Options dialog box.

Using Color Palettes Throughout a Site

As you saw in Chapter 4, "Color Essentials," and earlier in this chapter, it's easy to specify using the Web-safe color palette when saving a graphic in the Save for Web interface or in the Indexed Color mode. This ensures that your Web visitors on Windows and Mac platforms see your images in the same colors. You can also create your own custom look-up table by modifying the Swatches palette for all your Web graphics. This helps you establish a color-coordinated look to your Web pages.

To further the impression of color coordination, you can use some of the colors in your indexed color palette to set the colors of your links and the background color on your pages. When you specify these colors in your HTML documents, though, you can't use RGB values. You need to specify the colors in hexadecimal format instead, which uses three 2-character couplets to represent the red, green, and blue values of that color. As of version 5.5, Photoshop added a built-in method of converting between RGB and hexadecimal right in the Color Picker—you'll see a hexadecimal field that's labeled with a pound sign (#) underneath the RGB values (see Figure 12.25).

You can also ensure that only Web-safe colors are used through the Color Picker by clicking the Only Web Colors check box in the bottom-left corner of the Color Picker dialog box. Table 12.3 shows a quick way you can learn to recognize the RGB or hexadecimal values of all the colors in the Web-safe color palette by sight.

Just use any of the six RGB color values shown in this table (00, 51, 102, 153, 204, 255) in the red, green, or blue fields when choosing a

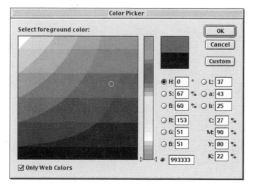

Figure 12.25

The hex value for the current RGB color is listed in the field labeled with a # sign. Check the Only Web Colors check box to allow only Web-safe colors to be picked.

color in Photoshop's Color Picker. So for example, the RGB triplet (255,255,0) is a Web-safe color, as is (102,51,153). You can string together the hexadecimal equivalents of the RGB triplets to generate the complete hex value. Accordingly, the hexadecimal representation of the RGB value (255,255,0) is written as #FFFF00, and the hexadecimal representation of the RGB value (102,51,153) is written as #663399.

Protecting Your Web Graphics

If you use your Web site to showcase your art creations, you might well worry about unscrupulous Web page creators copying and reusing your

Table 12.3 Converting Nondithering Web Colors from RGB to Hexadecimal Values

RGB VALUE	HEXADECIMAL VALUE
0	00
51	33
102	66
153	99
204	CC
255	FF

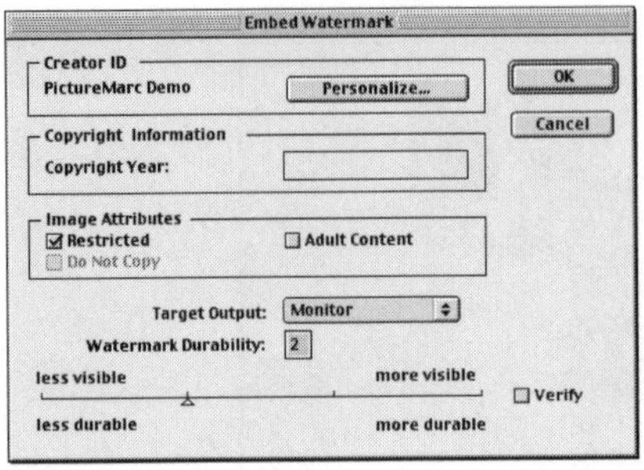

Figure 12.26

The Embed
Watermark
dialog box.

work without your permission or knowledge. One solution is to use the Digimarc watermarking filter built into Photoshop. This filter is fully functional only if you register with Digimarc Corporation for a unique creator ID. There's no fee if you're registering to use this on fewer than 100 images; you can find the fee schedule on Digimarc's site at **http://www.digimarc.com/**.

The watermarking filter embeds information into your image as background noise that is invisible to the casual observer. Once embedded, though, this identifying information stays with the image even if it's rescanned or filtered in other ways, so theoretically it can be used to catch copyright violators in the act even if they go to some lengths to hide the evidence.

You can register with Digimarc by choosing Digimarc from the Filter menu, and then choosing Embed Watermark (see Figure 12.26). Click the Personalize button and then click Register. This should launch your Web browser and point it to Digimarc's registration page. You'll also see a toll-free (within the U.S.) and international telephone number that you can call instead.

Summary

I hope I've piqued your interest with this introduction to working with Web graphics in Photoshop—in the next chapter, you learn how you can create more advanced Web effects—from image maps to animated GIFs to a variety of rollover effects—using ImageReady, Photoshop's companion program.

13

Using ImageReady

IN THIS CHAPTER

ImageReady's Tools & Palettes

Creating Image Maps

Using Animated GIFs

Creating Rollover Effects

There are many accomplished professional graphic designers who might have used Photoshop for years but are still unfamiliar with ImageReady's operations. Perhaps you're upgrading to version 6.0 from a version before 5.0, which was when ImageReady was first distributed with Photoshop. Or perhaps you're only just beginning to be tapped for Web assignments, after years of print design work. Or here's another familiar scenario: maybe you learned workarounds for creating rollovers through manual kludges in an earlier version of Photoshop, and then never got around to learning the "real" way to create these Web effects in ImageReady when it was finally bundled with Photoshop.

If you *have* used ImageReady before, I still have news for you—there's a new version of the program bundled with Photoshop 6.0. This is ImageReady 3.0—until now, version 2.0 was bundled with Photoshop 5.5.

For all these reasons, I think you'll gain a lot by adding the new ImageReady 3.0 capabilities to your computer graphics repertoire. In this chapter, you learn how to do the following:

- ◉ Determine when to use Photoshop and when to switch to ImageReady in your Web graphics work.

- ◉ Build image maps and designate their hot spots.

- ◉ Design and save your own animated GIFs.

- ◉ Create the different states for rollover graphics.

- ◉ Turn nontiling patterns into seamless tiles for backgrounds more easily than in Photoshop.

Assessing When to Use ImageReady vs. Photoshop

For each of the advanced Web effects discussed in this chapter, there may be some tasks that you can accomplish in either Photoshop or ImageReady, but there's a clear point at which completing the effect is best done in ImageReady.

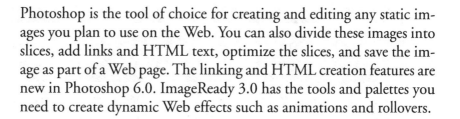

Photoshop is the tool of choice for creating and editing any static images you plan to use on the Web. You can also divide these images into slices, add links and HTML text, optimize the slices, and save the image as part of a Web page. The linking and HTML creation features are new in Photoshop 6.0. ImageReady 3.0 has the tools and palettes you need to create dynamic Web effects such as animations and rollovers.

 note

> The only exception to choosing Photoshop over ImageReady for any static file-manipulation is when turning nontiling patterned images into seamless tiles. Although you can accomplish this in Photoshop using the Offset filter and judicious application of the Clone Stamp tool, it's a bit easier with the Tile Maker filter (found in the Filter, Other submenu) in ImageReady.

Table 13.1 sums up how you might arrange your workflow process for each effect.

Examining ImageReady's Tools and Palettes

When you first launch ImageReady—remember, you can jump to the program from the icon at the bottom of Photoshop's toolbox—you might feel like you're experiencing déjávu. ImageReady's interface is very similar to Photoshop's, as shown in Figure 13.1.

Its toolbox (see Figure 13.2) is largely a pared-down version of Photoshop's, missing such tools as the Magnetic Lasso, Background Eraser, History Brush, Art History Brush, Pattern Stamp, Custom Shape, Annotations, Measure, most of the gradient tools, path-selection tools, and the pen tools. Some tools that had previously been solely in ImageReady's domain, such as the slicing tools and the vector-based Rounded Rectangle, have been integrated into Photoshop 6.0.

The tools you find only in ImageReady include the following:

The Rounded Rectangle Marquee tool, for easily creating round-cornered buttons.

Table 13.1 ImageReady and Photoshop's Capabilities, Side by Side

EFFECT	WHAT YOU CAN DO IN PHOTOSHOP	WHAT YOU CAN DO IN IMAGEREADY
Image maps	Prepare by placing each hot spot on its own layer, wherever possible.	Place each hot spot on its own layer—and then create layer-based hot spots. Carve out tool-based hot spots using one of the Image Map tools in circular, polygonal, or rectangular shapes.
Animations	Create individual frames on separate layers with small variations on each layer that simulate motion, flipbook style.	Use the Animation palette to denote the order in which each layer's content is placed as a frame. Specify timing and looping, and use the Tween command to further blend frames.
Multistate JavaScript rollovers	Develop the static graphics for each state in Photoshop. Create custom button shapes in libraries.	Assign the rest, rollover, and mouse-down states in ImageReady's Rollover palette. Select rollover styles to shapes you created in Photoshop 6.0 to automatically slice buttons and apply a variety of new layer effects.
Seamless tile patterns from nontiling images	Use the Offset filter.	Use the Tile Maker filter.

 The Rectangle Image Map tool, for creating rectangular-shaped hot spots in image maps.

 The Circle Image Map tool, for creating circular hot spots in image maps.

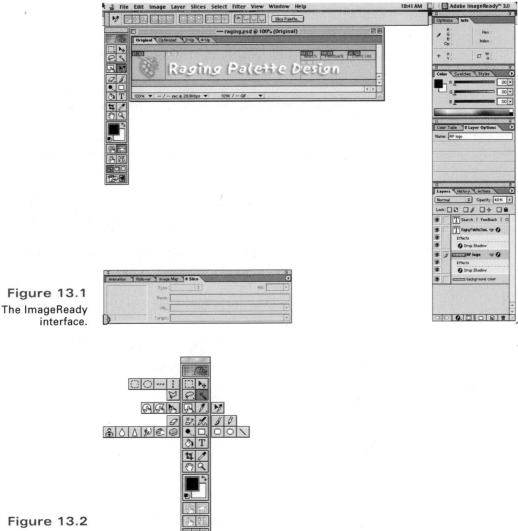

Figure 13.1
The ImageReady
interface.

Figure 13.2
The toolbox in
ImageReady.

 The Polygon Image Map tool, for creating polygonal-shaped hot spots in image maps.

 The Image Map Select tool, for selecting image maps.

The controls at the bottom of the toolbox include the same Color Picker used in Photoshop and the screen mode boxes for hiding or displaying

ImageReady's extras (such as the title bar, scroll bar, and status bar). In addition, there are controls for viewing image maps and rollovers.

These image map and rollover controls are covered further in their respective sections in this chapter:

The **Toggle Image Map Visibility** tool toggles between showing and hiding image maps.

The **Toggle Slices Visibility** tool toggles between showing and hiding slices in an image.

The **Rollover Preview** tool lets you preview rollover effects in ImageReady, without needing to launch a separate Web browser.

The **Preview in Default Browser** tool launches your Web browser to let you preview animation effects.

The options bar you see with each selected tool is the same as the one you see in Photoshop.

Several of the palettes in ImageReady are extended versions of the options in Photoshop's Save for Web interface. These include:

Color Table. Here, you can view and edit the colors in your image.

Layer Options. This functions like the Layer Properties dialog box in Photoshop. It lets you provide options for changing a layer's, or layer set's, name and opacity, among other options.

Figure 13.3
The Animation palette.

👁 **Animation**. With this palette (see Figure 13.3), you can create, view, and manipulate the frames in an animation one by one. You can also change the size of the thumbnail frames if they are too large.

👁 **Rollover**. You use the Rollover palette to create or save a new state to incorporate a new effect. Typical rollover states include Normal, Over (when users move the cursor over a graphic), and Down (when a button or graphic is pressed). Figure 13.4 shows an overview graphic where two states—Normal and Over—have been defined.

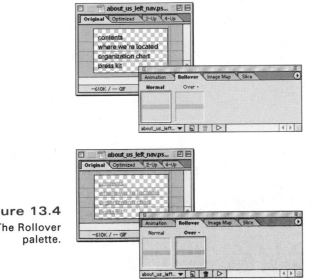

Figure 13.4
The Rollover palette.

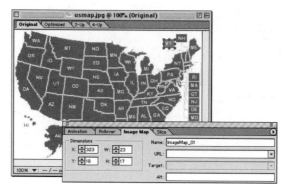

Figure 13.5
The Image Map palette.

👁 **Image Map.** You use the Image Map palette to specify a name, a URL, a target frame, and alternative text for an image map (see Figure 13.5).

👁 **Slice.** In the Slice palette (see Figure 13.6), you can see and edit the same information about your slices as you can in the Slice Options dialog box in Photoshop's Save for Web interface. You can edit slice names, the URL to link to, message text, and ALT text, among other options.

Now you can take a hands-on look at putting ImageReady's palettes and tools to work in creating advanced Web effects.

Figure 13.6
The Slice palette.

Creating Image Maps

Clickable image maps contain *hot spots* that link the users to different URLs at the click of a mouse button. This added capability lets your images serve as a visual index for your site's content or directory structure. With image maps, you avoid the choppy display of sliced-up Web graphics. The image appears as an integrated whole, and you can use interlacing to give the illusion that the image is coming through faster.

Image maps use the Cartesian (x-y) coordinate system to identify on what part of the image the user's cursor clicks. Just like the default coordinates in a Photoshop image, image maps place the point of origin (0, 0) in the upper-left corner of an image. You can use all kinds of shapes to define regions within your image: rectangles, circles, ovals, polygons, or even a single point (yes, really!—see Figure 13.7).

You can code the hot spots and corresponding URLs into your image maps in one of two ways—or use both methods, for good measure. The easier method—and the more popular one, naturally—is called the *client-side* image map; the hot spots are specified in your HTML.

The second and more complicated method is known as a *server-side* image map. In this case, ImageReady creates a map configuration file to identify the boundaries of each hot spot. When a user clicks an area of your image map, the request goes to the server that hosts your site.

Figure 13.7

You can specify irregularly shaped polygons as hot spots in an image map, as was done with the state borders in the image map shown here. To accommodate text-only users, consider placing text links to your hot spots underneath an image map.

However, you need to upload this map configuration file to the Web server and include the path to the map file in your HTML file. Ask your Webmaster or Internet service provider if they prefer you to use server-side image maps; otherwise, you'll be fine using client-side image maps.

Creating Hot Spots

Just as you can create two kinds of slices—those based on the contents of a layer and those you carve out with the Slice tool—you can create two kinds of hot spots for image maps in a similar way:

- 👁 **Tool-based hot spots** are created by clicking and dragging using one of the Image Map tools (Rectangle, Polygon, Circle) in the ImageReady toolbox. You can then manipulate these hot spots with the Image Map Select tool or enter values in the Image Map palette.

- 👁 **Layer-based hot spots** turn the contents of a layer into a hot spot area. If you edit or reposition the content layer, the hot spot area automatically updates. This affords you the most flexibility for continuing to edit your images after a hot spot has been designated.

Graphical navigation is prominent on many Web sites: you can click hot spots to drill down through an organization chart, find information about a particular region on a map or, as Exercise 13.1 shows, find out information about people by clicking on their likenesses. In this exercise, you learn how to designate the hot spot areas in a navigational area and specify what happens when the user clicks or rolls the mouse over that area.

note

If you intend to put a rollover effect in an image map area, a layer-based hot spot lends itself better to this task than a tool-based hot spot. The layer-based image map area (see Figure 13.8) automatically adjusts to include additional image data created through layer effects (or rollover effects, in ImageReady), such as glows or drop shadows.

To create a hot spot from a layer, you first need to target the desired layer. If you want to make multiple layers into a single hot spot, you need to merge the layers first. Then choose New Layer Based Image Map Area from the Layer menu in ImageReady.

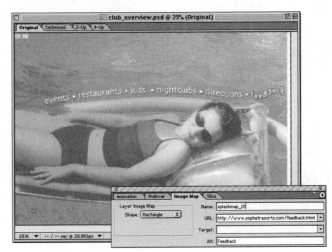

Figure 13.8
A layer-based
hot spot.

EXERCISE 13.1

Creating and Designating Hot Spots for an Image Map

①

②

③

④

1. Launch ImageReady and open an existing RGB or Indexed Color image you want to use for your image map. Here, I'm going to edit an image of some groomsmen and add clickable hot spots to each man's face. When a face is clicked, the user sees information about each member of the wedding party.

2. Because each face is fairly round, use the Circle Image Map tool ( ) to create the hot spot. Select the tool, and then drag over the area you want to define. Here, I've made my first selection around the third head from the left.

   For each hot spot, you can specify a name, a URL, a target frame, and alternative text. You'll see these fields in the Image Map palette. If you don't see the Image Map palette, choose Show Image Map from the Window menu.

3. Continue to click and drag—switching to one or more other Image Map tools as needed—to create additional hot spots. If you need to reposition or resize a hot spot after you've demarcated it, switch to the Image Map Select tool ( ). You can also select more than one hot spot at a time by clicking outside a hot spot, and then dragging across the areas you want to select.

   If you want to delete a hot spot after you've created it, just select it using the Image Map Select tool and press the Backspace key or the Delete key. You can also choose Delete Image Map Area from the Image Map palette menu.

4. At this point, you're ready to specify HTML output options for your image map. For example, will this be a client-side or server-side image map? (See the definitions at the beginning of this chapter's section on image maps.) Where in your HTML file do you want to place the image map information? You can update these settings by choosing Output Settings from the File menu, and then picking HTML.

Figure 13.9

The finished image map effect.

5. You can preview your image by clicking the Preview in Default Browser icon in the toolbox—you can choose either the Netscape or Microsoft icon. This icon launches your Web browser; you'll see your image with the hot spots activated. If you click any of the links, your browser connects to the Web page you specified in the URL for each hot spot (see Figure 13.9). The HTML code for the image map then follows—this markup needs to be included in the final HTML page for the image map effect to work.

Sliced Images vs. Image Maps

At first glance, sliced-and-diced overview graphics might sound like they serve essentially the same function as an image map, which is a single large graphic with embedded hyperlinks to various destination pages. But you can use sliced Web images and image maps for different ends:

◉ When a sliced Web graphic first shows up onscreen, it loads in bits and pieces—one segment at a time. As a result, you might lose the overall design effect because it might take a while for your readers to see the big picture, literally! One benefit of this approach, though, is that it gives visitors the illusion that the page is loading more quickly. Any real difference in speed is negligible, but if readers spot an early-loading graphic to a link that interests them, they can follow it immediately rather than waiting for the rest of the page to load.

👁 You might find it easier to update a portion of the sliced graphic than an image map. You need only generate a new image in the same dimensions as the original slice and update the link and graphic name in your HTML.

👁 With sliced images, your hot spots must be rectangular. If you have only rectangular shapes for hot spots, there's no need to use an image map. If, however, you want to create a circular or polygonal hot spot, you need to rely on image map capabilities.

👁 Sliced graphics can be more accessible to visitors with text-only browsers or browsers with graphics turned off. That's because you can specify alternative text (via the ALT attribute in your IMG tag), which describes each graphic. On an image map, you can only specify ALT text for the image as a whole.

Design Considerations for Image Maps

From a design standpoint, you need to make each hot spot visually discrete in your image, to avoid confusing users about the boundaries of where they should click. It's very frustrating when users misclick an image map and wind up at a URL other than the one intended. Besides making the hot spots visible, consider interlacing your image map graphics. If your visitors can find the right spot to click without enduring a long wait for the entire image map to load, they'll be happy to move to another part of your site that much more quickly.

Using Animated GIFs

An animated GIF is a low-hassle way to add motion effects to your Web pages. It's a single file with multiple images overlaid within it that is displayed over time, with preset controls for looping, timing, and backgrounds. Each frame should vary slightly from the preceding one to create the illusion of movement when the frames are viewed one

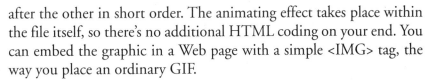

after the other in short order. The animating effect takes place within the file itself, so there's no additional HTML coding on your end. You can embed the graphic in a Web page with a simple <IMG> tag, the way you place an ordinary GIF.

You use the Animation palette—Choose Show Animation from the Window menu—to create animation frames. The Layers palette is also essential to creating good-looking animated GIFs, because the most efficient way to build slight frame-to-frame changes is to duplicate a layer and apply an effect or offset the image slightly.

You can even create animations that are just two or three frames long. By applying one or more layer effects, as Figure 13.10 shows, you can create instant blinking effects such as a light bulb going on or off or a neon sign.

You use the icons in the Animation palette to create and edit frames and play back your animation-in-progress.

◁◁ The Rewind icon returns you to the first frame in the series.

◁❘ The Backward icon takes you to the previous frame in the series.

☐ The Stop icon pauses the animation.

▷ The Play icon runs through all frames in the animation.

❘▷ The Forward icon advances you to the next frame in the series.

°°°° The Tween icon generates new frames.

Figure 13.10
The Animation palette in action.

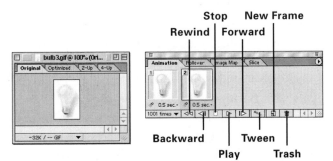

⊞ The New Frame icon adds a new frame that starts as a duplicate of the preceding one.

🗑 The Trash icon lets you delete a frame.

If you've ever created a flipbook on paper, you know that the key to fluid motion is adding subtle variations as you go from frame to frame. Any jerky motions ruin a realistic animation effect. You can use the Tween command to automatically add or edit a number of frames between two existing frames. You can vary position, opacity, or any effect evenly between the new frames to create the appearance of movement.

In this way, you can automate effects such as fading out a layer without needing to manually create the intervening frames between full opacity and the ending opacity. For example, you can set the opacity of the layer in the first frame to 100 percent, and then set the opacity of the same layer in the ending frame to 0 percent. When you tween between the two frames, you automatically reduce the opacity of the layer across however many new frames you create.

As you add more frames to achieve this subtlety of motion, though, you're increasing the file size of your animated GIF. Finding the right balance between a fluid effect and a manageable file size is an ongoing challenge you will face in your animated GIF creations. To learn how others have put together banners, visit free Web graphics archives such as ScreamDesign.com; download their sample files, and view the individual frames in ImageReady using the Animation palette. (See Appendix B, "Sources for Further Information," for a list of similar resources of free Web graphics.)

Animated Banners and Buttons

One of the most popular uses for animated GIFs is in Web advertising. These advertising images are usually referred to as *banners* or, when they're smaller, as *buttons*. Several standard sizes for Web advertising graphics have emerged and are listed in Table 13.2. These standard sizes have been recognized by the Internet Advertising Bureau (IAB) and Coalition for Advertising Supported Information and Entertainment (CASIE). Keep this chart handy if your animated GIF-creation work is mostly for Web advertising purposes.

Table 13.2 Standard Internet Ad Sizes	
DIMENSIONS (IN PIXELS)	**DESCRIPTION OF GRAPHIC**
468×60	Full banner
392×72	Full banner/vertical navigation bar
234×60	Half banner
125×125	Square button
120×90	Button #1
120×60	Button #2
88×31	Microbutton
120×240	Vertical banner

In Exercise 13.2, you can try your hand at crafting an animated GIF—consider creating an advertisement for your Web site, perhaps, or an eye-catcher for your home page.

tip If your users experience delays in page loading, they might see the first frame of your animated GIF longer than intended, so be sure that the first (and last—if your image doesn't continuously loop) frames in your animated GIF are meaningful.

Creating Rollover Effects

A *rollover* is an advanced Web effect in which different versions of an image appear when users move or click the cursor over an image or part of an image on a Web page. These different versions are known as *states*, and can be configured in ImageReady using layer effects and other formatting styles.

EXERCISE 13.2

Preparing Your Own Animated GIF

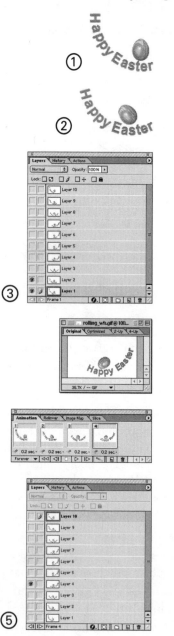

1. Launch ImageReady and open or edit an existing image to create the first frame in your animated GIF. If your animation is intended for publication as an ad banner, refer to Table 13.2 for standard Web ad-banner sizes. Make sure that the first frame's image data is on its own layer.

2. Now you need to duplicate the layer containing the first frame data to a new layer. You can drag the layer's icon down to the New Layer icon in the Layers palette or choose New Layer from the Layer menu. Apply the effect you want to appear in the second frame—if the effect you're looking to create can't readily be done in ImageReady, you can toggle back to Photoshop to apply the special effect you need.

3. Repeat this step of creating each new frame's data by duplicating the previous layer and making the necessary image data changes on the layer copy. When done, you should have a separate layer for each frame you want to add. In this example, I have five frames that appear and then appear again in reverse order, for a total of 10 frames.

4. Now launch the Animation palette in ImageReady. If it's not visible, choose Show Animation from the Window menu.

5. Click the New Frame icon, which will duplicate the preceding frame. Make sure that the target layer is visible, but all other layers are hidden. Continue to press the New Frame icon and make visible the layer that should appear in the next frame while hiding all other layers until all the necessary frames are created.

6. You can select a looping option to indicate how many times the animation should repeat. Click the looping option selection box in the lower-left corner of the Animation palette. Choose Once, Forever, or Other. If you click Other, you'll be prompted to enter a numeric value in the Set Loop Count dialog box.

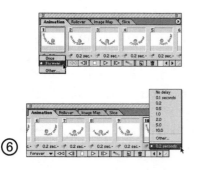

At this point, you can also specify a *delay*, which is the time that any frame is displayed. The delay time for each frame is displayed in seconds below the frame thumbnail in the Animation palette. Right-click on the time below each frame to select the delay interval.

7. Choose Save from the File menu when you're done; be sure to save in GIF format. Figure 13.11 shows the results.

Figure 13.11
The completed animation.

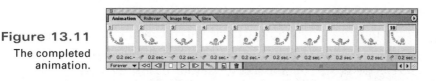

With the Rollover palette in ImageReady, you can make navigational buttons light up when a user moves the cursor over them (see Figure 13.12), or display an animation as a rollover state. You can also create secondary rollovers in which users move over one area and cause an image to change elsewhere on the Web page.

ImageReady adds JavaScript code to a resulting HTML file to specify the rollover states. All the rollover graphics must be uploaded to your Web site and the JavaScript code must be implemented in the final Web page for these effects to work.

Figure 13.12
The Rollover palette shows the effects that appear in each state.

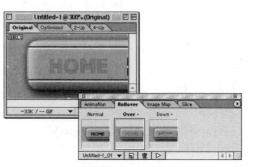

To define the active area for a rollover, you need to define the affected area as a slice or hot spot (if the image is an image map). The default state of every slice or hot spot area is Normal. When you add a new state to a rollover, you duplicate the slice or hot spot area in the previous state. You can then put the Layers palette to work to edit the image as appropriate for the new state—you might want to add a glow to type or a new color to your letterforms. You can also add animation to a rollover state.

When you save the HTML for an image with rollover states, each rollover state is saved as a separate image file. By default, rollover states are named using the corresponding slice name plus the mouse action (such as over or down) that triggers the rollover state. When you change the name of a slice, rollover states in the slice are automatically renamed.

In most cases, you'll have the best luck with layer-based slices rather than user-slices when creating rollovers. That's because the dimensions of a layer's content might change in the course of creating a rollover, and your layer-based slices will automatically adjust to include these new pixels.

To create or edit a rollover state, you need to display the Rollover palette by choosing Show Rollover from the Window menu. First, you need to select the slice or hot spot in your image that you want to affect. You then create a new state—duplicating the previous one—by clicking the New State icon at the bottom of the Rollover palette. You make the necessary changes to the appearance of the new state using the Layers palette, setting the layer visibility for the desired layer to visible.

ImageReady assigns a default rollover state to your slice or hot spot. You can change to these states using the pop-up menu above the rollover thumbnail:

- 👁 **Over** defines the rollover state when the users roll over the slice or hot spot but don't click. This is the default selection for any second rollover state.

- 👁 **Down** defines the rollover state when the users click the mouse on the slice or hot spot. This state appears as long as the viewers keep the mouse button pressed down on the area.

-  **Click** defines the rollover state when the users click the mouse on the slice or image map area.

- **Out** defines the rollover state when the users roll the mouse out of the slice or hot spot. Usually, the Normal state is used here.

- **Up** defines the state when the users release the mouse button over the slice or hot spot. The Over state is typically used here.

- **Custom** defines a new rollover state. You need to create your own JavaScript code and add it to the HTML file for it to function.

- **None** maintains the current state of the image.

Now you can combine the last two effects you'll learn about in Exercise 13.3—creating rollover effects that include an animation that plays when the cursor moves over a graphic.

Summary

If this has been your first experience using ImageReady, let me extend my warmest congratulations in breaking past those initial barriers and venturing into the unknown. You've truly expanded your Web design repertoire into the world of techieness—possibly without even realizing it!

Next up in Chapter 14, "Print Production Essentials," are some need-to-know guidelines for tackling thorny print production issues. Take a deep breath and dig in!

EXERCISE 13.3

Creating a Set of Animated Rollover Graphics

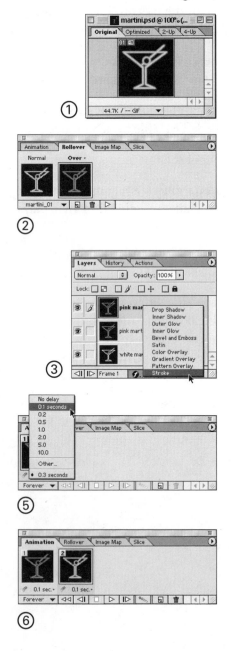

1. Launch ImageReady and open the initial graphic you want to create rollovers for. Use the Slice Select tool to choose the appropriate slice.

2. Now you add a new rollover state. Click the New State icon at the bottom of the Rollover palette. By default, the new state is an Over rollover, but you can set up another type of rollover if you want.

3. Using the Layer palette, select the layer to which you want to apply the rollover—usually a duplicate of your original layer. Now choose Layer Style from the Layer menu, and then pick an effect (I'm using Gradient Overlay) from the Layer Style submenu. Or, you can click the Effects button at the bottom of the Layer palette and choose Gradient Overlay from the Effects menu.

4. Tweak the layer effect until you have the right combination you want to add. When you're done, close the Layer Effect palette.

5. Now you can set up the brief animation effect. Switch over to display the Animation palette. You start by setting up a delay time from the Delay pop-up menu in the Animation palette. I've chosen Forever from the Looping pop-up menu. Try 0.1- or 0.2-second for the delay time—you'll have a chance to review the timing when you preview the animation, and you can return to tweak further if desired.

6. Click the New Frame icon at the bottom of the Animation palette to add a new frame. The animation effect shown here simply reverses the gradient. In the Layers palette, set the visibility of the new layer—the Gradient Fill Layer— to Not Visible. Now, when the animation frame displays during the rollover, the Over state will show the gradient first filling in, and then appearing in reverse.

7. Click the Preview in Default Browser icon in ImageReady's toolbox and pick the Netscape or Microsoft icon. If your preferred Web browser isn't shown, choose Preview In from the File menu, and then pick Other to locate your Web browser. You can change the delay time at this point if necessary. Now choose Optimize Animation from the File menu. Choose GIF in the Optimize palette and pick other options as desired for optimal display on the Web. Choose Save Optimized from the File menu to save your animated rollover. Figure 13.13 shows the results.

Figure 13.13
The finished animated rollover graphics.

14

Print Production Essentials

IN THIS CHAPTER

Preparing Graphics

◉

Helping Your Service Bureau

◉

Process vs. Spot Color

◉

On the Press

Ever since the advent of desktop publishing, prepress functions have largely become the responsibility of the desktop designer. Print design is more innovative than ever because of the ease with which type, graphics, and color elements can be placed on the page. Duotones and tritones, scan lines, spot varnish, and cutouts can all be specified through professional graphic design applications—and might already be high on your list of do-it-yourself projects.

Many designers, however, have overlooked how we're still using the same printing technology that was in use before desktop color. Although printing technology has improved and some publishers are experimenting with digital presses, most commercial printers are still using the same ink, plates, paper and high-speed presses as in years past.

To that end, as you'll see in the pages ahead, preparing your files correctly for print output and maintaining a good working relationship with a service bureau are crucial to getting your work to print the way you expect it to. This chapter focuses on good strategies for the following:

- 👁 Creating images that your page layout software can import correctly

- 👁 Working with a service bureau

- 👁 Getting the most out of your images for 1-, 2-, or 4-color print jobs

- 👁 Compensating for press conditions such as dot gain

Preparing Graphics for Use in Page Layout Programs

With desktop publishing, you usually import your images into a page layout program such as QuarkXPress or Adobe PageMaker to combine them with the publication's text and other page elements. You then send application files—or PostScript files generated from those application files—to a service bureau to output film (and perhaps color proofs). The film and accompanying proofs then go to your commercial printer, which uses them to produce your final print job.

Page layout programs have a wide range of image-handling capabilities—you can resize your graphics, rotate or crop them any number of ways, apply new colors, or change the contrast. But how do you decide which features to tweak in Photoshop and which you should leave for your page layout program? Your priorities here are twofold. First, you want to preserve the quality of your image, and second, you want to use each of your applications—Photoshop and your page layout program—to your best advantage. Here are a couple of examples of print issues best handled by page layout software:

👁 **Rotating graphics**. Rotating an image in Photoshop degrades its quality. If you don't know how much you'll need to rotate an image in your PageMaker or QuarkXPress document, you should use your page layout software's rotation capabilities first. However, graphics that are rotated in page layout programs take a long time to process, so to save printing time, you might want to consider going back to Photoshop, saving a copy of your document rotated to the same degree, and importing the rotated version into your pages.

👁 **Matching colors**. If you have an image that uses only a single color (line art) or shades of a single color (such as a grayscale image), you can apply a color to a TIFF within QuarkXPress or another page layout program. This is helpful when you want to match the color of an icon or other graphic to text in your page layout file. Because the color of the graphic and the color of the text—defined in Quark—are identical, you don't take any chances that the color you defined as 100C 40M in Quark will look any different from that same shade used in an image imported from Photoshop. (This is important only if you're printing in CMYK; you shouldn't have any color-matching problems if your Photoshop spot colors have the correct names.)

In both these cases, the original images remain untouched and you can use them just as easily for other purposes.

The following are some issues best handled by Photoshop before you import your graphics into your page layout program:

- 👁 **Converting from RGB to CMYK mode**. If you wind up printing separations of pages with RGB images embedded in them, you'll find out the hard way—and the expensive way—that these images will print on just one plate without separating.

- 👁 **Setting the resolution before resizing**. It's important to change the resolution of your image in Photoshop to twice the line screen at which you'll be printing. This helps the production team ensure that the size and percentage at which you're printing this graphic is appropriate.

tip

A good way to ensure that you've converted all RGB images to CMYK is to print color separations of each page in your DTP file. This produces four printed pages for every page in a CMYK document. Although this might send your laser printer into overdrive, especially for large four-color print projects, it's worth it to avoid paying for costly mistakes after your service bureau has output your film. If you notice that an image fails to print as expected on all four pages, the usual suspect is a wayward RGB image.

note

When you change the resolution of a Photoshop image you've already placed in a page layout application file, remember to go back and update the page layout file. The percentage at which the image should appear will change.

You also want to avoid drastically resizing your images in your page layout program—especially resizing upward, say, at 200 percent—because this can adversely affect the quality of your images. Your images will take on a pixelated look in print if you need to enlarge them significantly, which is another good reason to pay for high-resolution scans if high quality is the most important factor in your print work.

Another good reason to resize in Photoshop is that scaling in page layout programs compels the imagesetter to use much more processing time, sometimes called *RIP time* (named after the raster image processor that does the deed). Some service bureaus will charge you for excessive RIP time—or if they haven't so far, they might if your jobs start encroaching on their ability to do business.

Changing from RGB to CMYK

Forgetting to convert all your images from RGB mode to CMYK is a common mistake—but it can be a very expensive one if your service bureau winds up outputting a lot of film you can't use because the images didn't separate. Your service bureau can also hold up your job until you submit new CMYK images, resulting in great time delays.

Converting an RGB image to CMYK mode is a one-step process, but if you have a lot of images to convert it can eat a lot of time. You can use Photoshop's own Actions feature to speed up this kind of task—look ahead to Chapter 15, "Automation and Batch Processing Essentials," for details.

If, as in the RGB-to-CMYK conversion problem I just discussed, you have a number of images that need the same process performed on them, this kind of batch processing can really help you speed up your bulk Photoshop work. You can also use general batch processing utilities, such as CE Software's QuicKeys (for the Macintosh), to create a custom shortcut for any routine Photoshop task.

Changing File Formats

TIFF and EPS are the most commonly used graphic file formats in electronic print production. As you prepare TIFFs for final print production, you should check with your service bureau about whether it's all right to

Figure 14.1

The TIFF Options
dialog box.

use LZW compression—some service bureaus will ask you to leave this check box in the TIFF Options dialog box unchecked (see Figure 14.1).

As when converting color modes, it can be time consuming to convert a bunch of images from another file format to TIFF. The batch-processing shortcuts previously mentioned work great for changing file formats too.

For most of your print production needs, you'd do well to just use TIFF. By now you've seen one big exception—saving a clipping path with a graphic so you can silhouette it against another graphic or other elements in a page layout program file—where you should use EPS. You should also use EPS if you want to save custom halftone screening with an image—which is something you might want to do with your duotones, tritones, or quadtones. The EPS variants DCS 1.0 and DCS 2.0—introduced in Chapter 2, "File Format Essentials"—also support halftone screening (see Figure 14.2). However, you choose only one of the DCS formats if you have additional requirements:

👁 If your service bureau makes high-resolution scans of your artwork and returns the low-resolution version to you to work with in your page layout files, you might wind up using DCS 1.0.

👁 If you're printing more than four color channels—such as extra color plates for spot colors, die cuts, or other high-end printing needs—you need the later DCS 2.0 format. (See "Printing Spot Colors from Photoshop" a little later in this chapter.)

When you save a CMYK file in one of the DCS formats, you have the option to save it as one file (like any other graphics format) or as multiple files—one for each color channel (plus spot-color channels, with DCS 2.0), plus a low-resolution composite file. The composite file is the one your service bureau returns to you to work with. You don't

Figure 14.2
The DCS 1.0 and
DCS 2.0 Options
dialog boxes.

have to worry about swapping the high-res file with the low-res one; your service bureau will take care of that for you.

As helpful as it is to use DCS in this way to work with low-res files while your service bureau keeps the high-res ones, you have to be careful when you later archive all your images. If you lose one of the five files, you'll be in a jam if you ever need to restore that image.

Color Settings

The Color Settings command under the Edit menu lists configurable settings for the color spaces you use when editing or printing your images. (Review "Precision, Precision: Photoshop's Color Models" in Chapter 4, "Color Essentials," if you want to refresh your memory on color spaces.) From Color Settings, you can choose from a number of color-management settings, such as preparation for Web or offset press output. In most cases, these predefined settings should provide sufficient guidance for your color-management needs. Consult with your service bureau to determine whether you should alter any of these settings for your prepress workflow.

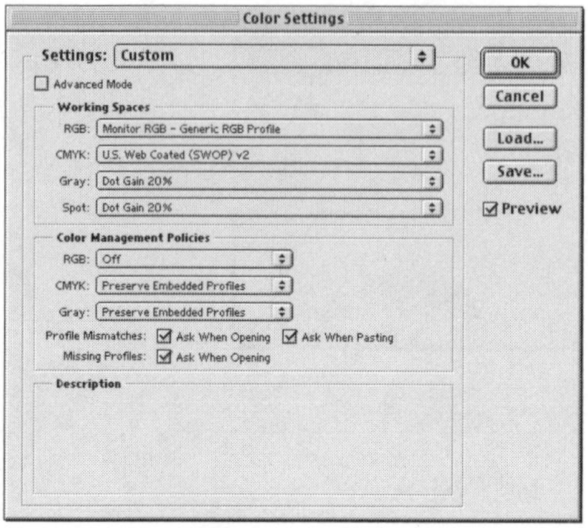

Figure 14.3

The U.S. Prepress Defaults settings in the Color Settings dialog box.

If you look around in the settings for U.S. Prepress Defaults (see Figure 14.3), you'll see the new options that Photoshop has built in for *working spaces*. These working spaces represent the color profiles that Photoshop associates with the RGB, CMYK, and Grayscale color modes.

If you don't know whether you should change any of Photoshop's default settings in the U.S. Prepress Defaults dialog box as you prepare work for professional printing, don't. For example, the U.S. Prepress Defaults setting already uses a CMYK working space that aims to preserve color consistency under standard Specifications for Web Offset Publications (SWOP) press conditions, and is the industry standard for color separation in the United States.

If your service bureau wants you to adjust your printing inks settings for a particular job, work hand in hand with your contact person there to determine the best parameters. For example, if your print job is using a different paper stock, you might be advised to change the default values for dot gain.

Helping Your Service Bureau and Yourself, Too

Planning ahead is the rule to live by when you're supplying your service bureau with everything they need to run your job. For completeness, I've included a run-down-the-list approach to making sure the folks at your service bureau have everything they need to output your job. It includes far more than just the admonition to send all the necessary graphics—but since when have you had a graphics project where you only had to send a couple of images? Usually your assignment is a little more complicated, so here's a checklist to help you make sure everything goes the way you want it to:

👁 **A transmittal form** specifying the services you need—for example, color-separated film output. Your service bureau probably has its own form it wants you to use. List by name all your application files, fonts, and graphics. Include appropriate information about line screen and printing resolution, emulsion specifications (for film), billing, and when you expect to have the work delivered.

👁 **A printed directory of disk contents**. This directory saves untold hours if your service bureau has any difficulty finding one of your graphic files or fonts. Be sure the contents of the folders appear in the file listing as well.

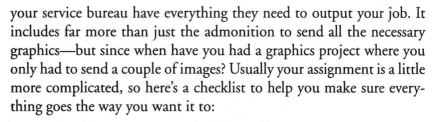

👁 **A copy of every graphic imported in your application file**. List on the transmittal form the file formats of the graphics you're sending—for example, so many TIFF files and so many EPS graphics.

👁 **Your page layout file**. If your page layout program generates its own Preferences file (such as the XPress Preferences file you can update in QuarkXPress), send that as well.

👁 **A hard copy final proof of every page in your job, printed at 100% size**. If you have any additional comments to mark on the laser proofs, use a high-contrast pen or marker so the folks at the service bureau don't miss them. If you have oversized documents that you can't print at 100 percent on your laser printer, print in tile mode rather than reducing the print size.

👁 **Screen and printer fonts**. Be sure to use PostScript fonts, not TrueType versions. You'll want to include all fonts used in both your page layout programs and in your Photoshop files.

👁 **Any additional artwork or transparencies that have not been scanned**. Label each piece of original art with page and column numbers, and write on the laser proofs indicating where you want the service bureau to scan an image and drop it in.

If you don't send page proofs, your printer won't accept responsibility if, for example, text reflows around images in your application file and changes all the page breaks.

note

Some desktop publishing applications have pre-flighting options that help you assess whether you have all the resources you need to print your job. For example, QuarkXPress's Collect for Output option simplifies gathering all the graphics, fonts, and other needed elements. There are also commercial pre-flighting programs available for use when collecting Photoshop files, such as Markzware's FlightCheck.

Here are some additional tips that, from the service bureau's perspective, should make you a joy to do business with:

- 👁 **Send color-separated laser proofs**. Time permitting, it's a good idea to send color-separated proofs if you're asking for film separations; your service bureau might even require them. Printing color separations is another way for you to ensure that everything shows up on different plates the way it should.

- 👁 **Flag all FPO (for position only) images**. Be sure to point out loud and clear if you expect your service bureau to put in some high-resolution images for the low-res versions in the document. That way, your vendor doesn't have to waste any time looking for files that you never intended for final output. Similarly, you should never change the name of any FPO file that your service bureau gives you.

- 👁 **Update all modified graphics in the page layout file**. This includes any image whose name you may have changed, as well as images where you changed the resolution or color mode at the last minute.

- 👁 **Match the names of spot colors in your Photoshop images with their counterparts in your page layout file**. You'll have printing problems if the two names don't match exactly. This shouldn't be a problem with predefined PMS colors in QuarkXPress or Adobe PageMaker.

- 👁 **Use clipping paths when you need images with a transparent background to overlap other page elements**. QuarkXPress has a misleading feature where you can specify an image's background fill as None; onscreen, your image's white background looks like it's been knocked out to transparency, but in reality, if such an image goes to press you'll see jagged edges form around it. Create a clipping path around the image in Photoshop if the image will overlap other graphics, rules, or type on the page. For other situations, it's a good idea to set the image's background fill to white or 0% black instead of None.

◉ **Add at least 1/8-inch for images that bleed**. If you have images that should print to the edge of the page (known as a bleed), you need to extend the image's display in your page layout file at least 9 points (⅛ inch) past the trim to account for slight movements on press.

◉ **Delete all unused colors in your page layout file's color palette**. Otherwise, your service bureau might inadvertently print blank color plates for these extra, unwanted colors.

Building Better Design from the Screen Up

So far, you've read about some good practices for handing off your completed work to your print shop or service bureau—but there are also a number of good design practices you can follow before your work leaves your screen. Here are some additional tips for ensuring your print projects look as good in print as they do on your computer—many of these tips can be applied to the color elements you add in your page layout program as well as your color work in Photoshop:

◉ **Background tints**. To ensure readability, keep dark-colored background images or tints under 30 percent opacity when black type is to print on top. If you are using knockout (or white) type, dark-colored backgrounds should appear at least at 70 percent opacity. Similarly, don't use tints of less than 5 percent—they simply won't reproduce on the printing plates. (These percentages might vary slightly depending on your ink colors or type size, so be sure to run a print test with your printer or service bureau.)

◉ **Avoid knockout type in small point sizes**. Below 10 point, reversed type can become illegible because of potential variations in color registration. Similarly, fine lettering and fine rules should be screened with a low opacity.

◉ **Limit colors used in fine lines**. Again, to avoid registration problems, restrict to a single color plate any thin lines (under ½ point) and small type (10 point or less).

👁 **High-percentage tints or screens should not exceed 90 percent**. Printing presses cannot distinguish subtle differences in screen percentages. Such high-percentage screens should be set solid (at 100 percent opacity) instead.

How Your Service Bureau's Imagesetter Works

After you submit your application files to your service bureau, they use them to generate PostScript files. If your company is trying to save money, you might be responsible for generating those PostScript files yourself, although that opens up possibilities for errors on your end. PostScript-based imagesetters have a raster image processor that translates the instructions in the PostScript files to dot patterns for each color. A recorder in the imagesetter uses a laser beam to reproduce the dot patterns on the film or paper loaded in the machine.

Halftone Screening

These imagesetter dots are organized into a system of cells that make up the halftone dots in the finished work. The more imagesetter dots that can fit into one of these cells, the larger the printed halftone dot will look in print. These variously sized but evenly spaced dots help create the appearance of *continuous tone* in your printed images. By default, the dots are actually shaped like little diamonds. However, you can choose from six dot shapes included in Photoshop—diamond, round, ellipse, line, square, or cross—or you can specify a custom shape.

You probably don't have any need to change the spot shape of the halftone dots. Depending on the circumstances of your print job—for example, if you're printing on newsprint at very coarse line frequencies—you might find that changing the shape of the dot helps you to capture more of an image's fine details.

To change the halftone screen settings for an image, first choose Page Setup from the File menu; the Page Setup dialog box appears. Next click the Screen button in the printer's Page Setup dialog box (see Figure 14.4) to open the Halftone Screens dialog box. Then, uncheck the Use Printer's Default Screens check box to set the dot shape or screen angle used in your image's halftones.

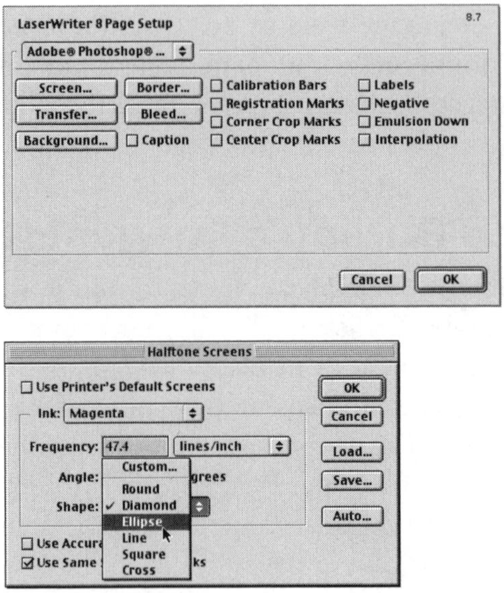

Figure 14.4

Specifying
custom halftone
screens for your
Photoshop
images.

Stochastic Screening

Besides halftoning, you can also simulate the appearance of continuous tone with stochastic screening. In stochastic screening, the dots are all the same size. The distance between the dots, not their varying size, helps create a realistic-looking image.

note

> **Don't change your default angle settings until you've checked with your service bureau to determine the best frequency, angle, and dot settings to use.**

To create stochastic screens in Photoshop, you need to adjust the line screen values set in the Page Setup dialog box for every plate. Choose Print Options from the File menu. Select the Show More Options check box; you will see the dialog box expand at the bottom (see Figure 14.5). With the Output pop-up menu showing, choose the button marked Screen. The Halftone Screens dialog box appears. You then uncheck the Use Printer's Default Screens check box to choose your own screen settings. Again, please check with your print shop before changing any of these settings on your own!

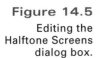

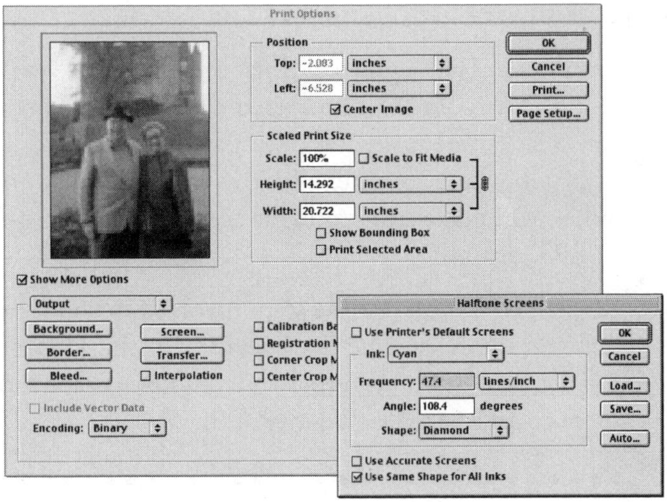

Figure 14.5
Editing the
Halftone Screens
dialog box.

You then need to save your file in EPS format so you can check the Include Halftone Screen check box; this embeds custom halftone screen information within the file.

You can also, however, create a decent stochastic effect when you convert an image from Grayscale to Bitmap and choose the Diffusion Dither option. You might have to play with increasing the resolution to get it right.

Process vs. Spot Color

Whatever form your print project will take, you'll want to plan well ahead of time how you'll be using color in the job. For example, will you use process color (CMYK) or spot color? Remember that commercial printers charge you for each ink you use for printing, so you or your company will save money by choosing spot color if you're printing only a small number of colors—three or fewer. A typical 2-color job uses black ink and a spot color, such as an ink from a predefined color system like the Pantone Matching System (PMS). Even when you're using just two inks, you still have a lot of flexibility—you can stretch your color range by making use of varying percentages of both those inks, blends, and duotones—areas where both inks print.

Duotones

A duotone is like a grayscale image, except that two inks—usually black and a PMS color—print over the same area. This added color depth can create some really interesting images, and add interest to a 2-color print job where all other elements appear in just one ink or the other. When you make a duotone for use in a print job, you'll need to save it in EPS format.

In Chapter 4, you saw the steps involved in choosing a second ink and saving a duotone. The live previews to the Duotone Options dialog box let you view and refine your duotone color settings as you apply them to an image (see Figure 14.6).

Using Short Pantone Names

Be sure that the Short PANTONE Names check box in Photoshop's General Preferences dialog box is checked. PMS color names in Photoshop can otherwise not match their counterparts in page layout programs. Older versions of some page layout programs define PMS colors with two-letter suffixes, as in Pantone 199 CV; but by default, Photoshop names that same color Pantone 199 CVC. If you check the Short Pantone Names check box, you can stave off this miscommunication between the programs.

Preferences	
General	OK
Color Picker: Adobe	Cancel
Interpolation: Bicubic (Better)	Prev
Redo Key: Cmd+Z (Toggles Undo/Redo) History States: 20	Next

Options
- ☐ Export Clipboard
- ☑ Short PANTONE Names
- ☑ Show Tool Tips
- ☑ Keyboard Zoom Resizes Windows
- ☐ Auto-update open documents
- ☐ Show Asian Text Options
- ☐ Beep When Done
- ☑ Dynamic Color Sliders
- ☑ Save Palette Locations
- ☑ Show Font Names in English
- ☑ Use Shift Key for Tool Switch

Reset All Warning Dialogs

Reset All Tools

Printing Spot Colors from Photoshop

What if you're fine-tuning some images for a 2-color print job and want to print spot colors, not duotones, from Photoshop? You can do

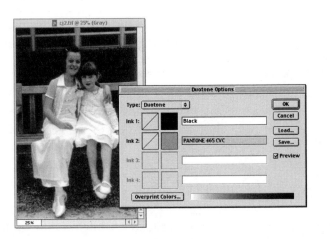

Figure 14.6
Click the Preview
check box in the
Duotone Options
dialog box to
inspect your
duotone
settings.

this by saving your file in the DCS 2.0 format, which supports multiple spot colors in extra channels.

First, you need to select the area or portions of your image that you want filled with a spot color. Then display the Channels palette and select New Spot Color from the drop-down menu. Click the color swatch to open the Color Picker dialog box. Now, click the Custom button to open the Custom dialog box, and toggle among the selections to choose the spot color you want. When you finish, click OK to close all the dialog boxes. Your new spot-color channel will automatically contain your selected area, and the selection will fill with that spot color.

Because both QuarkXPress and Adobe PageMaker support DCS 2.0, you can include images with spot colors that are not duotones. Check with your service bureau before submitting DCS 2.0 files for the first time. They can tell you which preferences, if any, they want you to use when you save your files in DCS 2.0 format.

Quick Tips for 2-Color Print Jobs

Here are some additional tips for getting the most from your 2-color projects:

◉ **Consider not using black.** This can definitely differentiate your printed piece from other 2-color projects. Use a color wheel or

consult with your service bureau to determine which 2-colored inks would work best together for the job at hand.

👁 **Consider using a colored paper stock**. This has the visual effect of adding a third color to your project, and might let you create even more color combination with your two inks. Consult with your print shop to ensure that the subject matter in your images will look good against the color in question.

On the Press

Until now, this chapter has focused only on how to prepare your work for imagesetter output, but you should also be aware of the kinds of printing problems that can crop up. This section covers such problems.

Dot Gain

When your job is on the press, the neat little halftone dots the imagesetter puts on film for you can show up as much bigger dots of ink on your paper (see Figure 14.7). Dot gain describes an increase in dot size; as a result, your job can print too dark or intense. It's attributable in part to the kind of inks or paper the job involves; newsprint, for example, is especially absorbent, so it can print darker than you intended.

Photoshop has a built-in method for safeguarding against dot gain on the press. Choose Color Settings from the File menu, and then choose CMYK Setup from the Color Settings submenu. The CMYK Setup dialog box displays a value for the percentage of dot gain expected during printing.

Figure 14.7

An example of dot gain. Halftone dots can change in size from the time they are output on film when printing plates to when the job is printed on paper.

Trapping

If you've ever seen slight gaps between colors in a document, you've seen what poor trapping does—it's a result of misalignment between printing plates. Like many desktop publishing programs, Photoshop has its own method of trapping. It can print one color slightly larger so as to overlap another color; this way, the telltale white gap won't appear even if the press gets the two colors slightly out of register. Figure 14.8 shows an image with trapping (right) and without trapping (left). Notice there are no unsightly gaps in the right example in Figure 14.8—these two colors are in register.

Trapping is a technique of overlapping colors to ensure that slight misalignment or movement of the plates while printing doesn't affect the final appearance of the print job. Therefore, if you have distinctly different colors in your image butt up against one another, you'll want to overprint them slightly to prevent gaps from appearing when the image is printed. Photoshop's trapping method spreads lighter colors under darker ones.

Here are some general rules for when two abutting elements require trapping:

- The two elements in question are two different spot colors (such as PMS 116 and PMS 295)

- One element is a PMS color and the other(s) are process colors (such as a CMYK combination and PMS 256)

Figure 14.8

Without trapping, you will see gaps in the color if the printing press cannot maintain perfect registration, as in the left picture. With trapping, one layer of ink is slightly printed over another one, as at right, to avoid such problems on press.

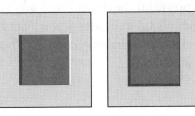

Figure 14.9
Photoshop's
Trap options.

If the two abutting elements use the same colors, trapping is not necessary (for example, both use CMYK colors at different percentages). For most of your Photoshop imagery, such as photographs, trapping should not be a cause for concern.

Spread and *choke* are two other terms you might hear used to describe trapping. Spread increases the size of an image for trapping, whereas choke reduces the image's size.

You can access Photoshop's Trap dialog box by choosing Trap from the Image menu. This menu item will appear only when you're working with a CMYK image. You can then select a unit of measurement and enter a value for the width of the trap (see Figure 14.9). Your print shop can help you determine the values to enter in the Trap dialog box.

Summary

The strategies covered here should help you work better with your service bureau and get the kind of results that you're after in your print production. Now brace yourself for the final chapter, which covers how Photoshop's Actions feature can streamline all the core Photoshop techniques you've learned about into batch process commands. As you learn to build your own powerful shortcuts—and acquire collections of actions from other thoughtful designers—you'll see how you can realize your Web, print, and multimedia projects using Photoshop in advanced and truly efficient ways.

15

Automation and Batch Processing Essentials

IN THIS CHAPTER

The Actions Palette

Recording and Editing Actions

Drag-and-Drop Actions

Automate Commands

As you take on more and more Photoshop work, you're bound to find yourself repeating certain routine tasks over and over again. If you work in print production, for example, you might receive dozens of RGB screen shots a day that you must convert to CMYK color mode, or BMP files that you must convert to TIFFs. Because it's not very efficient to open, edit, save, and close numerous images in the same way by hand, Photoshop has several built-in features that you can use to streamline your most repetitive chores. In this way, you can make your changes automatically—to one image or a hundred—with little or no human intervention.

In this chapter, you learn how to record a task as a set of scripted steps that Photoshop calls an *action*. An action is a series of Photoshop operations you record using the Actions palette, and then play back in order to apply those steps to another image or a series of images. I've already mentioned Photoshop's Actions palette a number of times in earlier chapters; this palette can store your most frequently used actions so they're always within easy reach. You'll also turn to the Actions palette to play existing actions or load actions you've acquired elsewhere. If you've ever used a macro utility such as QuicKeys, you're already familiar with how actions work.

Photoshop's Automation plug-ins help you accomplish certain tasks automatically—from creating a clipping path to resizing an image, for example. Now that you've seen in earlier chapters how to do these kinds of tasks by hand, you'll be in a good position to judge how and when you'll want to put these time-saving assistants to work instead. This chapter focuses on the following techniques for using Photoshop more efficiently:

- Recording a set of steps in a given task as a Photoshop action

- Adding more steps to any prerecorded action

- Putting a "stop" in the middle of an action to make Photoshop wait to receive some input from you before continuing

- Preparing and running an action as a batch process on numerous files at a time

👁 Organizing your actions into sets and acquiring new ones from other sources

👁 Using the onscreen assistants to guide you through accomplishing tasks

Exploring the Actions Palette

If the Actions palette isn't already visible, choose Show Actions from the Window menu to open it (see Figure 15.1). Inside the Actions palette, the actions shown are grouped in sets, indicated by folders. You should see a folder called Default Actions, for example. If you don't, you should be able to load it from your Photoshop 6.0 CD. Notice that many of the menu commands you've used in Photoshop appear as Command Actions.

The check box at the left of each command's row toggles that step in the action on or off. If you uncheck the check box next to a command name, you cannot activate that step in the action. A check box next to the name of an action shows that the action is active and will play as part of a set. The check box turns red if one or more commands in that action are not active and won't play.

The second column indicates if that action includes any "stop" points whereby a dialog box appears and asks you to enter some information or requires you to press Enter or Return before continuing. If the action stops at least once, a little red dialog box icon appears in that

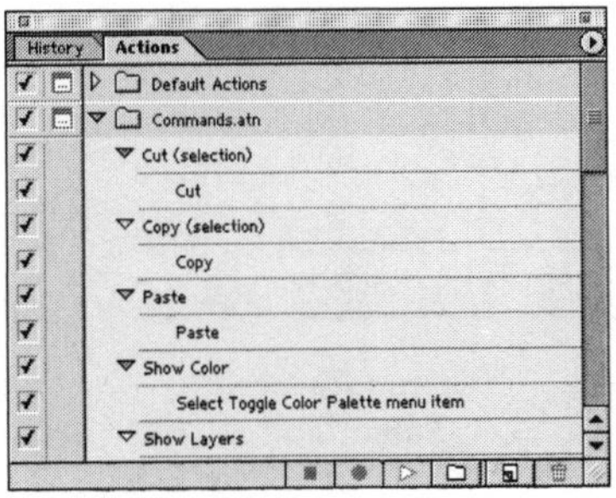

Figure 15.1

The Actions palette.

column. If the dialog box icon is black, this indicates that there is a stop at every step that asks for input.

note

Because some actions stop midway through to wait for some kind of input from you, it's important that you don't try to do anything else onscreen while an action is running. You might inadvertently stop the action or enter an improper value.

You can toggle the triangle next to the folder reading Default Actions to view all the predefined actions contained therein or hide the list again. Each action in this list also has a triangle to the left of its name. Click this triangle to see the sequence of commands that make up this action. Some of these commands might also have their own triangles, which you can click to see additional steps that make up that command.

tip

• •

You can move an action's position in a set by dragging the action's name to a new position within the Actions palette. You might want to use this to move the actions you use most frequently to the top positions in a set so that you don't need to hunt for them when you want them.

• •

Six icons appear at the bottom of the Actions palette to let you play and manipulate your actions. These include Stop Playing/Recording, Record, Play, Create New Set, Create New Action, and Delete Selection (see Figure 15.2).

The commands represented by these icons can also be selected using the pop-up menu that appears when you click the black triangle in the upper-right corner of the Actions palette (see Figure 15.3). This pop-up

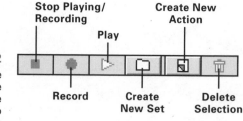

Figure 15.2
The icons at the bottom of the Actions palette allow you to manipulate Photoshop actions.

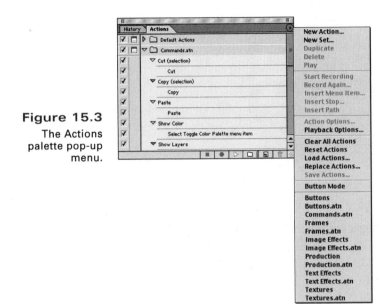

Figure 15.3

The Actions
palette pop-up
menu.

menu includes a number of additional commands related to recording
and playing Photoshop actions, which I'll talk about in more detail later
in this chapter.

Playing an Action

By now, you've seen two ways you can play an Action. You can highlight
its row in the Actions palette and click the Play (▷) icon. Alternatively,
you can choose Play from the Actions palette pop-up menu.

note

**While an action is playing, the Play icon turns red. After all steps
are complete, the icon turns black again.**

There's also a third method that involves displaying your actions as buttons. If you choose Button Mode from the Actions palette pop-up menu,
you'll see each action appear as a long, shallow rectangular button (see
Figure 15.4). In Button Mode, you can just click a button to play it.
Because you can assign different colors to your Actions buttons, you can
make a favorite action of yours visually pop out on the list by assigning it
a color that contrasts greatly with the surrounding buttons.

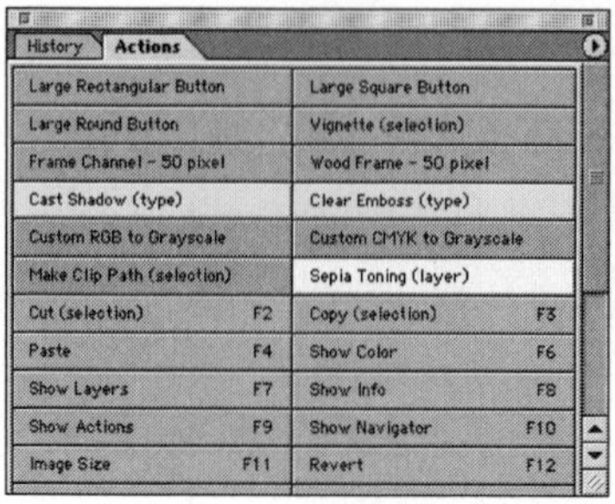

Figure 15.4

Viewing your actions in Button Mode.

If you play a lot of actions but don't spend much time recording new ones, the Button Mode display is easier to use. Function key commands are visible only when you're viewing your actions in Button Mode. To exit Button Mode, click the Actions palette pop-up menu again, and then choose the Button Mode menu item to uncheck it.

Finally, you can assign a function key to your favorite actions, so you can play them by simply pressing a keyboard combination. This might sound familiar to you if you've used keyboard shortcuts or macros in other programs. You might not have realized it before, but some Photoshop commands already have keyboard shortcuts assigned to them. You can see preassigned keyboard shortcuts when viewing Command Actions in Button Mode. For example, you can press the F8 key to activate the Show Info command; if you prefer to use a different keyboard shortcut, you can assign another function key in its place.

To assign a function key or a button color, highlight your action's row and choose Action Options from the Actions palette pop-up menu; you'll need to exit Button Mode if you're still in it. The Action Options dialog box opens (see Figure 15.5).

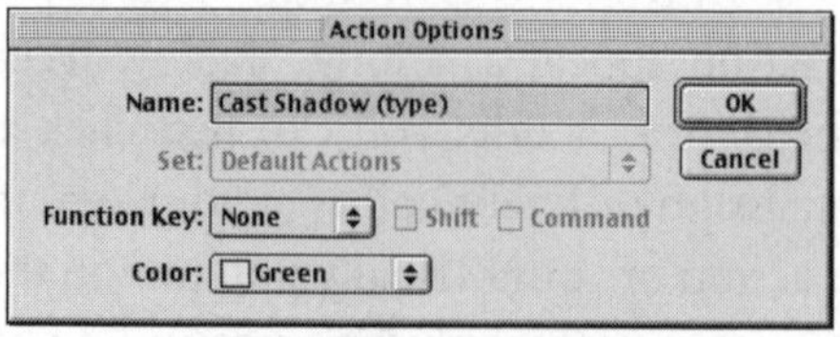

Figure 15.5

The Action Options dialog box.

You can also double-click any action's name in the Actions palette in standard mode to open the Action Options dialog box. This dialog box is also used to change your actions' names and indicate which set, if any, they belong to. Just like layer sets, action sets can be color-coded so that you can store related actions together in a visual way.

Predefined Actions

The default actions included with Photoshop help you gain an understanding of what kinds of tasks an action can do, and how you can extend actions' usefulness by making them stop at certain points to await your further instructions.

As you look over Photoshop's default actions (shown in Figure 15.1), the first thing you should note is that it's very important to give each of your actions a clear, succinct name. You might load numerous sets of custom actions, and you need to be able to pick out the action you want quickly from your list. Notice how some of these default actions include information in their names in parentheses—such as Cast Shadow (type), Vignette (selection), and Sepia Toning (layer). This helps indicate that the action must meet certain requirements first—for example, you might need to target a type layer or make a selection first—and you'll receive an error message if you try to play that action when it's not appropriate.

Take some time now to try some of the default actions to see what they do. First, create a new RGB document with a white background and choose a bright foreground color. Highlight one of the first three default actions—Large Rectangular Button, Large Square Button, or Large Round Button—and press the Play icon at the bottom of the Actions palette (see Figure 15.6).

Make sure that action's steps appear in the Actions palette. As the action plays, you can see each step highlighted in turn. When the action is complete, you'll see the final result: a new embossed button or rectangle (depending on what shape you selected) filled with your foreground color and appearing on a new layer in your document (see Figure 15.7).

Now look at each step in the action: Make layer, Set Selection, Fill, Set Selection, Set Layer Styles of Current Layer. Follow along with each step

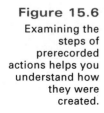

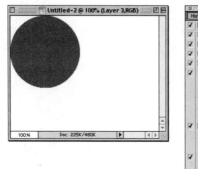

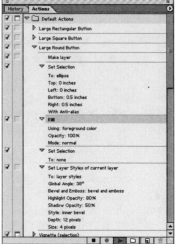

Figure 15.6
Examining the steps of prerecorded actions helps you understand how they were created.

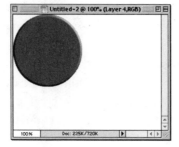

Figure 15.7
The results of applying the Large Square Button action.

in the predefined process to see what happened behind the scenes when you executed this command. After Make layer, all the commands in this action have additional steps where certain values are specified. The first Set Selection step specifies the dimensions of the selected area, and then the Fill step specifies the use of the foreground color, and so on.

The default Photoshop action that I find singularly useful is Make Clip Path (selection). This action generates a clipping path based on any current selection in your image, so you can easily create images for print publication that have a transparent background when placed in a page layout program. Without this Photoshop action, you have to convert your selection to a path and then use the Paths palette pop-up menu to

specify settings for the clipping path. Avoiding those steps can add up to real time savings, especially when you have a lot of images to deal with.

note   If you want to undo an action, use the History palette and its multiple levels of undo to return most quickly to the pre-action image state. The regular Undo command undoes only the last step in the action, and you need to repeat the Step Backward command under the Edit menu several times (once for each command in the action) in order to return to your pre-action state.

Recording and Editing Actions

Although the default Photoshop actions discussed so far are quite straightforward, they're probably not perfectly suited to your needs. The real value in the Actions feature comes in automating the specific tasks you do every day, so this section shows you how to record your steps as you meticulously accomplish a given task, and then apply that recorded action to a number of images stored in the same folder.

note   You can record steps you take in the Paths, Layers, and History palettes, as well as tool activities using the Gradient tools, the Marquee and Crop tools, and the Lasso, Move, Magic Wand, Paint Bucket, and Type tools. You can also save commands using Lighting Effects, Calculations, Apply Image, File Info, and Free Transform as steps in your actions.

Take some time to think about which repetitive Photoshop tasks are taking up too much of your time. For example, if part of your job calls for preparing the images from each new issue of your company's magazine for the Web, one good action to keep handy is the process you use to convert an image's color mode from CMYK to RGB, and then to Indexed Color, and then save it as a GIF file instead of a TIFF. This is an example of a very simple action—but one that can greatly improve your quality of life if you currently perform these steps on a manual basis dozens of times a day or week.

note You can even create an action that runs another action. To do so, record the process of choosing an action and pressing the Play icon at the bottom of the Actions palette as steps in a new action.

Actions are also very useful for capturing the steps involved in creating complex special effects. By recording the steps as an action, you're ready to apply the effect on an as-needed basis and don't need to keep a stack of how-to articles handy. In Exercise 15.1, you'll record the steps involved in creating a custom cutout border effect.

You might need to redefine how you think of some of your everyday Photoshop tasks in order to generalize them enough to record in an action. For example, when I create the effect described in Exercise 15.1 manually, I don't use steps 4 though 6—I just eyeball the image and create a rectangular marquee selection that's somewhat smaller than the entire image as a whole. But that framework doesn't work well when you're trying to generalize the process for an action. If I want to apply this action to an image of any dimension, I can't hard-code an exact size for the selection. The steps I added are a more roundabout way of getting the selection I want, but they can be applied to many images, not just the sample image I used in Exercise 15.1.

Duplicating Actions

It's useful to make a copy of an existing action when you want to tweak it; if you take a wrong turn, you can trash the flawed duplicate and start over again from the original. To duplicate an action, you can choose the command by that name in the Actions palette pop-up menu. Alternatively, you can drag the row of the action you want to duplicate down to the Create New Action icon at the bottom of the Actions palette.

Deleting Actions

You have two options at your disposal for deleting actions. First, you can choose the Delete command from the Actions palette pop-up menu. Alternatively, you can drag the row of the action you want to delete down to the Trash icon at the bottom of the Actions palette.

EXERCISE 15.1

Creating Custom Photo Edges Automatically

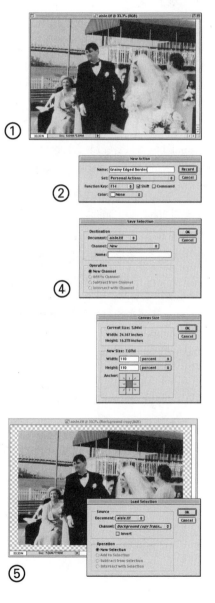

1. Open the document to which you plan to add a custom border.

    If you want to create a new set in which to place this action, now's the time—choose New Set from the pop-up menu at the right of the Actions palette and give your new set a name. If you're okay with placing this new action in the Default Actions set or another action set you've already created, go to step 2.

2. Click the Create New Action icon (🔲) at the bottom of the Actions palette. Assign the action a name; here, I'm calling this action "Grainy Edged Border." If you think you'll use this action frequently, assign it a function key that will run the action when you press it.

    The Record icon (⬤) at the bottom of the Actions palette will turn red. Everything you do now within Photoshop will be recorded until you click the Stop icon (⬛).

3. This effect involves creating a layer mask, so your image needs to be on any layer other than the Background layer. One easy way to automate this is to display the Layers palette by choosing Show Layers from the Window menu. Next, drag the Background layer down to the Create New Layer icon to duplicate it, and then drag the Background layer down to the Trash icon. The layer that's left is called Background copy.

4. Choose Select All from the Select menu, and then choose Save Selection from the Select menu to save this as an alpha channel.

5. Choose Canvas Size from the Image menu and increase the height and width to 110 percent. (It really doesn't matter what additional percentage you choose here; you'll restore the original dimensions before you're through.)

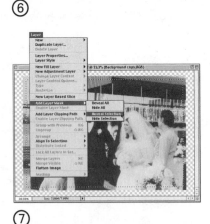

This deselects the area you had selected, so you need to choose Load Selection from the Select menu to restore the alpha channel you saved.

6. Now choose Modify from the Select menu and choose Contract. You can contract a selection by a maximum of 16 pixels, so if you want to create an even smaller selection within the image window, you need to repeat the Contract command one or more times.

7. Choose Add Layer Mask from the Layer menu, and then pick Reveal Selection from the Add Layer Mask submenu. Now you see only the contracted portion of the selection.

8. Next, choose Show Channels from the Window menu and verify that the mask channel is targeted.

9. Now you're going to apply the filters that will create the cutout border effect. Feel free to experiment with your own filter effects or just use the values shown here. Here, I applied the Gaussian Blur filter (under Blur in the Filter menu) with a value of 10 pixels, and then applied the Graphic Pen filter (under Sketch in the Filter menu) with a Stroke Length of 15 and a Light/Dark Balance set to 90.

10. Choose Flatten Image from the Layer menu. Now restore your image to its original dimensions. That is, reload your alpha channel by choosing Load Selection from the Select menu, and then choose Crop from the Image menu.

11. Click the Stop icon to finish recording the action. Figure 15.8 shows the result.

Figure 15.8

If you record complex Photoshop effects like this layer mask as single actions, you'll be inclined to use them more frequently.

Editing Actions

By editing actions, you can get more use out of actions you created previously as well as out of Photoshop's default actions and any that you might have acquired through other resources. To return to Photoshop's default actions, for example, I usually need to create buttons that are somewhat larger than the ones these actions create if left to themselves.

To insert one or more new steps in an existing action, make sure you display all the steps in that action in the Actions palette. (Remember to work on a duplicate if you think there's any chance you'll want the original action.) Click the task that immediately precedes the point where you want to add the new steps. Now click the Record icon and perform the steps that you want to add. Click the Stop icon when you finish.

If you need to delete a step in an action, you can click just that step in the Actions palette to highlight it and drag it down to the Trash icon.

Using the Insert Menu Item Command

When you record an action, there are some Photoshop commands that cannot be recorded as you perform them. These include entering View menu commands and setting Photoshop preferences. However, you can still insert these nonrecordable commands into your Photoshop actions by using the Insert Menu Item command from the Actions palette pop-up menu.

You can also use the Insert Menu Command to make your Photoshop action stop when a command causes a dialog box to open (see Figure 15.9). This is good to do when you want to add different values to the dialog boxes that appear in your actions, instead of hard-coding those values as part of your action.

In the Grainy Edged Border example in Exercise 15.1, for example, you might want to decide on a case-by-case basis how much to contract your selection. Click the task right before this menu item should appear. Choose Insert Menu Item from the Actions palette pop-up menu. The Insert Menu Item dialog box opens. With the Insert Menu Item dialog box open, you choose a command from its menu. Click OK to insert the new menu item in the action. If you automated that step with hard-coded values when you first created the action, you'll want to delete the old step.

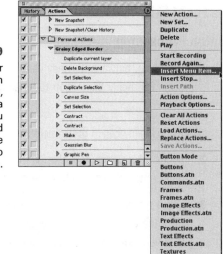

Figure 15.9

To make your actions even more flexible, you can add a stop when you reach a command in which you're prompted to input a value.

Hold It! or Stopping Actions

Sometimes you might want to pause your action in its tracks so you can carry out a task that can't be performed by rote—for example, touching up stray pixels after applying a filter. You can do this by including a stop in your action; when you're done making individual adjustments, you then click the Play button in the Actions palette.

To add a stop to an action, click the task that takes place just before the point where you want to insert the stop. Choose Insert Stop from the Actions palette pop-up menu. The Record Stop dialog box opens (see Figure 15.10); here, you can even enter a message that should appear at this point when the action is running. This is useful for reminding you (or another user, if you share your actions) what you need to do before continuing. If you want the option of continuing the action without stopping, you should also check the Allow Continue check box. Click OK; the new stop is inserted in the action.

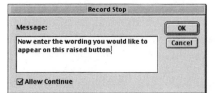

Figure 15.10

The Record Stop dialog box.

EXERCISE 15.2

Batch Processing

The custom photo edges from Exercise 15.1 look very striking, but face it—they were a real chore to create. Good thing you saved this effect as an action! Now you can apply this action to an entire folder of images without repeating any of the work.

1. Place all the images to which you want to apply the Grainy Edged Border action in a single folder.

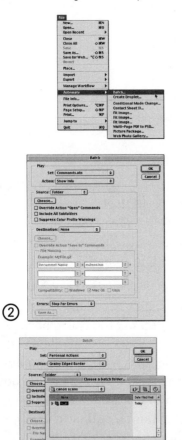

2. Choose Automate from the File menu, and then choose Batch. The Batch dialog box opens.

3. Make sure you see "Folder" in the Source drop-down list. Click the Choose button to toggle through the folders on your hard drive. Select the folder containing your images.

4. Click the Action drop-down list and select the action named Grainy Edged Border. Because this action doesn't have a step that involves choosing Open from the File menu, you don't need to click the Override Action "Open" Commands check box. (If your action did have an Open command, failing to check this box could create an endless loop that opens the same file over and over.) If your source folder has subfolders that contain images you want to batch process, make sure you check the Include All Subfolders check box.

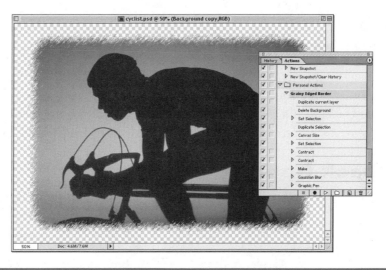

5. The Destination drop-down list lets you choose how you want Photoshop to save the affected files. Choosing None will leave all the files open and unsaved, because there's no Save step in the Grainy Edged Border action. Choosing Save and Close will do just that, overwriting the originals. Choosing Folder will save the modified files in a separate folder, thus preserving the originals—generally a wise precaution. Click OK when you finish.

Figure 15.11 shows the finished product.

Figure 15.11

You might want to watch the batch process in action for a little while—and estimate how much time you're saving!

Acquiring Additional Actions

As you've seen, the real value of Photoshop actions shows up when you create your own actions to speed up the specific tasks that you do repeatedly. One of the easiest ways to acquire new actions quickly is from Web sites devoted to Photoshop tips and tricks. As of this writing, for example, the Planet Photoshop portal site (**http://www.planetphotoshop.com/**) lists close to two dozen sites that specialize in giveaways of Photoshop actions. Appendix B, "Sources for Further Information," lists a number of useful sources for Photoshop actions.

Droplets: Drag-and-Drop Actions

Once you start creating your own Photoshop shortcuts and collecting additional actions for creating special effects, you'll really come to appreciate what a time-saver they can turn out to be. For even greater ease of use, you'll want to discover *droplets*, which are small applications that act as a drag-and-drop version of your Photoshop actions. You can save a droplet anywhere on your desktop or hard drive, and then drag images to the droplet icon (🔻) to apply the action.

Exercise 15.3 walks you through the steps to create your own instant droplets.

When Actions Go Wrong

Sometimes after downloading a new action or using a new droplet for the first time, I have trouble getting it to work the way I hoped it would. And sometimes actions I created work as expected during the action's creation—but produce bizarre results when I try to reuse them.

Playback Options

One good way to see where the problem is happening is to slow down the playback. Choose Playback Options from the Actions palette pop-up menu (see Figure 15.12). You have three speeds to choose from:

- 👁 **Accelerated** is the default option; it plays the action at a normal speed.

- 👁 **Step by Step** completes each command while you watch, redrawing the image before going on to the next command in the action.

- 👁 **Pause** lets you enter an amount of time that Photoshop should wait before performing each command in an action.

Figure 15.12
The Playback Options dialog box.

Playback Options
Performance
● Accelerated
○ Step by Step
○ Pause For: ☐ seconds
☑ Pause For Audio Annotation
OK Cancel

EXERCISE 15.3

Creating a Droplet

For this exercise, you need an action of your own or one you've downloaded from the Internet. You can also use one of the default Photoshop actions that came bundled with the application.

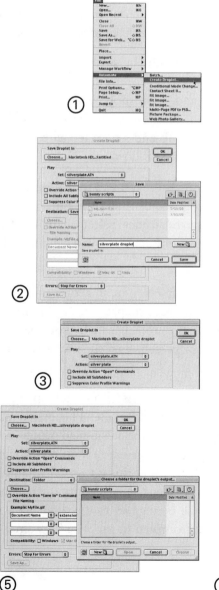

① ② ③ ⑤ ⑥

1. Choose Create Droplet from the Automate submenu under the File menu.

2. Select Choose in the Save Droplet In portion of the dialog box to choose a folder or location in which to save the droplet.

3. Pick the appropriate set, and then the name of the desired action.

4. Add any necessary options for this droplet. For example, if your action involves choosing Open from the File menu, you need to click the Override Action "Open" Commands check box. You also choose the Include All Subdirectories option to apply the droplet's action to all subdirectories within the appropriate folder.

5. You need to pick a destination for the files once the droplet's action has been applied. If you choose None, the files will remain open and unsaved (unless the action includes a Save command). Choosing Save and Close will cause the original files to be overwritten. If you select a new destination folder, the originals will remain untouched and the processed files will be saved in the new folder you specify. This last option might require a file-naming convention.

6. Leave the Photoshop application temporarily to return to your desktop view (Macintosh users return to the Finder). Drag the icons of one or more image files onto the droplet icon to see your action in action, so to speak. This has to be the fastest way to apply any given Photoshop effect—or most realistically, any tedious file-saving chore—to a large number of files at once.

silverplate droplet
swatch1.tif
swatch2.tif
swatch3.tif

Troubleshooting Tips

If you're still getting inconsistent results, try the following tips:

- Remember that when you're playing an action, the results might depend on variables that you overlooked when you recorded it. For example, do you need to set the background and foreground colors to specific values first? Will the color mode, height and width, or resolution of the image make a difference in the results?

- Some Photoshop activities still cannot be saved as steps in actions. These include the painting and toning tools, setting tool options, the View commands, and Photoshop preferences. However, you can still incorporate these steps with the Insert Menu Item command, or by adding a Stop and a message with explicit instructions on which activity should follow.

- If you add to an action any command that uses a transform box—such as any of the Transform commands under the Edit menu or the Transform Selection command under Select—you need to apply an Insert Menu Item to stop the action so you can make the necessary manual adjustments.

- Changing an image's dimensions as a step in an action can create less-than-ideal cropping if you don't anticipate the size of images you might one day apply this action to. That's why your best bet is to edit dimensions in terms of percentages, the way you did in Exercise 15.1.

- When you record an action with a Save As or Save a Copy command, make sure you don't enter a file name. Photoshop will dutifully record that file name as part of the automated process and save that file name every time you run that action, thus overwriting one file again and again. The way around this is to specify a folder name for saving the copy of the image, not an actual file name. When the action is played, you'll be toggled to the directory you wanted to save your file in and prompted to supply a file name.

◉ You might need to guarantee your image is in a particular color mode—for example, you must be working with a grayscale image before you can choose the Duotone menu item from the Image menu's Mode command. To do so, choose Automate from the File menu, and then choose Conditional Mode Change to change the image's mode based on the source mode.

Using the Automate Commands

The Conditional Mode Change command you've just seen is one of several assistants created with Adobe's automation plug-in architecture. The other menu items that appear under the File menu's Automate command are additional examples of onscreen assistants that come bundled with Photoshop. Although these onscreen assistants don't automate the process entirely, they take the grunt work out of it by asking you to indicate, through a series of dialog boxes, what result you're looking for.

Once you've specified the necessary parameters, these assistants automatically enact the necessary steps in Photoshop; you only see the result. Here's what each of the Automate commands packaged with Photoshop 6.0 does:

◉ **Conditional Mode Change** can change the color mode of a document to any other you specify, based on the original.

Conditional Mode Change

Source Mode

☐ Bitmap ☑ RGB Color

☐ Grayscale ☐ CMYK Color

☐ Duotone ☐ Lab Color

☐ Indexed Color ☐ Multichannel

[All] [None]

Target Mode

Mode: [CMYK Color ⬥]

[OK]
[Cancel]

👁 **Contact Sheet** creates a series of thumbnail previews of all images stored in a selected folder. It's a godsend for projects in which you need to send hundreds of images to your service bureau and need a no-hassle way of ensuring you've supplied print versions of all graphics.

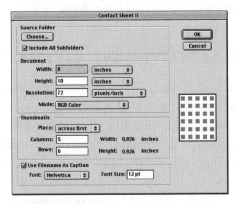

👁 **Fit Image** changes the size of your image to a new height and width you specify. Be cautious about using this one, though; it will resample your image, which can degrade its quality.

👁 **Convert Multi-Page PDF to PSD** turns each page in a PDF file into a separate Photoshop file. I like to use this for creating good-looking thumbnail images of page layout files.

👁 **Picture Package** places multiple copies of a single image at the sizes you want on a page in the style of photo packages traditionally sold by portrait studios.

👁 **Web Photo Gallery** turns a collection of images in a folder into an instant Web site. This command generates an index with thumbnail images that can be clicked to reach the full-size images.

Organizing Your Actions

If you use Photoshop for distinct kinds of graphics projects—a little Web design plus some print production, for example—you might wind up creating actions that you use for one kind of assignment but not another. Using *action sets*, you can put your actions for editing Web graphics in one set and place print production actions in another.

It's useful to organize these actions into different sets so you can load the ones you need without wading though extraneous ones. Creating sets of actions also makes sense if you share your workstation with others and want to make sure nobody inadvertently alters or moves your saved shortcuts.

To create a new set of actions, choose New Set from the Actions palette pop-up menu and enter the name of the set in the resulting dialog box, or click the Create New Set icon at the bottom of the palette (see Figure 15.13). You can move preexisting actions into this set by clicking the action's row in the Actions palette and dragging it over the new set's row.

You'll find several other options in the Actions palette pop-up menu for organizing your sets of actions. For example, you can rename a set of actions by choosing Set Options from the Actions palette pop-up menu, and then enter a new name for the set in the resulting dialog box. To save a set of actions, select those actions in the Actions palette and then choose Save Actions from the Actions palette menu. Enter a name for the set, choose a folder on your hard drive for storing the set, and click Save. By default, your saved actions are placed in a file called Default Actions in the Required folder within your Photoshop directory. Replace Actions displays a new chosen set of actions in the Actions palette, whereas Load Actions adds a new set to the bottom of the list.

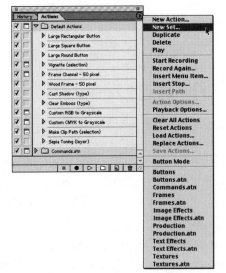

Figure 15.13

Creating a new action set.

Summary

With this chapter's coverage of using Photoshop to automate repetitive tasks, you've made it through 15 chapters of need-to-know information for gaining Photoshop expertise. You should be very proud of yourself—you've taken the initiative to become proficient in a high-profile, essential skill for graphic designers.

The appendices and glossary that follow include a great deal of at-your-fingertips reference material that you can use to explore tweaking Photoshop's default settings. You'll also discover prominent Web sites, publications, and vendors that cater to Photoshop users.

From here, you'll have many doors open to you. Professionally, you can use your Photoshop skills to build up your portfolio and command a better position. For fun, you can entertain your friends and family with bizarre composite images worthy of the supermarket tabloids. But most of all, for yourself, you've demonstrated you're a successful self-motivator. Let me congratulate you on your perseverance, and I wish you all the best in your graphics ventures!

Setting Photoshop Preferences

You can customize many of the default settings in Photoshop's interface to make the program easier for you to work with. These specifications—ranging from the file extensions you like to use when saving your files to the way you want Photoshop to display transparent backgrounds—are set in Photoshop's Preferences file. You can change them on the fly at any point by choosing Preferences from the Edit menu, shown in Figure A.1.

Click the words General Preferences in the drop-down menu near the top of the Preferences dialog box; you'll see there are eight screens of preferences you can set here:

- General Preferences
- Saving Files
- Display & Cursors
- Transparency & Gamut
- Units & Rulers
- Guides & Grid

Figure A.1

You can customize a number of default settings in Photoshop by choosing Preferences from the Edit menu.

👁 Plug-ins & Scratch Disks

👁 Image Cache

On any screen you can click Next to display the next preference set in the menu list, or click Prev to display the previous preference set.

* *

Preferences Shortcuts

To display Photoshop's General Preferences screen quickly, press ⌘+K (for Mac users) or Ctrl+K (for Windows users). To toggle through the various preference screens that follow—for Saving Files, Display & Cursor, and so on—press ⌘+2, ⌘+3, and so on, up to ⌘+8. These keyboard shortcuts are for Mac users; Windows users press Ctrl+2, Ctrl+3, and so on.

* *

* *

Resetting Preferences

To reset all your Photoshop preferences at once, Mac users can open the Adobe Photoshop Settings folder inside your Photoshop application folder and just delete the Adobe Photoshop 6.0 Prefs file and the Color Settings file. Photoshop will automatically generate a new one the next time you launch the program. Windows users should press and hold Alt+Ctrl+Shift immediately after launching Photoshop, and then click Yes to restore preferences.

* *

General Preferences

As the name implies, these settings apply to general features that come into play at any point in your Photoshop editing (see Figure A.2).

👁 **Color Picker.** Here, you can choose between your system's built-in color palette options (Windows or Macintosh) or Photoshop's Color Picker—which is by far the more comprehensive of the two.

👁 **Interpolation.** When you resize an image or invoke a transform command, Photoshop rearranges and adds to the pixels in your image using a process called *interpolation*. The default setting, Bicubic, is the highest-quality option you have here.

Figure A.2

The General
Preferences
dialog box.

⊙ **Redo Key**. This setting assigns a keyboard shortcut to help you toggle back and forth between steps in the History palette. You can indicate how many steps should be contained in the History palette—the default is 20. For example, you can use Cmd+Z (for Mac users) or Ctrl+Z (for Windows users) to toggle back and forth directly between a state eight or nine steps ago and your current state. Alternatively, you can press Cmd+Y (for Mac users) or Ctrl+Y (for Windows users) to come back to your current state one step at a time.

⊙ **Export Clipboard**. When this option is checked, your computer will hold whatever data is on Photoshop's Clipboard in memory after you quit the program. It's better to leave this option unchecked, because exporting the Clipboard slows down your machine every time you quit Photoshop. If you do need to copy data between Photoshop and another program, you can always turn this option back on.

⊙ **Short Pantone Names**. As pointed out in Chapter 12, "Web Graphics Essentials," you should check this option if your page layout programs use short Pantone names (such as Pantone 264 CV). This option ensures that the Pantone colors you select in Photoshop show up properly when you export your image files to your page layout programs.

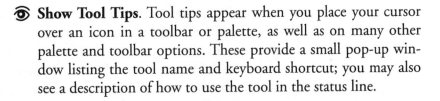

- **Show Tool Tips**. Tool tips appear when you place your cursor over an icon in a toolbar or palette, as well as on many other palette and toolbar options. These provide a small pop-up window listing the tool name and keyboard shortcut; you may also see a description of how to use the tool in the status line.

- **Keyboard Zoom Resizes Windows**. This lets you set whether document windows should resize when you use keyboard short-cuts for zooming in and out—[Cmd]++ and [Cmd]+- for Mac users; [Ctrl]++ and [Ctrl]+- for Windows users.

- **Auto-Update Open Documents**. This setting determines whether Photoshop automatically re-reads documents opened outside of the program—for instance, if you have a document open in Photoshop and then launch and edit the same document in ImageReady or Illustrator.

- **Show Asian Text Options**. Check this box to turn on Chinese, Japanese, and Korean type options in the character and paragraph type palettes.

- **Beep When Done**. If you turn this option on, Photoshop sounds an alert whenever a command finishes processing. This may be useful if you frequently run slow-to-process filtering commands and turn your attention to other tasks for the duration; the beeping can alert you that Photoshop is ready. I usually find that the repeated beeping gets annoying in short order, though.

- **Dynamic Color Sliders**. This option affects the active preview of colors formed using the sliders in the Color Picker dialog box.

- **Save Palette Locations**. On by default, this option lets you find your floating palettes right where you left them on your Photoshop desktop. It's worthwhile to rearrange or separate the palettes to suit the way you work, because you'll only have to do it once.

- **Show Font Names in English**. This setting, on by default, shows the name of non-Roman-alphabet fonts using their Roman names. This lets you view the actual name of fonts such as Wingdings or Symbol in the font menu instead of seeing a series of glyphs.

👁 **Use Shift Key for Tool Switch**. For those who rely on keyboard shortcuts for switching between tool icons, this setting indicates whether you need to press Shift when switching between grouped tools. To switch between the History Brush tool and the Art History Brush when this setting is turned on, for example, you have to press Shift+Y instead of just Y.

👁 **Reset All Warning Dialogs**. If you have suppressed any warning dialog boxes through their Don't Show Again check box options, you can click this button to bring them back.

If you change your mind about any changes you've made to your General Preferences, click the Reset All Tools button to start over.

Saving Files

These settings relate to several issues involving saving Photoshop files: naming conventions, image previews, and file compatibility (see Figure A.3).

👁 **Image Previews**. Saving an image preview with your image allows Photoshop to render a small preview version in one of several ways. If you're using a Mac, you have the option of creating an icon that appears as the image's icon on your computer desktop. Check the Thumbnail option to create a preview that appears in the Open dialog box.

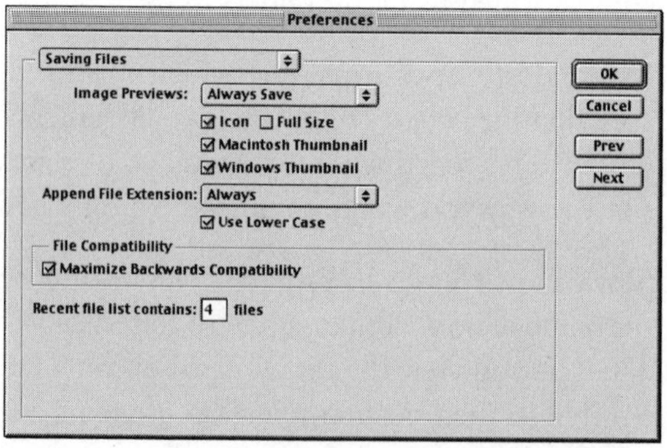

Figure A.3
The Saving Files dialog box.

- **Append File Extension**. Although this is optional on the Mac, it's necessary under Windows and is always a good convention to use for easy format identification.

- **Use Lowercase**. Does your naming convention call for files named image.gif or image.GIF? Choose your preferred case here and you don't need to rename files later.

- **Maximize Backwards Compatibility**. Checking this box ensures that your images with layers (introduced in Photoshop 3.0) can be opened in Photoshop 2.5 by generating an additional flattened composite image in your file. Unless you need to share files with someone who's using that older version of Photoshop, you can leave this unchecked; by doing so, you'll greatly reduce the size of your files.

- **Recent file list**. The number shown here indicates how many of the files you opened most recently in Photoshop will open on the submenu associated with Open Recent under the File menu. The default is 4.

Display & Cursors

These settings affect how colors and your cursors appear during your image editing sessions (see Figure A.4).

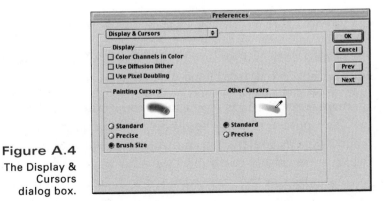

Figure A.4

The Display & Cursors dialog box.

- ☻ **Color Channels in Color.** If you check this option, you'll see the data in each of your color channels appear in the actual color (such as cyan or magenta) instead of in black and white (like a film negative). This eliminates worries you might have about editing the wrong color channel, but the data can be much harder to see or edit—look at the Yellow channel in a CMYK document with this option checked to see what I mean. As a result, I leave this unchecked.

- ☻ **Use Diffusion Dither.** If you're using an 8-bit (256-color) monitor, check this option to use an improved, randomized pixel diffusion method.

- ☻ **Use Pixel Doubling.** This setting uses a faster, reduced resolution display when you're moving data.

- ☻ **Painting Cursors.** Here, you can change the way the cursor looks when you use one of the painting tools that has a brush—from the Airbrush and Eraser to Smudge and the Rubber Stamp tools. The Standard setting uses the image of the icon as your cursor; the Precise option identifies the center of your cursor more easily. The Brush Size option (the default) sets your cursor to the size and shape of the selected brush; you might find this gives you more control over the tool as you edit your images.

- ☻ **Other Cursors.** This option affects the cursors used for all tools that don't use brushes. The Standard setting uses the image of the icon as your cursor; the Precise option identifies the center of your cursor more easily.

Transparency & Gamut

Use the transparency and gamut options to control how transparent areas of your image look (see Figure A.5).

- ☻ **Transparency Settings.** You can customize the gray-and-white gridlike appearance that Photoshop gives to transparent parts of your image. I wouldn't recommend setting Grid Size to None, which turns off the grid altogether—this way, transparent parts of your image are too easily confused with areas of solid white.

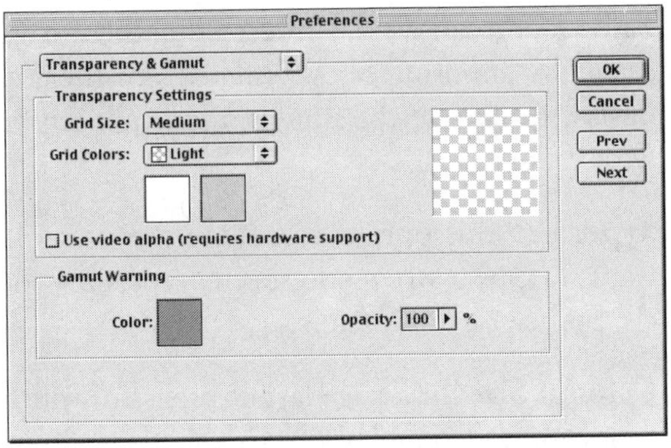

Figure A.5

The Transparency & Gamut dialog box.

- ⊚ **Use Video Alpha.** This option applies only if you use a video editing package and a 32-bit graphics card. With it, you can display a video signal in an alpha channel.

- ⊚ **Gamut Warning.** Here, you can choose the color used by the Gamut Warning command under the View menu to highlight any areas in your image that use an *out-of-gamut color* (one that can be displayed onscreen but can't be output in CMYK printing).

Units & Rulers

The units and rulers options set the unit of measurement used when you choose Show Rulers from the View menu (see Figure A.6).

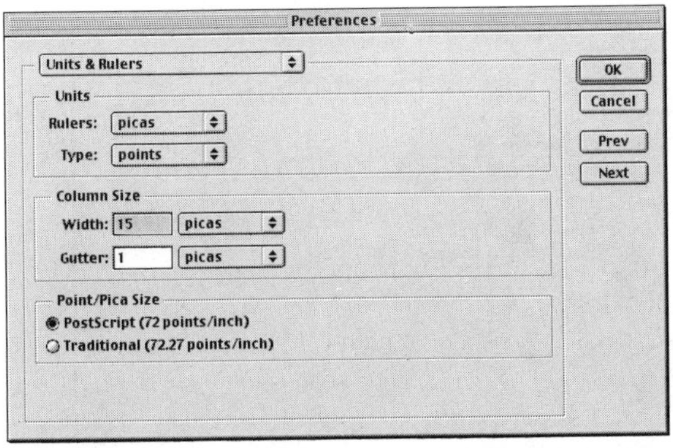

Figure A.6

The Units & Rulers dialog box.

◉ **Rulers**. You can display rulers along the top and left sides of your image by choosing Show Rulers from the View menu. Use this option to choose the unit of measurement you want to appear with these rulers.

◉ **Type**. Use this option to choose the unit of measurement you want to appear when you specify type size—options include pixels, points, or millimeters.

◉ **Column Size**. In a page layout program, you might measure how wide an image should be in terms of how many columns (and gutters in between) it should span. You can use this option to specify how wide a column is, and then use the Canvas Size command under the Image menu to specify an image's dimensions in terms of columns.

◉ **Point/Pica Size**. As the Traditional setting here shows, the traditional ratio is 72.27 points to one inch. In modern usage, described here as the PostScript setting, that's frequently rounded to a ratio of 72 points to an inch. If you're using a PostScript output device—like most laser printers or an imagesetter—there's no need to futz with this setting.

Guides & Grid

Use these settings if you want to customize the way movable guides and gridlines appear in your image (see Figure A.7). Guides can be laid down anywhere in your image where you need a baseline or point of

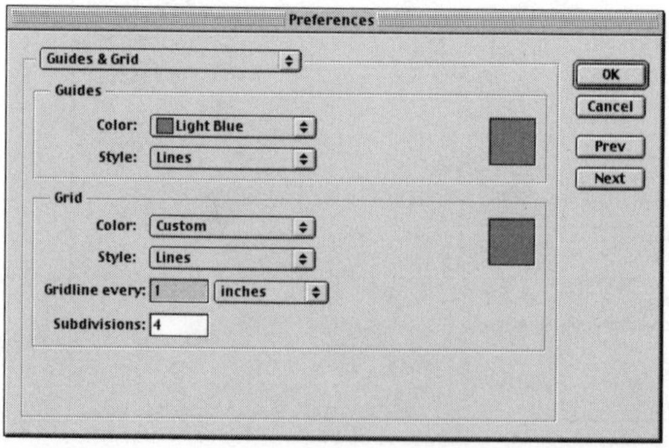

Figure A.7

The Guides & Grid dialog box.

reference for aligning elements. To place a guide, first choose Show Rulers from the View menu. You can then drag down from the horizontal or drag right from the vertical ruler to create a guide.

The Grid setting fills your image with evenly spaced vertical and horizontal lines; the options in this section show how and where you can specify the spacing.

- **Guides**. Use the Color drop-down menu or click the color swatch—which launches the Color Picker dialog box—to choose a color for your vertical and horizontal guidelines. Click the Style drop-down menu to choose between a solid rule or dashed lines.

- **Grid**. Much like the Guides options, you can choose a color and line style for your vertical and horizontal grid lines.

- **Gridline.** Enter a measurement to specify the distance between the gridlines in your image.

- **Subdivisions**. You can enter a value here to place thinner lines between your gridlines.

Plug-Ins & Scratch Disks

As you learned in Chapter 1, "System Essentials," you can specify up to four scratch disks for Photoshop's virtual memory to use when you run out of RAM during your image editing session. Use this dialog box to identify those additional scratch disks (see Figure A.8).

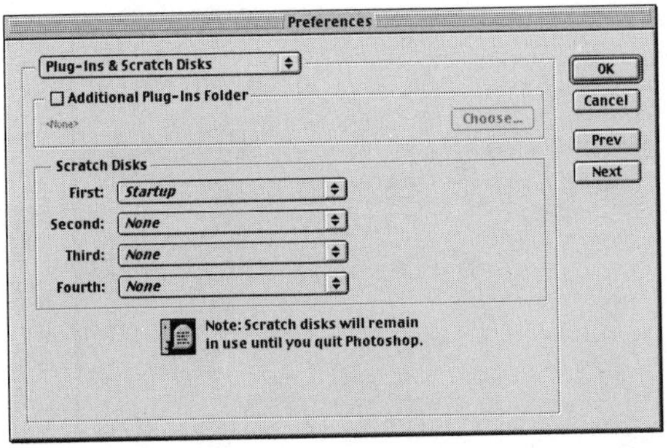

Figure A.8

The Plus-Ins & Scratch Disks dialog box.

You also use this dialog box if you need to tell Photoshop to look in a different place for an additional plug-in folder. By and large, the only time this is necessary is if you use other applications that support plug-ins that Photoshop can share. Premiere and Photoshop, for example, have a number of common plug-ins.

Image Cache, or Memory & Image Cache

The image cache settings affect the speed at which Photoshop redraws high-resolution images and how fast it generates your image histograms (see Figure A.9).

- 👁 **Cache Levels**. Enter a value between 1 and 8. Higher values increase image caching, so your screen redraws faster but requires more RAM. The default is 4; if a shortage of RAM is adversely affecting Photoshop's performance on your machine, lower this setting.

- 👁 **Use Cache for Histograms**. If you check this box, Photoshop uses the information in one of its cache levels to capture the information used when generating the histograms in the Levels and Histogram dialog boxes. (The cache levels are otherwise used to hold previews for different zoom percentages.)

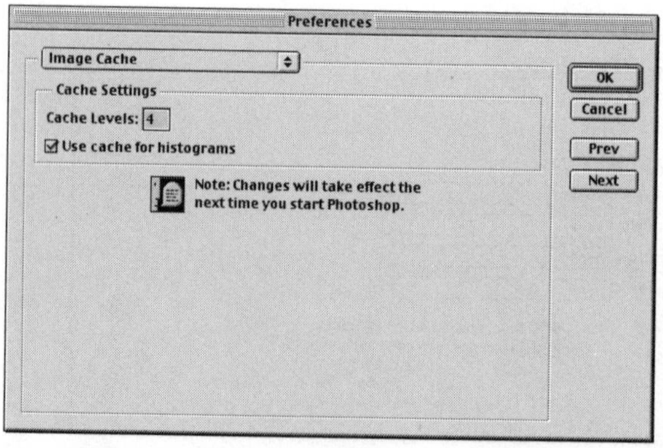

Figure A.9
The Image Cache dialog box.

If you're using Windows, you'll also see a setting for Physical Memory Usage. As Chapter 1 explained, you can enter a value in this field to alter how much RAM is allocated to Photoshop. By default, this is set to 60 percent.

Preset Manager

You can use the Preset Manager under the Edit menu to create, store, load, and remove the available set of brushes, swatches, gradients, styles, patterns, contours (for warping text), and custom shapes. Each of these sets has its own custom file extension and default folder in Photoshop, and a number of predefined sets of extra brushes, patterns, and so on that you can load or save.

When you first launch the Preset Manager dialog box, the Brushes set is the first to display. You can click any set's name in the drop-down menu to see the current choices for that set (see Figure A.10).

To load a predefined set, click the load button and select a set from the list that displays (see Figure A.11). If you have created sets in another folder, you might need to navigate to that folder to select the desired value. Or, if you click the black triangle in the Preset Manager dialog box, you can display a pop-up menu that lists the predefined sets available for that preset type (see Figure A.12). At this point, you just select a set to load from the pop-up menu.

You can also save and rename sets, as well as delete individual items from a set. You cannot delete the default items, however. To reset to the default set for that type, choose Reset from the pop-up menu.

Figure A.10
The Preset Manager dialog box.

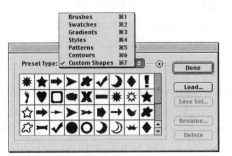

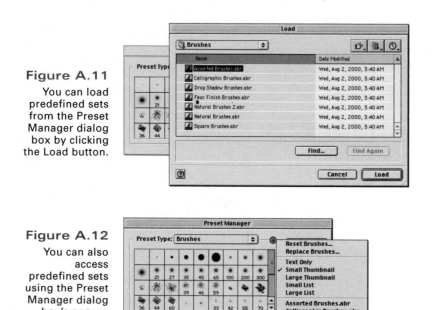

Figure A.11

You can load predefined sets from the Preset Manager dialog box by clicking the Load button.

Figure A.12

You can also access predefined sets using the Preset Manager dialog box's pop-up menu.

Color Settings

If you're looking for quick-start instructions for setting up your color-management settings, you should follow these steps in order:

1. **Calibrate your monitor—ASAP!** You might have put this off before, but it's an essential step for getting up and running with Photoshop. You can calibrate your monitor either using the Adobe Gamma control panel (see Figure A.13) included with Photoshop or with any calibration program included when you bought your monitor. If you're using a Mac, Apple's ColorSync is another good choice for color calibration.

2. **Determine whether you need to alter Photoshop's color-management settings.** Most of Photoshop's color-management controls are found in a single Color Settings dialog box. You can display this box by choosing Color Settings from the Edit menu (see Figure

Figure A.13
The Adobe Gamma control panel.

A.14). Here, you can choose from a list of predefined color-management settings that aim to produce consistent color for a common publishing workflow, such as Web publishing or print production. If your print service bureau specifies that you should customize color settings for your own specific workflow, you will probably find most of the configurations to change right here.

The configuration options available in the Color Settings dialog box include:

👁 **Color Management Off.** This option uses minimal color-management settings to emulate applications without support for color management. It's best used for images that will be output on video or used only as onscreen presentations.

Figure A.14
The Color Settings dialog box.

- 👁 **Emulate Photoshop 4.** This setting simulates the color workflow used by Adobe Photoshop 4.0 and earlier, before Photoshop revamped its color-management process in version 5.

- 👁 **U.S. Prepress Defaults.** This setting provides color management for images output under common press conditions in the U.S.

- 👁 **European Prepress Defaults.** This setting provides color management for images output under common press conditions in Europe.

- 👁 **Japan Prepress Defaults.** This setting provides color management for images output under common press conditions in Japan.

- 👁 **Web Graphics Defaults.** These color-management settings are designed for content that will be published on the Internet (see Figure A.14).

- 👁 **ColorSync Workflow (Mac OS only).** Manages color using the ColorSync 3.0 CMS with the profiles in the ColorSync control panel. This color-management configuration is not recognized by Windows systems, or by earlier versions of ColorSync.

You might not need to use color management if you are creating graphics for one medium only—say, if you're working in the graphics department of an online interactive agency and only create Web graphics. If you reuse graphics in both print and online production, though, or if your images go to print on both U.S. and non-U.S. presses, you should consult with your service bureau and printers to ensure that your color-management settings are consistent with those of your vendors.

B

Sources for Further Information

As you continue using Photoshop in your graphic design work, you may have a need for more up-to-the-minute information than this book can provide. That's where these Web sites and other resources can come to the rescue—you'll find fellow Photoshop users who have faced the same issues you're currently confronting, or who can save you time by providing shortcuts to creating good-looking Photoshop effects.

Photoshop-Related Tips, Tricks, and Techniques

Adobe Photoshop Tutorials,
http://www.adobe.com/products/tips/photoshop.html

CerealKiller's Help Desk, **http://www.cerealkiller.com/pshop/**

Deep Space Web, **http://www.deepspaceweb.com/**

DiP, **http://www.algonet.se/%7Edip/photoshop/tips/tips_00.html**

dsigning.com, **http://www.dsigning.com/**

The Elated Web Toolbox, **http://www.elated.com/toolbox/**

EyeWire Tips, **http://www.eyewire.com/tips/**

Graphic Design at About.com, **http://graphicdesign.about.com**

Hand's-On Training by Doc Ozone, **http://www.handson.nu/**

The Internet Eye How-To, **http://the-internet-eye.com/HOWTO/**

Photoshop Central, **http://www.photoshopcentral.com/**

The Photoshop Gurus' Handbook,
http://gurus.onlinedesignschool.com/

The Pixel Foundry, **http://www.pixelfoundry.com/**

PlanetPhotoshop.com, **http://www.planetphotoshop.com/**

StewartStudio Photoshop Tutorials,
http://www.stewartstudio.com/phototip.htm

Ultimate Photoshop, **http://www.ultimate-photoshop.com/**

PS Workshop, **http://rainworld.com/oe_99/forge/ps_tut/**

Photoshop-Related Actions

These sites offer recorded Photoshop actions—these are a prerecorded series of steps for creating a certain effect. You'll find these sites helpful when you're in a hurry to find a quick-and-dirty method to create a particular visual result.

Action Addict, **http://www.actionaddiction.com/**

ActionFX, **http://www.actionfx.com/**

Action XChange, **http://www.actionxchange.com/**

actions.8m.com, **http://actions.8m.com/**

DigitalThread: Photoshop,
http://www.digitalthread.com/photoshop/

The Elated Web Toolbox, **http://www.elated.com/toolbox/**

Mockensturm Art & Data Studios,
http://www.primenet.com/~mock/actions.html

Photoshop Action!, **http://home.sol.no/~liknes/Photoshop/**

Screenz (in both German and English), **http://www.screenz.de/**

Free Filters and Plug-ins for Photoshop

Adobe Downloads for Photoshop (Macintosh),
http://www.adobe.com/support/downloads/psmac.htm

Adobe Downloads for Photoshop (Windows),
http://www.adobe.com/support/downloads/pswin.htm

The Filter Factory Compendium, **http://pluginhead.i-us.com**

Furbo Filters, **http://www.furbo-filters.com/**

Greg's Factory Output filters, **http://mars.ark.com/~gschorno/gfo/**

Perfect Pixels, **http://www.perfectpixels.com/**

Plugin Com HQ, **http://thepluginsite.com/**

Plugin Head, **http://pluginhead.i-us.com/**

Plugins.com, **http://www.plugins.com/plugins/photoshop/**

PlugPage (Boxtop Software), **http://www.plugpage.com/**

Red Prince Atelier, **http://www.redprince.net/atelier/**

Free Web Graphics

If you're looking for inspiration in creating graphics for your Web site, there are many sites that can provide basic images for every purpose: navigation buttons, bullets and icons, animated GIFs, lines, logos, and overall interfaces. You may find a few icons that are perfect for your needs—and many that'll inspire you to create better-looking versions.

Buttons and Icons

FreeGraphics.com, **http://www.freegraphics.com/**

MediaBuilder Icon Library, **http://www.mediabuilder.com/graphicsicon.html**

Nebulus Designs, **http://www.nebulus.org/**

Samples from Artbeats WebTools, **http://www.artbeatswebtools.com/samples1.html**

Station4 Button Factory, **http://www.station4.com/buttonfactory**

Tazem Design's Free Graphics, **http://www.barndog.com/tazem/**

Backgrounds and Textures

Axem Textures, **http://axem2.simplenet.com**

Eyeball Design, **http://www.eyeball-design.com/**

TheFreeSite, **http://www.thefreesite.com/freegraphics.htm**

Goranation, **http://www.goranation.com/**

Kewlpack Software, **http://www.kewlpack.com/**

Nebulus Designs, **http://www.nebulus.org/**

Tazem Design's Free Graphics, **http://www.barndog.com/tazem/**

Animated GIFs

Animation Factory, **http://www.animfactory.com/**

TheFreeSite, **http://www.thefreesite.com/freegraphics.htm**

Graphics Kingdom, **http://www.graphxkingdom.com/**

MediaBuilder, **http://www.mediabuilder.com/**

Scream Design, **http://www.screamdesign.com/**

Free HTML Templates and Interfaces

BigNoseBird, **http://www.bignosebird.com/sets.shtml**

The Elated Web Toolbox, **http://www.elated.com/toolbox/**

Free Web Templates, **http://www.freewebtemplates.com/**

NavWorks, **http://navworks.i-us.com/**

NetJane, **http://www.netjane.com/**

Free Stock Photos and Clip Art

About.com's On Site Clip Art Collections,
**http://webclipart.about.com/internet/webclipart/library/weekly/
blclpmen.htm**

Artists' Exchange Clipart Co-op,
http://artistexchange.about.com/blclipart1.htm

ArtToday, **http://www.arttoday.com/**

Barry's Clipart Server, **http://www.barrysclipart.com/**

Clipart.com, **http://www.clipart.com/**

ClipArtConnection.com, **http://www.clipartconnection.com/**

TheFreeSite, **http://www.thefreesite.com/freegraphics.htm**

PhotoDisc, **http://www.photodisc.com/**

Free Fonts

Chankstore Fonts, **http://www.chank.com/**

Fontastic, **http://people.wiesbaden.netsurf.de/~kikita/**

Fonts & Things, **http://www.fontsnthings.com/**

Free Fonts for Web Viewing,
http://www.will-harris.com/fonts/freefonts.htm

Free QualiType Fonts, **http://qualitype.com/freefont.htm**

GraphxEdge Free Fonts,
http://www.graphxedge.com/freefonts.htm

Tazem Design's Free Graphics, **http://www.barndog.com/tazem/**

Virtual Free Fonts, **http://www.virtualfreesites.com/free.fonts.html**

Periodicals

Adobe Magazine
801 N. 34th Street
Seattle, WA 98103
800-771-9951
http://www.adobe.com/store/products/adobemag.html

AIGA Journal of Graphic Design
http://www.aiga.org/

Before & After Magazine
2007 Opportunity Drive #7
Roseville, CA 95678
916-784-3880
http://www.pagelab.com/

Computer Graphics World
c/o Pennwell Publishing Company
98 Spit Brook Rd.
Nashua, NH 03062-5737
603-891-0123
http://www.cgw.com/

PEI Magazine
229 Peachtree St. NE
Suite 2200, International Tower
Atlanta, GA 30303
404-522-8600
http://www.peimag.com/

Publish
462 Boston Street
Topsfield, MA 01983
978-887-7900
http://www.publish.com/

Professional Organizations

National Association of Photoshop Professionals
(publishes *Photoshop User* magazine)
http://www.photoshopuser.com/

AIGA (publishes *AIGA Journal of Graphic Design*)
http://www.aiga.org/

Related Usenet Newsgroups

Usenet newsgroups offer bulletin-board-style discussion threads on specific subject topics. You can read the messages posted to these newsgroups and post your own viewpoints with newsreader software or through the newsreading functionality that's built into most popular Web browsers. Read the latest buzz. Post your own viewpoint.

alt.design.graphics—A range of Photoshop-related graphics questions and discussions.

comp.graphics.apps.photoshop—Discussions of Adobe Photoshop techniques and problem solving.

rec.photo.digital—Discussions of graphic design for fun as well as profit.

To find answers to specific questions—for example, if you're looking for reviews on a specific scanner model or a custom filter effect—

tryDeja.com's Usenet Discussion Service at **http://www.deja.com/ usenet/**. On Deja.com, you can search the current library of newsgroups based on specific keywords.

Discussion Groups and Forums

Adobe Photoshop Discussion on i/us,
http://www.i-us.com/pshop.htm

Discussions: The Photoshop Guru's Handbook,
http://www.i-us.com/photoshopguru.htm

Graphic Design Bulletin Board,
http://graphicdesign.about.com/arts/graphicdesign/ mpboards.htm

The Pixel Foundry Forums,
http://www.pixelfoundry.com/cgi-bin/Ultimate.cgi

Ultimate Photoshop Forums,
http://www.ultimate-photoshop.com/forum/

Photoshop Discussion List

The Photoshop Discussion List, an Internet discussion group about Adobe Photoshop, is currently sponsored by Lyris Technologies. To subscribe to the list, visit **http://clio.lyris.net/cgi-bin/lyris.pl?join=photoshop** or send e-mail to **join-photoshop@clio.lyris.net**. To unsubscribe from the list, send e-mail to **unsubscribe-photoshop@clio.lyris.net**.

You can read archived messages without joining the list at **http:// clio.lyris.net/cgi-bin/lyris.pl?visit=photoshop**. The Photoshop Discussion List also has a Web site: **http://lists.lyris.net/photoshop/**.

Vendor Directory

Employment Services

Acquiring expertise in Photoshop is just one important step in kick-starting your career as a graphic design professional or Web designer. Knowing where to go to connect with employers who need your services—or locating resources for developing a business as a freelance consultant—is the next logical step. The Web sites listed in this appendix can get you started in circulating your portfolio online, submitting resumes, tracking the companies to which you've submitted resumes, or finding your next employer.

Adobe Job Connection
URL: **http://www.adobejobconnection.com/**

Aquent
PHONE: 877-PARTNER
URL: **http://www.aquent.com/**

eWork Exchange
URL: **http://www.eworkexchange.com/**

FindCreative.com
URL: **http://www.findcreative.com/**

FreeAgent.com
URL: **http://www.freeagent.com/**

Guru.com
URL: **http://www.guru.com/**

Silicon Alley Job Board
URL: **http://www.nynma.org/jobs/**
(For New York City area positions; search under "Design")

SkillsVillage.com
URL: **http://www.findcreative.com/**

Hardware and Software Products

Here are a bunch of outlets—mostly commercial—offering products that you can use with Photoshop. If the vendors have links to freeware and demo software on their Web sites, I've included a note about what they offer.

A Lowly Apprentice Production, Inc.
5963 La Place Court Suite 206
Carlsbad, CA 92008-8823
PHONE: 888-818-5790
FAX: 760-438-5791
E-MAIL: support@alap.com
URL: **http://www.alap.com/**
(ImagePort program for importing native
Photoshop files directly into
QuarkXPress.)

Adobe Systems Incorporated
345 Park Avenue
San Jose, CA 95110-2704
PHONE: 408-536-6000
TOLL-FREE: 800-833-6687
FAX: 408-537-6000
FEEDBACK: **http://www.adobe.com/misc/
comments.html**
URL: **http://www.adobe.com/**
FREEWARE: Patches and plug-ins are
available at **http://www.adobe.com/
support/downloads/main.html**
(For a complete roundup of Adobe
products, try the Adobe Products and
Applications Index at **http://
www.adobe.com/products/main.html**.)

Alien Skin Software LLC
1100 Haynes St., Suite Zero
Raleigh, NC 27604
PHONE: 919-832-4124
TOLL-FREE: 888-921-7546 (U.S. sales only)
FAX: 919-832-4065
E-MAIL: alien-skinfo@alienskin.com
URL: **http://www.alienskin.com/**
(Eye Candy and Xenofex Photoshop filters)

Altamira Group
1827 West Verdugo Avenue, Suite C
Burbank, CA 91506
PHONE: 818-556-6099
TOLL-FREE: 800-913-3391
FAX: 818-556-3365
URL: **http://www.altamira-group.com/**
(Genuine Fractals plug-in for scanning.)
DEMO SOFTWARE: Follow links from main
home page.

Andromeda Software Inc.
699 Hampshire Road, Suite 109
Thousand Oaks, CA 91361
PHONE: 805-379-4109
FAX: 805-379-5253
URL: **http://www.andromeda.com/**
(Andromeda series Photoshop filters)
DEMO SOFTWARE: **http://
www.andromeda.com/info/
getdemoform.html**

Auto F/X Corp.
Box 1415, Main Street
Alton, NH 03809
PHONE: 603-875-4400
FAX: 603-875-4404
E-MAIL: custservice@autofx.com
URL: **http://autofx.com/**
(Universal Animator, WebVise Totality,
Photo/Graphic Edges, Typo/Graphic
Edges, Photo/Graphic Patterns, The
Ultimate Texture Collection, Page/Edges,
Photo/Graphic Frames)
DEMO SOFTWARE: Follow links from main
home page.

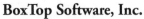

BoxTop Software, Inc.
P.O. Box 2347
Starkville, MS 39759
PHONE: 662-263-5410
FAX: 662-236-5412
URL: **http://www.boxtopsoft.com/**
(PhotoGIF, ImageVice, ColorSafe,
GIFmation, ProJPEG, and SuperGIF
utilities)
DEMO SOFTWARE: Follow links from main
home page.

Chroma Graphics
577 Airport Blvd., Suite 730
Burlingame, CA 94010-2020
PHONE: 650-685-6800 or
888-8CHROMA
FAX: 650-685-6818
E-MAIL: info@chromagraphics.com
URL: **http://www.chromagraphics.com/**
(Chromatica color engine, Magic Mask
and EdgeWizard plug-ins)

Corel Corporation
P.O. Box 706
Jericho, NY 11735-8918
PHONE: 800-772-6735
E-MAIL: custserv2@corel.com
URL: **http://www.corel.com/**
(Corel Professional Photos CD-ROM
collections)
FREEWARE: **http://www.corel.com/
freebies/index.htm**

Cytopia Software
812 Ninth Avenue
Redwood City, CA 94063
PHONE: 650-364-4594
FAX: 650-364-4592
E-MAIL: custerv@cytopia.com
URL: **http://www.cytopia.com/**
(Cytopia PhotoOptics filters)
DEMO SOFTWARE: Follow links from
home page.

Diaquest, Inc.
1226 Powell Street
Emeryville, CA 94608
PHONE: 510-594-9455
FAX: 510-654-8370
E-MAIL: support@diaquest.com
URL: **http://www.diaquest.com/**
(Diaquest DDR for Photoshop—video
capture/layoff for digital disk recorders)

Extensis Products Group
1800 SW First Avenue, Suite 500
Portland, OR 97201
PHONE: 503-274-2020 or 800-796-9798
FAX: 503-274-0530
E-MAIL: info@extensis.com
URL: **http://www.extensis.com/**
(PhotoTools, Intellihance, PhotosFrame,
and Mask Pro plug-ins for batch-correct-
ing scanned images, Portfolio 5 digital
asset manager)
DEMO SOFTWARE: **http://
www.extensis.com/download/**

Getty Images
701 N. 34th Street, Suite 400
Seattle, WA 98103
PHONE: 206-268-2000
FAX: 206-268-2000
URL: **http://www.gettyone.com/**
(Licensed and royalty-free imagery;
content brands include Stone, The Image
Bank, PhotoDisc, Artville, and EyeWire)

Human Software Inc.
14510 Big Basin Way
Saratoga, CA 95070
PHONE: 408-399-0057
FAX: 408-399-0157
E-MAIL: gn@humansoftware.com
URL: **http://www.humansoftware.com/**
(AutoMask plug-in, Squizz distortion
filter, OttoPaths for flowing text along
paths, Select filter, Swap color-editing
filter, and Textissimo text effects filter)

ImageXpress
P.O. Box 465867
Lawrenceville, GA 30242
PHONE: 770-995-6644
FAX: 770-995-7497
E-MAIL: info@ixsoftware.com
URL: **http://www.ixsoftware.com/**
(ScanPrep Pro colorization plug-in,
AutoPilot plug in, Alius posterization
plug-in, and Deep-Bit filters for applying
filters to 16-bit images.)
FREEWARE: Download trial versions by
following links to product pages.

Iomega
1821 West Iomega Way
Roy, Utah 84067
PHONE: 800-MY-STUFF (800-697-8833)
AUTOMATED fax-back help: 801-332-5763
E-MAIL support: **http://
www.iomega.com/support/
nav_techemail.html**
URL: **http://www.iomega.com**
(Zip and Jaz storage drives)

Markzware Software
1805 E. Dyer Road, Suite #101
Santa Ana, CA 92705
PHONE: 800-300-3532 or 949-756-5100
FAX: 949-756-5108
E-MAIL: info@markzware.com
URL: **http://www.markzware.com/**
(FlightCheck prepress application scans
documents created with QuarkXPress,
PageMaker, Photoshop, Illustrator,
Freehand, Multi-Ad Creator, PDF, and
PostScript.)
DEMO SOFTWARE: **http://
www.markzware.com/elements/data/
download/**

Metacreations Corporation
498 Seventh Avenue, 18th Floor
New York, NY 10018
PHONE: 212-201-0800
FAX: 212-201-0801
E-MAIL: info@metastream.com
URL: **http://www.metacreations.com/**
(Kai's PowerTools and KPT X)

Pantone, Inc.
590 Commerce Boulevard
Carlstadt, NJ 07072
PHONE: 201-935-5500 or
1-877-COLOR64 (1-877-265-6764)
FAX: 201-896-0242
URL: **http://www.pantone.com/**
(Pantone ColorSuite, ColorWeb, and
OfficeColor Assistant)

PhotoDisc
701 North 34th Street, Suite 400
Seattle, WA 98103
PHONE: 800-528-3472
FAX: 206-268-2001
E-MAIL: sales@photodisc.com
URL: **http://www.photodisc.com/**
(PhotoDisc royalty-free digital stock
photography)

Pictographics
2216 East 117th Street
Burnsville, MN 55337
PHONE: 952-894-6247
FAX: 952-894-0784
URL: **http://www.picto.com/**
(CandelaColor Suite and Color Synergy
color-management software)

Play, Inc.
2890 Kilgore Road
Rancho Cordova, CA 95670
PHONE: 916-851-0800
FAX: 916-851-0801
E-MAIL: snappysupport@play.com
URL: **http://www.play.com/**
(Snappy Video Snapshot video capture
device)

Ricoh Corporation
5 Derick Place
West Caldwell, NJ 07006
PHONE: 973-882-2000
FAX: 973-244-2768
URL: **http://www.ricoh.com/**
(Ricoh printers and digital cameras)

Second Glance Software
7248 Sunset Avenue NE
Bremerton, WA 98311
PHONE: 360-692-3694
FAX: 360-692-9241
E-MAIL: info@secondglance.com
URL: **http://www.secondglance.com/**
(Chromassage, PhotoSpot, PhotoCell
animation, and ScanTastic scanning
plug-ins)
DEMO SOFTWARE: Follow links from
home page.

Spinwave
E-MAIL: info@spinwave.com
URL: **http://www.spinwave.com/**
(JPEG Cruncher Pro, GIF Cruncher, HVS
Animator, HVS series products, and
OptiVerter batch utility for converting files)
DEMO SOFTWARE: **http://
www.spinwave.com/demos.html**

Total Integration, Inc.
600 North First Bank Drive
Palatine, IL 60067
PHONE: 847-776-2377
FAX: 847-776-2378
E-mail: sales@totalint.com
URL: **http://www.totalint.com/**
(IRIS/CT plug-in module)

UMAX Technologies, Inc.
3561 Gateway Blvd.
Fremont, CA 94538
PHONE: 510-651-4000
URL: **http://www.umax.com/**
(UMAX scanners and digital cameras)

VR Toolbox, Inc.
P.O. Box 111419
Pittsburgh, PA 15238
PHONE: 877-878-6657 or 412-767-4947
FAX: 412-767-4090
E-MAIL: info@vrtoolbox.com
URL: **http://www.vrtoolbox.com/**
(VR Worx, suite of QuickTime VR
authoring tools)

Wacom Technology Corporation
1311 SE Cardinal Court
Vancouver, WA 98683
PHONE: 800-922-9348
FAX: 360-896-9724
E-MAIL: support@wacom.com
URL: **http://www.wacom.com/**
(Wacom Intuos graphics tablets)

Xaos Tools, Inc.
582 San Luis Road
Berkeley, CA 94707
PHONE: 510-525-5465
FAX: 208-247-1261
URL: **http://www.xaostools.com/**
(Segmation, TypeCaster, Paint Alchemy,
Terrazzo, Total Xaos)
DEMO SOFTWARE: Follow links from
home page.

Glossary

24-bit color. A computer color system that allocates 1 byte (8 bits) of information each for red, green, and blue hues. This yields graphics that can have over 16.7 million colors in them—far more than the human eye can differentiate.

32-bit color. A computer color system that allows for 24 bits of RGB color information, plus another 8 bits to describe information in an additional color channel or alpha channel.

Additive color. A color model that mixes colors of light instead of pigments. For example, a color monitor creates color by adding the light from red, green, and blue phosphor dots that combine to form the onscreen pixels. Red, green, and blue are also known as the additive primaries because they create white light when fully combined.

Alpha channel. An additional 8 bits of pixel data saved in an image in conjunction with the 24 bits of color channel data. You can save multiple alpha channels with your Photoshop documents.

Animated GIF. *See GIF89a.*

Anti-aliasing. A method of smoothing out the appearance of jagged lines ("jaggies") created by the limited resolution of a computer graphics system. This method calculates intermediate colors and gives your lines a smooth appearance.

Banner. An advertisement—often animated—in the form of a graphic image on the Web.

Bézier curve. A type of curve defined by specifying anchor points that lie on the curve and control points positioned to set the shape of the curve.

Bit. Short for binary digit, this is the smallest unit of data that a computer works with. A bit can have one of two values, signaling that it is on or off. Eight bits make up a byte, another standard unit of digital data.

Bitmap. A type of graphics format made up of a number of dots, or bits, arrayed on a closely spaced grid. The term also refers to 1-bit graphics.

Black point. The heaviest shade of black that your monitor can display.

Bleed. The extension of a printed image beyond the edge of a page, usually one-eighth of an inch, to allow for slight variations in the page trim.

Brightness. One of the three major dimensions of color, along with hue and saturation. Brightness refers to a color's capability to reflect light.

Browser. A software program that enables you to surf the Web. The leading commercial Web browsers are Netscape Navigator and Microsoft Internet Explorer.

Burn. A traditional photographic technique for darkening an image by concentrating light on it.

Byte. A set of 8 bits that represents a number from 0 to 255. *(See bit.)*

Calibration. Adjusting a device, such as a computer monitor or scanner, to produce accurate and predictable output.

Channel. An 8-bit grayscale (256 tones) component of a Photoshop document. An RGB image is composed of three channels, red, green, and blue, each with 256 values that can be combined to create over 16 million possible colors. A CMYK color image is composed of four channels, cyan, magenta, yellow and black. Additional channels (also known as alpha channels) may be used for masking and special effects.

Clipping path. A shape or path that creates a silhouette to mask out the background or other parts of an image when combined with other elements in a page layout program.

CMYK. The acronym for the basic ink colors used in four-color process printing: cyan, magenta, yellow, and black. (The letter K stands for black to avoid confusion with blue.)

Color cast. An overall shift in color that gives an image an unnatural appearance. This is usually unintentional and can be caused at any point in the photographic or scanning processes.

Color channel. All the color information for a single primary color (for example, red, green, or blue) in an image.

Color correction. The process of adjusting the hue, saturation, and brightness of an image. This work is often necessary to compensate for the shortcomings of printing inks or paper stock.

Color depth. The number of colors used in an image. GIF is an 8-bit color format that can contain up to 256 colors, for example; if a GIF contains only 32 colors, though, its color depth can be reduced to 5 bits.

Color gamut. The available range of colors for a particular input, display or output device or process. For example, color monitors have a different gamut (viewed onscreen) than do CMYK inks (viewed in print).

Color separation. The process of dividing full-color photographic images into the four-color components needed to create CMYK printing plates. This generates a series of single-color images based on each of these colors.

Complementary color. This term refers to the relationship between the additive primaries (red, green, and blue) and the subtractive primaries (cyan, magenta, and yellow). Any two additive colors combine to create a subtractive color, and vice versa. For example, red and blue combine to produce magenta. Cyan and yellow combine to produce green.

Contrast. The tonal gradation in an image between highlights, mid-level tones, and shadows. Images with too little contrast appear dull or flat, whereas those with too much contrast look stark and overexposed.

Crop. The process of selecting only a desired area of an image.

Density range. The gamut or range of tones from the lightest to the darkest printing tone. The term also describes the difference in density from the lightest to the darkest portion of an image.

Displacement map (dmap). An image whose lightness values are used by the Displace filter to distort and add texture to another image.

Dither. To place or combine small dots in an area of an image to simulate a color that can't be represented directly by the available color range.

Dodge. A traditional photographic technique for lightening an image by diffusing the amount of light that reaches a piece of film during exposure.

Dot gain. An increase in the size of halftone dots that occurs naturally in the printing process as the ink spreads and is absorbed by the paper stock.

DPI (dots per inch). A measure of the resolution of printers and other output devices. *See also PPI.*

Duotone. A halftoned image created by printing two ink colors over the same area. The most common color combinations are black plus a second ink, usually a spot color such as a Pantone Matching System (PMS) ink.

Dye sublimation. A high-end digital proofing process in which CMYK dye solutions are applied to a paper carrier to approximate the final color images. The amount of heat determines the amount of dye transferred to the paper.

Dynamic range. The total range of visible tone, normally used as a measure from one scanner or imaging system to another. The greater your scanner's dynamic range, the more tone it can reproduce and the more realistic an image will look.

Emboss. The process of creating a raised image by stamping a paper sheet with a metal die; this effect is simulated by a Photoshop filter of the same name.

Feather. The process of blending or smoothing the edge of an object in an image into a background or another object to achieve a more realistic-looking transition.

Filter. An effect applied in Photoshop to mathematically move, alter, combine, and replace pixels in an image. The name is derived from how these effects simulate placing a photographic filter in front of the lens on a camera to distort or modify the light rays.

Flatness. A measure of how much a curve can deviate from the best fit the output device can deliver. In Photoshop, you set a flatness value when defining a clipping path around images that will appear in print with a transparent background.

Gamma. A measure of how your monitor displays the transition from dark to light color in the midtones.

GCR (Gray Component Replacement). The process of substituting black for the grays produced in a printed image where all three process colors (cyan, magenta, yellow) combine.

GIF (Graphics Interchange Format). The common file format for storing Web graphics. This format can display 256 colors (8 bits) at most.

GIF89a. This variation of the GIF standard lets you specify one or more transparent colors, so that you can create images with irregularly shaped borders in your Web graphics. You can also store multiple images in a single GIF89a file, which results in an animation-like effect (called an animated GIF).

Gigabyte. Abbreviated as GB, this standard unit of measuring data is equal to about 1 billion bytes (or 1,073,741,824 bytes exactly).

Gradient. An even transition of intermediate shades between two or more colors.

Grayscale. A tonal scale graduated from white to black, measured in density from 0 to 100 percent.

Halftone. A technique for reproducing photographs or artwork through a digital screening process that converts shaded images into solid ink dots of various sizes and concentrations. A few tiny dots will produce highlight areas. Heavier concentrations of large dots will produce midtone and shadow areas.

Hickies. Imperfections in presswork due to trapping errors or dirt or dust caught on the press.

Histogram. A type of bar chart used to show the amount of color used in an image across the tonal range.

Hot spot. A graphically defined area in an image that contains a hyperlink. When viewed in a Web browser, this area when clicked will deliver the Web visitor to another page or other type of file on the Web. An image with hot spots is called an image map.

Hyperlink. A jump from text or from an image map to a page or other type of file on the Web. In Web pages, hyperlinks are the primary way to navigate between pages and among Web sites.

Hue. The property of a color defined by the wavelength of light it transmits or reflects. This is what distinguishes red from green or any other color.

IBC. Inside back cover.

IFC. Inside front cover.

Image map. A single image on a Web page that contains multiple "hot spots," or areas that can be clicked to link to other Web pages.

ImageReady. A companion program bundled with Photoshop that contains more extensive Web-production capabilities, such as generating HTML and code for rollover effects (in which a graphic changes to a highlighted state as a user's cursor passes over it).

Imagesetter. A digital output device, such as the Linotronic and Agfa models, that produces high-resolution film or paper from electronic files.

Inkjet printer. A printing device that operates by spraying inks onto paper.

Interlaced. The method of displaying images onscreen using two fields of even and odd lines that oscillate back and forth. Images saved as interlaced (typically using the GIF file format) first appear rather blurred onscreen and then acquire sharper focus.

Interpolation. A process used to resample images to a larger size or resolution by adding pixels.

JPEG (Joint Photographic Experts Group). This image compression standard for still photographs is a common file format for Web graphics.

Kerning. The amount of spacing between two neighboring text characters.

Kilobyte. Abbreviated as KB, this standard unit of measuring data is equal to 1,024 bytes.

Lab color. A system for describing, measuring, and controlling color using hue, luminance, and brightness; established by the International Committee on Illumination (CIE).

Layer. A plane of an image, similar to a transparent overlay. You can draw, edit, paste, and reposition elements on one layer in a Photoshop file without disturbing the others.

Layer mask. A means of controlling how different areas within a layer or layer set are hidden and revealed. You can apply a variety of special effects to the layer without actually affecting the pixels on that layer. You can then apply the mask and make the changes permanent or remove the mask without applying the changes.

Line screen. The number of lines of dots per linear inch on a halftone screen.

Lossless compression. A scheme for reducing the file size of an image that incurs no loss of data when you compress or decompress the file.

Lossy compression. A destructive compression scheme that reduces the quality of an image in order to reduce its file size.

LPI (lines per inch). A measure of the number of lines of halftone dots in an inch. It's used as a halftone screen designation (for example, 133lpi or 150lpi).

Luminance. The brightness of a pixel's color as perceived by the human eye.

LZW (Lempel-Ziv-Welch). A lossless compression scheme and TIFF compressed file format. The standard CompuServe GIF file format is also based on an LZW scheme.

Mask. The process of blocking out part of an image so that it isn't affected by color-correction or editing.

Megabyte. Abbreviated as MB, this standard unit of measuring data is equal to 1,024 KB, or 1,048,576 bytes.

Midtone. Tonal values that are seen in the mid-level range between highlight and shadow. These are broadly defined within the 25 to 75 percent range (quarter tone to three-quarter tone).

Moiré. An undesirable pattern in printed halftones and screen tints. It's usually caused by incorrectly aligned screen angles, a pattern in the original digital image, or a rescanned halftoned image.

MPEG (Moving Picture Experts Group). A compression standard for video.

NTSC (National Television Systems Convention). The color television transmission standard used in the United States.

OBC. Outside back cover.

OFC. Outside front cover.

Offset. The transfer of ink from one material to another.

Opacity. The degree of translucency of an object atop the rest of an image.

PDF (Portable Document Format). This file format created by Adobe lets you share highly formatted documents with readers across computer platforms.

Phosphors. The values for your monitor's pure red, green, and blue hues.

Pica. A standard of measurement for print production, equivalent to 12 points or one-sixth of an inch.

Pixel. Short for picture element, the smallest object that can be changed in an electronic display.

Plate. A metal, plastic, or paper carrier of images that is printed on paper. One printing plate is required for each ink color printed.

Plug-in. Software often developed by third-party vendors that can be added to Photoshop. It adds functions not normally available in the standard Photoshop application.

PMS (Pantone Matching System) colors. A commercial system developed by Pantone, Inc., for specifying colors by means of numbered color samples provided in swatch books. PMS colors are also referred to as spot colors.

Point. A standard of measurement for print production. Traditionally, 72.27 points equal one inch, but in modern usage this is rounded to a ratio of 72 points to an inch.

Posterize. To greatly reduce the number of color shades in an image.

PPI (pixels per inch). A measure of monitor or image resolution. Although the dimensions of electronic images are often commonly described in terms of dpi, the correct terminology is really ppi because these images are made up of square pixels. *See also DPI.*

Process color. The four standard ink colors used in full-color printing: black, yellow, cyan, and magenta. Controlled screen tint combinations of the four basic colors allow nearly the full spectrum of colors to be produced on a printing press. *See also spot color.*

Quick Mask. A Photoshop mode that lets you edit any selection as a mask without using the Channels palette and while viewing your image.

Random access memory (RAM). The built-in readable and writable data storage that comes with (or can be added to) a computer. Having more RAM in your computer (such as 128 MB of RAM versus 64 MB of RAM) reduces the number of times that the computer processor has to read data in from your hard disk, an operation that takes much longer than reading data from RAM. RAM is called "random access" because data is placed in and obtained from memory in a nonsequential fashion.

Rasterize. To change a drawing held in an object-oriented (or vector) form to the pixel-based form used by most video displays and printers.

Register. To position printing in proper relation to the edges of the paper and other printed images on the same sheet.

Resolution. A measure of the packing of the dots or lines that make up an image. It's usually measured in dots per inch (dpi) when applied to paper output and in lines per inch (lpi) when applied to film output.

RGB. An acronym for red, green, and blue, the primary colors displayed by color monitors and color televisions. These devices use red, green, and blue electron guns that cause phosphor on a screen to glow.

RIP (raster image processor). A device for rasterizing digital output into a format that can be imaged on film or paper within an imagesetter.

RIP time. The amount of time used by an imagesetter in processing a print job.

Rollover graphics. Buttons or other Web graphics that offer an alternative version (such as for indicating a highlighted or selected state) when the user passes the cursor over one of these images or clicks with the mouse.

Saturation. The degree to which a color is made purely of a selected hue rather than a mixture. The higher the saturation, the brighter and more vivid the image. The lower the saturation, the duller and grayer the image.

Scratch disk. A term used by Photoshop to refer to the hard disk it's using for virtual memory.

Splash page. A introductory, often graphics-intensive, entry point to a Web site.

Spot color. A specific color applied only in regions where ink colors can be individually specified, rather than mixed through process CMYK printing. *See also process color.*

Subtractive color. A process of printing colors with colored inks, so called because inks block the reflection of certain colors by absorbing light in their wavelengths.

TIFF (Tagged Image File Format). This scanning standard for high-resolution images is a common file format for print production.

Tonal range. The full spectrum of brightness values from pure black to pure white.

Trap. A slight amount of overlap between two adjacent colors in printing.

UCR (Under Color Removal). The full or partial replacement of overprinted dark colors with additional black.

Varnish. A clear finish applied like ink on a press that provides additional protection and sheen to a printed piece. A varnish may have a dull or glossy appearance, and may be tinted with colored ink. A flood varnish is applied to the entire page; a spot varnish is applied only to selected image areas and requires a printing plate (and a separate alpha channel in a Photoshop image).

Vector-based image. An image composed of mathematical descriptions of lines, curves, objects, and type outlines.

Virtual memory. The memory space separate from the main memory (physical RAM), such as hard disk space. Virtual memory lets you work on large documents when you are running low on RAM.

Web-safe color palette. A 216-color palette, available within Photoshop as a built-in indexed color palette, that contains the colors common to the standard Macintosh and Windows 8-bit color system palette.

White point. The lightest shade of white that your monitor can display.

3D graphics, overlaying images on, 429–432
3D objects
  adding shadows to, 436–437
  creating, 120–121
    cones, 424–426
    cubes, 421–423
    edges, 433–435
    lettering, 436
    rods, 427–428
    spheres, 418–420
  perspective projection, 416
  rotating, 433
  viewing from other angles, 432
3D Transform filters, uses for, 314

A

Accented Edges filter, 296
accessing
  Channels palette, 246
  Color palette, 153
  Layers palette, 175
  Marquee tools, 82
  Paths palette, 209
Actions
  acquiring additional, 543
  deleting, 536
  duplicating, 536
  editing, 540
  Options dialog box, 532
  Playback Options, 544
  playing, 531–533
  predefined, 533–535
  recording, 535
  saving, 550
  sets, 549–550
  stopping, 541
  troubleshooting tips, 546–547
Add Anchor Point tool, 100
  keyboard command for, 138
Add Layer Mask (Layer menu), 203
Add Noise filters, 308–310
adding
  anchor points, 216
  audio to images, 81
  clipping paths to images, 241–242

raised text to textured surfaces, 438–439
recessed text to textured surfaces, 440–441
to selections, 83, 90
shadows to objects, 234–235, 436–437
Adjust command (Image menu), 193
adjustment layers
  creating, 193
  editing contents of, 194–195
Adobe Photoshop, system requirements for, 4–5
Adobe Photoshop 6.0 Info dialog box, 10
Airbrush tool, 111–112
  keyboard command for, 139
aligning images, 80
alpha channel, 244
Amiga IFF file formats, 52
anchor points, 216
Angle Strokes filters, 297
Angular fills, 114
animation, 496–498
anti-aliasing *versus* **feathering,** 85–86
Arrange command (Layer menu), 184
arranging layers
  by dragging, 183–184
  by using Arrange commands, 184–185
Art History Brush tool, 133–134
  keyboard command for, 139
Artistic filters
  Colored Pencil, 284
  Cutout, 286
  Dry Brush, 286
  Film Grain, 286–287
  Fresco, 287
  Neon Glow, 287
  Paint Daubs, 287–288
  Palette Knife, 288
  Plastic Wrap, 289
  Poster Edges, 289
  Rough Pastels, 289
  Smudge Stick, 289
  Sponge, 290
  Underpainting, 290
  Watercolor, 290–291
audio, adding to images, 81
Audio Annotation tool, keyboard command for, 137
Auto Resolution dialog box, 40, 350

auto slices, 97, 478
Automate commands
  Conditional Mode Change, 547
  Contact Sheet, 548
  Convert Multi-Page, 548
  Fit Image, 548
  Picture Package, 549
  Web Photo Gallery, 549

B
Background Eraser tool, 130
  keyboard command for, 139
background matting, 448
backgrounds
  editing, 406
    Background Eraser, 407–410
    Extract command, 407
  removing items from, 408–409
  tiling, 470–473
banners, animated, 498
Bas Relief filters, 321
baseline shift, 103
Behind mode, 165
Bitmap color mode, 56
Bitmap dialog box, 268
bitmapped file formats, 37
bitmapped graphics, 33–35
black point
  defined, 24
  setting options for, 345
blemishes, removing, 401–404
blending layers, 202–203
Blur filters
  Blur More, 291
  Gaussian Blur, 291–292
  Motion Blur, 292–293
  Radial Blur, 293
  Smart Blur, 294
Blur tool, 134
  keyboard command for, 140
BMP file formats, 51
bounding boxes, creating, 104–105
brightness, setting, 360–362
Brightness/Contrast dialog box, 361
Brush Strokes filters
  Accented Edges, 296
  Angled Strokes, 297
  Crosshatch, 297
  Dark Strokes, 297
  Ink Outlines, 297–298
  pictures of, 295

  Spatter, 298
  Sprayed Strokes, 298
  Sumi-e, 298
brushes. *See* paintbrushes
Burn tool, 135
  color corrections, 399–400
  keyboard command for, 140
buttons, animated, 498

C
calibrating
  monitors, 23–27
  terminology for, 24
cameras
  acquiring images from, 29–30
  digital, 29–30
  examining, 368–369
  video, 29–30
CD-ROM drives, system requirements, 5
central processing unit. *See* CPU
Chalk & Charcoal filters, 321
changing. *See also* editing
  magnification of images, 78
Channel Mixer, 251–253
channels, 246–247
  adding to, 262
  alpha, 244
  capturing hard-to-select areas, 251
  copying, 264
  deleting, 264
  editing combinations of, 251
  Green, 248
  intersecting, 262
  key combinations for, 249
  merging, 266
  New Spot Channel dialog box, 255
  overview, 245
  Red, 249
  removing from, 262
  saving selections in, 255–259
  selecting, 248–249
  shortcuts for, creating, 257
  source, 253
  splitting, 265
  spot-channel, 244, 254–255
  storing, saving memory, 263
  target, 249
Channels palette, 59
  accessing, 246
  menus
    Channel Options, 265

Delete Channel, 264
Duplicate Channel, 264
Merge Channels, 266
Merge Spot Channel, 264–265
New Channel, 263
New Spot Channel, 264–265
shortcuts for, 60
Split Channel, 265
Options dialog box, 266
Charcoal filters, 321–322
Choose Layer Style command (Layer menu), 190
choosing. *See* selecting
Chrome filters, 322–323
Clear mode, 165
client-side image maps, 491
clip art, acquiring images by, 27–28
clipping groups, creating, 199
Clipping Path dialog box, 239
clipping paths, 35, 214
adding to images, 241–242
creating silhouettes with, 237–241
defined, 237
closed paths, creating, 212
closing selections, 88–89
Clouds filter, 314
CLUT (color look-up table), 37, 155
CMYK color mode, 60–61
converting from RGB color mode, 511
overview, 145–147
primary colors of, 145
Color Balance dialog box, 393–394
Color Burn mode, 166
color casts, removing, 362–363
color channels. *See* channels
color depth, 37
Color Dodge mode, 166
Color Halftone filters, 312
color look-up table. *See* CLUT
color models
CMYK, primary colors of, 145
HSB, 147
Lab, 148–149
RGB, 144–145
Web colors, 149
color modes, 55
Bitmap, 56
CMYK, 60–61
Duotone, 57–58
Grayscale, 57
Indexed color, 58–59
Lab, 61–62

Multichannel, 62
RGB, 59–60
Color palette
accessing, 153
changing, 154
Color Picker dialog box, 116, 143
Alert symbol, 152
Color Slider, 151
Custom button, 152–153
"Not Web Safe" warning, 152
Select Color field, 150–151
Color Sampler tool, 128
keyboard command for, 139
Color Settings command (Edit menu), 171
color systems, list of, 157
Colored Pencil filters, 284
colors
correcting, 391
Color Balance command, 393–394
Curves, 399
Histogram command, 395–396
Hue/Saturation command, 394–395
out-of gamut colors, 392
previewing, 399–400
using Burn tools, 399–400
using Dodge tools, 399–400
Variations, 397
editing mode options, 164–166
managing consistency of, 167–171
painting mode options, 164–166
commands
Edit menu
Color Settings, 171
Define Brush, 109
Define Custom Shape, 127
Define Pattern, 113
Fade, 281
Fade Variations, 384
Fill, 113, 236
Free Transform, 429
Paste, 36
Paste Into, 199
Preset Manager, 107
Purge, 10, 282, 374
Step Backward, 371
Step Forward, 371
File menu
Get Info, 9
Import, 341
Open, 35
Place, 35

commands (continued)
  Image menu
    Adjust, 193
    Image Size, 39, 349
  Layer menu
    Add Layer Mask, 203
    Arrange, 184
    Choose Layer Style, 190
    Flatten Image, 177
    Group Linked, 199
    Group with Previous, 199
    Layer Style, 187
    Lock All Layers in Set, 187
    Merge Down, 205
    Merge Visible, 205
    New, 176
    New Adjustment Layer, 193
    New Fill Layer, 191
    Rasterize, 206
  Select menu
    Inverse, 93
    Load Selection, 260
    Save Selection, 267
    Similar, 93
  tools, keyboard commands for, 137–140
  View menu, Show Rulers, 216
  Window menu
    Show Actions, 529
    Show Channels, 246
    Show Color, 153
    Show History, 372
    Show Info, 216, 378
    Show Layers, 175
    Show Paths, 209
commercial inking systems, 156–159
complementary colors, 146
compression, 53
  lossless, 55, 447
  lossy, 54
  maximizing, 463
computer systems, minimum requirements, 4–5
cones, creating, 424–426
Conté Crayon filters, 323
contrast, setting, 360–362
Convert Point tool, 100
converting
  paths to selections, 231–232
  selections to paths, 232–233
copying
  channels, 264
  layers between documents, 183
corner points
  defined, 222

  drawing curves with, 222–223
corrections. *See* retouching images
CPU (central processing unit)
  clock speed, 7
  defined, 6
  system requirements, 4
  upgrading, 7
Craquelure filters, 330
creating
  bounding boxes, 104–105
  channels, shortcuts for, 257
  clipping groups, 199
  closed paths, 212
  cones, 424–426
  cubes, 421–423
  drop shadows with Layer Styles, 189
  droplets, 545
  Duotones with custom commercial ink, 158–159
  edges, 433–435
  effects with masked type option, 267–271
  gradients
    new, 116
    noise, 118–119
  hotspots, 492–494
  image maps, 491–494
  layer masks, 203–204
  layers
    adjustment, 193
    fill, 191–192
    new, 174–177
    sets, 185–186
  lettering, 3D, 436
  paintbrushes, custom, 108–109
  paths, 229
  rods, 427–428
  rollover effects, 499–503
  selections
    of fixed dimensions, 85
    subset, 84
  silhouettes with clipping paths, 237–241
  slices, 96–97
  snapshots, 373
  spheres, 418–420
  stencil-images with masked type option, 271
  texture from scratch, 308–310
  translucent overlays, 192
Crop tool, 87–88
  keyboard command for, 138
cropping
  images, 87–88, 464
  setting option for, 344
Crystallize filters, 312
cubes, creating, 421–423

curves
  color corrections, 399
  combining with lines, 223–225
  constraining lines in, 222
  drawing, 219–223
  sine waves, 221–222
  tonal corrections, 388–391
Curves dialog box, 390–391
Cutout filter, 286

D
Dark Strokes filters, 297
Darken mode, 166
DCS (Desktop Color Separation), 50–51
De-Interlace filters, 332
Define Brush command (Edit menu), 109
Define Custom Shape (Edit menu), 127
Define Pattern command (Edit menu), 113
Deja.com Web site, 338
Delete Anchor Point tool, 100
  keyboard command for, 138
deleting. *See also* removing
  Actions, 536
  anchor points, 216
  channels, 264
  layers, 180
  paths, 230
descreening, setting options for, 344
Desktop Color Separation. *See* DCS
Despeckle filters, 310
dialog boxes
  Actions Options, 532
  Adobe Gamma, 26
  Adobe Photoshop 6.0 Info, 10
  Auto Resolution, 40, 350
  Bitmap, 268
  Brightness/Contrast, 361
  Channel Mixer, 253
  Channels Options, 266
  Clipping Path, 239
  Color Balance, 393–394
  Color Picker, 116, 143
    Alert symbol, 152
    Color Slider, 151
    Custom button, 152–153
    "Not Web safe" warning, 152
    Select Color field, 150–151
  Curves, 390–391
  Duotone Options, 158
  Duplicate Channel, 264
  Duotone Curve, 159
  Effects, 189
  Embed Watermark, 335

  EPS Options, 159
  Fade, 282, 385
  File Info, 47
  Fill Path, 235
  Fill Pattern, 192
  Filters, 281
  GIF Options, 453
  Gradient Editor, 115
  Histogram, 383
  History Options, 374
  Hue/Saturation, 168, 394–395
  Image Size, 350
  Indexed Color, 450
  Info Options, 379
  JPEG Options, 449
  Layer Styles, 189
  Layers Palette Options, 178
  Layers Properties, 186
  Levels, 194, 385
  Load Selection, 261–262
  Make Selection, 231
  New Brush, 109
  New Layer, 176
  New Path, 229
  New Snapshot, 373
  New Spot Channel, 255
  Offset, 334
  Paint Daubs, 288
  Paste, 36, 230
  Plug-Ins & Scratch Disks, 280
  Preferences, 73
  Preset Manager, 108
  Quick Mask Options, 273
  Radial Blur, 293
  Rasterize Generic EPS Format, 35
  Raw Options, 53
  Record Stop, 541
  Rename, 229
  Rough Pastels, 290
  Save Path, 229
  Save Selection, 257, 262
  Settings, 346
  Shear, 302
  Slice Options, 99
  Smart Blur, 294
  Stroke Path, 237
  Twirl, 303
  Variations, 361
  Warp Text, 102
DIC Color Guide, 157
Difference Clouds filter, 314
Difference mode, 166
Diffuse filters, 325

Diffuse Glow filters, 298–299
Digimarc Corporation Web site, 482
digital cameras. *See* cameras
digital clip art, acquiring images by, 27–28
Digital Watermarking filters
    Embed Watermark, 335
    Read Watermark, 336
direction handles, 219
direction points, 219
Direction Selection tool, 100
    keyboard command for, 138
directional light type, 316
disks
    scratch, 12–13
        assigning additional, 14
        defined, 11
    USB (Universal Serial Bus), 14
Displace filters
    demonstration of, 306
    displacements maps, 305
    pixel assessment, 305
Dissolve mode, 165
distorting images, 411–413
Distortion filters
    Diffuse Glow, 298–299
    Displace
        demonstration of, 306
        displacement maps, 305
        pixel assessment, 305
    Glass, 299
    Ocean Ripple, 300
    Pinch, 300
    Polar Coordinates, 301
    Ripple, 301
    Shear, 302
    Spherize, 302
    Twirl, 303
    Wave, 303–304
    ZigZag, 304
DitherBox filters, 333
dithering, 452–453
documents, copying layers between, 183
Dodge tool, 135
    color corrections, 399–400
    keyboard command for, 140
dot gain, 380
download time, minimizing
    creating thumbnails, 464
    cropping, 464
    by using fewer colors, 455–457
dragging layers, 183–184
drawing
    curves, 219–223

    lines, 217
    sine waves, 221–222
drop shadows, creating, 189
droplets
    creating, 545
    defined, 544
drum scanners, 22–23
Dry Brush filters, 286
Duotone color mode, 57–58
Duotone Curve dialog box, 159
Duotone Options dialog box, 158
Duotones, creating, 158–159
Duplicate Channel dialog box, 264
duplicating. *See* copying
Dust & Scratches filters, 310
dust spots, removing, 401–404
dye-sublimation printers, 20

E
edges, 3D, creating, 433–435
Edit menu commands
    Color Settings, 171
    Define Brush, 109
    Define Custom Shape, 127
    Define Pattern, 113
    Fade, 281
    Fade Variations, 384
    Fill, 113, 236
    Free Transform, 429
    Paste, 36
    Paste Into, 199
    Preset Manager, 107
    Purge, 10, 282, 374
    Step Backward, 371
    Step Forward, 371
editing. *See also* changing
    Actions, 540
    adjustment layers, contents of, 194–195
    backgrounds, 406
        Background Eraser, 407–410
        Extract command, 407
    layer masks, 204–205
    lines, 218–219
    modes, color options in, 164–166
    Swatches palette, 155
effects, creating with masked type option, 267–271
Effects dialog box, 189
Embed Watermark filters, 335
Emboss filters, 326
EPS (Encapsulated PostScript) file format, 49–50
EPS Options dialog box, 159
Eraser tool, 129
    keyboard command for, 139

Exclusion mode, 166
exporting paths, 230
Extrude filters, 328
Eyedropper tool, 127–128
  keyboard command for, 139

F

Facet filters, 312
facial corrections, 404
  naturalizing, 405–406
  red-eye, 406
Fade command (Edit menu), 281
Fade dialog box, 282, 385
Fade Variations command (Edit menu), 384
feathering
  adjusting values of, 86
  versus anti-aliasing, 85–86
  defined, 84
  selections, 85
  for smoothing transitions, 404
file formats, 32–33, 41, 62, 447
  Amiga IFF, 52
  bitmapped, 37
  BMP, 51
  choosing for Web graphics, 454
  DCS (Desktop Color Separation), 50–51
  EPS (Encapsulated PostScript), 49–50
  filmstrip, 51–52
  FlashPix, 52
  GIF (Graphics Interchange Format), 43, 447, 450
  JPEG (Joint Photographic Experts Group), 44–45, 449–450
  matching
    with File menu options, 64
    uses with image modes, 63
  online standards, 42
  PCX, 51
  PDF (Portable Document Format), 48
  PICT, 51
  Pixar, 52
  PNG (Portable Network Graphics), 46, 448–449
  Scitex CT, 52
  Targa, 52
  TIFF (Tagged Image File Format), 46–47
File Info dialog box, 47
File menu commands
  Get Info, 9
  Import, 341
  Open, 35
  Place, 35
Fill command (Edit menu), 113, 236
fill layers, creating, 191–192
Fill Path dialog box, 235

filling paths, 236
fills, types of, 114
Film Grain filters, 286–287
filmstrip file format, 51–52
filters
  Artistic
    Colored Pencil, 284–285
    Cutout, 286
    Dry Brush, 286
    Film Grain, 286–287
    Fresco, 287
    Neon Glow, 287
    Paint Daubs, 287–288
    Palette Knife, 288
    Plastic Wrap, 289
    Poster Edges, 289
    Rough Pastels, 289
    Smudge Stick, 289
    Sponge, 290
    Underpainting, 290
    Watercolor, 290–291
  Blur
    Blur More, 291
    Gaussian Blur, 291–292
    Motion Blur, 292–293
    Radial Blur, 293
    Smart Blur, 294
  Brush Strokes
    Accented Edges, 296
    Angled Strokes, 297
    Crosshatch, 297
    Dark Strokes, 297
    Ink Outlines, 297–298
    picture of, 295
    Spatter, 298
    Sprayed Strokes, 298
    Sumi-e, 298
  defined, 278
  Digital Watermarking
    Embed Watermark, 335
    Read Watermark, 336
  Distortion
    Diffuse Glow, 298–299
    Displace, 305–308
    Glass, 299
    Ocean Ripple, 300
    Pinch, 300
    Polar Coordinates, 301
    Ripple, 301
    Shear, 302
    Spherize, 302
    Twirl, 303
    Wave, 303–304

filters (continued)
 ZigZag, 304
 Noise
  Add Noise, 308–309
  Despeckle, 310
  Dust & Scratches, 310
  Median, 311
 Other, 332
  Custom, 334
  DitherBox, 333
  High Pass, 333
  Maximum, 334
  Minimum, 334
  Offset, 334
 overview, 278–280
 Pixelate, 311
  Color Halftone, 312
  Crystallize, 312
  Facet, 312
  Fragment, 313
  Mezzotint, 313
  picture of, 312
  Pointillize, 313
 reapplying, 281
 reducing intensity of, 281–282
 Render, 313
  3D Transform, 314
  Clouds, 314
  Difference Clouds, 314
  Lens Flare, 315
  Lighting Effects, 315–319
  Texture Fill, 315
 selecting, 279
 Sharpen
  Sharpen Edges, 320
  Sharpen More, 320
  Unsharp Mask, 320–321
 Sketch
  Bas Relief, 321
  Chalk & Charcoal, 321
  Charcoal, 321–322
  Chrome, 322–323
  Conté Crayon, 323
  Graphic Pen, 323
  Halftone Pattern, 323
  Note Paper, 324
  Photocopy, 324
  pictures of, 322
  Plaster, 324
  Reticulation, 324
  Stamp, 325
  Torn Edges, 325
  Water Paper, 325

 speeding up, 282–284
 Stylize
  Diffuse, 325
  Emboss, 326
  Extrude, 328
  Find Edges, 328–329
  pictures of, 326
  Solarize, 329
  Tiles, 329
  Trace Contour, 329
  Wind, 329
 Texture
  Craquelure, 330
  example of, 331
  Grain, 330
  Mosaic Tiles, 330
  Patchwork, 330–331
  Stained Glass, 331–332
  Texturizer, 332
 Video
  De-Interlace, 332
  NTSC, 332
Filters dialog box, 281
Find Edges filters, 328–329
finding layers
 by title bar, 178–179
 using Layer thumbnails, 177–178
FlashPix file format, 52
flatbed scanners, 22
Flatten Image command (Layer menu), 177
flattening layers, 206
Focoltone color system, 157
Fragment filters, 313
Free Transform command (Edit menu), 429
Freefrom Pen tool, 99
 keyboard command for, 138
Fresco filters, 287

G
gamma, 24
Gaussian Blur filters, 291–292
Get Info command (File menu), 9
GIF (Graphics Interchange Format), 43, 447
 animated, 496–498
 for Web graphics, 450
GIF Options dialog box, 453
Glass filters, 299
glowing effects, 298–299
Gradient Editor dialog box, 115
Gradient tool, 114–115
 creating 3D shapes with, 120–121
 keyboard command for, 139

gradients, 119
  creating
    new, 116
    noise, 118–119
  loading predefined, 115
  reopening, 116
  saving, 116
Grain filters, 330
Graphic Pen filters, 323
graphics. *See also* Web graphics
  bitmapped, 33
  object-oriented, 33–36
Grayscale color mode, 57
Group Linked command (Layer menu), 199

H

Halftone Pattern filters, 323
Halftone scanning, 354–357
Hand tool, 77
  keyboard command for, 137
hard disk space, system requirements, 4
Hard Light mode, 166
hiding
  layers, 182
  marching ants border, 82
  palettes, 69
  paths, 209
  toolbox, 71
High Pass filters, 333
Histogram dialog box, 383
histograms, 361
History Brush tool, 132–133
  keyboard command for, 139
History Options dialog, 374
History palette, 131
  icons for, 132
  Step Backward, 371
  Step Forward, 371
hot spots, 491
  creating, 492–494
  types of, 492
HSB color model, 147
Hue mode, 166
Hue/Saturation dialog box, 168, 394–395

I

image maps
  client-side, 491
  coordinates for, 491
  creating, 491–494
  design considerations for, 496
  server-side, 491
  versus sliced images, 495–496

Image menu commands
  Adjust, 193
  Image Size, 39, 349
Image Size command (Image menu), 39, 349
Image Size dialog box, 350
image states, 131, 372
ImageReady
  palettes
    Animation, 489
    Color Table, 488
    Image Map, 490
    Layers Options, 488
    Rollover, 489
    Slice, 490
  tools
    Circle Image Map, 486
    Image Map Select, 487
    Polygon Image Map, 487
    Preview in Default Browser, 488
    Rectangle Image Map, 486
    Rollover Preview, 488
    Rounded Rectangle Marquee, 485
    Toggle Image Map, 488
    Toggle Slices Visibility, 488
  when to use, 484–485
images. *See also* selections
  acquiring
    by digital cameras, 29–30
    from digital clip art, 27–28
    by drawing tablets, 30
    by online image archives, 28
    by scanning, 27
    by video cameras, 29–30
  adding
    audio to, 81
    clipping paths to, 241–242
    spot-color channel to, 256
  aligning, 80
  colorizing with hand-tinted effects, 168–169
  cropping, 87–88, 464
  distorting, 411–413
  enlarging resolution for, 352–353
  lightening, 387
  magnification of, changing, 78
  metallic, 322
  moving, 94–95
  overlaying on 3D graphics, 429–432
  posterizing, 390
  resizing, 78–79
  restoring, 375–376
  silhouetted, 35
  touching up. *see* retouching images
  zooming, 78–80

imagesetters, 21
Import command (File menu), 341
importing paths, 230
Indexed Color dialog box, 450
  Adaptive, 452
  Custom, 452
  Exact, 451
  Perceptual, 451
  Previous, 452
  Selective, 451
  System, 451
  Uniform, 451
  Web, 451
Indexed color mode, 58–59
Indexed color palettes, 160–163
Info Options dialog box, 379
Ink Outlines filters, 297–298
ink sets, 156–157
inkjet printers, 20
Input Levels, tonal corrections, 386–387
installing scanning software, 341–342
interlacing, 43
  for Web graphics, 453–454
interpolation, 22, 348
Inverse command (Select menu), 93

J

JPEG (Joint Photographic Experts Group), 44–45, 447
  for Web graphics, 449–450
JPEG Options dialog box, 449

K

kerning, 103
keyboard shortcuts
  for image magnification, 80
  moving between layers, 182–183
  for tools, 72

L

Lab color mode, 61–62
  overview, 148–149
laser printers, 20
Lasso tools
  editing selections with, 90
  keyboard command for, 138
  Magnetic Lasso, 89
  Polygonal, 88–89
layer-based slices, 475
layer masks
  adding, 203
  creating, 203–204
  editing, 204–205

  removing, 205
Layer menu commands
  Add Layer Mask, 203
  Arrange, 184
  Choose Layer Style, 190
  Flatten Image, 177
  Group Linked, 199
  Group with Previous, 199
  Layer Style, 187
  Lock All Layers in Set, 187
  Merge Down, 205
  Merge Visible, 205
  New, 176
  New Adjustment Layer, 193
  New Fill Layer, 191
  Rasterize, 206
layer styles
  applying, 187–188
  choices for, 187–188
  creating drop shadows with, 189
Layer Styles dialog box, 189
layers
  adding to layer sets, 185
  adjusting, 194–195
  arranging
    by dragging, 183–184
    by using Arrange commands, 184–185
  assigning colors to, 186
  blending options, 202–203
  clipping groups, 199
  copying between documents, 183
  creating
    adjustment, 193
    fill, 191–192
    new, 174–177
    sets, 185–186
  deleting, 180
  finding
    by title bar, 178–179
    using Layer thumbnails, 177–178
  flattening, 206
  hiding, 182
  leveraging, 125
  linking, 181
  locking, 186–187
  merging, 205
  mode settings, 196–198
  moving, 181
  pasting into, 199
  renaming, 177
  saving, 177
  switching between, 182–183

target, 179
viewing, 182
Layers palette, accessing, 175
Layers Palette Options dialog box, 178
Layers Properties dialog box, 186
leading, 103
Lens Flare filters, 315
levels, tonal corrections for, 385–386
Levels dialog box, 194, 385
leveraging layers, 125
Lighten mode, 166
Lighting Effects filters
exercise, 318–319
light type properties, 315–316
style properties, 315–316
uses for, 315
line art, scanning resolution for, 353
Line tool, 123–124
Create filled region, 123
Create new shape layer, 123
Create new work path, 123
keyboard command for, 139
Linear fills, 114
lines
combining with curves, 223–225
drawing, 217
editing, 218–219
linking layers, 181
Load Selection dialog box, 261–262
loading
gradients, 115
paintbrushes, 107–108
selections, 260–261
locking layers, 186–187
lossless compression, 55, 447
Luminosity mode, 166

M

Mac OS X, features of, 6
Magic Eraser tool, 129–130
keyboard command for, 139
Magic Wand tool
keyboard command for, 138
tolerance levels, setting, 91–92
Magnetic Lasso tool, 89
keyboard command for, 138
Make Selection dialog box, 231
maps. *See* image maps
marching ants
defined, 81–82
hiding, 82
Marquee tools

accessing, 82
Constrained Aspect Ratio setting, 85
keyboard commands for, 138
Single Column, 86
Single Row, 86
masked type option, creating
effects with, 267–271
stenciled images with, 271
Maximum filters, 334
Measure tool, 80
keyboard command for, 137
Median filters, 311
memory. *See* RAM
merging
channels, 266
layers, 205
metallic images, 322
Mezzotint filters, 313
mezzotints, creating, 268–269
Minimum filters, 334
modes. *See* color modes
monitors
basics of, 16–18
calibrating, 23–27
system requirements, 5
Mosaic Tiles filters, 330
Motion Blur filters, 292–293
Move tool, 94
keyboard command for, 138
moving layers with, 181
moving
images, 94–95
layers, 181
slices, 98
Multichannel mode, 62
multimedia applications, 66
Multiply mode, 165

N

Navigator palette controls, 79
Neon Glow filters, 287
New Adjustment Layer (Layer menu), 193
New Brush dialog box, 109
New Fill Layer command (Layer menu), 191
New Layer dialog box, 176
New Path dialog box, 229
New Snapshot dialog box, 373
New Spot Channel dialog box, 255
Noise filters
Add Noise, 308–310
Despeckle, 310
Dust & Scratches, 310
Median, 311

noise gradients
  creating, 118–119
  editing, 119
Non-Linear History, 374
Normal mode, 164
Note Paper filters, 324
Notes tool, 81
  keyboard command for, 137
NTSC Colors filters, 332

O
object-oriented graphics, 33–36
objects, as bitmaps, 34–35
Ocean Ripple filters, 300
Offset filters, 334
omni light type, 316
opacity settings for paintbrushes, 110
Open command (File menu), 35
Output Levels, tonal corrections, 387–388
Overlay mode, 165

P
page layout programs, print issues handled by, 509
Paint Bucket tool, 113
  keyboard command for, 139
Paint Daubs dialog box, 288
Paint Daubs filters
  brush types, 288
  uses for, 287–288
Paintbrush tool, 110
paintbrushes
  active, 107
  creating custom, 108–109
  loading, 107–108
  New Brush dialog box, 109
  opacity settings, 110
  selecting, 107
painting modes, color options in, 164–166
Palette Knife filters, 288
palettes
  Channels, 59
    accessing, 246
    Channel Options, 265
    Delete Channel, 264
    Duplicate Channel, 264
    Merge Channels, 266
    Merge Spot Channel, 264–265
    New Channel, 263
    New Spot Channel, 264–265
    Options dialog box, 266
    shortcuts for, 60
    Split Channels, 265

Color
  accessing, 153
  changing background color of, 154
  changing foreground color of, 154
  hiding, 69
  History, 131
    icons for, 132
    Step Backward, 371
    Step Forward, 371
  Indexed color, 160–163
  Layers, accessing, 175
  Navigator, controls, 79
  Paths
    accessing, 209
    icons in, 214–215
  Swatches, 154
    editing, 155
    Load Swatches, 155
Pantone Matching System (PMS), 157
Paste command (Edit menu), 36
Paste dialog box, 36, 230
Paste Into command (Edit menu), 199
pasting into layers, 199
Patchwork filters, 330–331
Path Component Selection tool, 100
  keyboard command for, 138
paths, 208
  adding shadows to objects with, 234–235
  clipping. *see* clipping paths
  constraining lines in, 217
  converting
    to selections, 231–232
    selections to, 232–233
  creating
    closed, 212
    new, 229
  defined, 99, 209
  deleting, 230
  exporting, 230
  filling, 213, 236
  hiding, 209
  importing, 230
  renaming, 213, 229
  restoring, 209
  rotating, 233
  saving, 213, 228–229
  scaling, 233
  segments, cutting in two, 225
  skewing, 233
  stroke, 213
  stroking, 236–237
Pattern Fill dialog box, 192

Pattern Stamp tool
keyboard command for, 139
uses for, 112–113
PCX file formats, 51
PDF (Portable Document Format), 48
Pen tools, 99
creating anchor points with, 211
Freeform, 99
keyboard command for, 138
Pencil tool
Auto Erase, 122
keyboard command for, 139
phosphors, 24
Photocopy filters, 324
Photoshop
bringing object-oriented graphics into, 35–36
speeding performance of, 15
PICT file format, 51
Pinch filters, 300
Pixar file formats, 52
Pixelate filters, 311
Color Halftone, 312
Crystallize, 312
Facet, 312
Fragment, 313
Mezzotint, 313
picture of, 312
Pointillize, 313
Place command (File menu), 35
Plaster filters, 324
Plastic Wrap filters, 289
playing Actions, 531–533
Plug-Ins & Scratch Disks dialog box, 280
PMS (Pantone Matching System), 157
PNG (Portable Network Graphics) file format, 46
Pointillize filters, 313
Polar Coordinates filters, 301
Polygonal Lasso tool, 88–89
keyboard command for, 138
Portable Document Format. *See* PDF
Portable Network Graphics file formats. *See* PNG
Poster Edges filters, 289
Preferences dialog box, 73
Preset Manager command (Edit menu), 107
Preset Manager dialog box, 108
previewing color corrections, 399–400
printers, 19
dye-sublimation, 20
inkjet printers, 20
laser, 20
process colors, 21
Purge command (Edit menu), 10, 282, 374

Q
Quick Mask mode
editing in, 272–273
overview, 272
Quick Mask Options dialog box, 273

R
Radial Blur filters, 293
Radial fills, 114
RAID (redundant array of inexpensive disks), 14
RAM (random access memory)
allocating to Photoshop
on Mac, 9–10
under Windows, 9
clearing within Photoshop, 10
defined, 7
system requirements, 4
Rasterize command (Layer menu), 206
Rasterize Generic EPS Format dialog box, 35
Raw Options dialog box, 53
Read Watermark filters, 336
Record Stop dialog box, 541
recording Actions, 535
red-eye, removing, 406
redundant array of inexpensive disks.
See RAID
Reflected fills, 114
removing. *See also* deleting
background items, 408–409
blemishes, 401–404
color casts, 362–363
dust spots, 401–404
layers masks, 205
red-eye, 406
from selections, 83, 90
Rename Path dialog box, 229
renaming
layers, 177
paths, 213, 229
Render filters, 313
3D Transform, 314
Clouds, 314
Difference Clouds, 314
Lens Flare, 315
Lighting Effects
exercise, 318–319
light type properties, 316–317
style properties, 315–316
Texture Fill, 315
resampling, 348
Resize Windows To Fit check box
(Zoom tool), 78

resizing
images, 78–79
slices, 98
resolution, 37–39
defined, 20
issues to consider, 346
enlarging images, 352–353
file size, 349–350
interpolation, 348
Onscreen Production, 347
print production scanning, 347
scanning line art, 353
Web scanning, 347
setting options for, 346
Web graphic design considerations, 446–447
restoring images, 375–376
Reticulation filters, 324
retouching images
blemishes, 401–404
color values, 369–371
dust spots, 401–404
snapshots, creating, 371–373
RGB color modes, 59–60
converting to CMYK color mode, 511
overview, 144–145
Ripple filters, 301
RLE (Run-Length Encoding), 55
rods, creating, 427–428
rollover effects, creating, 499–503
rollovers, 499
rotating
3D shapes, 433
paths, 233
Rough Pastels dialog box, 290
Rough Pastels filters, 289
Rubber Stamp tool, 112
Run-Length Encoding. *See* RLE

S
Saturation mode, 166
Save for Web interface
optimization settings, 460–462
Output Settings, 459
tools for
Eyedropper, 459
Eyedropper Color swatch, 459
Hand, 458
Slice Select, 458
Slice Visibility button, 459
Zoom, 458
Save Path dialog box, 229
Save Selection command (Select menu), 267
Save Selection dialog box, 257, 262

saving
Actions, 550
gradients, 116
layers, 177
paths, 213, 228–229
selections in channels, 255–259
scaling paths, 233
scanners
cleaning, 23
drum, 22–23
flatbed, 22
options
cropping, 344
descreening, 344
sharpening, 344
prices of, 21
purchasing tips, 21–22, 338
settings, 342
black point, 345
color mode, 343–344
Preview, 343
resolution, 346
white point, 345
slide, 22
specifications for, 339–340
bit depth, 339–340
color scanning method, 340
dynamic range, 339
registering light, 339
resolution, 339
scanning area, 340
scanning
acquiring images by, 27
Halftone, 354–357
installation software, 341–342
material used for, 340–341
quality factors, 338
resolution issues, 346
enlarging images, 352–353
file size, 349–350
interpolation, 348
onscreen production scanning, 347
print production scanning, 347
scanning line art, 353
Web scanning, 347
tonal improvements
black point settings, 357
brightness settings, 360–362
color cast, removing, 362–363
contrast settings, 360–362
sharpening, 362
white point settings, 357
Scitex CT file formats, 52

scratch disks, 12
  assigning additional, 14
  defined, 11
  memory for, 11
Screen mode, 165
searching. *See* finding
Select menu commands
  Inverse, 93
  Load Selection, 260
  Save Selection, 267
  Similar, 93
selecting
  channels, 248–249
  filters, 279
  paintbrushes, 107
selections. *See also* images
  adding to, 83, 90
  closing, 88–89
  converting
    to paths, 232–233
    paths to, 231–232
  creating
    of fixed dimensions, 85
    subset, 84
  feathering, 85
  loading, 260–261
  removing from, 83, 90
  saving in channels, 255–259
server-side image maps, 491
service bureaus, 514–516
Settings dialog box, 346
shadows
  adding to objects, 234–235, 436–437
  lightening, 387
Shape tools, 126–127
Sharpen filters
  Sharpen Edges, 320
  Sharpen More, 320
  Unsharp Mask, 320–321
Sharpen tool, 134
  keyboard command for, 140
sharpening
  setting option for, 344
  with Unsharp Mask filter, 362
Shear dialog box, 302
Shear filters, 302
shortcut keys
  for image magnification, 80
  moving between layers, 182–183
  for tools, 72
Show Actions command (Window menu), 529
Show Channels command (Window menu), 246
Show Color command (Window menu), 153

Show History command (Window menu), 372
Show Info command (Window menu), 216, 378
Show Layers command (Window menu), 175
Show Paths command (Window menu), 209
Show Rulers command (View menu), 216
silhouetted images, 35
  creating with clipping paths, 237–241
Similar command (Select menu), 93
sine waves, drawing, 221–222
Sketch filters
  Bas Relief, 321
  Chalk & Charcoal, 321
  Charcoal, 321–322
  Chrome, 322–323
  Conté Crayon, 323
  Graphic pen, 323
  Halftone Pattern, 323
  Note Paper, 324
  Photocopy, 324
  pictures of, 322
  Plaster, 324
  Reticulation, 324
  Stamp, 325
  Torn Edges, 325
  Water Paper, 325
skewing paths, 233
Slice Options dialog box, 99
Slice Select tool, 96–98
  keyboard command for, 138
Slice tool, 96–98
  keyboard command for, 138
sliced images *versus* **image maps,** 495–496
slices, 474
  auto, 97, 478
  creating, 96–97
  icons, list of, 477
  layer-based, 475
  moving, 98
  resizing, 98
  unattaching numbers to, 97
  user, 97, 476–477
slide scanners, 22
Smart Blur filters, 294
smooth points, 222
Smudge Stick filters, 289
Smudge tool, 134–135
  keyboard command for, 140
snapshots, 132
  creating new, 373
Soft Light mode, 165
Solarize filters, 329
source channels, 253
Spatter filters, 298

speeding up filters, 282–284
spheres
  creating, 418–420
  placing photographs on, 429
Spherize filters, 302
splash pages, 444, 468–469
splitting channels, 265
Sponge filters, 290
Sponge tool, 135
  keyboard command for, 140
spot-color channel
  adding to images, 256
  saving images with, 255
spot colors, 21
spotlight light type, 316
Sprayed Strokes filters, 298
Stained Glass filters, 331–332
Stamp filters, 325
stamping. *See* Rubber Stamp tool
stenciled images, creating, 271
Step Backward command (File menu), 371
Step Forward command (File menu), 371
stopping Actions, 541
Stroke Path dialog box, 237
stroke paths, 213
strokes. *See also* Brush Strokes filters
stroking paths, 236–237
Stylize filters
  Diffuse, 325
  Emboss, 326
  Extrude, 328
  Find Edges, 328–329
  pictures of, 326
  Solarize, 329
  Tiles, 329
  Trace Contour, 329
  Wind, 329
Sumi-e filters, 298
Swatches palette, 154
  creating out of custom ink sets, 156
  editing, 155
  Load Swatches, 155
switching between layers, 182–183

T

Tagged Image File Format. *See* TIFF
Targa file formats, 52
target channels, 249
target layers, 179
text, raised, 438–439
Texture Fill filters
  Grain, 330
  Mosaic Tiles, 330
  uses for, 315
Texture filters
  Craquelure, 330
  examples of, 331
  Patchwork, 330–331
  Stained Glass, 331–332
  Texturizer, 332
textures, creating from scratch, 308–310
three-dimensional. *See* 3D
Threshold mode, 165
thumbnails, 177–178
TIFF (Tagged Image File Format), 46–47
Tiles filters, 329
tiling patterns, 470–473
tolerance, 233
tonal corrections, 378–382
  Curves, 388–391
  Input Levels, 386–387
  Levels, 385
  Output Levels, 387–388
  variations, 383–385
tones, improving
  black point, setting, 357
  brightness, setting, 360–362
  color cast, removing, 362–363
  contrast, setting, 360–362
  sharpening, 362
  white point, setting, 357
tool tips, 72
toolbox, 69
  controls
    Color Selection box, 74
    Jump to button, 75
    Mask Mode box, 74–75
    Screen Mode box, 75
  hiding, 71
  icons, 71
  location of, 68
  tool tips, 72–73
tools
  Add Anchor Point, 100
  Airbrush, 111–112
  Art History Brush, 133–134
  Audio Annotation, 81
  Background Eraser, 130
  Blur, 134
  Burn, 135
    color corrections, 399–400
  Color Sampler, 128
  Convert Point, 100
  Crop, 87–88

Delete Anchor Point, 100
Direct Selection, 100
Dodge, 135
  color corrections, 399–400
Eraser, 129
Eyedropper, 127–128
Gradient, 114–115
  creating 3D shapes with, 120–121
Hand, 77
History Brush, 132–133
for ImageReady. *see* ImageReady
keyboard commands for, 137–140
keyboard shortcuts for, 72
Lasso
  editing selections with, 90
  Magnetic Lasso, 89
  Polygonal, 88–89
Line, 123–124
Magic Eraser, 129–130
Magic Wand, 91
Marquee
  accessing, 82
  Constrained Aspect Ratio setting, 85
  Single Column, 86
  Single Row, 86
Measure, 80
Move, 94
  moving layers with, 181
Paint Bucket, 113
Paintbrush, 110
Path Component Selection, 100
Pattern Stamp, 112–113
Pen, 99
  creating anchor points with, 211
  Freeform, 99
Pencil, 122
Rubber Stamp, 112
Shape, 126–127
Sharpen, 134
Slice, 96–98
Slice Select, 96–98
Smudge, 134–135
Sponge, 135
tool tips, 72–73
Type
  exercise, 104–105
  uses for, 100–102
Zoom, 78
Torn Edges filters, 325
touchups. *See* retouching images
Toyo Color Finder color system, 157
Trace Contour filters, 329

tracking, 103
translucent overlays, 192
trapping, 525
troubleshooting Actions, 546–547
Trumatch color system, 157
turning off tool tips, 73
Twirl filters, 303
Type tool, 100
  exercise, 104–105
  keyboard command for, 137
  uses for, 100–102

U
Underpainting filters, 290
Universal Serial Bus. *See* USB
Unsharp Mask filters, 320–321
USB (Universal Serial Bus), 14
user-slices, 97, 476–477

V
Variations
  color corrections, 397
  dialog box, 361
  Fade Variations command (Edit menu), 384
  tonal corrections, 383–385
video accelerators, 16
video cameras. *See* cameras
video display cards, 16–17
Video filters, 332
View menu commands, Show Rulers, 216
viewing layers, 182
virtual memory, 8–9

W-X-Y
Warp Text dialog box, 102
Water Paper filters, 325
Watercolor filters, 290–291
Wave filters, 303–304
Web graphics, 66, 444
  color inclusion, 452
  design considerations
    color issues, 446
    design information, 445
    file size, 446
    interacting, 447
    layout, 446
    page dimensions, 446
    resolution, 446
  dithering, 452–453
  download time, minimizing
    creating thumbnails, 464
    cropping, 464

Web graphics (continued)
   image compression, 463
   low-resolutions, 464–467
   by slicing, 474–477
   using fewer colors, 455
  file formats for
   choosing best, 454
   GIF, 447
   JPEG, 447, 449–450
  functions of
   background colors, 469–470
   background images, 470–473
   background patterns, 469–470
   background tiling, 470–473
   splash pages, 468–469
  interlacing, 453–454
  protecting, 482
  safe colors indication, 462–463
Web sites
  Deja.com, 338
  Digimarc Corporation, 482

whirling effects. *See* Twirl filters
white point
  defined, 24
  setting options for, 345
Wind filters, 329
Window menu commands
  Show Actions, 529
  Show Channels, 246
  Show Color, 153
  Show History, 372
  Show Info, 216, 378
  Show Layers, 175
  Show Paths, 209

Z
ZigZag filters, 304
Zoom tools
  keyboard command for, 137
  Resize Windows To Fit, 78
zooming images, 78–80